D1267211

International
Economic
Cooperation

A National Bureau
of Economic Research
Conference Report

International Economic Cooperation

Edited and with an Introduction by

Martin Feldstein

The University of Chicago Press

Chicago and London

MARTIN FELDSTEIN is the George F. Baker Professor of
Economics at Harvard University and president of the National
Bureau of Economic Research. He is the author of more than 200
scientific papers and four books, including *Inflation, Tax Rules,
and Capital Formation* (1983) and the editor of *The American
Economy in Transition* (1980), *Behavioral Simulation Methods in
Tax Policy Analysis* (1983), *The Effects of Taxation on Capital
Accumulation* (1987), *Taxes and Capital Formation* (1987), and
The United States in the World Economy (1988), all published by
the University of Chicago Press in association with the National
Bureau of Economic Research.

The University of Chicago Press, Chicago 60637
The University of Chicago Press, Ltd., London
© 1988 by the National Bureau of Economic Research
All rights reserved. Published 1988
Printed in the United States of America

97 96 95 94 93 92 91 90 89 88   5 4 3 2 1

Library of Congress Cataloging-in-Publication Data

International economic cooperation / edited and with an introduction
  by Martin Feldstein.
        p.   cm. — (A National Bureau of Economic Research conference
  report)
     Bibliography: p.
     Includes index.
     ISBN 0-226-24075-4.   ISBN 0-226-24076-2 (pbk.)
        1. International economic relations—Congresses.   I.   Feldstein,
Martin S.   II. National Bureau of Economic   Research.   III. Series:
Conference report (National Bureau of Economic Research)
  HF1359.I58 1988
     337.1—dc19   88-1883
                                                                    CIP

Since this volume is a record of conference proceedings, it has been exempted from the rules governing critical review of manuscripts by the Board of Directors of the National Bureau (resolution adopted 8 June 1948, as revised 21 November 1949 and 20 April 1968).

Contents

Preface

In April 1987 the National Bureau of Economic Research (NBER) held a conference on international economic cooperation. The conference focused on four general areas: macroeconomic policy, exchange rate policy, trade, and the international debt of developing countries. In preparation for this conference, NBER Research Associates prepared nontechnical background papers on each subject. At the conference itself, the discussion of each of these subjects was launched by prepared personal statements by individuals who have played leading roles in government or business in either the United States or another country. This volume brings together the background papers, the personal statements, and a detailed summary of the discussion at the conference.

The authors of the background papers met as a group on two occasions before the final conference to discuss the approach to be taken in each paper and to review critically the preliminary drafts of the papers. Each of the authors also benefited from the comments of an outside reviewer.

The fifteen individuals who prepared the remarks that launched the individual sessions included former government officials who held key positions dealing with international economic issues, current officials from Japan, France, and the International Monetary Fund with international responsibilities, and American business leaders who are actively involved in international business and finance. Their willingness to share their experiences and to participate throughout the conference made for a uniquely interesting series of discussions. The summaries of the discussions were prepared by Professor Kenneth Froot.

I am grateful to The Ford Foundation for financial support of both this conference and the research presented in the background papers.

I am grateful also to the members of the NBER staff for their assistance with all of the details involved in the planning and execution of the meeting and this volume, particularly to Kirsten Foss Davis, Ilana Hardesty, Mark Fitz-Patrick, and Carolyn Terry.

Martin Feldstein

International Economic Cooperation: Introduction

Martin Feldstein

Although some form of economic cooperation has been a part of international political relations during most of this century, American interest in international economic cooperation has increased substantially in recent years. This heightened desire to coordinate economic policies with the other major economic powers is in part a response to the special problems of the 1980s: the sharp fluctuations in exchange rates, the massive shifts in the trade balance, and the explosive growth of debt among many of the developing countries.

The increased interest in international economic cooperation also reflects the more fundamental changes in the world economy that have been evolving over a longer period of time. The world economy has become more interdependent: international trade has increased relative to production for domestic markets and international capital markets have become larger and more active. In addition, the United States has lost the dominant economic position that it enjoyed in the early postwar years. Japan and the European Economic Community (EEC) have become major economic powers that compete effectively in trade and finance.

How has policy coordination evolved in this changing environment? How have the changes in the world economy altered the problems and possibilities of international economic cooperation? What are the prospects and potential benefits and costs of increased cooperation in the future?

To assess these questions, I asked four NBER Research Associates—Stanley Fischer of the Massachusetts Institute of Technology, Richard Marston of the University of Pennsylvania, David Richardson of the University of Wisconsin, and Jeffrey Sachs of Harvard—to prepare background papers that discussed the academic research and the historic experience in four areas of international economic cooperation: macroeconomic policy, exchange rate policy, international trade, and developing country debt. I also asked a distinguished group of individuals who have played leading roles in business and government to write personal statements on their own perceptions of these issues. This group then gathered for several days of intense discussions in April 1987.

The background papers and the discussion at the conference made it clear that the first two subjects—macroeconomic cooperation and exchange rate coordination—are very different from cooperation in international trade and in dealing with the international debtors. Cooperation in macroeconomic and exchange rate policies generally means redirecting and increasing the economic role of governments. In contrast, cooperation in international trade involves reducing the interference of governments in private markets. Experience with the international debt problem has shown little explicit intergovernmental cooperation except for the Paris Club negotiations that deal with debts to the governments themselves. It is useful therefore to begin by considering the macroeconomic and exchange rate coordination and then to turn to cooperation in international trade and in dealing with international debt.

Coordination of Macroeconomic Policy and Exchange Rates

Senior economic officials of the major governments talk with each other frequently in the context of Organization for Economic Cooperation and Development (OECD), International Monetary Fund (IMF), and Group of 7 (G-7; i.e., the seven largest economies in OECD) meetings as well as in bilateral sessions. In addition, the heads of the central banks meet monthly at the Basel meetings of the Bank for International Settlements (BIS). These meetings inevitably alter the way officials think about their own macroeconomic policies and increase their understanding of the policies being pursued by other governments. Since all of this is bound to influence each government's own policies, it serves as a type of implicit policy coordination. Such an exchange of information is clearly desirable and can help each country pursue its own policies more wisely.

It is useful, however, to focus on the more explicit types of macroeconomic and exchange rate coordination and, in this context, to consider two extreme positions. At one extreme is the idea that each country should manage its own domestic monetary and fiscal policies with a concern for its own well-being only and without trying to take into account the effect of its policies on the other countries of the world. A government may understand that its economy is affected by the policies adopted elsewhere and that its own policies affect other countries but still choose to make its policy decisions unilaterally. At the other extreme is the view that each (industrial) country should formulate its economic policies in explicit coordination with every other (industrial) country so that the policies are chosen to maximize world economic welfare as a whole, or at least to achieve a configuration of policies from which no country can be made better off without making some other country worse off.

Although this statement of the alternatives might suggest that international coordination is unambiguously better than the uncoordinated pursuit of national self-interest, it is important to distinguish between the theoretical possibilities of idealized coordination and the realistic potential gains of practical coordination. In practice, despite its aspirations, international coordination may produce results that are not as satisfactory as those that result from each country's uncoordinated pursuit of national self-interest.

One reason why coordination may fail to achieve an improvement in world economic performance is that, as Stanley Fischer notes in his background paper, extensive statistical studies indicate that the monetary and fiscal policies of each country have only a relatively small effect on the level of economic activity and inflation in other countries. The potential gain from even perfect coordination is therefore likely to be small and easily overwhelmed in practice when the policies are less than ideal.

International policy coordination may fail to improve overall economic performance simply because the political officials who participate in these international negotiations choose policies that are politically convenient rather than economically sound. We know that this happens all too frequently at the domestic level. Why should we expect the same officials to follow a higher standard just because they are engaged in an international negotiation?

The process of international negotiation may also be counterproductive because it diverts attention and action from needed domestic policy changes. Governments may explicitly delay painful domestic policy changes as part of an international negotiating strategy designed to induce policy changes abroad that would make the domestic changes unnecessary. The emphasis on international negotiations may also rechannel domestic political pressures away from needed reforms. Recent experience provides ample examples of both dangers. Germany and Japan have failed to stimulate domestic demand enough because of their reliance on expectations of continued exchange rate stability. The U.S. Administration has diverted attention from the need for budget deficit reduction by emphasizing the favorable effects on U.S. exports of greater fiscal expansion abroad.

The ability of international macroeconomic coordination to permit countries to pursue more expansionary policies than would otherwise be possible is both a potential benefit and a potential danger. When a single country tries to expand by itself, it may soon find that rising imports create a balance of payments problem. A coordinated expansion by a group of trading partners can eliminate this balance of payments constraint and permit all of the countries to expand more than any of them could have done alone. When all economies are operating well below capacity, such coordinated expansion can provide gains for all. But the ability of coordination to circumvent the balance of payments constraint on expansionary policies also creates the temptation to overexpand. Without the automatic market check of a deteriorating balance of payments, governments may pursue inflationary policies that would otherwise be avoided. On balance, whether one regards the ability to achieve an expansion that would not be possible without coordinated action as a reason to favor coordination or to oppose it depends on the likelihood that governments will use that ability to pursue inflationary policies.

There is a further problem that arises because it is generally far more difficult to alter budget and tax policies than to change monetary policy. Macroeconomic coordination may in practice be limited to a coordination of only monetary policies. This is particularly the case in the United States because fiscal policy is controlled by the Congress which, even when its majority is of the same party as the President, may be reluctant to enact the tax changes, particularly tax increases, that a President wants. But the reliance on monetary rather than fiscal policy will also be true in other countries because of the greater political attention generated by changes in fiscal policy and the greater difficulty of reversing expansionary fiscal changes if they turn out to be inappropriate.

A monetary expansion or contraction is not generally an appropriate substitute for a fiscal change. For example, while tighter monetary policy in the United States could offset the aggregate demand effect of large budget deficits, it would not reduce real interest rates. More generally, monetary and fiscal policies that have equal expansionary effects at home can have opposite effects on the rest of the world. A fiscal expansion that raises real interest rates and appreciates the currency will unambiguously raise foreign exports and thereby stimulate the foreign economy. In contrast, a monetary expansion that temporarily reduces real interest rates will depreciate the currency and thereby reduce foreign exports.

The need to rely on monetary policy rather than fiscal policy is particularly a problem when the international coordination focuses on exchange rate stabilization. If the United States had been induced to stabilize the dollar in the early 1980s, it would have done so by increasing the money supply rather than by cutting the budget deficit. This in turn would have increased the rate of inflation in the United States. Moreover, although the rise in inflation and in the price level would be sufficient to reduce the nominal value of the dollar, the real exchange rate might soon be back to the level that would have prevailed without any change in monetary policy. A commitment to exchange rate stabilization that leaves real exchange rates unchanged but causes higher inflation must be regarded as counterproductive.

Exchange rate targeting has become a central focus of all discussions of international economic cooperation. The sharp 80 percent increase in the value of the dollar between 1980 and early 1985 caused great distress to American firms that try to export or that compete with imports from abroad. Although the decline in the dollar that began in March 1985 started to shrink the real trade deficit about 18 months later, that deficit remains very large. The cries of pain continue to be heard from adversely affected American industries and regions, but these have now been joined by equally loud declarations of anguish and fear from Japan and Europe. As Richard Marston notes in his background paper, these currency misalignments are much more harmful than very short-term fluctuations in currency values.

But even while recognizing the serious damage caused by the dollar's sharp rise, it is important to ask whether the American economy would have been better off if the dollar had somehow been prevented from increasing in value in the early 1980s. Without the dollar's rise, we would not have had the trade deficit, but we also would not have had the major increase in capital inflow to the United States that automatically accompanied the increased trade deficit. The rise in the budget deficit would therefore have caused real interest rates to rise sharply, crowding out investment in housing and in industrial plants and equipment. The rise of the dollar acted like the opening of a safety valve, permitting the pressures that would otherwise have been concentrated on the domestic capital goods sector to spread to all parts of the economy that compete in international markets.

If a rise in government borrowing without the offsetting help of a strong capital inflow had caused a sharp rise in U.S. real interest rates, there would also have been strong political pressures on the Federal Reserve System to increase the monetary aggregates, a policy shift that would inevitably have increased the rate of inflation. While some have argued that the rise in interest rates would have forced the Administration and the Congress to reduce the budget deficit, I believe on the basis of my own experience within the Administration at that time that the substitution of the pain caused by higher interest rates for the problems caused by the strong dollar would not have changed the political response to the existing and projected budget deficits.

For those who want to evaluate whether a policy of stabilizing the real value of the dollar during the first half of the 1980s would have been better than permitting the dollar's rise that actually occurred, the relevant question is whether the adverse effects of the budget deficit would have been greater with or without the rise of the dollar. When government borrowing absorbed more than half of all U.S. domestic saving, was it better to attract capital from the rest of the world to maintain the relative level of investment in the United States or would it have been better to permit a sharp fall in U.S. domestic investment? Was it better to spread the crowding-out effects of the increased budget deficit to all parts of the manufacturing sector or would it have been better to concentrate them on the capital goods and construction sectors?

I think these questions are very difficult to answer, whether from the point of view of the United States or of the world economy as a whole. But in the absence of a clear demonstration to the contrary, I am inclined to believe that the market solution is likely to be better than one imposed by government controls. I believe therefore that allowing the dollar to rise, thus permitting the natural inflow of capital in response to the higher interest rates in the United States, was probably the preferable way of responding to the rapid increase in the budget deficit. But I hope that careful future research will eventually provide a more reliable basis for answering these questions.

The debate about the desirability of targeting the real level of the dollar presupposes that it is possible for governments to achieve such targets. The general consensus among economists, as Richard Marston indicates, is that exchange market intervention per se can have only a small and temporary effect on exchange rates. Several speakers at the conference emphasized that the recent expansion of global capital markets has further reduced the potential effects of government intervention. Shifts in monetary policy can have more substantial effects but only so long as monetary changes alone can alter real interest rates. In the longer run, exchange rates will respond only to the fundamentals of national saving rates, domestic investment demand, and trade competitiveness.

The experience during the first half of 1987 has raised some important questions about this consensus view. Although there was and still is wide agreement that the level of the dollar at the beginning of 1987 was too high to be sustainable,[1] the dollar has remained essentially unchanged between then and now (August 1987)—declining for a few months and then rising back to its earlier level. Although some or all of this might be attributed to the rise in the price of oil (which strengthens the dollar because the United States is less dependent on oil imports than Japan and Germany), to the greater than anticipated temporary decline in the U.S. budget deficit, to the reduction in the trade deficit, and to the continued strength of the American economy, the dollar's strength may also reflect the shift in international government policy toward the dollar.

In the fall of 1986, U.S. Treasury Secretary Baker, after a meeting with Japanese Finance Minister Miyazawa, adopted the position that the United States no longer favored a declining dollar. Subsequent multilateral meetings at the Louvre in February 1987 and at the Venice Summit meeting in June asserted an international consensus that a further dollar decline would be counterproductive. The leading central banks engaged in massive coordinated intervention in the first quarter of the year with central bank purchases of dollar bonds equaling or exceeding the U.S. current account deficit. The Federal Reserve announced that it had "snugged up" on monetary conditions, and U.S. interest rates rose while rates in Germany and Japan declined. It remains for future empirical research to sort out the extent to which intervention and the changes in monetary policies were responsible for the surprising behavior of the dollar during this period.

International Trade

Although the primary source of the unprecedented rise of the U.S. trade deficit between 1982 and 1986 was the increase in the value of the dollar and therefore indirectly the growth of the U.S. budget deficit, the political response to the trade deficit has been an increase in attention to the specific problems of foreign competition and international trade practices. Unfortunately, much of this response has been a harmful backsliding from free trade to various sorts of restrictions on the flow of goods to the United States. Recent years have witnessed the cartelization of key international markets, the introduction of so-called voluntary restraints on a wide range of exports to the United States, and the tightening of U.S. import quotas on textiles with the threat of much more protectionism to come as a result of the pending trade legislation.

Of course, not all of the political response to the trade deficit has been harmful. The concern about the U.S. trade balance has spurred a more assiduous pursuit of policies aimed at reducing foreign import barriers, especially those of Japan and some of its East Asian neighbors. Although these policies cannot eliminate the massive U.S. trade deficit as long as the dollar remains overvalued, they can increase the opportunity for American firms and employees to do more in those areas where they have a comparative advantage.

Cooperation in international trade requires not active comanagement of the economic environment but a negotiated reduction in government interference with private flows of trade and investment. The golden rule of international trade is the double negative injunction: "Do not unto others what you would not have them do unto you."

The major trade rounds of the past quarter century have been successful in achieving sharp reductions of tariffs and quotas. But now, as several of the conference participants noted, improving the international allocation of resources requires a reorientation of the trade negotiations.

Government subsidies to domestic industries engaged in international competition must be reduced. This is true of agricultural policies in every major industrial country. It is also increasingly true of a wide range of manufacturing industries in Europe as well as in many developing countries. Progress in these areas will be difficult not only because such subsidies restrain powerful domestic political interests but also because it will involve extending international trade negotiations outside traditional lines into subjects previously regarded as domestic concerns.

A similar extension of international trade negotiations into domestic policies is required to reduce purchasing restrictions of government buyers in transportation and telecommunications and to improve the international allocation of investment, the production of services, and the protection of patents and other forms of intellectual property. The current Uruguay Round of trade negotiations has recognized the importance of these issues. Only time will tell whether the potential gains from a better international division of labor and the negotiating skills of the parties will together be powerful enough to overcome the powerful domestic interests that stand in their way.

Developing Country Debts

Despite the conference's overarching theme of international cooperation and coordination, a striking feature of the presentations and discussion about the less-developed countries' (LDC) debt problem was the virtual absence of explicit references to intergovernmental coordination. That aspect of the conference is of course just a reflection of the way the international debt problem has been handled in practice.

Despite the desire of some commercial bankers, academic economists, and others to get governments individually and collectively to play a larger part in the resolution of the debt problem, the governments have been understandably reluctant to assume such a role. When governments have acted, they have generally acted in a largely independent role. The United States provided several "bridge" loans at an early stage in the debt crisis until commercial bank and IMF funding could be arranged. The Japanese government is now proposing to provide longer term credits on a unilateral basis and through the IMF, the World Bank, and the regional development banks. Individual governments have modified domestic banking rules to strengthen their domestic banks and to encourage those banks to continue lending to the debtor countries, with an informal, ad hoc coordination of these banking "reforms" through the regular meetings of central bankers at the Bank for International Settlements. The only explicit intergovernmental coordination of policy was through the Paris Club meetings at which the governments acted in their roles as creditors of the specific borrowing nations. The IMF was the only official participant that played an explicit major role in dealing with the debts to private creditors.

Despite the very limited official government coordination in this area, there has been extensive private coordination among the commercial banks around the world. The coordination committees of representatives of the major commercial banks have negotiated with the individual debtor governments on behalf of all the creditor banks. The debt problem has been managed by private international cooperation rather than by government coordination.

Looking ahead, the key role for official international cooperation in dealing with the debt problem should be maintaining open markers for the exports of the debtor countries. To service their debts while maintaining politically acceptable economic growth, the debtor countries must export. An increase in their exports will require a reorientation of domestic policies by the debtor nations, but it will only be possible if the creditor nations keep their markets open. Since the open markets of each creditor nation help all other creditors, and since the creditor nations as a whole have strong financial, economic, and political interests in the successful evolution of the debt problem, there is a powerful case for a coordinated agreement to maintain open markets for the products of these countries.

Concluding Comment

Economic cooperation is part of the more important process of international political cooperation. Successful coordination of policies in the economic arena can strengthen political and national security ties. Unfortunately, however, all too often the process of international economic negotiation creates new sources of conflict and tensions as each participating country seeks to impose its own preferences and judgments on the economic policies of the other governments. In recent months some governments have resented U.S. pressures to pursue more stimulative fiscal and monetary policies than they thought prudent, and they have complained about the implicit threat of using the exchange rate as a weapon to force compliance with American views. There is a danger that the process of international cooperation in macroeconomic and exchange rate management, despite its lofty aspirations, can be harmful politically as well as economically. While economic coordination and negotiation can, under the right circumstances, make a positive contribution to worldwide economic well-being, it is important not to exaggerate the potential gains from such coordination nor to pursue it in ways that threaten broader political harmony.

Note

1. For a nontechnical discussion of this, see Martin Feldstein, "Correcting the Trade Imbalance," *Foreign Affairs*, Summer 1987.

1 Macroeconomic Policy

1. Stanley Fischer
2. W. Michael Blumenthal
3. Charles L. Schultze
4. Alan Greenspan
5. Helmut Schmidt

1. Stanley Fischer

International Macroeconomic Policy Coordination

International cooperation in macroeconomic policy-making takes place in a multitude of settings, including regular diplomatic contacts, the IMF, the General Agreement on Tariffs and Trade (GATT), the European Monetary System (EMS), the OECD, the Bank for International Settlements (BIS), and summits. It takes a multitude of forms, from sharing information about current and future policies, through consultation about decisions, to actual coordination of policies. Coordination "implies a significant modification of national policies in recognition of international economic interdependence."[1]

Coordination holds out the promise of mutual gains resulting from the effects of economic policy decisions in one country on the economies of others. The Bonn Summit of 1978, in which Germany agreed to an expansionary fiscal policy in exchange for a U.S. commitment to raise the price of oil to the world level, is a much quoted example of policy coordination.[2] That agreement, followed by the second oil shock and increased inflation, was later viewed by many as a mistake. It was used in 1986 by German policymakers as an argument against the trade of fiscal expansion in Germany for fiscal contraction in the United States.

Both the potential and the incentive for economic policy coordination have increased as the world economy has become increasingly integrated since World War II. It was of course true during the entire period that other economies were significantly affected by U.S. economic performance. The impact of other economies on the United States has increased as both their share of the world Gross National Product (GNP) and the share of imports and exports in the U.S. GNP have risen. In section 1.1 of this paper, I trace the connections between economies and the impacts of foreign and U.S. fiscal and monetary policies on the respective economies. It remains true that the United States is the most independent of the major economies, that is, it is least affected by decisions made elsewhere, but even it can no longer make policy as if it is a closed economy.

Research, theoretical and applied, on policy coordination has proliferated in the last decade. The potential gains from policy coordination and the different types of possible coordination have been clarified by a theoretical literature that draws on the theory of games. Conditions under which coordination may even worsen economic performance have been identified. However, empirical work based on applications of these models implies that the potential gains from coordinating policies may be quite small. These developments are reviewed in section 1.2.

Countries have cooperated in macroeconomic policy-making since at least the interwar period when Britain's 1925 return to gold was urged and assisted by the Federal Reserve. The breakdown of cooperation and the world economy during the Great Depression served as a powerful spur to the creation in 1944 of the Bretton Woods system, the IMF, the World Bank, and GATT—institutions that would permit the resumption and growth of world trade. Those institutions, in place during a period of extraordinary growth and prosperity, were in many respects highly successful, even though in the end the Bretton Woods adjustable peg exchange rate system could not withstand the pressures of speculative capital flows.

The shift to flexible exchange rates in 1973 occurred because countries had been unable to coordinate their policies. It had been argued that flexible rates would insulate countries from foreign shocks, implying far greater freedom than under Bretton Woods to pursue domestic goals independently of foreign reactions and policies. But experience since the onset of floating rates has reaffirmed international interdependence and led to the current search for methods of cooperation. In section 1.3 I briefly describe macroeconomic policy cooperation and coordination since the 1920s and the institutions that have been put in place to facilitate that cooperation.

In section 1.4 I discuss and evaluate recent proposals for macroeconomic policy coordination, including those arising from the 1986 Tokyo agreement, the 1987 Paris agreement, and exchange rate target zones. I argue that continued systematic policy coordination on a grand scale among the major economies is unlikely, because the largest countries are still too insulated—particularly in the short run—from the foreign repercussions of their actions. The most that can be expected in the near future is occasional agreements, when a mutually advantageous bargain can be struck, and the continued exchange of information in the many formal and informal international meetings in which economic policy is discussed. But coordination on a smaller scale, as in the EMS, has developed significantly.

Eventually, but only in the very long run, as understanding of the operation of policy improves and interdependence grows, countries may begin systematically to coordinate their policy decisions for their mutual benefit. Even then, and certainly until then, the best that each country can do for other countries is to keep its own economy in shape.

1.1   The Extent of Interdependence

International trade has become increasingly important to all countries in the period since World War II. Table 1.1 presents data for the Group of 5 (G-5; i.e., five largest economies in OECD) countries.[3] Both exports and imports have risen sharply for Germany, France, and the United Kingdom. Japan's imports have not grown much as a proportion of GNP, though the export share has risen substantially. Although the proportionate increase in exports and especially imports has been high for the United States, it remains by far the most closed of the OECD economies. The importance of trade issues is seen clearly in the fact that the three largest OECD economies each had a trade gap of at least 3 percent of GNP in 1985.

More impressive even than the growth of trade in goods and services is the increasing integration of the world's capital markets. European currencies only became convertible in 1958;[4] now there is complete freedom of capital movements for the major economies, except France and Italy, and they have announced their intentions to remove controls.

Table 1.1   **Share of Exports and Imports in GNP (%)**

	U.S.	Japan	Germany	France	U.K.
1950 Exports	4.3	10.4[a]	11.4	15.6	22.3
Imports	4.1	10.5[a]	12.7	14.6	22.9
1970 Exports	5.6	11.3	22.6	15.2	22.3
Imports	5.4	10.2	20.6	14.9	21.4
1985 Exports	7.0	16.4	35.2	23.5	29.3
Imports	10.0	12.6	31.3	24.0	28.1

Source: IMF, *International Financial Statistics,* 1986.
[a]Figure is for 1955.

Whereas daily trading volume on the New York Stock Exchange averages less than $10 billion, foreign exchange transactions in Tokyo, New York, and London average more than $100 billion per day. Capital flows were the proximate cause of the death of the Bretton Woods system. They are a major and extraordinarily rapid mechanism for transmitting shocks in the international economy.[5]

Policy interactions among countries depend on the exchange rate regime. In the Bretton Woods adjustable peg system, expansionary monetary policy in the United States would cause domestic expansion, tending to raise the domestic price level, and a current account deficit. The current account deficit would cause an inflow of dollars to other countries requiring foreign monetary expansion to maintain the exchange rate. This was the source of the frequent charge that the United States exported inflation in the Bretton Woods period. With the lifting of capital controls, speculative capital flows provided a more immediate link among economies. Expansionary domestic policies could lead to the anticipation of devaluation, to a massive capital outflow, and to devaluation or an imposed change in policies.

Proponents argued that flexible exchange rates would reduce interdependence. Expansionary monetary policy in one country would lead to inflation and depreciation of that country's currency, but it would not affect other economies. There was little discussion of the international transmission, if any, of fiscal policy changes in one economy.

Interdependence has nonetheless increased in the flexible rate system. The missing element in the earlier analysis was the recognition of the slow adjustment of prices and wages. If prices and wages in the domestic economy were fully flexible, then an increase in the money stock would indeed lead immediately to a proportional increase in the price level and exchange rate. In practice, the slow adjustment of domestic prices and wages and the rapid adjustment of the exchange rate to policy changes have meant that monetary and fiscal policy changes in one country affect the real exchange rate rapidly. The real exchange rate changes are transmitted rapidly to foreign economies, affecting both the profitability of exports and the Consumer Price Index (CPI) as prices of imports change.

Policy decisions in today's flexible exchange rate world are transmitted to other countries through three main channels:

1. Policy decisions or their expectation affect interest rates and asset prices, including the exchange rate. U.S. fiscal expansion increases interest rates, attracting foreign capital and creating a demand for dollar securities. The capital inflow causes a dollar appreciation and, by drawing capital out of foreign economies, raises interest rates abroad too. U.S. monetary contraction likewise raises interest rates and causes a dollar appreciation.

2. The rapid interest rate and exchange rate responses are transmitted slowly to real variables. Exchange rate depreciation through the J-curve initially worsens the trade balance measured in domestic currency, taking up to two years (and perhaps more) to produce an improvement in the current account and, through the increase in net exports, to exert an expansionary effect on the domestic economy. By the same token, a depreciation of the domestic currency will take several years to reduce exports and real activity in foreign economies. Real interest rate movements likewise affect investment slowly.

3. Aside from their effects on trade flows, changes in exchange rates also affect domestic inflation. A depreciation directly affects domestic inflation by raising the prices of imports. Further, by increasing the profitability of exports and increasing aggregate demand, depreciation affects wage claims and thereby indirectly increases the inflation rate.

Commonsense evidence suggests these interactions are large enough to matter. The world economy recovered in 1984 and 1985 under the impetus of an expansionary U.S. fiscal policy despite restrictive European and Japanese fiscal and monetary policies. The massive appreciation of the dollar from 1980 to 1985 made large parts of U.S. industry and agriculture uncompetitive and generated strong political pressures for protection and, to a much more limited extent, for a reversal of fiscal policy.

Some econometric evidence on the extent of economic policy interactions is summarized in table 1.2, which shows the effects of fiscal and monetary policies in the United States and the rest of the OECD on their economies.[6] The data in the table are estimates of the effects of the policies in the second year after they have been introduced, by which time most of the impact of the policy change has taken place. They are based on the properties of twelve econometric models, representing a wide range of views about the operation of the economy and showing considerable diversity of results.[7]

To read table 1.2, consider a typical entry, say that for GNP in row I. Note 1 indicates that the policy action in row I is a sustained increase in U.S. government spending of 1 percent of GNP (with no change in tax rates). The entry 1.2 under "Own" means that the GNP in the United States is 1.2 percent higher in the second year after the policy has been put in place than it would otherwise have been. The entry 0.3 under "For." (Foreign) means that the GNP in the rest of the OECD in the second year after the U.S. policy change is 0.3 percent higher than it would otherwise have been. Similarly, moving across row I to the CPI column, the 1 percent of GNP increase in U.S. government spending raises the price level in both the United States and abroad by 0.3 percent (i.e., very little) relative to what it would otherwise have been.

Table 1.2   Policy Interactions, United States and the Rest of the OECD[a]

	GNP (%)		CPI (%)		Int. Rate (%)		Current Acc. ($billion)		Ex. Rate (%)
	Own	For.	Own	For.	Own	For.	Own	For.	
I.	1.2	0.3	0.3	0.3	1.1	0.4	− 13.1	6.9	+ 1.4
II.	1.5	0.2	0.3	0.5[b]	0.6	0.4	− 7.1	5.3	+ 0.4
III.	1.2	− 0.1	0.9	− 0.3	− 1.6	− 0.5	− 2.8	− 2.9	− 6.4[b]
IV.	0.6	0.1	0.5	− 0.5	− 1.1	− 0.3	− 0.2	0.1	− 3.2

Notes: 1. The policy actions are:

Row I. U.S. fiscal expansion, a sustained increase in U.S. government spending equal to 1 percent of GNP.

Row II. OECD fiscal expansion, a sustained increase in government spending in the rest of OECD by 1 percent of GNP.

Row III. U.S. monetary expansion, an increase in the U.S. money supply of 4 percent.

Row IV. OECD monetary expansion, an increase in the money supply in the rest of OECD by 4 percent.

2. "For." means foreign. In rows I and III, "Own" = U.S. and "For." = OECD; in rows II and IV, "Own" = OECD and "For." = U.S.

3. These results are averages, based on simulations of twelve econometric models. Some variables are not calculated in certain models, though in all cases there are at least ten estimates. Ranges of estimates vary; information on the ranges is reported in Holtham (1986).

4. The interest rate is a short rate.

5. The exchange rate is the value of the domestic currency. A depreciation registers as a negative number.

[a]These data are averages of data reported in tables 1a and 6a of Frankel and Rockett (1986). They are the changes in the variables shown in the second year after a policy change has been initiated. The GNP, CPI, and exchange rate data are percentage changes from a baseline value. The interest rate data are expressed as the change in the interest rate.

[b]These numbers are heavily influenced by one substantial outlier.

The strongest and most consistent results found by examining the twelve models are those for the effects of U.S. fiscal policy. The results for monetary policy show considerable divergence across the different models.

U.S. fiscal expansion, row I of table 1.2, is expansionary both in the United States and abroad, resulting in higher output and higher prices. Although the models concur in the inflationary effects in the United States, some models show U.S. fiscal expansion reducing foreign prices. U.S. fiscal expansion increases interest rates both at home and abroad and generally leads to a dollar appreciation. Note though that the interdependence between the United States and the rest of the OECD is limited: although U.S. fiscal expansion by 1 percent of GNP increases U.S. GNP by more than 1 percent, its impact in the rest of the OECD is only one-fourth of its direct U.S. impact. None of the twelve models studied shows GNP in the rest of the OECD rising by as much as 1 percent of its GNP.

The results of foreign fiscal expansion, summarized in row II of table 1.2 (here "Own" = OECD; "For." = U.S.), are consistent with the U.S. case. The foreign currency appreciation is much smaller than the dollar appreciation is in row I. This is consistent with the complaint by individual foreign countries that fiscal expansion in their countries would lead not to appreciation, as in the United States, but rather to depreciation, as a result of loss of confidence in the sustainability of their balance of payments deficit.[8] The failure of the Mitterrand expansion in 1981 is some evidence in favor of this view, though that period was marked by monetary as well as fiscal expansion. The spillover effects on GNP in the United States are quite small (0.2), though all but one of the models concur in showing these effects to be positive.

Monetary expansion in the United States is examined in row III ("Own" = U.S.; "For." = OECD). A 4 percent increase in the U.S. money stock leads to lower interest rates, a dollar depreciation, and an increase in U.S. GNP and price level. The U.S. current account is shown as worsening, probably because the effects of the increase in income on imports are more rapid than the effects of the dollar depreciation on the current account. Expansionary U.S. monetary policy is shown as having negative effects on the rest of the OECD. This must be largely due to the worsening of their current account. Note both that the table implies an improvement in the current accounts of non-OECD countries[9] and that there is a greater diversity of views among the models on the effects of monetary expansion—particularly the spillovers to the non-OECD countries—than about fiscal expansion.

Note also that foreign fiscal expansion (row II) has relatively small effects on the U.S. current account within the two-year horizon of table 1.2. An increase in government spending of 1 percent of GNP in all the rest of the OECD improves the U.S. current account by only $5.3 billion in the second year after the policy change. The table implies that the benefits of foreign expansion for U.S. exports are likely to be small.

The results of the effects of monetary expansion in the rest of the OECD (row IV; "Own" = OECD; "For." = U.S.) on those countries are in the same direction as the "Own" columns in row III. However, U.S. monetary expansion is more powerful in the United States than the rest of the OECD monetary expansion is for those countries.[10]

Table 1.2 confirms the interdependencies among economies. They are stronger—or at least more reliable—for fiscal than for monetary policy, but they also have to be qualified. In the first instance, the

"Own" effects on GNP are in all cases much larger than the "Foreign" effects, thus the interdependence is limited. This is a fundamental finding that will color much of the remainder of this paper. Second, the analysis of fiscal and monetary policy in the rest of the OECD implies a degree of coordination that simply does not exist. The major OECD countries, including Japan and Germany, do not necessarily pursue coordinated policies. Even if they did—together with France, Italy, the United Kingdom, Canada, and the smaller OECD countries—the effects of expansion in those countries on U.S. GNP would be limited, unless U.S. monetary and fiscal policies changed in response. The table therefore indirectly emphasizes the dominant role of the United States.

Significant as the basic results in table 1.2 are, recent experience suggests that they omit an important, sectoral aspect of policy interdependence. Exchange rate changes, and subsequent effects on trade flows and competitiveness, generate pressures for policy changes. In the case of an appreciation, the pressures are for protection, not for fiscal discipline. Despite the governments' commitment in principle— and, in a succession of negotiations, in practice—to increased freedom of trade, protectionist pressures from well-organized export- and import-competing sectors have been increasingly effective. That sectoral aspect of interdependence, and the dangers it brings of a breakdown of the world trading system that has been a major achievement of the entire post–World War II period, is as important for the well-being of the major economies as the direct macroeconomic interdependences that are the subject of table 1.2. Because the exchange rate adjusts very rapidly to expected and actual policy changes, the competitive effects of macroeconomic policies may begin to exert political pressures well before they have major macroeconomic impacts.

Slower moving interdependencies also deserve attention. Exchange rate changes move the location of production and international investment. The effects on the location of production go in both directions. Producers move to countries where wages, measured in international prices, are low—thus to countries with undervalued currencies. But some producers (e.g., Honda) move into countries where protectionist pressures may raise import barriers—thus to countries with overvalued currencies.

Structural interdependence arises from the growing integration of world markets and the mobility of firms to areas of least regulation and taxation. The United States and the United Kingdom have agreed to coordinate capital requirements for banks. The U.S. tax reform of 1986 may well spark similar reforms in other countries, not necessarily because the intellectual case is convincing, but because other countries want to retain the skilled and high-paid individuals affected by the reform.

1.2   Policy Coordination in Theory

The theoretical literature on macroeconomic policy coordination has grown rapidly in volume, sophistication, and complexity.[11] The basic argument for coordination can be seen in the following example. Consider two countries called, for the sake of concreteness, America and Europe, each constrained to use only fiscal policy. Suppose that fiscal expansion produces higher output and an appreciation for the expanding country. Each country is concerned about both its level of output and its current account.

In the most independent arrangement, each country chooses its optimal policy taking the policy action of the other country as given. Equilibrium in each country is reached at the point where the benefits of expansion are balanced by the costs of appreciation, given the other country's decision. This is a noncooperative equilibrium.[12]

In this situation, expansion in one country, say America, makes the other country better off. If America expands, Europe's output and current account improve, and vice versa. If both expand together, both will become better off, as output rises and the current account of each country deteriorates very little.[13] If the countries can agree on the expansion, both improve their situation. If only one country expands, it becomes worse off.[14] Without coordination or cooperation, a mutually beneficial expansion is prevented.

Perhaps the only mystery in this story is why the countries do not reach the cooperative equilibrium without coordinating. The explanation lies in the football spectator problem.[15] If everyone is sitting, someone who stands has a better view. People see equally well if everyone stands or if everyone sits. Sitting in the seats is more comfortable than standing. In the noncooperative equilibrium, everyone stands. That is because in the noncooperative case, each person does what is best for him or herself given the actions of others. If everyone sits, someone, taking what the others will do as given, will stand. If everyone is standing, then it is best to continue standing. The cooperative solution is for everyone to sit. The problem is that each person is tempted to get ahead by standing. Thus the cooperative solution will not be achieved without an explicit agreement on coordination—in this case that everyone stays seated.

Returning to the economic example, what happens if one country, say America, goes ahead in the hope that Europe will follow? After all, American expansion increases European income and improves its current account. Surely Europe will expand in response. What Europe does depends on its evaluation of American responses to its action. If it believes America will continue to act as the leader, it will likely expand, making both countries better off than they were in the noncooperative equilibrium.[16] If Europe does not respond, America is worse off for having expanded. But even if Europe does respond when America acts as leader, the final equilibrium is not as good for both countries as would be possible if each could make its policy decisions with the assurance that the other would be cooperating fully.

This example, which underlies the locomotive case for German expansion in 1977, captures the essential motivation for policy coordination. But it is not always true that coordination leads to more expansionary policies by both countries. Optimal cooperative policies depend on the objectives of the policymakers, the nature of the transmission mechanism between the economies, the policy tools that they have available, and the nature of the disturbances that hit their economies and call for policy responses.

Transmission between the economies in the locomotive example is positive: expansion in one country produces expansion and an improved current account in the other. Negative transmission is also possible: under some circumstances expansionary monetary policy in one country causes contraction in the other. If the exchange rate is viewed as an instrument of policy, competitive devaluation can produce so-called beggar-thy-neighbor outcomes in which a devaluing country gains exports and increases employment at the expense of the other, which increases its imports while it loses exports. Cooperation may then result in less active use of the policy than when the countries are independently pursuing their own interests. For instance, suppose the targets of policy are output and inflation, and monetary policy is the only instrument. In the noncooperative equilibrium, each country is balancing the costs of added inflation against the benefit of higher output. But an expansionary policy in each economy reduces output in the other. If monetary policy in each economy becomes less expansionary, the same income levels can be attained at a lower rate of inflation.[17]

Policies may also be transmitted asymmetrically between countries. As in table 1.2, monetary expansion in America may produce lower output in Europe while European money growth produces higher output in America. If the targets are inflation and output, the cooperative equilibrium is one in which Europe expands relative to the noncooperative case, while America contracts. Despite the prominence of the locomotive theory example, coordination does not necessarily mean more expansion all round.

Cooperative responses depend also, obviously, on the economic disturbances with which they have to deal. If transmission effects are positive, a shift of demand between countries will call for differing policies in the two countries. A worldwide disturbance will call for similar policy responses in different countries if transmission effects are positive.

Differences in objectives between countries affect the particular policy actions that should be taken in each country, but they do not affect the basic principle of gains from cooperation. Europe (or Germany) may be more hostile to inflation than America, but both countries can produce lower inflation rates by cooperating than by pursuing independent policies.[18]

So far it has been assumed that there is a once-for-all decision on policy which takes effect immediately. Policy analysis becomes more difficult when account is taken of both the time lags with which policy works and the fact that policy decisions are made period after period, not once-for-all. Empirical evidence shows long lags in the effects of policy decisions. The J-curve is a relevant example. When lags are long and uncertain, as they are, optimal policy is cautious. The danger is that strong actions taken today will come into effect at an uncertain later date, when they might be totally inappropriate to the economic situation.[19]

It is sometimes argued that the best policy is entirely inactive—that the government should set a constant growth rate of money, fix tax rates and government spending at levels appropriate for the long run, and not respond at all to disturbances to the economy. The argument is not entirely resolved,[20] but there is a clear case for active monetary policy to counteract shifts in money demand that would cause inflation or deflation. Similarly, the short-run inflexibility of prices combined with the rapid adjustment of the exchange rate means that foreign monetary disturbances change the real exchange rate, also creating a possible need for active monetary policy to prevent the shocks from being transmitted to the domestic economy.

Once we recognize the ongoing nature of policy interactions among countries, reputational considerations make cooperative equilibria more likely. Each country knows it will be better off in the long run if the cooperative equilibrium is maintained. Countries may develop strategies both to punish those that do not cooperate, and to earn a reputation for reliability. It then becomes possible that countries will reach and stay at the cooperative equilibrium. This reduces the force of the one-period example by suggesting that there is more cooperation than the discussion of the football spectators suggests.

Coordination through reputation, without explicit international agreements, is less likely the more countries there are. When everyone is at the cooperative equilibrium, the temptation for one small country to break ranks is very strong. The potential cost to it of doing so may also be high, for it is more dependent on the world economy than is a larger country. But because it inflicts very little damage on the rest of the world by not cooperating, it is not certain that it will be penalized. Coordination is probably easier to achieve among larger countries, or among groups of countries that have coordinated policies internally, despite the inverse relationship between the size and openness of economies.

What happens to cooperation when countries have different views about the effects of policy? Frankel (1986) and Frankel and Rockett (1986) have examined cooperative policy-making when nations have different models of the economy. Given each country's model, it is possible to find a set of policies that each nation believes will improve its welfare. Whether those policies will actually improve economic performance in their countries depends on the true model of the economy. Frankel and Rockett use the twelve models of the economy whose properties are summarized in table 1.2 to examine the outcome of policies that might be agreed to. Assume that each country believes in one of the twelve models, and further that one of the models is correct, but that no one knows which it is. Frankel and Rockett show that it is quite likely that cooperation makes an economy worse off than it would be if it pursued a noncooperative strategy, doing what it regarded as best given the actions of other countries.

The force of this calculation is that the twelve models examined have each been advanced by reputable scholars, they come from several countries, and several might be used in choosing policies in their countries. If policy coordination agreements were made on the basis of those models, they would be quite likely to turn out badly. Just how powerful this result is depends on whether there are policies whose effects are widely agreed upon and which work in the agreed upon manner. It is then possible that policies that are not optimal in any model, but that do well in all of them, would perform well in the real world.

Rogoff (1985) and Kehoe (1986) have shown another condition under which cooperative policy may produce a worse outcome than the Nash equilibrium. In the Rogoff example,[21] domestic wage setting depends on the expected price level. The policy variable is the money stock. In the absence of cooperation, each central bank is constrained from trying to raise output through expansionary policy by the inflationary impact of the resultant depreciation. When the central banks cooperate, that constraint is removed. Expecting more inflation, wage setters set a higher nominal wage, and on average the price level is higher. If the central banks could precommit themselves not to attempt to expand the money supply excessively after the wage has been set, cooperation would produce better performance than uncoordinated policy.[22]

Many of the qualifications to the locomotive theory example raise doubts about the potential gains from cooperative policy-making. Another source of doubt is the weak interaction effects examined in table 1.2. Several authors have attempted to estimate potential gains from cooperation using econometric models. The best-known work is that of Oudiz and Sachs (1984), who used the Federal Reserve's multi-country model (MCM) and the Japanese Economic Planning Agency (EPA) model to study coordination among the United States, Japan, and Germany.

Oudiz and Sachs assumed that governments target the level of GNP, the inflation rate, and the current account. They estimated the trade-offs that each country was willing to make among the three goals on the basis of experience in those countries. Japan, for instance, appears to put the highest weight on the current account, Germany on the inflation rate.

Using these trade-offs, Oudiz and Sachs (1984) calculated the gains that would have been obtained in 1984–86 by pursuing cooperative policies. Their basic result is that the gains for the United States and Germany would have been small (averaging, across the two models, less than 0.2 percent of GNP per year) while those for Japan were larger (averaging nearly 0.7 percent of GNP per year across the two models).[23] Surprisingly, cooperation involved expansionary fiscal and monetary policies in the United States, and fiscal contraction with monetary expansion in Germany and Japan. Oudiz and Sachs argued that the improvement from cooperation would increase if the entire OECD, or the major European countries, were added to the model.

In a subsequent paper, Oudiz (1985) examined policy coordination within the EMS. Interaction effects are stronger than they are between the United States and the rest of the OECD in table 1.2. Nonetheless, the gains from coordination are again quite limited, except in the case of France which would gain nearly 1 percent of GNP per year. Hughes Hallett (1986) finds small gains from cooperation between the United States and Europe, with most of the gains accruing to Europe.

The game theory literature on policy coordination, then, makes a convincing case that coordination is generally superior to noncooperative policy-making. But beyond that general principle, it provides no simple results showing how cooperative rules should operate. It shows also that there are exceptions to this principle, most important that the application of cooperative policies calculated in incorrect models may worsen rather than improve economic performance. It may be better to look for robust rules that perform well in many models than rules that are optimal in a particular model. Finally, calculations imply that the gains from coordination per se would be small, even if the correct model of the economy were known.

1.3 The Historical Background

International cooperation in economic policy extends back at least to nineteenth-century cooperation between central banks. The Bank of England and the Bank of France, the major repositories of gold in Europe, helped each other out in several nineteenth-century crises, starting as early as 1825 (Clapham 1944).[24] Russia and France, economically linked through French loans to Russia, also cooperated in maintaining the convertibility of gold in France.

The nineteenth-century gold standard imposed discipline on monetary policies. As has often been remarked, the system was far from automatic.[25] Supposedly, a set of "rules of the game" developed to describe the policies central banks should have followed. The standard account of the operation of the gold standard, in which an expansionary shock in one country leads to a gold outflow, implies that central banks should have permitted the money stock to be determined by gold flows. However, Bloomfield (1959) has shown that gold inflows were typically offset rather than allowed to produce automatic changes in the domestic money supply. Although policy had discretionary elements, one rule was followed consistently: tighten interest rates to defend the convertibility of gold. Thus the indirect effects of high interest rates on domestic activity substituted for the gold flow mechanism which Hume argued equilibrated the system. Explicit cooperation between central banks was episodic, associated with crises, but nonetheless effective. The coordination of nonexistent fiscal policies was not an issue.

Cooperation between central banks became much more active in the 1920s.[26] After Britain decided in 1918 to return to gold at the prewar parity, international conferences in 1920 and 1922 laid the foundation for the return to gold in a gold exchange standard. The conclusions of the 1922 Genoa Conference noted the need to avoid a competitive struggle by central banks to acquire gold but did not specify how such a cooperative solution was to be obtained.

Britain's return to gold in 1925 was actively encouraged by both the League of Nations and the Federal Reserve System. Benjamin Strong of the New York Federal Reserve Bank and Montagu Norman of the Bank of England were in very close touch throughout the 1920s, and the New York Fed supported Britain's return to gold with a $300 million loan. Strong and Norman's attempts to restore the gold standard system seemed to have succeeded by the end of the 1920s when over fifty countries were back on gold.

But by that stage the weakness of the system was already becoming clear. Britain had gone back to gold with an overvalued exchange rate and struggled through the rest of the 1920s to bring prices down further. Tight monetary policy, meaning high interest rates, was under constant attack from the U.K. Treasury, implying that the coordination imposed by the discipline of the inappropriate exchange rate might not withstand domestic political pressures. France in 1926 undervalued the franc and began accumulating gold with the intention of building Paris as a major financial center. This was the competitive struggle for gold that the Genoa Conference had warned against. Fixed exchange rate systems create an asymmetry between creditors and debtors that enables the former to avoid adjusting, and that creates the incentive for competitive beggar-thy-neighbor devaluations.

The fixed parities could not withstand the shocks of the Great Depression and the persistent attempts of France to accumulate gold.[27] By 1931 Britain was off gold, floating its exchange rate and beginning a period of relative recovery. In 1933 the United States left gold, in the process torpedoing that year's World Monetary and Economic Conference meeting in London that had on its agenda the stabilization of exchange rates. In 1934 the dollar attained de facto stability against gold at $35 an ounce. All through this period France stayed on gold, devaluing eventually in 1936. A tripartite agreement was reached in that year to set exchange rates among the franc, dollar, and sterling, and it operated successfully through 1939, permitting devaluations of the franc while maintaining stability of the dollar-sterling exchange rate.

The lessons of the interwar period for cooperation are mixed. The cooperative return of Britain to gold at the prewar parity—chosen by Britain itself—was a mistake. France's lack of cooperation in competing for gold showed the potential weakness of a fixed-rate system. And the unwillingness of Britain and the United States to subordinate their domestic policies to maintenance of the gold standard when the going got tough is a warning of the effective limitations of international constraints on domestic policy. Issues of fiscal policy coordination did not arise in this period either, aside from general agreement that budgets should be balanced.

The most significant breakdown of international cooperation during the interwar period came in the competitive devaluations and growth of protection that sharply reduced the volume of world trade during the Great Depression. That breakdown, more than the failures of monetary coordination, is the shadow hanging over the international economy, warning of the continued need for cooperative policy.[28]

An important question that arises from the interwar period is that raised by Kindleberger (1986): Was the Great Depression itself largely due to a failure of international monetary leadership? Kindleberger argues that the international system cannot operate successfully unless some country or institution takes the responsibility of acting as lender of last resort in times of distress.

There can be little doubt that vigorous Federal Reserve policy in 1931, directed at stopping the domestic recession, would both have prevented the worst of the Great Depression in the United States and reduced its impact in other countries. But given that the Fed already had the clear task of sustaining domestic stability, it is difficult to see that agreements on international coordination would have led it to be more expansionary than it was.

Bretton Woods in 1944 was the first, and probably the last, occasion that the entire structure of the international economy could be considered anew. The IMF, as it emerged, was closer to the American (White) plan than to the British (Keynes) proposal. The Keynes plan was more ambitious, particularly in encouraging adjustment on both surplus and debtor countries. Reserves were to be held in international currency (Bancor) units at the IMF, and interest would have been paid on both excess and deficient balances. A country holding excess reserves would have had to discuss with the IMF its plans for adjustment, including appreciation or expansion of the domestic economy. However, the IMF had no power to enforce policy decisions. The IMF would have been required to expand the total of reserves at a rate appropriate to the expansion of world trade.

The adjustable peg exchange rate system was common to both proposals. Under the Bretton Woods agreement, countries could adjust the exchange rate if they were in "fundamental disequilibrium." Except for adjustments within a 20 percent band of the parity first established, members would change exchange rates only with IMF approval—it was not anticipated that they would be adjusted often. Convertibility was expected to be restored after an initial adjustment period. The IMF could lend to deficit countries but was not expected to finance capital outflows, which were instead to be handled through capital controls.[29] Policy coordination would come from the discipline of the fixed exchange rates, and from discussion and consultation within the IMF. "What had been created was the embryo of a world central bank" (Solomon 1977, p. 13), but it did not control the world supply of money or even high powered money.

The IBRD, also set up at Bretton Woods, was expected to help finance postwar reconstruction, but supplanted by the Marshall Plan, it has devoted itself to development. A stillborn International Trade Organization to promote free trade, negotiated in 1946 and 1947, was not ratified. The GATT, a surprising success, has served much that same purpose.

Bretton Woods was followed by a quarter century of substantial exchange rate stability, rapid economic growth, and the growth of world trade. From 1949 to the 1960s, only France and Canada among the major countries adjusted their exchange rates. In 1958 the major countries moved to convertibility, with Japan following in 1964. The dollar had become the world's main reserve currency; the dollar shortage was by the end of the 1950s giving way to concerns about the U.S. balance of payments deficit. Triffin (1960) had begun to warn of the need for a more systematic basis for regulating reserve creation than

U.S. balance of payments deficits. Despite the omens, the system had given the world economy one of its most impressive periods of growth.

In the early 1960s the United States built up a set of measures to defend the dollar, including swaps with other central banks, the issue of foreign-currency-denominated bonds, and the Interest Equalization Tax. The U.S. current account deficit declined during that period and went into surplus, but capital outflows and later foreign (mainly French) gold purchases kept up the pressure. Domestic policy was affected by the position of the dollar: expansionary policy was inhibited at the beginning of the Kennedy Administration, and their monetary policy's "Operation Twist," intended to raise the short interest rate relative to the long, was an attempt to encourage investment without causing a capital outflow. The investment tax credit had the same aim.

The 1960s also saw the development of regular consultation on economic policy among the OECD countries outside the framework of the IMF. The OECD's Economic Policy Committee meets three times a year with senior government officials (e.g., the Chairman of the Council of Economic Advisers from the United States) in attendance. Working Party 3, to which the ten largest members of the OECD (G-10) belong, meets even more frequently. There is no lack of discussion or information about their current economic policies among the major industrialized economies—although countries are less likely to discuss future policy changes in these forums.

The shift of consultations to the OECD reflected both the increase in the membership of the IMF and the European countries' desire to meet on more equal terms with the Americans. The possibility arose in the early 1960s that the United States would have to borrow from the IMF to support the dollar, but IMF resources were inadequate. The G-10 was the locus for discussions that set up the General Arrangements to Borrow (GAB), which would provide—with G-10 approval—loans to the IMF.

In the 1960s the Europeans used Working Party 3 meetings to pressure the United States to deal with the dollar problem. The Europeans attributed the problem to expansionary U.S. monetary policy which, it was argued, was exporting inflation to Europe. Robert Solomon (1977) emphasizes that there was remarkably little discussion of possible exchange rate adjustments. Americans believed the dollar could not be devalued against gold without completely changing the nature of the monetary system by putting the reserve currency role of the dollar in doubt. The Europeans did not want to revalue because the United States had a current account surplus; the problem at that stage was one of capital flows, not the current account.

The discipline imposed by the fixed exchange rate system in the 1960s is worth emphasizing. Germany and the Netherlands revalued in 1961. The next major adjustment was the British devaluation in 1967. That came after a three-year struggle by the Labor government to avoid the stigma of devaluation. A massive loan package assembled from the GAB, IMF, the United States, and other sources in 1964 preserved the $2.80 parity, but crises recurred in the next two years. Despite cooperative attempts to starve off the devaluation, including both intervention by and loans from the Fed and other central banks, and restrictive domestic policies, Britain in the end succumbed. The Bretton Woods system unquestionably enforced policy coordination—though not to the benefit of the British economy at the time.

Purchases of gold from the London gold pool accelerated after the British devaluation, culminating in the closing of the pool and the institution of the two-tier price system. The United States remained committed to buy and sell gold at the official price in intercentral bank dealings, but not to sell to private buyers. Dollar reserves were still claims on gold, but the agreement was that those claims would not be pursued. Negotiations for the establishment of the SDR were proceeding at the same time.[30] The first SDR's were created in 1970, giving the IMF the ability to create a reserve asset, and opening up the possibility of the IMF developing eventually into a world central bank, as the Keynes plan had envisaged.[31]

Exchange crises became more regular after 1968. Capital flowed into Germany, creating pressure for revaluation. French political problems created pressures for devaluation. In an Alphonse and Gerhardt routine repeated in 1987, each preferred the other to act. Both acted in 1969, when the mark was allowed to float for a time before a new parity was set. In 1970 the Canadian dollar was set afloat. Despite a current account surplus of $2 billion, capital outflows produced a U.S. balance of payments deficit (before official transfers) of $10 billion, 1 percent of GNP.

The Bretton Woods system succumbed in 1971. Massive capital flows forced the mark to float in May. In August the United States imposed the wage-price freeze, a 10 percent import surcharge, and suspended gold convertibility. In subsequent negotiations, the United States agreed to raise the price of gold as part of a package leading to the return to fixed rates. The December 1971 Smithsonian agreement established a new set of parities, which lasted, with strains, for the next fifteen months. During that period the European currency snake, the forerunner of the EMS, was established.

In February 1973, Japan, Italy, and Switzerland floated their currencies. The snake currencies followed, and the worldwide fixed exchange rate system was dead. It had operated successfully until the mid-1960s and had continued to put pressure on domestic policies into the 1970s. It was a victim fundamentally of the failure of countries fully to coordinate their macroeconomic policies. The system imposed discipline on countries in deficit as they faced an increasing probability of running out of reserves. But because its liabilities were the main reserve currency, there was not the same discipline on the United States when it ran deficits. The surplus countries were unwilling to expand at a rate sufficient to make revaluations unnecessary; alternatively, they were unwilling to accept foreign rates of inflation. Nor were the deficit countries willing to accept the contractionary policies that would have been needed for them to protect the exchange rate.

Proximately the Bretton Woods system succumbed to massive international capital flows. Capital flows fast in the international monetary system, and it is doubtful that macroeconomic policies to cure the imbalances of the early 1970s would have taken effect quickly enough to maintain the exchange rate. Perhaps a firm commitment by all countries to pursue exchange rate targets, firmly believed, would have been self-sustaining. But it is hard to imagine that all the major countries will ever firmly commit themselves to exchange rate targets unless they use the same money. Thus it is difficult to see among the major countries the successful return to a fixed exchange rate system with free capital flows.

The fact that the capital flows precipitated exchange rate changes does not establish that they were destabilizing. They may rather have recognized the inevitable. In some cases capital flows were beaten back. In 1964 Italy refused to devalue despite capital outflows, obtained international loans, and prevailed. So for a time did Britain. The Italian refusal to devalue, followed by rapid growth, was probably wise; the British decision followed by three years of slow growth was not. It can be concluded neither that speculative capital flows should always be resisted, nor that they should always be succumbed to.

The outstanding feature and the major surprise of the new era that began in 1973 is the volatility of both nominal and real exchange rates, as illustrated in figure 1.1. Exchange rates fluctuate more than prices of goods but less than stock prices. Table 1.3 presents measures of the variability of the month to month changes in the exchange rate.[32] Equally surprising have been the massive cumulative, and ultimately reversed, movements in the dollar, dominated of course by its movements in the 1980s. Note though that the real value of the dollar is only now returning to its value at the start of the decade.

The issue of whether exchange rates fluctuate excessively has been extensively though inconclusively researched.[33] Pre-1970s theoretical discussion argued that speculation was inherently stabilizing because successful speculators would have to buy low and sell high. More recently it has been shown that speculative bubbles can exist without anyone necessarily losing money. Excessive volatility of exchange rates

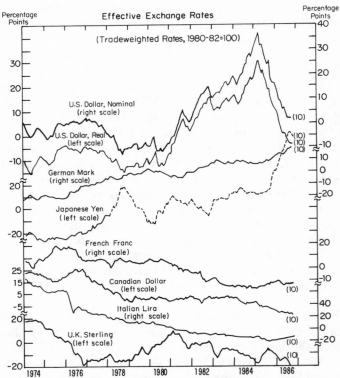

Figure 1.1   Exchange rates, 1974–1987. *Source:* Goldman Sachs Economic Research.

is thus a theoretical possibility, but empirical research has not been able to show that rates have fluctuated more than they should have, given economic policies, the shocks hitting the economy, and the information available to market participants. In particular, the system had to deal with the strains of two massive oil shocks and unprecedented divergences between fiscal policies in the United States and the rest of the world.[34]

Exchange rate movements in 1973 and 1974 led to discussions of intervention among the central banks, which agreed to maintain orderly conditions in the markets. It was already becoming clear that floating rates did not insulate countries from each other's policies and that the same conflicts that had led to the breakdown of Bretton Woods could reappear in the new floating rate world.

Policy discussions and the sharing of information continued in the OECD forums and in the IMF. Policy coordination continued to be discussed and little acted upon. It was during this period that the Economic Summits emerged as vehicles for policy discussions and decisions.[35]

Table 1.3   **Exchange Rate Variability**

	Exchange Rate	CPI	New York Stock Exchange
United States	22.8	5.0	53.9
Germany	19.3	3.9	
Japan	33.1	35.3	

Notes: 1. Data are standard deviations of monthly change in the variables, expressed as a percentage at an annual rate from July 1973 to December 1986.
2. Exchange rate is a trade-weighted (MERM) index from *International Financial Statistics.*
3. Standard deviation of Japanese CPI inflation is very high in part because of high and variable Japanese inflation up to 1975. The standard deviation of Japanese CPI inflation for the period starting July 1976 is only 8.3.
4. The New York Stock Exchange index is Standard & Poor's 500.

Participants in the first Summit, at Rambouillet in 1975, accepted floating exchange rates, giving up the notion that a restoration of fixed parities was likely, and agreed to intervene to maintain orderly markets.

After remaining reasonably stable in the first year of the Carter Administration, the dollar began to slide in 1978 as the U.S. economy, with the aid of active fiscal and monetary policies, continued its rapid recovery from the 1974–75 recession. With the U.S. expansion helping other countries, but the dollar under pressure, the call for international coordination began to be heard. Germany, the strongest economy in Europe and the leader of its currency bloc, was the main focus of attention, seen as the potential locomotive for the world recovery. Japan was under less pressure because it had agreed at the 1977 Summit to seek annual growth of 7 percent and had introduced an expansionary budget.

The Europeans, in turn, regarded U.S. policy as too expansionary. In addition, they argued that the U.S. failure to adjust the price of oil to world levels was worsening its balance of payments and strengthening the Organization of Petroleum Exporting Countries (OPEC). As the 1978 Bonn Summit approached, the dimensions of a deal could be seen. The deal was that Germany would increase government spending by 1 percent of GNP, while the United States would put in place a program to reduce oil imports. In addition, the United States agreed to undertake anti-inflationary measures, including a reduction in a planned 1979 tax cut.

In their analysis of the bargain reached in Bonn, Putnam and Henning (1986) point to domestic disagreements on policy as an important reason for success of the international agreements. In neither Germany nor the United States was there a consensus for the policies agreed to by the governments at the Summit. Oil price decontrol was unpopular in the U.S. Congress; expansion was opposed by important segments of the German political and economic system. Putnam and Henning argue that the domestic proponents of the policies were able to use the Summit process to move the decision their way, inviting the pressure exerted by foreign governments. They suggest that Chancellor Schmidt may have been quite willing to expand but preferred to conceal his preferences for domestic political reasons. This analysis does not encourage the view that international coordination can easily be achieved on a regular basis.

Whereas the previous London Summit had reached agreed but not plausible growth targets, the Bonn Summit agreement was more specific, and was thus verifiable and credible, in specifying policy actions for the United States and Germany.[36] Japan was specific in agreeing to hold exports to no growth, a commitment that was achieved, but the communique again specified a Japanese growth target rather than specific fiscal or monetary actions. Germany passed the expansionary budget package within a month of the Summit. The United States was slower in following through, but the commitment was an important factor in strengthening the resolve of the Carter Administration to decontrol oil prices.

The Bonn Summit is credited by de Menil and Solomon (1983) with also contributing to the successful conclusion of the 1979 Tokyo Round of tariff negotiations. The London Summit had expressed the desire of the participants for a prompt and positive conclusion of the tariff negotiations, a commitment that was exploited by the U.S. representative to force final agreement by the time of the Bonn Summit.

The second oil shock struck between the Bonn and Tokyo Summits. Both the Tokyo and the 1980 Venice Summits were dominated by the energy problem, and no macroeconomic policy agreements were reached. This was not only because the Germans had begun to regard the Bonn agreement as a mistake, but also because there were no obvious macroeconomic bargains to be reached.

Despite the German expansion, the dollar continued to fall after the Bonn Summit. U.S. inflation was rising. The United States pressured Germany to intervene in support of the dollar, but the Bundesbank resisted, pushing instead for a change in U.S. domestic policy. In October the President announced an anti-inflationary package that included voluntary wage-price restraints. In response the dollar declined sharply. By November the Fed had assembled an announced $30 billion fund which it would use in support of the dollar. This time the dollar responded favorably and continued to rise through the middle of 1979.

In November 1979 the United States made the basic decision to fight inflation through restrictive monetary policy. Although the decision commanded wide international support, it was made largely for domestic reasons as inflation was increasingly recognized as the number one problem facing the nation.

The cast of summit characters changed in the 1980s. With widespread agreement that the fight against inflation was first priority, there was at first little need to discuss macroeconomic policy. At the beginning of the Reagan Administration, the United States adopted a hands-off policy on the exchange rate, showing remarkable equanimity about the rise of the dollar. The vigor of the 1984 recovery kept the dollar problem concealed from the political process through that year. But as the nature of the U.S. twin deficit problem became clearer, and as the political pressures of declining exports and rising imports mounted, echoes of the 1976–78 debate were heard.

With the change of U.S. Treasury Secretary in 1985, and growing protectionist pressure in Congress, the Reagan Administration began to look for ways to reduce the trade deficit and to move the dollar down. Japan-bashing became a popular if ineffective political activity. The Administration was unwilling to raise taxes and was unable to cut spending. Unable to attack the trade deficit through fiscal policy,[37] it was constrained to fight for the opening of foreign markets and to attempt to push down the dollar. The dollar slide that had begun in February 1985 was briefly accelerated by the announcement of the Plaza G-5 agreement of September 1985 that agreed to intervene to push down the dollar. The dollar continued its decline into 1986.

Déjà vu arrived in 1986. Germany and Japan were being pressured to expand to help the United States. Neither wanted to expand, putting the onus of the problem on U.S. fiscal policy. Economists could see a clear bargain: U.S. fiscal contraction offset by domestic monetary expansion and Japanese and German expansion. But the Reagan Administration was not taking that route. There were of course differences between the 1986 and 1976–78 debates. Among them: the inflation rate was low—close to zero in Germany and Japan; the United Kingdom was far less expansionary than it had been a decade earlier.

Talk of policy coordination increased. The 1986 Tokyo Summit agreed that the G-7 finance ministers would meet at least once a year to review the compatibility of their economic objectives. They were to consult a large set of indicators, including policy variables. The finance ministers were "to make their best efforts to reach an understanding on appropriate remedial measures whenever there are significant deviations from an intended course." The significance of this agreement is discussed in section 1.4.

There was also some action. In October 1986 the finance ministers of the United States and Japan agreed that Japan would reduce its discount rate, in that the United States would continue to fight protectionism and that the then-current yen-dollar exchange rate [154 yen to the dollar] was "broadly consistent with the present underlying fundamentals." The agreement noted and strengthened the fiscal expansion package Japan was undertaking and recorded the U.S. tax reform act. The agreement was also thought to be a signal to the Germans that they might lose their seat at the very top levels if they failed to cooperate.

In February 1987, the G-7 met in Paris and issued a communique stating that exchange rates were currently appropriate given the economic policies being followed. The Germans agreed to increase slightly the tax cut they were planning for 1987, and the Japanese pledged to pursue fiscal expansion, as previously agreed. The United States for its part would attempt to bring its budget deficit down. There was no explicit mention of intervention to attempt to enforce the current levels of exchange rates.

The concentration on U.S.-Europe-Japan relations should not be allowed to obscure the importance of the EMS, set up in 1978. The EMS can be viewed as an agreement by France and Italy to accept German leadership in monetary policy, imposing constraints on their domestic monetary and fiscal policies. The EMS has been surprisingly successful, withstanding even the Mitterrand expansion in 1981–82. With the announcement in 1986 that Italy and France plan to lift capital controls, the EMS now faces a crucial test.[38] British membership, which appears increasingly likely, would also significantly change the nature of the organization by adding another capital-control-free currency to the system. British and German policies would have to be closely coordinated if the fixed exchange rate within the EMS were to hold for any length of time, otherwise capital flows between the two currencies would quickly force changes in the parity.

Discussions of economic policy also take place in the framework of the IMF, under the general heading of surveillance. The end of the Bretton Woods system left the IMF's responsibilities for dealing with exchange rates undefined. The IMF's Article IV, dealing with exchange rates, was amended in 1978. Members recognized their obligation not to manipulate exchange rates unfairly, and the IMF was given the responsibility of exercising "firm surveillance over the exchange rate policies of members." Bilateral Article IV discussions between the IMF and members take place annually, but the Article IV reports are not published.

Multilateral surveillance is less regular and formalized. The IMF Managing Director attends some G-5 meetings but is not apparently in a position to exercise influence. The *World Economic Outlook,* published since 1980, is discussed at Executive Board meetings, but this is not known to influence policy in individual countries. In 1985 both the G-10 and the Group of 24 developing countries published proposals for multilateral surveillance, with a greater emphasis on the international economy and policy coordination. With the Tokyo Summit agreement, these proposals are presumably moving toward implementation.[39]

1.4   The Prospects for Coordination

The historical record suggests the following generalizations:

- The Bretton Woods system imposed significant constraints on domestic policies, including on occasion U.S. domestic policy.
- Under Bretton Woods, countries were not willing to subordinate domestic policies entirely to maintenance of the exchange rate. The same was true under the gold exchange standard of the interwar period.
- Increasingly massive capital flows made maintenance of fixed rates progressively more difficult, perhaps because it was clear countries were not absolutely committed to maintaining the exchange rate.
- Information sharing about economic policy has been extensive since the 1960s and has moved to increasingly authoritative levels of government.
- Interdependence among economies did not markedly decline as a result of the move to floating exchange rates. Countries were revealed not to be indifferent to the behavior of their exchange rates, and they sometimes took domestic policy actions in response. Exchange rate crises occurred, not in the form of an attack on a fixed rate, but rather as a rapid shift out of a currency and rapid depreciation.
- Policy coordination under the Bretton Woods system occurred more as a result of the constraints imposed by the system than by explicit agreement.
- Explicit coordination has been rare in the post–Bretton Woods period. The Bonn Summit is a clear example of such coordination. International political pressures to change economic policy have been common, especially in the last few years, as the magnitude of the U.S. trade deficit problem became clear. Apparent agreements on policy coordination were reached in October 1986 and February 1987, but it is not yet clear whether any policy actions will follow.

The bewildering array of organizations, meetings, plans, and activities described in the previous section should not be allowed to obscure the basic question of what is to be gained by international coordination. The evidence of section 2.2 is that the gains at best would be modest and that there is a possibility that the gains would be negative.

I will now discuss the prospects for four different types of coordination, in the order of the increasing constraints imposed on individual countries.

1.4.1   Surveillance and Information Exchange

Information exchanges already take place on a broad scale. The shift to regular consultation among finance ministers envisaged in the Tokyo

Summit agreement makes it more likely that the international implications of domestic policy decisions will be weighed, as the finance minister contemplates explaining the decision to his counterparts at the next meeting.

Multilateral surveillance can bring an outside perspective to economic discussions that may be clouded by domestic political considerations. In this connection, it could be helpful if a way were found to publish some version of the IMF's Article IV reports, which are of a generally high standard and could serve as an outside technical evaluation of domestic policies. These reports could eventually exercise some influence over domestic policy decisions if they turned out over the years to provide a good analysis of the state of the world economy.

Useful as this type of information exchange is, it cannot be expected to exert more than a marginal influence on policy.

1.4.2   Discretionary Policy Deals

Occasionally there is a clear international policy deal to be made. That was true in 1978; it appears to be true in 1987. Regularly scheduled OECD meetings, those among finance ministers set up at Tokyo, special meetings such as that at the Louvre in February 1987, and the Summits are the appropriate places for such deals to be made. They will and should continue to occur.

It is doubtful though that continuing coordination, "significant modification of national policies in recognition of international economic interdependence," will emerge from these meetings. The domestic political process is sufficiently complicated that the international input cannot be more than a small factor in regular policy-making. Putnam and Henning's (1986) analysis of the Bonn agreement suggests the importance of the domestic political configurations in that case.

In both the Bonn Summit case and the possible February 1987 trade of German and Japanese expansion for a reduction in the U.S. budget deficit along with increased resistance to protection, the proposals involve a change in American policy that looks untenable in the long run. The supporters of coordination in the United States call on the international factor to help change American policy of which they disapprove. It is doubtful that they would be as enthusiastic if in 1982 coordination had required them to accept the current German view that there is very little to be done about high unemployment and that budget balance is the main criterion for good policy.

There is nothing in either the Bonn Summit or the 1987 examples to refute the view that there would be little need for coordination if each country were taking good care of its own domestic policies.

1.4.3   Policy Harmonization through Rule Changes

The rules of the Bretton Woods system enforced more coordination than the successor regime. A return to fixed exchange rates among all the major economies now looks unlikely, but suggestions for changes in the international rules are frequent. I briefly discuss two proposals.

The McKinnon Monetary Rule: Ronald McKinnon (1984) has suggested that money growth rates be coordinated among the United States, Japan, and Germany. His proposal can be phrased alternatively as tieing national money growth rates to the behavior of the exchange rate. An appreciation of a currency is a cause for greater money growth in that country and less money growth elsewhere. The assumption underlying this rule is that international shifts in the demand for money are the main causes of exchange rate changes. The rule could have unfortunate consequences; for instance, expansionary fiscal policy would induce an increase in the money stock.

The rule approach to monetary and fiscal policies, exemplified by the McKinnon monetary rule, is attractive in providing certainty about policy. If optimal rules for all countries could be calculated, taking into account the interactions among economies, it would be sensible to implement them, perhaps even by law. The Bretton Woods system can be seen as an example of such a system, which, while not prescribing policy, put in place an immediate target of policy—maintenance of the exchange rate—that tightly constrained policy choices. That system ultimately broke down; there has been no similar simple replacement suggested; and the state of knowledge about the effects of monetary and fiscal policies is not such as to commend the implementation of monetary and fiscal policy rules any time soon.

The Target Zone Proposal: Seeking to combine the virtues of floating rates with the benefits of fixed rates, John Williamson (1985) has proposed target zones for exchange rates. Countries would announce wide bands within which the exchange rate could move, but they would have to take corrective action as the exchange rate approached the limits of the bands. Williamson's proposals have received widespread attention.[40] The elusive character of the zones suggests they will not much constrain domestic policies unless the exchange rate reaches the limits of the zone. At that point countries will face the same choices they faced in the Bretton Woods system, and it is not clear why they will not then move their zones. The proposal is a subtle and probably ineffective way to introduce gentle discipline on players who have been impervious to rigorous discipline in the past.

1.4.4   A Three-Currency Bloc World

The international economy appears increasingly to be evolving into three currency blocs: the yen, the dollar, and the mark or the EMS currency. There are fixed rates within each bloc, implying coordination of fiscal and monetary policies within the blocs, and flexible rates between them.

Those countries that are sufficiently willing to coordinate their policies to maintain a fixed exchange rate indicate their willingness by joining the bloc. That is what the decision to join the EMS means, and, if it continues to develop successfully, it may eventually evolve into a truly fixed exchange rate regime.

The three-bloc system is very close to the notion of optimal currency areas discussed by Robert Mundell (1971) in 1961. Mundell asked what characteristic defined an area or group of countries in which it was optimal to maintain a fixed exchange rate. He argued that the key was the mobility within that area of factors of production (i.e., capital and labor).

Consider, for instance, the United States. If each state had its own currency, the Texas dollar would have appreciated in the 1970s and depreciated in the 1980s. Because there is factor mobility in the United States, the adjustment came instead by labor and capital moving into Texas in the 1970s and out in the 1980s. So long as factors are mobile, adjustment can come through movements of factors rather than changes in the real exchange rate.

Why would adjustment through factor mobility be preferable to adjustment through exchange rate changes? Ultimately the argument comes down to risk sharing. If every region in the country were an independent currency area with no factor mobility, individuals' incomes would fluctuate with the state of the local economy. They would do better than average sometimes and less well at other times. With factor mobility, individuals reduce the variability of their incomes by retaining the right to move on to other markets when the local economy shrinks.

On the basis of the mobility of factors of production, Europe may eventually become a natural currency area. Japan and the United States already are. It seems unlikely that full freedom of factor movements, including labor, will develop among the three areas. That is the reason why the world is more likely to see three currency blocs rather than just one, and that is why exchange rates among them are likely to remain flexible.

1.5 Concluding Comments

The notion of international policy coordination is appealing and appears to hold out the promise of major improvements in economic performance. However, estimates of the quantitative impacts of policy decisions in one economy on other economies are quite small. These results, together with explicit calculations of the benefits of coordination, suggest the gains will rarely be significant. Further, theoretical analysis finds many circumstances under which coordination worsens rather than improves economic performance.

The interest in policy coordination in the United States has been strongest when advocates of coordination were hoping to use international policy agreements to bring about changes in domestic policies that they regarded as either undesirable or eventually untenable. It is entirely possible though that formal coordination would sometimes require a country to undertake policy actions of which it disapproved.

So long as exchange rates remain flexible—and they will likely remain flexible among the three major currency areas—macroeconomic policy coordination among the major blocs is unlikely to advance beyond the provision of mutual information and occasional agreements for specific policy trade-offs. Both information interchanges and occasional policy agreements when the circumstances are right are useful and should be encouraged.

But more consistent ongoing policy coordination in which countries, including the United States, significantly modify national policies "in recognition of international policy interdependence" is not on the near horizon. Fortunately, the evidence suggests that the potential gains from coordination are in any event small: the best that each country can do for other countries is to keep its own economy in shape.

Notes

I am indebted to Geoffrey Carliner, Rudiger Dornbusch, and Martin Feldstein for comments.

1. This definition is from Wallich (1984).

2. Putnam and Henning (1986) provide a comprehensive analysis of this episode.

3. Except for the United Kingdom, the share of exports for each country in 1950 was below its 1929 level. U.S. imports, which amounted to 10 percent of GNP in 1985, have risen more rapidly than exports.

4. Germany has allowed its residents to export capital since 1957; convertibility in 1958 applied to external holders of other European currencies, while capital controls continued for domestic residents.

5. They played this role too in the heyday of the gold standard from 1880 to 1914.

6. The properties of twelve international econometric models were discussed at a Brookings Conference on Empirical Macroeconomics for Interdependent Economies, March 1986. Frankel and Rockett (1986), Hickman (1986), and Holtham (1986) all present summaries of some of the properties of those models.

7. The twelve models are: DRI multicountry; Compact (European Economic Community); EPA (Japanese Economic Planning Agency); Project Link; Liverpool (a rational expectations monetarist model); MSG (McKibbin-Sachs

global); MCM (Federal Reserve Board's Multicountry Model); Minimod (based in the IMF); Interlink (from the OECD); Taylor (from Stanford University); VAR (a minimally structured vector autoregressive model); and Wharton mode.

8. Oudiz and Sachs (1984) show that fiscal expansion may cause depreciation for countries whose liabilities are not held internationally.

9. If the current accounts of both the United States and the rest of the OECD worsen, the current accounts of other countries must improve.

10. The "foreign" effects of the monetary expansions have different signs in some columns. However, estimates of these effects show a wide range, and the precise numerical magnitudes should not be given significant weight.

11. Mundell (1971) is an influential contributor. Hamada (1985), Buiter and Marston (1985), and Cooper (1986) are useful general references to the theoretical literature. This section draws in particular on Canzoneri and Gray (1983), and Canzoneri and Henderson (1987); the latter provides a comprehensive view of recent developments.

12. In game theory jargon, it is called a Nash equilibrium.

13. The mutual expansion cannot continue without limit, either because expansion worsens current accounts (vis-à-vis the rest of the world) or because full employment is reached.

14. The reasoning is as follows: The country had previously expanded to the point where the benefits of expansion were balanced by the cost of appreciation. If it now expands further, the costs of the appreciation outweigh the benefits of the expansion.

15. The usual example is the prisoners' dilemma. Here two suspects, questioned separately, are each offered a better deal if he confesses than if he remains silent while the other confesses. If neither confesses, the prosecution fails to convict. Fearing that the other will confess, each prisoner confesses. If they had been able to coordinate, neither would have confessed. Since it is not clear whether to be on the side of the prisoners (in which case the cooperative equilibrium is better) or the law (when the noncooperative solution is socially preferable), I give a slightly less familiar example.

16. Technically, America is acting as a Stackelberg leader, and the new equilibrium is a Stackelberg equilibrium. See Canzoneri and Henderson (1987) for more precise definitions and a discussion of some problems with the Stackelberg equilibrium.

17. Canzoneri and Gray (1983) analyze this example in detail.

18. It is often pointed out in the literature that the coordination problem disappears if each country has as many policy instruments as targets. With perfect certainty, each country can then attain its targets exactly, and need not worry about foreign decisions. When the effects of policy are uncertain, international coordination may still be useful, even if each country has as many policy instruments as targets.

19. This is what happened after the Bonn Summit in 1978 when an expansionary German fiscal policy began to take effect as the second oil shock hit.

20. It is reviewed at length in Fischer (1988).

21. This is closely related to the Barro-Gordon (1983) analysis in which discretionary policy raises the average rate of inflation.

22. Kehoe's (1986) example is also based on the government's inability to precommit, in his case not to tax capital heavily.

23. The differences between the results using the two models are large, e.g., 0.99 percent of GNP per year gain in the MCM for Japan, versus 0.37 percent per year in the EPA.

24. The assistance from the Bank of France to the Bank of England in 1825 was indirect, the British Foreign Secretary finding assistance from so recently defeated an enemy difficult to acknowledge (Clapham 1944, p. 101).

25. Fischer (1988) discusses the automaticity of the system.

26. Eichengreen (1985) provides an interesting account of this period, drawing on the theoretical developments described in section 1.2 above.

27. Einzig (1937) sharply criticizes French international monetary policy in the interwar period.

28. Devaluations per se were actually expansionary, since by raising the value of gold they increased the nominal value of the world money stock. It should also be noted that there are no estimates of the cost to individual economies of the reduction in the volume of trade. At the macro level, protectionism diverted demand from the international to the domestic economy, and it is not certain that the total loss of demand was necessarily high. At the micro level, protectionism reduced welfare by denying economies the benefits of comparative advantage.

29. In this section I draw freely on Robert Solomon's (1977) account of the period.

30. The creation of the SDR was the culmination of a process that started with a G-10 group set up in 1964 to study the creation of reserve assets.

31. Fischer (1983) discusses this possibility.

32. In table 6.2 of his paper in this volume, Richard Marston presents related data. Apparent differences are a result of my expressing the rates of change as percentages of annual rates.

33. Richard Marston discusses the possible excess volatility of exchange rates in section 6.1 of his paper in this volume.

34. I take up in section 1.4 the question of whether the floating rate system itself made these divergent policies possible.

35. The six largest countries in the OECD participated in the first two Summits; since then, Canada has become a member of the group (G-7). De Menil and Solomon (1983) describe and analyze the Summits through 1982.

36. The appendix of de Menil and Solomon (1983) summarizes the communiques of the first eight Summits.

37. Unless one counts the 1984 *Economic Report of the President* as an administration document, there was no administration recognition through the end of 1986 that the trade deficit is linked to the budget deficit.

38. Giavazzi and Giovannini (1986) argue that capital controls have been essential to the success of the EMS.

39. Kenen (1986) and Solomon (1987) contain insightful discussions and proposals on the prospects of multilateral surveillance.

40. See, for instance, Brainard and Perry (1986).

References

Barro, Robert J., and David B. Gordon. 1983. A positive theory of monetary policy in a natural-rate model. *Journal of Political Economy* 91:589–610.

Bloomfield, Arthur I. 1959. *Monetary policy under the international gold standard: 1880–1914.* Federal Reserve Bank of New York.

Brainard, William C., and George L. Perry, eds. 1986. Symposium on exchange rates, trade and capital flows. *Brookings Papers on Economic Activity* 1:165–235.

Buiter, Willem H., and Richard C. Marston, 1985. *International economic policy coordination*. New York: Cambridge University Press.

Canzoneri, Matthew, and Joanna Gray. 1983. Two essays on monetary policy in an interdependent world. Federal Reserve Board, International Finance Discussion Paper no. 219.

Canzoneri, Matthew, and Dale W. Henderson. 1987. Strategic aspects of macroeconomic policymaking in interdependent economies. Georgetown University. Typescript.

Clapham, John. 1944. *The Bank of England*. Vol. 2. London: Cambridge University Press.

Cooper, Richard N. 1986. *Economic policy in an interdependent world*, chap. 11. Cambridge, Mass.: MIT Press.

de Menil, George, and Anthony M. Solomon. 1983. *Economic summitry*. New York: Council on Foreign Relations.

Eichengreen, Barry. 1985. International policy coordination in historical perspective: A view from the interwar years. In *International economic policy coordination*, ed. Willem H. Buiter and Richard C. Marston. New York: Cambridge University Press.

Einzig, Paul. 1937. *World finance 1935–1936*. New York: Macmillan.

Fischer, Stanley. 1983. The SDR and the IMF: Toward a world central bank? In *International money and credit: The policy roles*, ed. George von Furstenberg. Washington, D.C.: International Monetary Fund.

———. 1988. Rules versus discretion in monetary policy. Forthcoming in *Handbook of Monetary Economics*, ed. B. Friedman and F. Hahn. Amsterdam: North-Holland.

Frankel, Jeffrey A. 1986. The sources of disagreement among international macro models and implications for policy coordination. NBER Working Paper no. 1925. Cambridge, Mass.: National Bureau of Economic Research.

Frankel, Jeffrey A., and Katherine Rockett. 1986. International macroeconomic policy coordination when policy-makers disagree on the model. NBER Working Paper no. 2059. Cambridge, Mass.: National Bureau of Economic Research.

Giavazzi, Francesco, and Alberto Giovannini. 1986. The EMS and the dollar. *Economic Policy* 1(2):455–74.

Hallett, A. J. Hughes. 1986. International policy design and sustainable policy bargains. University of Newcastle upon Tyne, England. Mimeo.

Hamada, Koichi. 1985. *The political economy of international monetary interdependence*. Cambridge, Mass.: MIT Press.

Hickman, Bert G. 1986. The U.S. economy and the international transmission mechanism: A structural comparison of twelve multicountry models. Center for Economic Policy Research, Stanford University, no. 78.

Holtham, Gerald. 1986. International policy co-ordination: How much consensus is there? Brookings Discussion Papers in International Economics, no. 50.

Kehoe, Patrick J. 1986. International policy cooperation may be undesirable. Federal Reserve Bank of Minneapolis, Staff Report no. 103.

Kenen, Peter B. 1986. What role for IMF surveillance? *World Development*.

Kindleberger, Charles P. 1986. *The world in depression*. 2d ed. Berkeley: University of California Press.

McKinnon, Ronald I. 1984. *A new international standard for monetary stabilization*. Washington, D.C.: Institute for International Economics.

Mundell, Robert A. 1971. European and American monetary policy. In R. A. Mundell, *Monetary theory.* Pacific Palisades, Calif.: Goodyear.

Oudiz, Gilles. 1985. European policy coordination: An evaluation. Centre for Economic Policy Research, London, England, Paper no. 81.

Oudiz, Gilles, and Jeffrey Sachs. 1984. Macroeconomic policy coordination among the industrial economies. *Brookings Papers on Economic Activity* 1:1–64.

Putnam, Robert D., and C. Randall Henning. 1986. The Bonn Summit of 1978: How does international policy coordination actually work? Brookings Discussion Papers in International Economics, no. 53.

Rogoff, Kenneth. 1985. Can international monetary policy cooperation be counterproductive? *Journal of International Economics* 18:199–217.

Solomon, Robert. 1977. *The international monetary system 1945–76: An insider's view.* New York: Harper & Row.

———. 1987. IMF surveillance. Brookings Institution. Mimeo.

Triffin, Robert. 1960. *Gold and the dollar crisis.* New Haven: Yale University Press.

Wallich, Henry C. 1984. Institutional cooperation in the world economy. In *The world economic system: Performance and prospects,* ed. Jacob A. Frenkel and Michael L. Mussa. Dover, Mass.: Auburn House Publishing.

Williamson, John. 1985. *The exchange rate system.* Policy Analyses in International Economics no. 5. Washington, D.C.: Institute for International Economics.

2. W. Michael Blumenthal

Two Perspectives on International Macroeconomic Policy Coordination

I thought that perhaps I, as someone who is responsible for what is probably the prototype for a large, modern, computer-age, multinational firm, could make a modest contribution to begin with by injecting, if you will, a note of reality into this discussion. Then I'd like to describe to you what it is governments face as they wrestle with macroeconomic policies and as they attempt to coordinate and collaborate on matters relating to macroeconomics.

I will very briefly tell you what Unisys Corporation does and how a company like ours functions. But, of course, this is not intended to be a commercial at all.

Unisys has annual sales of roughly $10 billion, half in the United States, half outside. Our activities are distributed through one hundred different countries, with major concentrations in the European Economic Community, Japan, Canada, Mexico, Brazil, Korea, and Taiwan, in addition to the United States.

We sell information systems and services that consist of totally intermingled products and components. Memory chips come from Japan, logic chips from the United States, cables and similar accessories from Mexico, the heads for the storage gear are assembled in Singapore, central processors are assembled in the United States, the United Kingdom, France, Brazil, Belgium, Canada, and several other places. The software is produced all around the world, including Asia and the Middle East. Media are produced in Ireland. And so it goes.

The point is that our products, both hardware and software, are composed of subsystems and parts and services that come from all over the world, and they are totally intermingled when they reach the user.

Our financial operations are also worldwide. The best example of this was our need to raise about $5 billion quickly last year when we acquired another company. Three leading banks put together a consortium; the telegrams went out at about 4:01 PM on a Monday afternoon, right after the markets closed; and by the next morning a consortium of more than fifty banks had been assembled and the $5 billion had been oversubscribed. This involved Japanese banks, eleven banks in Europe, and the rest in the United States and Canada.

We immediately hedged our interest rate exposure, since these were in large part floating rate loans. Of course, we are constantly in the foreign exchange markets to hedge our foreign exchange rate exposure relating to our regular day-to-day activities in the various countries where we operate.

The executive team of Unisys is multinational. The top forty or fifty people in the company include Americans, British, Swedes, Swiss, Japanese, Germans, Indians, Chinese, Canadians, and probably a few other nationalities.

Production can shift very rapidly in our kind of business. We made a decision just before Christmas of 1986 to move a complex operation from Santa Clara, California, to Singapore. There had been nothing done on this except a feasibility study. The first storage gear heads are being assembled in Singapore this month (April 1987). In something like 90 to 120 days, we were able to move a critical production operation literally halfway around the world.

Our products are usually shipped by air. Since quarterly results are important in the United States, where we're measured on quarterly report cards, I can tell you that we put systems on airplanes on the 29th of March to reach customers all over the world and that they were billed on the 31st. Within 24 to 36 hours, our equipment can go anyplace in the world and reach the customer.

Our computer systems in customer sites are often linked one with the other. For example, large systems in Hong Kong or Taiwan can be monitored through customer service centers established in Sydney, Australia. If anything goes wrong with a customer anywhere in Southeast Asia, our service centers can monitor, fix, and keep the systems going across national boundaries.

Patents are freely exchanged. They are royalty free, for much of the technology in our industry is pretty well internationalized. Because investments in technology are very heavy, there is an enormous intertwining of companies. To put it another way, everybody in this industry is in bed with everybody else. We buy from our major competitors and they buy from us. Most of us are interlinked with one another. We are, all at the same time, suppliers, customers, and competitors. We joint venture, we co-produce, we share, we compete.

This is the reality of a modern, high-technology corporation, and, of course, there are many, many others like us. Though there are many industries and companies whose focus is much more domestic, I think that this international pattern is becoming more common, whether in automobiles, pharmaceuticals, or even in more traditionally domestic industries such as textiles.

Now I will make a few comments about what I believe this picture of the Unisys Corporation illustrates. First, there is indeed an increasingly high degree of structural interdependence between companies operating across national subsidiaries with regards to products and components, manufacturing operations, the mobility of various factors of production, and the intertwining of operations.

Factor mobility, unthinkable fifteen or twenty years ago, is now a reality, a fact of life. This applies, and I did not stress it, even to assembly labor for both hardware and software. In the case of software, for example, we have arrangements with countries in which the cost of labor is low since labor costs are important in the software area. Throughout the world, therefore, you will find, say, Indian nationals brought from India on temporary duty to do software work in other countries. They are employed in their own countries, as a kind of contract labor, and they remain based in their own countries. This shows that factors of production previously considered immobile have now become quite mobile.

National boundaries have lost much of their meaning for us because of the scope and character of our operations. As far as our operations are concerned, national boundaries have become a hindrance and a nuisance, but we tend to find ways to get around them.

When you think about it, the concept of a "national" corporation is perhaps becoming obsolete. It is difficult to think of Unisys as an American corporation, given the kind of organizational pattern I have described. That argument is even more properly applied to our major competitor, IBM. They have long been one of the larger Japanese computer exporters, and their products are probably more totally in-termingled as to origin than is true for us. Thus, the concept of a national corporate entity in this kind of world is becoming increasingly anachronistic.

The final critical point is that all of this has become possible because in the last ten or fifteen years accelerating technology has fundamentally altered the way we do business.

I will turn now to the government perspective. Thinking about the kind of culture shock I had to go through as I moved from the government sector to the private sector in 1980 clearly brings home to me the widening gap between government thinking, government organization, and government concerns, on the one hand, and the way many key elements in the private sector actually function, on the other. This leads me to two rather important conclusions.

First, technology has made it extraordinarily difficult to understand, let alone manage, our economic affairs and our macroeconomic problems. Perhaps this is self-evident. I think we've all experienced this difficulty during our various tours of duty. I'm not sure that I fully appreciated the width of the gulf that has opened up between practices and requirements when I last served in the government, or that I fully understood the complexities of the new issues we have to face.

The second fundamental conclusion that one would have to reach, except that I don't quite know what to do with it, is that national sovereignty as an underlying basis for the conduct of either domestic or international economic affairs is increasingly inefficient and inapplicable to the kind of economic environment that governments have to face. Or, to put it another way, technology has outstripped or over-taken the kind of political economy that we have been used to in the past.

What are the implications of all this? I'm not suggesting that we ought to strive for world government as a solution, although one could argue that that is where the ultimate logic might lead us. That's obviously not a rational guide for future research, although it does raise interesting questions about where we may ultimately come out. All this does imply that political economists must urgently focus on the means and the mechanisms for the management of either domestic or international economic relations that better take into account the realities of the private sector that I have described.

I should note parenthetically that I have read with interest the debate in the literature about whether international collaboration is useful and the interesting descriptions of cases where coordination of economic policies internationally may in fact be counterproductive. No doubt that's possible. But I would have to say that, at least in the world in which I function, there is little doubt in my mind that the internationalization of operations and the efforts to coordinate policies are not zero-sum games. This is true as much for the government sector as it is for the private sector, if it is done right.

The problem that we will be discussing here is, of course, that so far the record of our efforts to cope with the new economic environment is a pretty modest one and that there is, to put it mildly, ample room for improvement.

Based on my experience in government under three presidents during the last twenty-five years, I would say that up to the early 1970s we weren't doing all that badly. We had a reasonably functioning regime for international collaboration suited reasonably well to the then-prevailing circumstances, which were, of course, among others, the paramount importance of U.S. economic power in the world system, Bretton Woods, and the fact that we were operating, in the premicroelectronic era, a point I keep coming back to over and over again.

We had a GATT that functioned reasonably well in trade matters. It was well suited to a world where merchandise trade was of key importance, factors of production were much less mobile, the capital markets were nationally distinct, and tariffs were a critical form of protection, although even then agriculture, nontariff barriers, invisible trade, and similar areas were not really handled well. But these were merely imperfections in a system that otherwise was reasonably efficient.

Similarly, the IMF, the World Bank, and the OECD (as a forum for a discussion of national economic policies) all served us reasonably well during that period. When it came to developed and less-developed country (LDC) relations, by the early 1970s the system was getting rather creaky, as witnessed by the growing dissatisfaction of LDCs leading to the creation of UNCTAD, lack of progress in agriculture, worries about technology transfers, the American challenge, and so forth.

It seems to me that today we have to conclude that most of these institutions have been rendered substantially less effective. They have been overtaken by events. In the trade area, with a bow in Bob Strauss's direction, I would have to say that the last truly far-reaching trade negotiation successfully completed under the GATT was the Kennedy Round which ended in 1967. Since then, really substantive negotiations have become very difficult to complete because such matters as non-tariff barriers, intellectual property, agriculture, and transport investment simply are not suitable for negotiation in that kind of forum, and we have not found a successful substitute as yet.

The IMF has been no more successful than the central banks and the ministries of finance in working to keep order in the world financial markets and to keep international exchange rates from overshooting and undershooting and making life difficult for those in the private sector such as myself.

And, of course, these institutions have also proved inadequate to deal with the implications of the debt crisis or to cope with the burgeoning problem of the debt of the developing countries.

So, clearly, we need to think about what steps can be taken, gradually no doubt, to improve the institutional framework. We do need to improve these institutions and to develop new institutions that are better able to cope with the kinds of problems I have described. I would think that this will involve (and presumably this will be discussed here) new and better coordination of the world banking system, perhaps with an information exchange among the central banks with more policy coordination on elements of national monetary policy and a closer coordination with the activities of the IMF. A new regime is needed to limit excessive exchange rate fluctuations, and a better framework to deal with agricultural matters is also long overdue. Here again, technology has been the major factor. If there's any truth to the basic rule that it is the sight of the gallows that clarifies the mind and that it is only in periods of exigency that governments begin to focus on how they can better work together, then it seems to me that the time has come to do more. Clearly, an expanded and improved trade and investment organization that can deal with some of the new issues that I have referred to is needed. And, of course, international collaboration in the security markets and in their regulation—recognizing the fact that these markets are totally tied together and are really functioning as one—would be most helpful.

Let me just say one more thing about the Summits, since I participated in three of them. I have very little to add to what I think has been an excellent summary report by de Menil and Solomon (1983). I agree, based on my experience, that though the Summits are imperfect, they do provide a useful basis on which to build; they are important from the point of view of public education on these issues; they do expose world leaders to each other; and they do get the bureaucracies in the various countries energized and counteract national with international concerns. Thus, it seems to me that even if they do not show any concrete progress, they do serve to keep us from sliding back. And they do allow national governments to focus on and bring to a head disputes, disagreements, and policies that are deadlocked. Thus, Summits can become a convenient political mechanism for national leaders to push forward their own policies. I think that is the story of the Bonn Summit. Obviously, Chancellor Schmidt can speak to this with greater authority.

My impression, looking back on the Bonn Summit as a successful Summit in which something was really accomplished, is that most of the things decided upon were really matters that the various governments at that point wished to do anyway. I know that was true with regard to the United States on the energy commitment, and it is my impression, at least in looking back (and I'm sure Helmut Schmidt will comment on this), that by the time the Summit had come around, he and his government were also anxious to move on the commitments they had made. The Summit provided a convenient way of accomplishing that. So the notion that the Summits are a true bargaining forum, at least based on the three that I have attended, strikes me as somewhat unrealistic. But they can be an important way for the various government leaders to get their domestic constituencies to go along with what they feel needs to be done. I think that is a technique that ought to be built on, perhaps in a variety of ways. I see that there are two Summit models that are mentioned—one a very informal one just for the top leaders and their deputies to come together; the other a more permanent institutional framework. My own view is that, based on my experience, it's not really a question of one or the other. We probably need both in order to make some progress.

Reference

de Menil, George, and Anthony M. Solomon. 1983. *Economic summitry.* New York: Council on Foreign Relations.

3. Charles L. Schultze

International Macroeconomics Coordination— Marrying the Economic Models with Political Reality

Stanley Fischer's background paper provides a balanced and highly useful exposition of recent economic research into the problem of macroeconomic policy coordination. Precisely because it is an excellent analytic summary of the state of the art from the professional economist's standpoint, it highlights how drastically the theoretical discussion is forced to simplify the complexities of the political forces and motivations which actually drive macroeconomic decision making in both the domestic and international arenas. I want to use the analytic framework that Fischer lays out as a starting point and then try to see what happens, along various dimensions, as we introduce some easily recognizable political and institutional realities that do not square with the usual assumption of the theory. In the process I will make some specific observations about several past and present efforts to achieve macroeconomic policy coordination.

The Theoretical Model

The framework within which macroeconomic policy is typically analyzed has the following characteristics. In each country there is a monolithic decision-making entity, "the government." The government has a relatively limited number of macroeconomic policy objectives; they are usually three in number: output, inflation, and the foreign balance. The government also has a small number of policy instruments to use in nudging the economy toward its targets. (The number of policy instruments is at least one less than the number of macroeconomic targets.) Those instruments are almost always fiscal policy and monetary policy. Finally, all governments agree in broad outline on how the world works with respect to such key matters as the short-run trade-off between inflation and unemployment, the interconnections between domestic policy actions, exchange rates, and the trade balance, and the current economic outlook. Given these underlying assumptions and recognizing that the setting of policy dials by one country affects the economic performance of other countries through trade balances and exchange rates, the theoretical models attempt to show how, and under what specific circumstances, countries can all do a better job of achieving their own macroeconomic goals when they act in concert and in ways that engender mutual trust, compared to the outcome when they act alone. Indeed, in these models macroeconomic policy coordination does not constitute a "deal" or "trade" in which one party gives up one thing to get another. Given the assumptions, each party can, through coordination of policies, have more of what it wants in one or more macroeconomic dimensions without giving up anything in the other.

If the major elements of the policy coordination game were, in fact, as I have sketched out, we should have seen a lot more macroeconomic coordination among countries than we have in recent decades. Why, if there are possibilities of clear gains from coordination that can be identified by all parties, do we not have more of it? Stanley Fischer gives us the analogies of the football spectators and the prisoners' dilemma. Everybody in the football stands would be better off if everyone sat down, but acting alone each spectator finds it in his self-interest to stand. The two prisoners would be better off if both kept their mouths shut, but acting alone each is better off to inform on the other. But this will not do as an explanation. We are not dealing with 50,000 football spectators but with the top officials of only five—or at most seven—

countries. And, unlike the prisoners, no one is keeping these officials from talking to each other.

Some Political Realities

In my judgment macroeconomic policy coordination is so hard to come by and its costs and benefits are so hard to assess because decision makers do not act the way the models require. There are four major ways in which political reality tends to deviate significantly from the underlying assumptions of the theoretical model. Let me first describe them and then suggest how they substantially complicate the problem of both thinking about and carrying out international policy coordination.

First, it is quite common, if not universal, that presidents, prime ministers, cabinet officers, parliamentarians, and congressmen do not think of macroeconomic and other policy instruments solely as instruments but very often treat those instruments as very important ends in themselves, or at least as way stations on the road to some other important end with little relationship to macroeconomic demand management. President Reagan does not think of taxes as an instrument of fiscal policy. Low tax rates are in themselves his highest priority domestic objective on structural supply-side grounds. The shadow price at which he would trade off fiscal deficits for low taxes is, I think, very close to infinite. To the U.S. Congress, spending programs are not fiscal policy instruments but ends in themselves. While I am less familiar with Japan, it is my impression that for Prime Minister Nakasone, reducing the Japanese budget deficit to zero by 1990 is an ultimate objective; Japanese fiscal policy is not for him an instrument to be used for other macroeconomic ends. A bit later on I will try to show how the fact that macroeconomic policy instruments are often themselves political goals usually makes the process of international policy coordination much more difficult, but occasionally it can have the opposite effect.

A second way in which the world differs from the assumptions of theoretical models is that political decision makers in the various countries (and their economic advisers) often do not share a common view of how the economic world works. It is my strong impression, for example, that current German political leaders believe some combination of two things: (1) The scope for faster German expansion is still severely limited by structural rigidities and by an excessive level of real wages. Any substantial demand stimulus from the government would do little to raise output and would mainly be dissipated in higher inflation. (2) Despite the expected fall in exports, overall economic growth in Germany is likely to proceed at a satisfactory pace without the need for additional stimulus from the government. These views are obviously not shared by the U.S. Treasury (or at least they do not believe them to be applicable to Germany). Similarly, from their public statements and private conversations, top Japanese officials apparently believe strongly that the long-run equilibrium value for the yen to be somewhere in the range of 150 to 160 to the dollar (or higher). They resist a further drop in the dollar not merely because they think it has been going down *too fast,* but rather because it has already reached or fallen below its equilibrium value. It is hard to find anyone in U.S. officialdom who agrees with that conclusion. Fischer recognizes and indeed emphasizes the difficulty that arises for the theoretical analysis of policy coordination when decision makers have significantly different economic models in mind. He cites several articles which conclude that such differences hinder the making of mutually acceptable macroeconomic bargains, and, according to one study, can make them dangerous.[1]

A third way in which the simplifications needed for the theoretical models importantly fail to represent reality is their implicit assumption that for each government there is a single unitary decision maker with a well-defined set of policy preferences.[2] In fact, as we all know, government decisions are the outcome of a tug-of-war within the government itself. On some issues the differences are small and the decisions overwhelmingly one-sided. But sometimes the differences are wide and deep with the power balance fairly evenly divided. In those cases the final decision is a close one and is usually a compromise among the warring factions.

This departure from the theoretical model lends itself at least occasionally to the striking of international bargains and enlarges the possibility of macroeconomic coordination. When part of one government is, for purely domestic reasons, pushing for a change in some macroeconomic policy, the fact that the change can be used to extract a favorable move from other governments can tip the balance toward the proponents of change.[3] It is much more difficult to model this process, however, and because different power centers within a single government have differently weighted objectives and different views of how the world works, it is also more difficult to show that a deal will necessarily improve each country's performance.

The fourth way in which the world of international political bargains differs from the analytic models of policy coordination is that some of the most important possibilities for coordination involve a "deal" in which some countries trade commitments to change macroeconomic policy for concessions from other countries in areas that have little to do with macroeconomics. The 1978 Bonn Summit agreement was a case in point.[4] In fact, the world is even more complicated than this, as we shall see, because even here a "deal" can usually be struck only when there are important *differences of opinion within countries* about the policies that are being "traded."

Let me try very briefly to formulate a few generalizations about how these characteristics affect the prospects for and the potential benefits and costs of different types of policy coordination.

Various Kinds of Policy Coordination

It is useful in thinking about this problem to distinguish two kinds of policy coordination: First, there is coordination through continuing adherence to an agreed upon rule (or set of rules) to guide macroeconomic policy. Bretton Woods provided such a set of rules at the core of which was the commitment so to conduct policy as to maintain fixed exchange rates. Second, there is discretionary coordination based on case-by-case bargaining that produces a specific agreement to do certain specific things on a one-time, or at least time-limited, basis. The agreement reached at the Bonn Summit and, arguably, the Plaza agreement of September 1985 are examples of this second type.[5]

Coordination by Rule: Exchange Rate Target Zones

One prominent proposal that has been circulating in recent years is for a return to a modified and softened form of a fixed exchange rate. Countries would agree to keep their rates within an agreed upon target zone and implicitly undertake to conduct their macroeconomic policies to meet this commitment.[6] One major benefit claimed for such a system is that it would create a political commitment powerful enough to keep countries from embarking on macroeconomic policies that tend to drive exchange rates far away from their long-run equilibrium and create tremendous temporary disturbances in trade and capital flows and industrial structures. The extreme mix of U.S. fiscal and monetary policies of the last five years is a key example of the kind of policy that presumably would be prevented. There are economic reasons to be chary of a target zone system,[7] but I want to concentrate on the political implications. In a world in which political leaders treated the components of fiscal policy—tax rates and expenditure programs—as instruments, and, within limits, attached no overriding importance to their level, then conceivably honoring the commitment to a target zone might over time begin to acquire some weight as a political goal. But, in fact, it is hard for me to imagine that President Reagan would have given up his twin commitments to increased defense spending and cutting taxes for the sake of keeping the dollar within the target zone. The whole job of trying to meet the target zone commitment would have fallen on the Federal Reserve System, which in order to keep the dollar from appreciating would have been committed to a policy of keeping U.S. nominal interest rates low, despite the huge budget deficits. The result would have been the creation of substantial inflationary pressure within the United States and quite possibly after a year or two a dollar which violated the target zone agreement on the downside!

To generalize, on those not infrequent occasions in which the instruments of fiscal policy are treated by political leaders as high-priority objectives in themselves, a country loses the ability to vary the mix of fiscal and monetary policies to meet the exchange rate commitment without substantial damage to domestic output or inflation objectives. In those circumstances, to try to enforce macroeconomic policy coordination through an agreement to fix exchange rates could lead to highly undesirable consequences. Granted that the size of the U.S. fiscal deficit was determined by other than macroeconomic considerations, it was far better to have suffered the divergent macroeconomic and wide exchange rate swings that resulted than to have coordinated policy with a large inflationary bias. And I can imagine political circumstances where the results could be deflationary in nature. More generally, the lesson to be drawn from this is that if one of the instruments of macroeconomic policy is subject to being fixed by considerations other than macroeconomic objectives, adhering to any kind of an exchange rule will sometimes lead to highly undesirable consequences.

Discretionary Coordination: The "Pure" Case

There are several types of discretionary macropolicy coordination. One of these is the "pure" case along the lines of theoretical models that Fischer presented, in which all countries can gain on one or several fronts through coordination without having to give anything up. There are situations where the political realities do match the simplifying assumptions of the model. One example would be an agreement among countries, in the face of a serious recession, not to use competitive beggar-thy-neighbor devaluation as a means of exporting employment.[8] A closely related real world example was the generally well-observed agreement among the OECD countries at the onset of the 1975 recession that they would not resort to protectionist measures. Generally, in a deep recession common to all countries, various kinds of policy coordination can be arranged and can pay off. But these are easy cases. In a deep recession, not complicated by a previously inherited inflation, almost all economic models will at least point in the same direction, even if they disagree over magnitude—aggregate demand expansion can raise output without significant costs in higher inflation. Coordination expansion can remove potential current account and exchange rate problems that might constrain any one country from acting alone. Moreover, while political leaders often treat fiscal policy instruments as ends, the treatment is asymmetric. Low tax rates are an end in themselves, but high tax rates are not. Mutatis mutandis, the same is true of expenditures. In a deep recession political leaders are less likely to balk at fiscal expansion because they have independent goals of high tax rates and low spending programs.[9]

Outside of a deep worldwide recession, however, the existence of the political realities I outlined earlier will usually make the analysis and the execution of purely macroeconomic policy coordination quite difficult.

Fischer, for example, tells us that economists can see a clear potential bargain at the present time—it would consist of, on the one side, reduction in the U.S. budget deficit accompanied by U.S. monetary expansion and, on the other side, Japanese and German expansion of domestic demand. The logic behind this concerted action presumably is that the United States could reduce its budget deficit and its trade deficit at a smaller cost in a depreciated exchange rate if only Germany and Japan would expand domestic demand more rapidly. On the other side, Germany and Japan could raise domestic demand and absorption without risking additional inflation. But here the fact that fiscal policy instruments are treated as goals gets in the way of the macroeconomic bargain. The reason the U.S. budget deficit remains high is *not* because U.S. leaders fear the additional dollar depreciation that deficit reduction would bring. Far from it. Fear of a depreciated dollar is not why President Reagan refuses to agree to a tax increase nor why the Congress refuses to cut spending programs by enough to do the job. The potential bargain is irrelevant to them because it treats as an instrument to be costlessly changed what they consider a policy goal. Since substantial downward pressure on the dollar continues despite the current U.S. budget impasse, the U.S. Treasury and the Federal Reserve would prefer to have more of the relief on the trade deficit come from European and Japanese expansion and less from a depreciating dollar. And it is, of course, quite conceivable that Germany and Japan may end up taking stimulative action on their own. But their actions will not be taken in order to generate faster demand growth than they earlier forecast, but rather to keep demand and output from slipping badly below that forecast.

On the other side of the ledger, the fact that one instrument of economic policy is frozen, because it has been fixed in pursuit of other goals, may increase the need for macroeconomic policy coordination. Several of Fischer's examples have to do with situations in which countries can use only one of the two fiscal policy instruments. Richard Cooper has argued, with respect to European countries, that the emergence of a full-fledged international capital market has increased the freedom of individual countries to expand on their own without the constraint generated by fears of a depreciating currency.[10] Fiscal expansion, partially offset by tight money and higher interest rates, would make it possible to finance the resulting current account deficit without the necessity of a large devaluation. But if, as appears to be the case, most European governments during the past four years set their sights on a policy of long-run "consolidation" of their budget deficits, expansive fiscal policies were anathema to them. In that case, reliance on a "go it alone" monetary policy for expansion could indeed lead to problems of currency depreciation and great inflationary pressure. Expansion requires coordination of monetary policies. Thus, turning instruments into goals sometimes precludes and sometimes increases the need for policy coordination.

The fact that different governments, and different groups within the same government, often do not agree about how the economic world works makes a big difference to the prospects of policy coordination. In extreme situations—deep worldwide recession or deep inflation—there is more likely to be agreement within and among countries about causes and consequences. But in other situations, different economic models may well give different signals even with respect to direction. So the pure model of mutual gains from cooperation breaks down. At this point what is critical is likely to be whether or not governments internally have unified or strongly competing views about macroeconomic policy. As I said earlier, if there are differences of opinion within a country about the proper course of internal policy, the additional gains from cooperation could tip the balance in one or several countries toward the internal policy needed to complete the coordination agreement. In this case, so long as one agrees with the economic model and the policy objectives of the winners, the well-being of all countries can be improved. There are only two morals I can draw from this. First, a coordinated set of macroeconomic policy changes will be much more difficult both to arrange and to justify in periods that are closer to equilibrium. Second, unless there is a significant group within a particular country that is leaning toward the proposed policy change anyway for purely internal reasons, it may be useless or even counterproductive to try to push a coordinated strategy.

Discretionary Coordination: The "Deal"

The second type of discretionary policy invokes a "deal" in which some countries offer up changes in macroeconomic policy that they may not have otherwise undertaken (or *say* they would not undertake) in return for changes by other countries in areas of policy outside the macroeconomic field.[11]

The 1978 Bonn Summit represented that kind of a deal. The components of the deal were threefold: First, a commitment to expedite the then-lagging MTN discussion leading to the Tokyo Round, which was a particularly significant concession from the French. Second, U.S. agreement to move domestic oil prices up to the world market levels by the end of 1980, a concession wanted by all the other participants. Third, German and Japanese agreement to stimulate their economies, a policy change especially wanted by the United States and France. That Summit has been widely written about and will, I am sure, be talked about much at this conference. I want to make only three comments.

In the first place, the 1978 Bonn Summit, if not quite unique, was very special. It was, I said, not essentially an exercise in macroeconomic coordination enabling each partner to achieve better performance in its macroeconomic goals, but a trade between macroeconomic and other goals. Only very occasionally, I suspect, will a concatenation of circumstances arise making such a deal possible.

Second, the 1978 Bonn Summit was influenced to an important extent by the existence of differences of opinion. According to Putnam and Henning (1986, 63–69) there existed within the German government some important proponents of fiscal expansion. Equally, within the American government there were those who believed that oil prices should, in any event, be raised toward world levels. I know less about Germany, but in the case of the United States it is almost certain that without the potential gains from a Summit deal the proponents of oil price decontrol would have been far less successful in reaching their objective.[12] I suspect a deal would not have been struck had there not been important groups in both the German and U.S. governments who actively wanted to pursue the very policies which their governments, with alleged reluctance, eventually offered up at the Summit. This makes the 1978 Bonn Summit deal even more unique.

Finally, my own reflections about the 1978 Summit preparations suggest to me that it is in the very nature of such bargaining that each party gradually assigns a more and more unrealistic importance to the concessions it hopes to wring from the other party. Let me quote from a Council of Economic Advisors memorandum to President Carter just before the Summit, entitled *Economic Effects of Alternative Outcomes at the Summit:*

> "If as a result (of German and Japanese economic stimulation and other actions) industrial countries increased domestic growth rates by an average of 1 percent, U.S. exports would grow by about $2 billion a year faster for each year in which the higher growth was sustained. Although it is impossible to predict exchange rates, a depreciation on the order of 1 to 2 percent would be needed to obtain the same effect on the trade balance.

Those were scarcely earthshaking results. But after months of hard negotiation and persuasion, success became much more important as a symbol and for the sake of "having won" than, in the cold light of hindsight, the potential economic gains warranted.

The Current Case for a "Deal"

This leads me to a final observation about policy coordination in the context of today's economic scene. Fischer's table 1.2, which is quite similar to other findings, suggests that the actual gains from purely macroeconomic coordination are not very large. From the standpoint of the United States, for example, the improvement in its current account balance and the slowdown in dollar depreciation from a 1 percent fiscal stimulus in other OECD countries is quite small. It alone would hardly seem to justify the pressure the United States is putting on other countries to undertake additional stimulus.

But there is a more compelling case for coordinated action in Japan, Europe, and the United States—a coordination that is not purely macroeconomic in character and that incorporates large political elements. Japan and Europe have only recently begun to feel the depressing impact on the demand for their output of the falling dollar and the soon-to-be declining U.S. trade deficit. But private economic forecasts and current economic data increasingly suggest, for most of them, a significant slippage in the rate of expansion. The world is already on the edge of substantial economic difficulty on two fronts: First, protectionist pressures did not really subside in the wake of recovery from the 1982 recession; in Europe the recovery has never been strong, and in the United States the effect of recovery in moderating protectionist pressure was, after a time, offset by the growth in the trade deficit. I am not sanguine about the consequences if macroeconomic policy outside of the United States allows already modest economic growth to slip even further and unemployment to begin rising again, while the United States itself is fighting an only partially successful rearguard action against the protectionist pressures engendered by its own trade deficit. Second, the LDC debt situation continues along the precarious edge between muddling through and collapse. Again, failure of Europe and Japan to offset the macroeconomic consequences of the declining U.S. trade deficit could tip the balance.

If political leaders in Europe and Japan and their economic advisers are united in a view that growth prospects remain good, or that macroeconomic stimulus will be largely dissipated in inflation, there is little room for action. But if this is not the case, there is a role for coordinated policy and the possibility of making a deal. First, with respect to protectionism, the gains from the coordination of stimulative action do not rest on the trade or exchange rate spillovers contained in the usual macroeconomic models. As noted above, these are not large, at least among the three major blocks—Europe, the United States, and Japan.[13] Rather the gains arise from the interaction between domestic expansion and protectionism. For one country to maintain or increase growth on its own—even if feasible from a macroeconomic standpoint—would not generate sufficient spillover effects in world trade to counter mounting protectionist pressures stemming from stagnating growth in other OECD countries. And if such measures begin, even the expanding country would not be able to resist its own internal pressures for retaliation. But this would not be true in a concerted expansion. Thus, even though the purely macro spillovers from coordination are relatively modest, the gains could still be significant when the dynamics of protectionism are taken into account. In the case of the LDCs, faster expansion in Europe and Japan (combined with U.S. action to reduce real interest rates, as indicated below) would generate political and economic gains that could be important in preventing a tipping of the balance in some countries toward financial and political crises.

Second, in contrast to the political situation of the past few years, there are now some American political leaders who believe there is a glimmering hope that enough pressure can be brought to bear on President Reagan that he might agree to accept an overall package of deficit reduction measures, including a moderate-sized tax increase. The recent clamor by the United States for economic expansion in other countries has raised this issue in the consciousness of American public opinion, to the point where other governments have decided that some economic stimulus is in any event warranted in their own countries, and might be able in the upcoming Summit to add an important new set of pressures on the President and the Congress, sufficient to make that glimmering hope a reality. Thus, this year's Summitry might exploit some of the political realities I have listed and try to moderate others: using nonmacroeconomic issues to bargain for macroeconomic concessions, taking advantage of differences of opinion within governments, and converting U.S. tax and expenditure policies from goals to fiscal policy instruments.

Notes

The views set forth in this chapter are solely those of the author and do not necessarily represent the opinions of the trustees, officers, or other staff members of the Brookings Institution. The author has benefited from comments by George L. Perry and Robert Solomon.

1. See Fischer, p. 22, in this volume. See also Cooper (1986b), who says: "But I would conjecture that the major stumbling block to close macroeconomic cooperation is sharp continuing disagreement on means-ends relationships, on the technology of macroeconomics, and the influence of instruments of policy on national economies" (p. 98).

2. This lack of a unitary decision process and its importance on the Bonn Summit is stressed by Putnam and Henning (1986, 104–14). On this and other points, I have drawn importantly from their analysis.

3. Although, paradoxically, if the other governments mistakenly forecast that the proponents of change will win anyway, they may (wrongly) try to get a "free ride," thereby aborting that agreement.

4. See Putnam and Henning (1986).

5. I say "arguably" because some people contend (and I agree) that the Plaza agreement was mainly in terms of changing the rhetoric with no real commitment on macropolicy action.

6. Williamson (1985).

7. For a discussion of the pros and cons of target zone systems, see Brainard and Perry (1986), especially the papers by Cooper, Dornbusch, Branson, and Williamson.

8. However, as Sachs points out in his background paper for this conference (see chap. 15, this volume), once the concern of political leaders in most OECD countries shifted to inflation control in the late 1970s and early 1980s, there was some evidence of beggar-thy-neighbor policies to appreciate currencies and export inflation.

9. But see the argument by Cooper (1986a, 13).

10. Cooper (1986a, 4–8).

11. Putnam and Henning (1986, 114–18) analyze some of the implications of adding issues other than macroeconomic to the bargaining table.

12. This was clearly evidenced in early 1979 after the Summit when internal negotiations were underway over the scope and speed of oil decontrol. The political White House advisers wanted to move as late and as gradually as possible. But in every meeting, participants from the Treasury and other agencies would wave the Bonn Summit commitment, with a decisive effect on the ultimate decision.

13. Within Europe, on the other hand, if fiscal stimulus is blocked by a drive to continue budget consolidation so that only monetary policy is available, the standard case for coordinating expansive monetary policies will hold.

References

Brainard, William C., and George L. Perry, eds. 1986. Symposium on exchange rates, trade, and capital flows. *Brookings Papers on Economic Activity* 1:165–235.

Cooper, Richard N. 1986a. External constraints in European growth. Paper prepared for the Conferences on Impediments to European Economic Growth, Brookings Institution, October 9–10.

———. 1986b. International cooperation in public health as a prologue to macroeconomic cooperation. Brookings Discussion Papers in Macroeconomics, no. 44.

Putnam, Robert D., and C. Randall Henning. 1986. The Bonn Summit of 1978: How does international policy coordination actually work? Brookings Discussion Papers in International Economics, no. 53.

Williamson, John. 1985. *The exchange rate system.* Policy Analyses in International Economics no. 5. Washington, D.C.: Institute for International Economics.

4. *Alan Greenspan*

Prospects for International Economic Cooperation

Economists generally argue that the ideal international economic order would include a single currency and free trade. Such a regime would maximize economic efficiency and lead to all of the textbook benefits of comparative advantage and optimum allocation of capital. The fifty separate states of the United States achieved that, at least to a large extent, and certainly the Common Market supported by the European Monetary System (EMS) is a noteworthy effort. But common currencies and open borders to goods and services are too often in conflict with national sovereignty.

The concept of international economic coordination is essentially a notion in which sovereignty is traded off for the economic benefits of an international division of labor. One could argue, as indeed I would, that it is to everyone's advantage to engage in the benefits of international trade and finance, and that the exercise of sovereignty would best serve a nation's people over the long run by freer trade and co-ordinated international economic policies. The problem is that national politics seemingly require a much shorter time frame for fulfillment than it takes for international cooperation to yield benefits to individual countries and their citizens.

This tendency is underscored by the sequence of negotiations that generally are supposed to lead to international cooperation. All too often heads of government, finance ministers, or trade negotiators meet to hammer out an international agreement *after* much of the crucial negotiating leeway has been sharply delimited by previous domestic political compromises. An American presidential candidate, for example, who promises upon election to initiate a trade bill that would double the tariffs on goods competing with industry x is scarcely left with a useful negotiating position when multinational trade talks are on the agenda at his first economic summit as president. A democratic system functions through a series of domestic political compromises and agreements. Too often those agreements significantly preclude avenues for effective compromise over similar issues in later international forums.

Unless some means is found to introduce international considerations in the context of the striking of domestic political agreements, the potential areas of meaningful compromise over real policy alternatives at international meetings is severely limited. At the extreme, economic summits, or their equivalent at lower levels, produce communiques that are merely the rephrasing of already agreed upon domestic economic initiatives of the individual countries.

Much of the extraordinary economic cooperation of the early post–World War II period was initiated by the United States as part of its domestic political agenda. Our purpose was to support the economic recovery of Europe and Japan and, hence, develop a viable Western economic community. American participation in the IMF, World Bank, OECD, and other economic forums was part of a policy agenda developed within the context of our domestic political system.

Now that the United States is no longer as preeminent in economic affairs as it was a generation ago, it is no longer capable of virtually unilaterally dictating the conditions of Western economic cooperation.

Principal Obstacle

Coordination is particularly difficult in the face of very strong market forces. This is especially the case in the foreign exchange markets. Unless exchange rate coordination is workable, policies attempting to affect interest rate levels and differentials become ineffective. In such an environment, fiscal and trade policy coordination is unlikely to achieve much. Hence, at the risk of spilling over into the subject matter that may be the province of other sessions, I should like to especially focus on this key aspect of macroeconomic policy coordination in today's environment.

The EMS has been able to hold the cross rates among the major European currencies in a relatively narrow band. No such stabilization, however, is likely to be initiated soon for any of the major exchange rates relative to the U.S. dollar. The principal obstacle is the extraordinarily large stock of U.S. dollar assets held in international currency portfolios. Of the approximately $2.5 trillion in international bank claims on nonresidents, more than two-thirds are denominated in dollars. Moreover, about three-fourths of international bond issues are denominated in dollars. Despite Japan's dramatic rise as an international financial power, international claims denominated in yen remain a small fraction of those in dollars.

When there are relatively small amounts of cross-border claims in foreign currencies and, hence, little in the way of financial assets held in other than domestic currencies, the demand for foreign exchange tends to mirror intercountry demand for goods and services. Under those conditions, markets generally tend to arbitrage the currencies toward levels consistent with purchasing-power parity, that is, to equalize what currencies can purchase in the way of goods and services originating in various countries. Such conditions exist, more or less, among the European currencies, and this is a major reason for their relative success in maintaining exchange rate stability.

When substantial cross-border holdings of financial claims exist, however, the demand for one currency relative to another is the combination of demand for transaction and investment purposes. In recent years, it has become ever more obvious that investment demand is virtually swamping transactions demand in all dealings with respect to the dollar. This results from the extraordinary buildup of dollar-denominated financial assets in world markets, the demand for which changes sufficiently rapidly to overwhelm changes stimulated by shifts in the underlying purchasing power of the U.S. dollar relative to other currencies. This is not the case with other currencies, even such "strong" currencies as the yen and the mark, and this is one reason it is so difficult to reach the "right" value of the dollar vis-à-vis major U.S. trading partners.

The very size of dollar investment holdings implies that relatively small random changes in the propensity to hold dollar-denominated assets create flows that swamp transaction demand shifts. Such shifts obscure pressures on the value of the currency stemming from changes in purchasing power parities. And the limited supply of alternative currencies means any moderate change in the propensity to hold dollars will create a disproportionate change in demand for yen or mark securities relative to the available stock of such securities. This results in a major change in these currencies' bilateral exchange rates relative to the dollar. If the aggregate supply of yen among international currencies, for example, were equal to that of the U.S. dollar, exchange rate fluctuations between the yen and the dollar would moderate, although their volatility vis-à-vis other currencies would remain.

Hence, any realistic effort to reduce the volatility of exchange rates is likely to require equalizing the available stocks of the major currencies in international financial markets and/or lowering the aggregate levels.

The recent instability in exchange rates itself has probably induced added flows of cross-border liabilities as a currency hedge, which in turn has tended to increase exchange rate instability. In a hypothetical international monetary system of fixed exchange rates, the hedging requirements would largely disappear and the need to hold balanced currency portfolio positions would be reduced. Fixed rates, if believed, reduce the risk premiums in holding claims in foreign currencies.

Obviously, it is undesirable to reduce cross-border claims between the originators of savings and the ultimate users of those savings. However, the huge interbank market proliferated beyond any expectation in the past 20 years, in part because of the differing regulatory environments for international banking. Many of these interbank deposits are vehicles to avoid national and central bank regulations and reserve requirements (which, of course, are equivalent to taxes on banking claims).

How much reduction in redepositing is either desirable or feasible isn't clear. Should a substantial reduction occur, it also is unclear that the net demand for any currency relative to the dollar would change significantly. A good part of interbank depositing is merely a passive process to facilitate intermediation between the final user of funds and the initial saver.

Anticipatory claims or liabilities in the interbank market that are not immediately supported by final demand do tend to build up, however. For example, a bank anticipating a fall in the exchange rate of the dollar could accept dollar deposits, convert them to another currency, and redeposit them in another bank. The transaction would weaken the dollar's exchange rate, but of course, the subsequent reconversion would strengthen the dollar.

Undercutting Efficiency

In the long run, this expectation-based inventorying of funds cannot have an effect on exchange rates, since net demand and supply of funds ultimately will prevail. Nevertheless, fluctuations in interbank depositing beyond those that passively reflect underlying demand almost surely impose some degree of volatility on the foreign exchange market.

Redepositing cannot be suppressed significantly and effectively, it would appear, without undercutting the extraordinary efficiency of international financial markets. It is possible, however, that less regulation of capital flows could reduce the need for multiple redepositing in the Caribbean or other havens from regulation and taxation.

Minus some attention on this front, exchange rates against the dollar are likely to continue to be volatile. Whether anchored with some fixed standard or not, efforts at international coordination of macroeconomic policies as a consequence will be difficult.

My final concern about the efficacy of economic policy coordination is in a way more fundamental and disturbing. Coordination presupposes a conceptual framework that specifies how economic events in one country affect another and, more generally, how all such events interact internationally. Obviously lacking such a conceptual framework, governments would not know what to cooperate about to achieve even agreed upon goals.

It was implicitly assumed during the formation of the OECD and, specifically, its Economic Policy Committee that the then-accepted Keynesian structure, in its international context, appropriately described the lines of relationship from policy to policy impact.

But as econometric models tied to domestic economies began to run into explanatory difficulties so have their counterparts in the international arena. Stanley Fischer's discussion (see above) on the use of models to lead international coordination is scarcely encouraging on this score.

I would not, however, conclude that the effort of coordination is without value. If we aver that cross-border trade enhances world living standards, we are of necessity asserting that independent economies significantly affect each other. If our tools for influencing coordination are less effective than we would like, it means only that we should sharpen our conceptual understanding of how our constantly evolving economies are changing. We have no choice but to keep trying.

5. Helmut Schmidt

Prospects for International Cooperation

I would like to start with a question. When was it that the political elites first understood the necessity of international economic cooperation of governments, central banks, and so on? When did that happen?

It seems to me it happened at the end of World War II, when the political leaders remembered the domino-type of deflationist recession and depression of the early 1930s, and when they, at the same time, understood the necessity of rebuilding—economically rebuilding—the world after World War II. This was done in Europe as well as in East Asia, even in the former defeated enemy countries like Japan and Germany due to the enormous generosity of the United States. These two motivations did flow into each other.

This then led to the already mentioned institutions like Bretton Woods, the World Bank, IMF, GATT, OECD. I think Mike Blumenthal has described it correctly (see above).

The backbone of these institutions was the overwhelming economic and political strength of the United States of America. There was no question of who was to lead the Western world. It was self-understood. There was no other possibility, and there was no question inside the U.S. elites that they had to take the lead.

Later on the strength of the United States started to wither away—due to Mao Tse-tung; due to de Gaulle; due to the Vietnamese war in the 1960s; due to OPEC; due to many other factors including the fact that those countries whom you had helped to regain their economic strength really did regain some strength and you were no longer the one and only overwhelming factor in the world's economy. But this loss of economic strength was also due to the political mistake which you made when you in a so-called benign way neglected not only the monetary developments and the currency developments, but also the deterioration of the functioning of the world's economy as a whole in the late 1960s and early 1970s. The phrase "benign neglect" was coined for a specific situation, but it was neglect of the interdependence of the economic functioning of the world.

Since at least the late 1960s (you might also say since 1973, when the free floating of currencies started and when the first oil price explosion was started), we have been faced with a growing disorder of the world. The Third World politicians ask us time and again to create a new economic order of the world; this seems to presuppose that there is an old order or a present order. But there is not. We don't have an order in the world. We might call it a fluctuating or fluid constellation, but there is no order. There are almost no rules any longer being kept now.

This was possible even after the beginning of the general currency float in the early 1970s, and there were at least two men in Europe who seem to have understood it. I think there were many more in the world who understood, but we, Giscard and myself, happened to have some influence because by coincidence we were leaders of our governments at the time. We used the peak of this period of détente, which had been brought about by Nixon and Brezhnev at the Helsinki Conference of 1975, to try to influence the other leaders of the Western countries to convene what later became known as an economic summit.

It was not very easy to convince Harold Wilson, he was difficult to convince of anything, anytime. It also was not very easy to convince Gerry Ford, but Gerry Ford let himself be convinced. All of us were aware that the whole thing would run into the rocks if we let it get into the hands of the national bureaucracies, ministries, and what have you. Therefore, it was prepared by personal representatives; people like Raymond Barre, who was then an unknown quantity even in France, who acted as the personal representative of Giscard, who so far knew him only superficially; people like George Shultz, who was with Bechtel in San Francisco at the time and was internationally experienced since he had been Secretary of the U.S. Treasury; or Wilfried Guth, to just remember a third example, who then was a member of the executive of Deutsche Bank and had never been in government.

They were successful in preparing the groundwork, and the first meeting happened in Rambouillet. I think that this was the most successful one. I have participated in eight such Summit meetings, but I think the first one was the best one. I will come back to this qualification a little later.

I would just like to mention that Giscard and the German Chancellor of those years also invented a number of other international, semi-official international groupings. Together with George Shultz, we invented the Group of 5, then called the Library Group. Why? Because the first meeting was held in the library in the basement of the White House.

We invented the Euro-Council, which since 1974 meets three times a year. We also invented the European Monetary System, which has been staggering along after some initial success, since other people have taken over and do not propel it further.

In all these meetings we were very eager to include the Japanese from the beginning, because we did foresee the growing isolation of Japan, which now is greater than it was twelve years ago.

So the feeling in leaders at the time, and this does include Gerry Ford and George Shultz, was that we needed some more international elbow rubbing and some exchange and mutual influencing of ourselves regarding, for instance, our monetary and fiscal policies.

The question is: What did we achieve? We did bring the Japanese into the fold and made them feel a little bit more at home, at least in the beginning. More important was the fact that we achieved some economic education of political leaders, but you have to start this business all over again every once in a while once you get a new prime minister, a new chancellor, or a new president.

Normally political leaders of a country have no knowledge of economic interdependence. They have learned some prejudices in their college years, some of their political friends have added some prejudices, and this is the equipment they bring with them once they enter the national political scene. Moreover, they have been learning over their political career to be responsible to national or regional or local pressure groups.

So we had a little success in educating political leaders. And I think Mike Blumenthal is right, sometimes the participants used each other in order to take legitimate economic steps they had already intended to take but which had run into domestic opposition, and now they could make them look like a result of an international meeting or an international compromise and consensus.

The most important achievement, I think, was that we were able over a long period of years to avoid open economic warfare. This was not inevitable. It could have happened easily. But we were able to avoid open economic warfare, one against the other.

Now there is a long list of what we have not achieved. We did not achieve, as has been hinted at by Alan Greenspan and Charles Schultze and others, exchange rate reliability. Which may not seem like much in the eyes of the Americans or maybe—formerly—in the eyes of the Germans and the Japanese; nowadays I have come to understand that it is a great menace to exporting industries. If you have to export rice or grain, or if you have to export conventional commodities or conventional manufactured goods, international exchange rates matter much.

If you right now try to conquer, as an American enterprise, a new share of the market in Europe or in East Asia, only to see five years later that the dollar goes up again and you lose your market totally, you will be discouraged for the rest of your life from trying it a second time. This is exactly what is happening now in the United States. There is an enormous chance to regain market shares in the world, but people have become discouraged by the ups and downs of the dollar in the last fifteen years.

We did not achieve a world monetary system. What we have is a monetary nonsystem of the world that is much worse than the Bretton Woods system and that is categorically worse than the international gold standard before 1914. It is an invitation to all kinds of trite political practices over the counter and under the table, as it were.

We did not achieve a well-organized cooperation regarding the structure of intermeshed domestic development in the Third World and foreign development aid toward the Third World. We have a lot of organizations in that field, starting with the World Bank and what have you, but the actual development in most countries of the Third World is just chaotic. For instance, there is a handful of bankers in this country and in my country who think that to make the Third World pay interest is much more important than to look at their domestic economic development.

We have failed to coordinate our energy policies. In a time when oil prices were exploding, a big country started to hamper other countries in their development of nuclear reactor branches.

We failed to foresee the debt crisis. We failed to foresee the enormous process of integration of public and private financing all over the world. Central banks have been unable to control the so-called Euro-currencies. Who fifteen years ago would have understood a term like "Euro-dollar"? Anybody would have thought that the dollar comes out of Washington. What is a Euro-dollar? But it does exist. The Euro-currencies have a volume nowadays of $1.8 trillion worth, or something on that order of magnitude, not under the control of our central banks.

We have also failed to prevent offshore banking. Grand Cayman is a sheet of banks nowadays, as is Luxembourg and all those places that are not under surveillance of our national banking regulatory agencies or our central banks, and mischief is brooding there. But since no major tragedy has happened so far, we live with it and think it's normal. It's not normal. Our central banks have abdicated to a great degree. They are not aware of it. All the admonishing of them has not led them to understand that they can solve these problems only if they cooperate much closer than they do. They ought to be the banks of banks. But things could happen in this world in which the central banks are not big enough and not close enough to each other to control the tragedies that might occur.

We also failed to address the biggest problem behind them all, namely, the world's population explosion. In 1925, I remember it exactly because that was the year when I was entering school, I learned that there were 2 billion people in the world. In the year 2025, there will be more than 8 billion. Right now it's 5+ billion, at the end of the century, twelve years and eight months ahead, there will be 6+ billion people. All these people not only want to be nourished, want to be fed, need water, but all these people will cook their meals and will use energy.There are two main forms of energy. One is nuclear, which entails a number of hazards like Three Mile Island, like Chernobyl, like the fact that no government in the world has yet invented a process that does away with the nuclear waste. The other form of energy is hydrocarbons, and hydrocarbons also cause a number of threats to the environment, including the greatest danger of all, which has not been understood by political leaders so far, but only by a number of physicists. This is the aggravation of the amount of carbon dioxide in the lower atmosphere, the so-called greenhouse effect. This is without any doubt to come. Without any doubt! This has not been understood by us political leaders, nor has it been really dealt with by the economists. Economists are talking about the next quarter or the next year. Their utmost foresight goes three to five years ahead. The greenhouse effect will become important in the middle of the lifetime of our children. Those who are 35 or 40 years of age will live long enough to see thousands of species die out and the level of the oceans come up. People who live in deltas, like the Dutch people or the people in Bangladesh, will have to flee from their homes because the surface of the ocean will go up. We have totally failed to address the population problem, and we still do.

After having overcome the balance of payments network upheaval due to the second oil crisis shortly, let us say, after 1981, we ought not to have failed to make Japan, Germany, Holland, and others aware of the fact that their economic policy mixes are more than 50 percent responsible for the permanent up-valuation of the yen, the Deutsche mark, the Dutch gulden, and others who follow that course.

We have been totally unable to make the political leaders in Japan and Germany understand that in the medium run the world will not be willing to accept a situation in which the great victor of World War II has become the greatest debtor of the world and the former axis powers have become the greatest creditors of the world—Japan in the first place and Germany in the second. This already is the case today. There is no way psychologically for the rest of the world to accept this. The leaders in both these countries have just begun to realize that they cannot afford to be the leaders of the Western world, a situation in which their debt becomes a greater menace to the rest of the world than the debt of Brazil or Mexico.

There are three triangles in the world of which people are aware. There is the economic triangle with the United States on one of the three corners, Japan on the second, and the so-called Common Market of Europe on the third. (I say "so-called" because it is a rather *uncommon* common market: eleven currencies in one market, twelve tax systems, twelve legal systems, twelve insurance systems, twelve different systems of all kinds of security regulations. You try to introduce an elevator that has been built in England into a newly built hotel in France; it's almost impossible!) But this triangle of economic leaders is well understood, more or less, in the world.

The power triangle is not as well understood. But by the end of the century everybody will perceive that there are two superpowers, America and the Soviet Union, and that there is, inevitably, a third world power: China. China already today could, of course, destroy Moscow with their nuclear rockets, and Moscow could not hope to avoid it; the same is true vis-à-vis the United States. Even if China will still be a developing country in twelve years time, maybe with a level of real income of $700 per capita per year, they will be a military world power.

I am mentioning these two triangles for one reason. It's the United States of America, only, that is part of both these triangles. Russia is not part of the economic triangle; as an economic factor Russia does not play any role and will not play any role in the near future. China will never play any role economically, except that all our exporters think that they are a huge market. But they don't realize that these Chinese have no huge exports nowadays or in the foreseeable future to pay for their imports. So China will not play a major role economically, nor will Russia.

America, of course, will. And America plays a role in this power triangle. America is the only country who participates in both these structures which govern the globe. That's the reason why America is in a position to lead the world in the future.

But if you don't lead the world, who then is going to do it? Probably Luxembourg.

You are in the process of abdicating leadership. The instinct of the United States is to go alone. I am a guest in your country five or six times every year. I seem to sense that the mentality here is isolationist again. Not necessarily in the political meaning of the word, but the instinct is to go alone.

Now you have to understand the reasons for this instinct. You are not really economically interrelated with the world. Take that little country of Germany, with just one quarter of your population; our exports in absolute figures are even a little bigger than yours. Take Japan, one half of your population; their exports are also a little higher than yours. Your exports are relatively small, less than 10 percent of your GNP. You are not really export-minded because your domestic markets are such huge markets. Why should General Motors try hard to export cars?

In the United States you consume about 3 percent more than you produce. This has been the case for more than just a couple of months; it has gone on now for years. You eat up more than you produce. Your consumption and domestic use of your GNP is 103 percent. You are the richest country in the world, yet, at the same time, you are already the greatest debtor in the world. At the end of Ronald Reagan's term you might have a net foreign debt on the order of, some people say, $700 billion. Early in the 1990s you will have a net foreign debt on the order of $1 trillion, because I can't foresee a U.S. presidential candidate promising to cut into the budget and raise taxation: He would not be elected. If he gets elected on some other promises and takes some time to reverse those promises into opposite actions and tries to undertake them, then the senators and the congressmen will beat him in the neck. So it will be very difficult to change this development in the early 1990s.

Your currency, in my eyes, has become a yo-yo, up and down, up and down. You might be capable of coping with such a yo-yo dollar. It may not mean so much if you are not so much interested in exports anyway. But the rest of the world cannot afford for the major currency of the world to behave like that. I happen to think that it is ridiculous that you have such an enormous deficit in your budget and let about three-quarters of it be financed by the savings of people outside the United States. You are importing about $140 billion in capital and credit, net per year, which is almost three-quarters of your budgetary deficit. This cannot go on for long. Just think about the way you expect the Brazils and the Mexicos to service their debts, namely, by export surpluses. You will have to service your debt to the rest of the world, but you don't have export surpluses, and you are not likely to arrive at export surpluses. You have export deficits. So I guess you will just print the dollar. You will print the interest. You will do away with Paul Volcker and others and change the composition of the open market committee, or whoever takes the decision, and you will just print the dollars. That's my fear for the early 1990s.

You will not be in a position, like Peru or Brazil, to declare a moratorium on servicing your debt. You will service your debt by easing up much further than hither to on your money supply. So there is no global economic leadership by the United States right now, although you are the only ones who could lead the world. Because you are not leading it, you are not legitimated to criticize the Japanese and the Germans, because you make as big mistakes as they make, only from the other side of the coin. There is no legitimization on the side of the Germans or Japanese to criticize you, and there is no legitimization on your side to criticize the Japanese or the Germans.

Now, are there prospects for improvement? I am uncertain. Governments are responsible enough to answer the demands and questions of national groups, national pressure groups, national public opinion, national parliaments, and then they have to enter into electoral campaigns every once in a while on national levels, local levels, state levels.

The Summits and the Euro-Councils, even the meetings of central bankers and finance ministers, have deteriorated into public relation events. Several thousand journalists come to a so-called summit meeting nowadays and make it impossible for the leaders to talk and listen to each other in confidence. Because every word, every fifteen minutes, is being carried outside of this room by some press speaker to inform the national press, and they print tomorrow "how strongly the chancellor has spoken" or what how he has told the American president or the Japanese prime minister or what evil things he has been committing. You should exclude the press from these meetings, this is my advice!

The greatest tragedy is brooding over Japan, I think, because of the isolation of Japan, which, on the other hand, is becoming the number one financial power house of this world. Please try to compare the capital formation of savings per year in Japan with the capital formation of savings in absolute figures in this country: Capital formation in Japan is double in absolute figures! They are obviously intellectually unable to use that enormous capital formation inside their own country. The instincts of not only Nakasone but the whole political elite in Japan to arrive at a nondeficit budget are ridiculously wrong. There is no choice for them, if they don't use the money by their own industry and by their own government, other than to export the capital. If there continues to be such a big capital demand in this country, the Japanese in a short while will own not only half of Hawaii, but also half of Puerto Rico. They don't understand, though, what they're doing to themselves.

China, on the other hand, will be successful, but economically, as I have said, they will not play a world role.

Turning to the Soviet Union: How good this great communicator Gorbachev may be I don't know, but he doesn't have any economic concept so far. He is opening up some of the rigidities in which they, in the last sixty or seventy years, have governed their public opinion and subdued the opposition intellectuals and other critical voices. He has good instincts there, but he lacks an economic concept.

In my view, there is a great danger of a backlash. Now the intellectuals and the press reluctantly, because they don't know how long such openness will last, start to speak up. They will get used to speaking up and articulating criticisms. Once it appears, in three or five years' time, that the economic promises will not come through, they will criticize that. Then, I guess, the government will clamp down on them again. So I am not too hopeful about the domestic government in Russia.

I am not too hopeful regarding the economic integration of Europe either, but I won't get into that issue because that one takes too much time.

All I would like to say in the end is: Be aware of the fact, ladies and gentleman, that if the United States should for a longer while not take up the reins of economic political leadership in the world, you will also lose your grand strategic leadership of the West. If it becomes common understanding in Europe and elsewhere in the world that you are not able economically to manage your affairs, nobody will believe what you tell them in the field of SDI or zero-zero option or whatever.

All this is not necessarily a cause for despair. I think it is still a good world, but one has to think of the question: What can one do? Mike Blumenthal has described a multinational enterprise. Mike, I was again impressed by what you said about your enterprise, but it is not a multinational one. It's an American enterprise that does business, that produces and sells and buys, in, I don't know, fifty countries of the world. It's a national enterprise, in my opinion.

Multinational enterprises hardly do exist. It's the wrong terminology. There are some binational enterprises, like Royal Dutch Shell or like Phillips. Multinationals do not exist so far. Siemens, for instance, or Hitachi—these are national enterprises spanning the globe, doing business all over the globe. They are not necessarily led by national instincts, that would be wrong to say, but the leadership will be either German, in the case of Siemens, or, in the case of Burroughs or Sperry or Exxon, it will be American.

What is needed, I think, are international meetings of CEOs of firms who do global business. Meetings like this—small groups where they can exchange their experiences, their grievances, their interests, their desires, and their apprehensions. Meetings between Japanese, Europeans, people from let us say Hong Kong, South Korea, America, the Latin American countries, and so on; multinational meetings of financial executives and agricultural leaders, for instance. The ridiculous agriculture policies of Japan, Europe, and the United States are due to the nationalist structure of the pressure groups. They never meet each other, these national pressure groups, they are never forced by economists to exchange their ridiculous prejudices. Meetings like the meeting of this group today, I think, are really worthwhile.

Summary of Discussion

De Menil began by pointing out that the disparity between economic theory and reality unfairly weakened the case for fixed exchange rates. Results of economic simulation models often show that the gains from coordination are implausibly small and that the degree of interdependence is limited; perhaps this is because so little is known about exchange rate expectations. Yet, de Menil argued, the discipline exerted by fixed rates is a powerful political tool. He expressed the opinion that had the Reagan Administration understood the effects of its proposals on the current account and the exchange rate, it might have proceeded differently. The Mitterrand experiment was reversed, largely due to the pressures imposed by the EMS. Of course, if coordination were completely effective, such an experiment would not have been attempted at all. Coordination at the worldwide level will be more difficult, however, since capital controls would not be as practical as they are in the EMS. It will be harder both to ensure that the chosen parities are credible and to guarantee that policies will be reformulated in order to salvage the exchange rate.

Ruggiero pointed out that the main task for the United States is to find a way to reduce fiscal and merchandise trade deficits while maintaining world growth. Any successful strategy will require more compatible economic policies. What steps should be taken? On the subject of the exchange rate, Ruggiero suggested that the dollar has depreciated enough. At current levels, the current account should improve by $20–$30 billion. Any further rapid and substantial depreciation of the dollar should be against the currencies of the newly industrialized countries. Further substantial depreciation against the EMS currencies and the yen would be counterproductive: inflation and interest rates would tend to rise in the United States, while growth in West Germany and Japan would fall and protectionist pressures abroad would mount.

Ruggiero also emphasized that there is no quick fix for the current situation and suggested five elements which any solution would necessarily contain. First, U.S. taxes must be raised. There are a variety of ways to do this without endangering high growth; a tax on oil is an example. Second, the rest of the European Community would have to find a better strategy for lowering unemployment and improving growth. Third, possibilities for a "reference zone" exchange rate system should be explored. He noted that despite the view of the experts (who were as pessimistic about the viability of the EMS as they are about world-wide exchange rate target zones), the political will had made the EMS a reality. Fourth, continued adherence to a policy of free trade is needed if developed and, especially, less-developed countries are to grow. Finally, Ruggiero stressed that the imperfect separation between global economic and political interests implied that policy coordination is essential to the survival of the Western alliance.

Robert Solomon asked Helmut Schmidt to clarify his earlier claim that the United States had shirked its leadership role in the world economy. Solomon pointed out that it is the United States that has been forced to lecture a recalcitrant West Germany and Japan on the need to lower unemployment and raise growth. It was the U.S. Treasury that initiated the Plaza agreement, the Baker Plan, the Louvre agreement, and important aspects of the Tokyo Summit.

Schmidt asserted that U.S. statesmen do not demonstrate enough ability to follow through and make their policy initiatives successful. The United States lacks credibility as a leader because its own house is not in order. These problems must be resolved before the United States can hope to fulfill its responsibilities as a world economic leader. Schmidt also contrasted leadership within the U.S. Executive Office with that of other countries. The U.S. president is an imperial figure; to get through, advisers must catch the emperor's ear. In other countries and in large corporations, leaders preside over frequent cabinet meetings and use them more as a forum for policy-making.

McNamar agreed with Schmidt's assessment of the benefits of a rule-by-cabinet system. The difficulty of economic leadership is enhanced in the United States by the separation of powers. Perhaps more prudent policy could be assured if the Secretary of the Treasury were required to have votes of confidence within the Congress. McNamar expressed disappointment that neither a consumption tax nor a value-added tax was passed. In view of this, he felt that as a result of the inability of the Reagan Administration to force a reduction in government spending, the Reagan Administration's economic policies have failed.

Branson asked Mike Blumenthal and Helmut Schmidt to account for their ostensibly contradictory views on world factor mobility. Blumenthal had stressed the ability of his company, and others like it, to arrange financing and to shift production rapidly around the world. If factors are so mobile, then why does Helmut Schmidt assign such importance to the policies of any single country.

Blumenthal agreed with the implications that Bill Branson had drawn from capital mobility, but he noted that factor mobility is far from being either perfect or uniform. He felt that mobility did not bear directly on the issue of leadership, and that a prerequisite for good leadership is having one's own house in order.

Foell asked the former chairmen of the Council of Economic Advisers (CEA) attending about the ability of economic and scientific advisers to affect the views of the president.

Greenspan felt that an adviser can influence decisions, but only when his views are solicited. *Schultze* added that a range of advice is required on all important issues; it is the responsibility of the CEA chairman to give advice from an economic viewpoint and not to posture in order to gain presidential influence.

Fischer noted that many conferees seemed unhappy with floating exchange rates and eager to consider target zone proposals. He reminded them, however, that the world came to floating rates from a system of fixed rates. The Bretton Woods arrangement collapsed because of acute policy divergences. It would be ironic if divergent policies were both the reason we came to a floating system and the reason we left it. Fischer also disagreed with George de Menil's contention that the Reagan Administration would have retreated from its fiscal strategy if the effects of the strategy had been known in advance. These policies reflect the philosophy that government is too big and depend on faulty folk wisdom which holds that spending follows taxes.

Feldstein agreed that the Reagan Administration would not have been induced by a fixed-rate system to change fiscal policy. He added that in 1981 the U.S. Administration did not believe that either government budget deficits or trade balance deficits were forthcoming. Even when substantial deficits began to appear, both the President and his Secretary of the Treasury clung to the view that the tax cut would increase growth enough to eliminate the budget deficit. The now familiar link between budget deficits, interest rates, the dollar, and the trade balance was not seen by the President and other key Administration officials until much later. While it takes time for individual political leaders to learn, their offices have no memory.

Schultze attacked the view that fixed exchange rates could begin to solve pressing international economic problems. Fixed rates have the potential to solve smaller problems associated with floating rates, such as excessive short-term volatility. But larger problems, primarily those of policy coordination, would not disappear with the adoption of fixed rates. Schultze felt that fixed rates might even have been dangerous, given the current Administration's entrenched views on U.S. expansionary fiscal policy.

Sachs argued that, under fixed rates, the U.S. fiscal expansion not only would have continued, but also would have required a large monetary expansion. The cost of fixing foreign exchange would have been substantial inflation in the United States at a time when inflation was already viewed as the major problem confronting the economy. Under this more realistic scenario of much higher U.S. prices, fixed rates would not even have prevented the real appreciation of the dollar. Sachs characterized as scandalous the lack of quantification behind the belief that expansion by U.S. trading partners would have an appreciable effect on the trade balance. Macroeconomic simulation models consistently yield transmission effects far too small to resolve the current account problem. He stressed that it is unfair to ask a country such as South Korea to appreciate its currency when the effects on U.S. GNP or trade would be negligible. Sachs also argued that a fiscal adjustment in the United States would need to be matched by expansion abroad. With inflation low and real interest rates high, the appropriate vehicle is monetary policy. Investment, particularly in LDCs, would benefit substantially from the lower interest rates.

Frenkel characterized as nostalgic the view that fixed exchange rates would indeed be credible if only the United States had control of its fiscal policies. He asked about the appropriate circumstances under which to consider revamping the international monetary system. He expressed the view that the international monetary system needs to be improved, but a reform should not be viewed as an instrument of crisis management. In the present context, the short-term crisis concerns the fiscal imbalances in the world economy. He stressed that the discipline required to make a fixed rate system work would not materialize simply by declaring parities to be rigid.

Kunihiro reiterated the need for coordination from Japan's perspective and argued that each country must attend first to those of its own policies which conflict with shared goals. In particular, he expressed concern over the U.S. temptation to use the exchange rate as a tool for macroeconomic action. The awareness in Japan of international transmission effects has generated a move toward a more expansionary fiscal policy. Kunihiro expressed further concern that the level of this international awareness is low in the United States, which is a much more closed economy than Americans generally believe, and that foreign conditions do not influence policies in the United States as much as they do in Japan.

2 Exchange Rate Coordination

1. Richard C. Marston
2. Guido Carli
3. Jacques Attali
4. John R. Petty
5. Robert Solomon

---

1. Richard C. Marston

Exchange Rate Policy Reconsidered

> I would regard it as a catastrophe amounting to a world tragedy if [this conference should] . . . allow itself to be diverted by the proposal of a purely artificial and temporary experiment affecting the monetary exchange of a few nations only. . . . The sound internal economic system of a nation is a greater factor in its well-being than the price of its currency in changing terms of the currencies of other nations. (From President Franklin D. Roosevelt's message to the London Economic Conference of 1933)

> It has been our task to find a common measure, a common standard, a common rule applicable to each and not irksome to any. . . . [W]e have perhaps accomplished here in Bretton Woods something more than what is embodied in this Final Act. We have shown that a concourse of 44 nations are actually able to work together at a constructive task in amity and unbroken accord. (J. M. Keynes at the conclusion of the Bretton Woods Conference in 1944)[1]

The Bretton Woods Conference of 1944, which fixed exchange rates for over twenty-five years, is often cited as a model of economic cooperation among countries. Indeed, the Bretton Woods agreement on exchange rates was a remarkable accomplishment, particularly when measured against the failures of earlier conferences such as the London Economic Conference of 1933. Yet over fifteen years have elapsed since the breakdown of the Bretton Woods system without any serious efforts to restore fixed exchange rates among the currencies of the major industrial countries. The last attempt to reconstruct the exchange rate system, the Smithsonian agreement of December 1971, broke down almost immediately. Recent Economic Summits have agreed on ad hoc policies to counter exchange rate movements and have considered modest proposals to modify the existing system, but these Summits have made no progress on more systemic changes in exchange rate arrangements. Governments may have refrained from "reforming" the system for good reasons. This paper will consider arguments for and against more far-reaching international agreements on exchange rate policy.

When considering possible reforms of the exchange rate system, it is natural to compare experience since 1973 with that of the Bretton Woods period. The difference in economic performance between the two periods would be startling if it were not so well known. Table 2.1 updates a table presented in Goldstein (1984, 10) that compares recent inflation rates, growth rates, and other economic variables with those of the Bretton Woods period. The period since 1973 is divided in two parts to highlight more recent developments in the 1980s.

Regardless of which indicator is chosen, the decade of the 1960s was a time of much superior economic performance. During the 1960s, inflation was markedly lower in all major industrial countries, with the

Table 2.1   **Comparison of Macroeconomic Performance in Three Recent Periods**

	U.S.	Canada	Japan	France	Germany	Italy	U.K.
Average Inflation Rates							
1961–71	2.8	2.7	5.6	4.1	2.8	3.9	4.4
1973–80	8.5	8.7	9.5	10.1	4.9	14.9	14.0
1981–85	5.3	7.2	2.7	9.1	3.8	12.9	6.9
Average GNP Growth Rates							
1961–71	3.6	5.2	10.4	5.4	4.2	5.2	2.8
1973–80	2.5	3.4	4.1	3.1	2.5	3.3	1.8
1981–85[a]	2.4	2.2	3.8	1.2	1.2	0.4	1.7
Average Productivity Growth							
1961–71	2.9	4.5	9.8	6.4	5.5	6.5	3.8
1973–80	1.6	2.1	6.1	4.6	4.0	4.6	1.8
1981–85	3.7	2.4	5.3	4.5	3.9	3.5	5.0
Average Unemployment Rates							
1961–71	4.8	4.9	1.2	1.6	0.8	5.1	2.6
1973–80	6.6	7.0	1.9	4.5	2.9	6.6	4.9
1981–85	8.3	10.4	2.5	8.7	7.1	9.6	11.9

Sources: CPI indexes and GNP: IMF, *International Financial Statistics;* productivity: U.S. Bureau of Labor Statistics; unemployment rates: OECD, *Labor Force Statistics.*
[a]Until 1984 for Italy.

notable exception of Japan where inflation in the 1980s is half what it was in the 1960s. A more recent trend toward lower inflation rates, however, is observed by comparing the 1981–85 and 1973–80 periods. Figure 2.1, illustrating the annual inflation rates for the three largest industrial economies, confirms this downward trend and also suggests that inflation rates for these countries may be converging. But these recent favorable trends in inflation are not matched by similar trends in output and other variables. Real growth in GNP was higher during the 1960s in all countries. Productivity growth was higher in all countries during the 1960s than during the 1973–85 period as a whole, although in the United States and in the United Kingdom productivity growth during the 1980s has exceeded that of the 1960s.[2] Finally, unemployment rates were in an entirely different range during the 1960s. In Germany, for example, unemployment averaged only 0.8 percent in the 1960s, but 2.9 percent in the 1970s, and a depressingly high 7.1 percent in the 1980s. In the United Kingdom, a 2.6 percent unemployment rate during the 1960s has turned into an 11.9 percent rate in the 1980s. Compared with the recent period of flexible exchange rates, therefore, the 1960s appear to have been a golden era of economic performance.

Yet we should hesitate before attributing recent economic performance to the switch from fixed to flexible exchange rates. Although flexible rates may help to explain high inflation rates in the 1970s, it is much more difficult to tie growth rates, unemployment rates, or productivity performance to a nominal variable like the exchange rate.

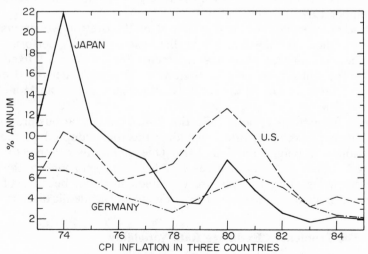

Fig. 2.1   Inflation rates since 1973. *Source:* IMF, *International Financial Statistics.*

Nor is it easy to say how the fixed rate system would have performed in response to the economic disturbances of the 1970s and 1980s, including the two oil shocks and the sharp changes in macroeconomic policies undertaken in Britain and the United States. Rather than try to account for this gap in economic performance, or to speculate about how a different exchange rate system might have performed, this paper will focus on the choices that are presented to policymakers today. One of these choices is to return to fixed exchange rates, but in today's economic environment this may prove as difficult as putting Humpty Dumpty together again.

This paper addresses a number of issues important to exchange rate policy:

Exchange rate variability: Section 2.1 examines the problem that exchange rate policy is designed to address, exchange rate variability. It distinguishes between two types of exchange rate variability, the short-run volatility of exchange rates characteristic of all asset prices and the misalignment of exchange rates which may persist for several years at a time. This distinction is crucial to an understanding of exchange rate policy, since actions designed to reduce volatility may not be well suited to countering misalignments.

Role of sterilized intervention: Casual observers may regard exchange market intervention as the primary tool of exchange rate policy, yet existing evidence raises doubts about the effectiveness of intervention unaccompanied by changes in money supplies. Section 2.2 reviews existing statistical evidence on so-called sterilized intervention, then studies two recent episodes of foreign exchange intervention in November 1978 and September 1985.

Fixed exchange rates: Those who look on the Bretton Woods system with nostalgia may not recall how that system actually performed in practice. Section 2.3 examines arguments for and against fixed exchange rates in general. It then reviews experience under the Bretton Woods system as well as the recently established European Monetary System (EMS).

Rules for managed floating: Section 2.4 considers various proposals for managing exchange rates, including the rules adopted by the International Monetary Fund in 1978. One ambitious scheme for exchange rate management involves establishing *target zones* for the major currencies. Target zones are examined in detail because of the attention given to them in recent government and academic discussions.

2.1   The Problem of Exchange Rate Variability

Variable exchange rates pose problems for an economy, but the problems vary widely depending on the nature of the variability. A useful distinction can be drawn between two types of variability: *volatility* and *misalignment*. Volatility is the day-to-day, month-to-month variability of exchange rates, a variability that may have no trend to it. Misalignment, in contrast, is the persistent departure of an exchange rate from its long-run competitive level. Misalignment thus refers not to month-to-month variability but to longer-lasting movements of exchange rates, and only to those movements that depart from relative price trends, thus altering the relative competitiveness of a country's goods.[3] This distinction is important for intervention policy because a case might be made that only one form of variability is harmful and therefore might justify intervention. It must be admitted at the outset, however, that this distinction between the two forms of exchange rate variability is more easily made in theory than in practice, since exchange rates may exhibit their greatest volatility during periods of misalignment.

2.1.1   Volatility

One of the lessons learned from the voluminous literature on exchange rate behavior written in the 1970s is that exchange rates behave like asset prices, displaying much more volatility than most macroeconomic variables such as output or the prices of goods and services.[4] This is not surprising given the dominance of asset trades in the determination of exchange rates. Table 2.2 examines the volatility of

Table 2.2   **Standard Deviations of Monthly Percentage Changes in Exchange Rates and Other Prices, July 1973–December 1985**

	U.S.	Japan	France	Germany	U.K.
Exchange Rates					
Nominal bilateral[a]	—	0.0274	0.0279	0.0288	0.0255
Real bilateral[a,b]	—	0.0256	0.0272	0.0302	0.0271
Nominal effective[c]	0.0166	0.0229	0.0120	0.0113	0.0195
Real effective[b,c]	0.0176	0.0208	0.0116	0.0118	0.0197
Prices					
Ratios of CPIs[a]	—	0.0094	0.0037	0.0039	0.0081
Ratios of WPIs[a]	—	0.0106	0.0123	0.0078	0.0090
Stock indexes	0.0388	0.0294	0.0580	0.0315	0.0597
Commodity	Copper	Cotton	Rice	Tin	Wheat
prices	0.0481	0.0656	0.0700	0.0546	0.0646

Sources: Monthly series: IMF, *International Financial Statistics* tape. Trade weights: Morgan Guaranty Trust, *World Financial Markets.*

[a]All bilateral comparisons are vis-à-vis the United States.

[b]Real exchange rates are measured using wholesale price indexes.

[c]Effective exchange rates are weighted averages of ten countries' exchange rates (G-5 plus Belgium, Canada, Italy, the Netherlands, and Switzerland); weights are based on total trade (imports plus exports) in manufactures.

exchange rates using one measure of volatility, the standard deviation of monthly percentage changes in exchange rates.[5] This measure of volatility, suggested by Lanyi and Suss (1982), counts as variable only those movements in exchange rates that depart from an average trend (measured as a percentage change).

Volatility Comparisons

Table 2.2 compares the volatility of exchange rates with the volatility of price ratios based on two aggregate price indexes, the Consumer Price Index (CPI) and the Wholesale Price Index (WPI), for the so-called Group of 5 (G-5) industrial countries: France, Germany, Japan, United Kingdom, and United States. According to this table, bilateral exchange rates are more than twice as volatile as these price ratios, in some cases more than five times as volatile.[6] This should not be surprising once it is recognized that, unlike many goods prices that are changed only infrequently, exchange rates are free to respond to any new information hitting the exchange markets.

Even though exchange rates are volatile when compared with price indexes, they are less volatile than some asset prices like stock exchange indexes. And exchange rate volatility is also generally lower than the volatility of commodity prices quoted on organized exchanges. Table 2.2 reports the volatility measures for both of these sets of variables. Notice that three agricultural commodities important to farming communities—cotton, rice, and wheat—have almost three times the volatility of exchange rates.

That exchange rates are so much more volatile than prices should suggest that the volatility of real exchange rates is also quite large. Table 2.2 also provides evidence that real rates are about as volatile as nominal rates. This table presents volatility measures of nominal and real bilateral exchange rates as well as nominal and real *effective* exchange rates. Throughout this paper, the real exchange rate (R_t) is defined as the ratio of the domestic price index (P_t) to the domestic currency value of the foreign price index $(X_t P_t^*)$, where X_t is the domestic currency price of the foreign currency:[7]

$$(1) \qquad\qquad R_t = P_t / (X_t P_t^*).$$

The domestic and foreign prices used are WPIs, which are available on a monthly basis for most industrial countries. Effective exchange rates are obtained by weighting the exchange rates of ten countries (G-5 plus five medium-size industrial countries) by the share of total trade in manufactures (imports plus exports) of one country with each of the other countries.[8] The lesson to be learned from table 2.2 is an important one: real exchange rates are volatile primarily because nominal exchange rates are volatile. That is, the relative stability of price levels means that nominal exchange rate volatility translates into real exchange rate volatility.

Excessive Volatility?

Recent studies have addressed the question of whether asset prices are *excessively* volatile relative to the underlying factors determining their values. Shiller (1979), for example, studies whether long-term interest rates are excessively volatile relative to interest rates on short-term bonds. He finds that the volatility of long rates exceeds the limits imposed by term-structure models, which represent long-term rates as averages of expected short-term rates. The same type of methodology can be used to investigate the volatility of exchange rates.[9] But the tests are valid only if the researcher uses the correct underlying model of exchange rates, and there is little consensus about the appropriate model to use.[10] Huang (1981) shows that exchange rates are excessively volatile relative to a monetary model of exchange rates. But exchange rate volatility has yet to be investigated in terms of other models, so whether exchange rates exhibit excessive volatility remains an open question.

Changes in Volatility over Time

We have lived with flexible exchange rates for over a decade now, but there is no evidence that exchange rate volatility has declined as traders have become more accustomed to flexibility. Figure 2.2 illustrates the pattern of volatility over time for the real effective exchange

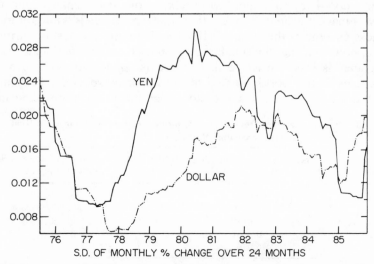

Fig. 2.2   Volatility of real effective rates. *Source:* Same as table 2.2.

rates for the yen and dollar. (The currencies in the EMS, including the Deutsche mark, are discussed in section 2.3.) Volatility is measured over the twenty-four months immediately prior to each time period. The yen and dollar experienced a decrease in volatility in 1976–77 before being hit by the second oil shock and by changes in U.S. policy (to be discussed below). There are no obvious trends in these series.

No doubt exchange rates are much more volatile than they were under the so-called fixed exchange rate regime of the 1960s. Table 2.3 uses quarterly data for real effective exchange rates to compare volatility during the 1960s with that of the more recent period from 1973 to 1985. Volatility is defined as the standard deviation of quarterly percentage changes. The results are quite clear: the Bretton Woods system's band around par values did constrain the volatility of real exchange rates. The two currencies experiencing only a marginal increase in volatility, the franc and mark, are those that have been tied together in European exchange rate arrangements, first the SNAKE and more recently the EMS.

Effects on Trade

To what extent should we be concerned with volatility per se? That question is difficult to answer. There is ample evidence that the movements in exchange rates reflected in the volatility measures are mostly *unanticipated*. (For example, forward premiums explain only a fraction of the variance of spot exchange rate changes.) So trading firms must cope with uncertainty about exchange rates. In drawing up contracts involving foreign exchange exposure, firms must take into account this uncertainty. They may elect to purchase forward exchange, but the forward market is limited to less than a dozen currencies, and for most of these currencies the market is thin for all but the shortest maturities. (Note, however, that limiting hedging alternatives to less than a dozen currencies is less restrictive than it seems, since most of the other currencies in the world are tied to the major currencies.) They may use the Eurocurrency markets to hedge their currency exposure,

Table 2.3   Standard Deviations of Quarterly Percentage Changes in Real Effective Exchange Rates

Country	Fixed Exchange Rate Period: 1960 I–1971 I	Flexible Exchange Rate Period: 1973 II–1985 IV
U.S.	0.0066	0.0281
Japan	0.0070	0.0377
France	0.0155	0.0185
Germany	0.0141	0.0193
U.K.	0.0162	0.0391

Sources: Same as table 2.2.

matching assets and liabilities in different currencies (the range of currencies available closely corresponding to the set available in the forward markets). They may take advantage of currency swaps which expand the range of foreign currency instruments available to the average company. Firms may also take advantage of the relatively new markets for options on foreign exchange, particularly when bidding on contracts. Finally, large multinational firms can diversify away much of the exchange risk. These hedging and diversification strategies are not without costs, including the additional managerial effort required to monitor exposure. These costs must be weighed against whatever benefits the present system affords.

Despite strong evidence that exchange rate volatility is much greater under flexible rates than under fixed rates, it has been difficult to establish statistically that this increase in volatility has seriously affected international trade. Hooper and Kohlhagen (1978) studied the effects of volatility on bilateral trade flows of the United States and Germany with other major industrial countries. They found "absolutely no significant effect of exchange risk on the volume of trade" (p. 505). Cushman (1983) found some evidence of reduced trade using the volatility of real rather than nominal exchange rates as his measure of risk. Kenen and Rodrik (1984), using multilateral trade data and effective exchange rates for eleven countries, also found some limited evidence of trade reduction. But for some countries in their sample, higher volatility seemed to increase rather than reduce trade. The strongest evidence of trade reduction effects was provided by Akhtar and Hilton (1984), who examined aggregate export and import behavior in the United States and Germany. Using a longer sample period than Hooper and Kohlhagen (1978), who studied the same two countries, Akhtar and Hilton found that German exports and imports were significantly reduced as a result of the increased volatility of nominal effective exchange rates, measured as the standard deviation of daily exchange rates. Even that study, however, found that U.S. imports were unaffected by volatility, and U.S. exports only marginally so. How is this evidence to be interpreted? It may be that opportunities for hedging and diversification are sufficient to limit the impact of volatility on trade. But it also may be that our econometric methods are not sufficiently powerful to determine the effects of volatility on trade.

Example of a Trading Firm

At this point it is useful to remind readers that volatility as defined is very different from the persistent *misalignment* of exchange rates that we have experienced recently. When the rise in the dollar leads to a loss of competitiveness for U.S. goods of more than 30 percent, as has happened over the last several years, trade is bound to be affected regardless of how successful firms are in reducing the effects of exchange rate volatility.

The distinction between the two concepts can be illustrated by a simple example. Suppose an American firm regularly exports goods to Germany for sale in that country. Whether these goods are invoiced in dollars or marks determines which firm, the American exporting firm or the German importing firm, bears the "transaction risk," the exchange risk associated with a particular export contract. If the mark/dollar (DM/$) rate fluctuates widely around an equilibrium value of DM2/$ (i.e., if the DM/$ rate is highly volatile), that risk can be considerable. The firm bearing the transaction risk, however, may elect to purchase a forward contract to hedge this risk. Alternatively, the risk can be reduced by appropriate financing or diversification strategies. Contrast the same American firm faced with a misalignment of the DM/$ rate at a level of DM3/$ (as occurred in the early 1980s). If this *misalignment* is persistent, then the firm will find its "economic exposure" cannot be hedged so easily. The firm may be faced with a choice between shutting down or shifting its production facilities abroad.

2.1.2   Misalignment

Economists writing on flexible exchange rates in the 1960s contemplated neither the magnitude nor the persistence of the changes in real exchange rates that have occurred in the last fifteen years, so the term "misalignment" is a relatively new one. In his recent study of exchange rates, Williamson defines misalignment as the "persistent departure of the exchange rate from its long run equilibrium level" (Williamson 1985, 13). Defining such a long-run equilibrium is no simple task. Williamson identifies the long-run equilibrium exchange rate as

> that which is expected to generate a current account surplus or deficit equal to the underlying capital flow over the cycle, given that the country is pursuing "internal balance" as best it can and not restricting trade for balance of payments reasons (p. 14).[11]

It is evident that such a definition refers to the real rather than the nominal exchange rate, so the nominal exchange rate has to be adjusted by relative prices through time if inflation differentials are significant. This is analogous to calculating a purchasing power parity (PPP) exchange rate relative to some base period. But Williamson's concept of the long-run equilibrium rate is more sophisticated than a PPP concept since it also takes into account real shocks such as the OPEC price increases of 1973–74 and 1978–79.

This paper will discuss some of the problems involved in defining long-run equilibrium when we analyze target zones for exchange rates (section 2.4). In this section, there is no need to be specific about what the equilibrium level of any exchange rate is in order to illustrate the extent of movement of real exchange rates over time for some of the major currencies. In figure 2.3, one commonly cited measure of real exchange rates, real effective exchange rates based on wholesale prices in manufacturing, is used to illustrate the movements of the dollar, yen, and pound sterling over the period since the start of floating rates in 1973. The figure illustrates clearly the wide swings in real exchange rates that have characterized these currencies.[12] In the period since 1973, the most serious cases of misalignment among the industrial countries occurred with respect to the pound sterling and the dollar. Between 1976 and 1980, the pound rose by over 40 percent in real effective terms. Between 1980 and 1985, the dollar rose more than 35 percent using yearly averages;[13] its peak in February 1985 was 42 percent above its 1980 average. Both cases of misalignment will be studied in detail in order to show the extent of the misalignment and its effects on the economies concerned. Before doing so, however, some of the costs associated with misalignment will be discussed to show why there is so much concern about it.

Costs of Misalignment

When real exchange rates are misaligned, there are incentives to shift resources both internally and externally. Internally, whenever the rate is overvalued, services and other so-called nontradable industries gain at the expense of export and import-competing or tradable

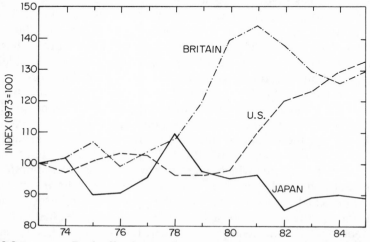

Fig. 2.3   Real effective exchange rates. *Source:* Morgan Guaranty Trust, *World Financial Markets.*

industries. Externally, foreign competitors gain at the expense of these same industries. These shifts in resources are costly.[14]

Misalignments of the size experienced recently, where competing countries gain a price advantage of 20 or 30 percent, can have very disruptive effects on firms producing traded goods. Since misalignments may persist for five years or more, production facilities in some tradable industries may be mothballed or scrapped altogether, even though these facilities might be internationally competitive at exchange rates closer to their long-run equilibrium levels. Short-run losses of competitiveness due to misalignment can easily become permanent in cases where foreign firms are able to establish themselves in an industry. Baldwin and Krugman (1986) have shown that such irreversible changes can occur in industries where costs of entry (e.g., investment in marketing and distribution) would deter foreign competition in the absence of the misalignment.

If a firm is a multinational, it might elect to shift the production facility threatened by the misalignment to lower-cost countries. That decision is not without peril, however, since today's undervalued exchange rate might swing to overvaluation as did sterling in the late 1970s. A firm electing to locate a production facility in Britain in the mid-1970s would have been unpleasantly surprised by the real appreciation that followed.

Even if domestic production facilities are merely mothballed, moreover, the resulting unemployment is costly. Given sufficient time, the labor force can be retrained and reassigned to nontradable industries. But even if such shifts of employment between industries can be effected, the costs involved are still significant. The decision to shift to a new industry is made more difficult by three factors. First, it is as unclear to the labor force as it is to firms how long the misalignment will last. The decision of employees to seek employment elsewhere or of firms to close facilities must be made despite the considerable uncertainty about the timing of any return to equilibrium. (Recall the uncertainty about the timing of the dollar's fall.) Second, it is hard to disentangle long-run shifts in comparative advantage from misalignment. The U.S. steel and automobile industries, for example, were no doubt hurt by the misalignment, but the growth of foreign production was important as well. Third, there is the uncertainty about future protectionist measures which might shield an industry from both misalignment and secular declines in competitiveness. These sources of uncertainty make it difficult for both the labor force and firms to make decisions. In the early 1980s auto workers, for example, had to decide whether to retrain and possibly relocate on the basis of their assessment of the duration of misalignment, the long-term prospects of the auto industry, and the political economy of protectionism. This was a formidable task indeed—one certainly beyond the skills of economists.

The costs of misalignment are not limited to the firms and labor force in the tradables sector. First, the economy as a whole must adjust its consumption of nontradables if the resources shifted to that sector are to be fully employed. Since the relative price of tradables has fallen, that shift in nontradables requires an increase in total consumption relative to its long-run sustainable level. A capital account surplus will finance this consumer surge, but at the cost of a buildup of debt. So one of the costs of the misalignment, as emphasized earlier by Hause (1966) and Johnson (1966), is a major shift in the time pattern of consumption.[15] The second cost is one alluded to earlier, the cost of tariffs and other protectionist measures which may be introduced in response to the misalignment. In his study of trade tensions between the United States and Japan, Bergsten (1982) points out that the three recent periods when protectionist pressures were at their height in the United States were times when the dollar was most overvalued relative to the yen. The costs of protectionist legislation, if enacted, which would be "justified" by the need to protect the tradable industries, are borne by consumers throughout the economy.

Some of the costs associated with misalignments are illustrated by the two most serious cases of misalignment among the major industrial countries, those of Britain and the United States.

The Misalignment of Sterling in 1979–82

The run-up of sterling began before the Conservative government led by Margaret Thatcher took office in June 1979, but during the first three years of that government the misalignment problem became severe. Sterling rose from $1.70/£ in 1976 to $2.40/£ in 1980. The rise in the nominal value of sterling, moreover, was matched by its rise in real terms. Figure 2.3 above shows a rise in the real effective exchange rate for sterling by 45 percent between 1976 and 1981. Recall that this series for the real exchange rate is based on manufacturing prices, so the rise in the index reflects a startling loss of price competitiveness in Britain's principal export sector. A real appreciation of this magnitude led to what was called at the time the "deindustrialization of Britain."

This appreciation is usually attributed to two main factors: the discovery and exploitation of North Sea oil and the commitment to tight monetary policy by the Thatcher government. Although North Sea discoveries began in the early 1970s, production rose sharply only in the late 1970s, from 16.6 million tons in (the financial year) 1976–77 to 79.6 million tons in 1979–80.[16] So the timing of sterling's rise coincides roughly with the rise in North Sea production (although not with the exchange market's anticipation of this rise). In a detailed study of economic policies under the first Thatcher government, however, Buiter and Miller (1983) find that at most 10 percent of the real appreciation can be attributed to the effects of North Sea oil.[17] The second factor, tight monetary policy, also undoubtedly played a role in the appreciation. The appreciation, however, may have been due more to the *announced targets* for money growth rather than actual money growth performance, since actual money growth (at least for the broader aggregates) repeatedly outran the targets. After evaluating these and other explanations of the appreciation, Buiter and Miller conclude that much of the appreciation remains unexplained; indeed, they "find the decline in competitiveness puzzling" (p. 317).

How much of this real appreciation represents misalignment of the real exchange rate from its equilibrium level? The discovery of North Sea oil shifted the equilibrium real exchange rate, so some of the loss of competitiveness of British manufacturing might be better termed "realignment" rather than "misalignment." That is, some of the real appreciation of sterling reflected the necessary adjustment of relative prices called for by this real shock. But what about the real appreciation due to the monetary tightening (or prospective monetary tightening)? If misalignment is defined as the departure of the exchange rate from its equilibrium level, then the overshooting of the exchange rate associated with monetary tightening should be labeled misalignment. The monetary policy itself may have been desirable as part of a disinflation policy, but the accompanying temporary overshooting of the exchange rate imposes adjustment costs which are just as severe as when the exchange rate becomes misaligned as a result of exchange market inefficiencies or speculative bubbles.

The effects of the appreciation on the British manufacturing sector were unusually severe. Value added in manufacturing fell by over 8 percent in 1980 and by over 6 percent in 1981, compared with declines of 2 percent or less in GDP in these same two years. The effects on employment in manufacturing were slower to develop, but they appear to be longer lasting. According to figure 2.4, employment in manufacturing declined by over 4 percent in 1980, but by over 10 percent in 1981, and it continued to decline in 1982 and 1983. The effects of sterling's loss of competitiveness were devastating for British manufacturing. The term "Dutch Disease" is used to describe the loss of competitiveness of a manufacturing sector when oil or gas discoveries drive up the exchange rate. Britain seems to have suffered from a particularly virulent strain of this disease, although as argued above, the causes of the illness cannot be attributed to North Sea oil alone.

Misalignment of the Dollar, 1981–85

The dollar has more recently been misaligned as seriously as the pound sterling was in 1980–82, but the effects of the misalignment on employment have been mitigated by strong domestic demand for U.S.

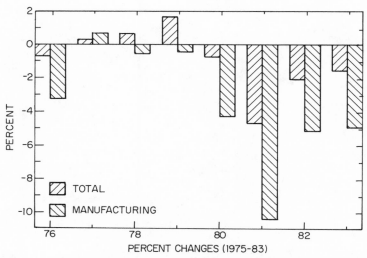

Fig. 2.4   Growth in British employment. *Source:* OECD National Accounts.

goods. Figure 2.5 traces three real effective exchange rates for the dollar, all based on prices in the manufacturing sectors of the United States and its trading partners. The three prices represented are wholesale prices, value-added deflators, and normalized unit labor costs. The real exchange rates measure U.S. relative to foreign prices or labor costs, so a rise in any of the real exchange rate series represents a real appreciation of the dollar and a loss of competitiveness for U.S. manufactures.[18] The sharp appreciation of the dollar from 1980 to 1985 is seen in all three series, appreciations of from 34 to 43 percent in five years.

The origins of the appreciation remain a controversial subject. Among the principal causes cited are the fiscal policies of the Reagan Administration, the tight monetary policies pursued by the Federal Reserve Board since Paul Volcker became Chairman in 1979, the rise in investment associated with the Tax Reduction Act of 1981, and the flight of capital to the "safe haven" of U.S. capital markets. Branson (1985) presents the argument in favor of attributing much of the rise to American fiscal policies. Although the defense buildup and tax cuts were spread out over several years, Branson argues that the Reagan Administration made credible "announcements" concerning this policy in 1981, a year when the dollar rose sharply. Obstfeld (1985) also attributes much of the rise to fiscal policy, but he emphasizes the separate contribution of foreign fiscal authorities. In a back-of-the-envelope calculation of fiscal effects, he attributes to fiscal policy a real appreciation of a little over 20 percent, but almost half of that appreciation is due

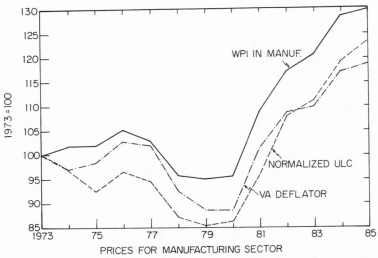

Fig. 2.5   Real exchange rates for dollar. *Source:* IMF, *International Financial Statistics.*

to *foreign* fiscal policy. Frenkel (1985) argues that the initial rise in the dollar (in 1980) was due more to *actual monetary* policy than to expected future fiscal policy. He cites the rise in short-term interest rates which could not have been due to fiscal actions several years in the future. Evidence for the role of investment and the "safe haven" flight of capital is harder to find. Branson (1985) points out that while the level of investment rose sharply in the 1983–85 recovery, the level of investment relative to GNP was not unusually high in that period. "Safe haven" effects may have been at work during the period, but it is hard to argue that the degree of political risk, in Europe at least, was higher in the 1980s than in earlier postwar periods.[19]

Unlike the origins of the misalignment, the effects on U.S. trade are unmistakable. The export- and import-competing sectors of the U.S. economy have been hard hit. Table 2.4 reports the trade balance by sector in two years, 1980 and 1985, as well as the percentage change in the trade balance over this period measured as a percentage of *exports* in 1980. According to this table, the sectors hardest hit by the misalignment were the auto and general consumer goods sectors; the trade balance in autos deteriorated by almost 180 percent of 1980 exports during this five-year period, while the trade balance in general consumer goods deteriorated by over 200 percent. Even the capital goods sector, normally the strongest of the U.S. manufacturing sectors, deteriorated sharply with the trade balance falling to $11.6 billion from a 1980 level of $43.4 billion. The trade balance as a whole went from a deficit of $27.7 billion in 1980 to an alarmingly large deficit of $122.1 billion in 1985.[20]

Table 2.4   **U.S. Trade Account (in billions of current $)**

	1980	1985	% Change 1980–85[a]
Merchandise Trade Balance	−27.7	−122.1	−43.3
Agriculture and raw materials	32.7	1.3	−30.5
Fuels	−79.1	−50.5	36.2
Manufactures	15.3	−81.2	−90.3
Capital goods	43.4	11.6	−43.3
Autos	−10.2	−40.6	−179.9
Consumer goods	−17.9	−52.2	−207.9
Other	3.4	8.2	57.8

Source: Survey of Current Business, National Income and Product Accounts.
[a]Measured as a percentage of exports in 1980 (imports in the case of fuels).

The misalignment, of course, was not the sole cause of this deterioration in U.S. trade performance. During the 1980–85 period, growth in Europe lagged behind that in the United States, causing faster growth of imports in the United States. In addition, the debt crisis forced Latin American countries to curtail their imports from the United States, a factor which may be particularly important in explaining the fall in U.S. exports of capital goods. But the trade sector had to have been seriously affected by a change in relative prices of the magnitude experienced.

The misalignment led to a fall in production and employment in many subsectors of manufacturing. Branson and Love (1986) have estimated disaggregated equations for production and employment in the United States to determine the effects of the dollar's appreciation. They attribute a loss of 1.3 million jobs in U.S. manufacturing to a 40 percent appreciation of the dollar. This job loss was concentrated in the durable goods sectors, with many of these jobs being lost in two of those sectors, primary metals and nonelectrical machinery. Nonetheless, the effects of the dollar's appreciation on industrial production and employment were not as severe as in the case of Britain for two reasons. First, the trade sector is much less important to the U.S. economy than it is to the British. Perhaps more importantly, the appreciation coincided with a defense buildup as well as a consumer boom which kept domestic demand for U.S. goods strong despite the inroads made by foreign goods.

These two case studies serve to illustrate the disruptive effects of sizable misalignments. One sector of the economy, the tradables sector, suffers inordinately during the period of the misalignment while the rest of the economy stumbles on. During the period of sterling's misalignment, the dichotomy between traded and nontraded sectors took a geographical form. The north of England, where traditional industries such as steel and automobiles were centered, suffered from severe unemployment, while the area around London remained relatively prosperous. In the United States, the contrast in fortunes between the rust-belt and the sun-belt can be explained at least in part by the deterioration of U.S. competitiveness associated with the appreciation of the dollar.

The problems associated with misalignment thus differ markedly from those associated with volatility. No simple hedging strategy can protect a firm from a loss of relative competitiveness of 30 percent or more.

Having defined these problems of exchange rate variability, we now turn to the search for solutions. Some observers might contend that the solution is obvious: governments must adopt policies designed to minimize the variability of exchange rates. Yet the fact that there are costs associated with volatility and misalignment does not in itself justify policies designed to limit exchange rate variability. Before discussing the arguments for and against exchange rate policies, let us review evidence on the effectiveness of the most common instrument used to control exchange rates, foreign exchange intervention.

2.2 The Effectiveness of Foreign Exchange Intervention

The central question addressed in this section is the following: Does foreign exchange intervention constitute a separate instrument of exchange rate policy, or does it work solely through its effects on domestic and foreign money supplies? If the latter is the case, then intervention must be considered in the broader framework of monetary policy.

2.2.1 Definition of Foreign Exchange Intervention

Intervention is difficult to define because there are many ways in which the monetary authorities can influence exchange rates. The Working Group on Foreign Exchange Intervention, commissioned by the Versailles Summit of June 1982, adopted a narrow definition of intervention modified to include certain "passive" operations. According to the Working Group's Report (1983, hereafter referred to as the Jurgensen Report),[21] the narrow definition consists of "any sale or purchase of foreign exchange against domestic currency which monetary authorities undertake in the exchange market" (p. 4). It includes all central bank purchases and sales of foreign exchange against domestic currency, whatever form of financing is used (reserves, swaps, official borrowing, etc.). The Jurgensen Report adds to this narrow definition three forms of "passive" intervention: sales concluded by the central bank with public sector entities including the central government (which would otherwise have undertaken the transactions in the exchange market), IMF drawings, and interest payments on international reserves. This definition makes intervention equivalent to the change in the monetary authorities' net foreign currency assets excluding any capital gains on existing assets. The definition specifically does not include exchange market transactions carried out by other private or public entities that might be considered to be "directed" by the government or central bank (such as Eurodollar loans to public authorities) because it is so difficult to establish the intent of the authorities in the case of such transactions.

More important than the precise definition of intervention is the distinction between sterilized and nonsterilized intervention. The Jurgensen Report defines *sterilized intervention* as a "change in the monetary authorities' net foreign currency assets which is offset by a corresponding change in their net domestic assets so that their monetary liabilities (or, specifically, the monetary base) remains unchanged" (p. 6). Nonsterilized intervention, in contrast, involves a one-for-one change in the authorities' net foreign currency assets and the monetary base. *Nonsterilized intervention* thus is a form of monetary policy, distinguishable from conventional open-market operations only in the type of asset being exchanged for money.[22] There is virtually unanimous agreement among economists that nonsterilized intervention can affect exchange rates, just as more conventionally defined monetary policy can undoubtedly affect exchange rates. The effectiveness of sterilized intervention, in contrast, is a much more controversial topic. Yet if foreign exchange intervention is to be regarded as a separate instrument of economic policy, distinct from monetary policy, then it must take the form of sterilized intervention.

2.2.2 Effectiveness of Sterilized Intervention

There are three distinct channels through which sterilized intervention can affect exchange rates.[23] The first is the most straightforward: sterilized intervention works by altering the supplies of assets in private portfolios, thus requiring a realignment of asset returns. This *portfolio balance* channel requires that foreign and domestic securities be imperfect substitutes. The more substitutable these securities are, the smaller the realignment of asset returns, and thus the smaller the change in the current exchange rate, required to rebalance portfolios. In the limiting case of perfect substitution between securities, where investors regard domestic and foreign bonds as interchangeable, sterilized intervention is completely ineffective, at least through this portfolio balance channel.

The other two channels operate through *announcement effects* requiring either market inefficiencies or superior information on the part of the authorities. If the market is inefficient, intervention operations may help focus the attention of the public on hitherto neglected factors even though the operation itself provides no new information. It is difficult to provide a convincing rationale for why market operators would neglect publicly available information, or why intervention would refocus their attention on this information. But we cannot rule out this possibility a priori. Alternatively, the intervention operation could provide new information by signaling the private market about the future monetary policies of the authorities.[24] This last channel could operate even if the market were efficient, in the sense that market participants incorporate all available information in forming their expectations, since the authorities naturally have superior information about their future intentions.

There is extensive empirical research on the effectiveness of sterilized intervention. Although this evidence is far from conclusive, it is strong enough to have led the Jurgensen Report to conclude that "there was broad agreement among the members of the Working Group that sterilized intervention alone did not appear to have constituted an effective instrument in the face of persistent market pressures" (p. 20). Whether or not sterilized intervention might have a short-term impact through announcement effects was less clear to the Working Group.

The Jurgensen Report's conclusion is based on two different types of evidence. First, there are tests of "speculative efficiency," which are actually joint tests of uncovered interest parity and market efficiency. Second, there are estimates of portfolio models designed to determine the influence of bond supplies on risk premia. These two sets of evidence reach sharply different conclusions.

Speculative Efficiency Tests

Tests of speculative efficiency are based on uncovered interest parity, the equality of *expected* returns on securities denominated in different currencies. If uncovered interest parity holds, the expected interest return on a dollar security should equal the expected return on a foreign currency security measured in terms of dollars (the expected return consisting of the foreign interest rate plus the expected capital gain or loss on the foreign currency).[25] The expected returns will be equal whenever investors regard the two securities as perfect substitutes. If investors are risk averse, on the other hand, then they will regard two securities denominated in different currencies as imperfect substitutes, and a *risk premium* will separate the two expected returns. In that case, sterilized intervention might be effective if it can change the relative supply of dollar and nondollar securities enough to affect the risk premium.

To determine whether uncovered interest parity holds, investigators must examine actual, not expected, returns (since expected returns are not observable). Uncovered interest parity does not ensure that *actual* returns are equal on securities denominated in different currencies. But the differential between these returns should be random as long as the forecast errors from predicting exchange rates are random, which will be the case if the exchange market is *efficient*. The speculative efficiency test, which tests jointly whether uncovered interest parity holds and the exchange market is efficient, thus examines whether actual returns on securities denominated in different currencies are equal except for a random factor.

During the 1970s, a score of investigators ran tests of speculative efficiency using different time periods and currencies. With few exceptions, they were unable to reject the speculative efficiency hypothesis. The evidence was strong enough for Mussa (1979) to conclude in his summary of empirical regularities in the foreign exchange market that "the interest differential in favor of domestic currency bonds is equal approximately to the expected rate of depreciation of domestic money in terms of foreign money" (p. 24).

Recent studies, however, have been able to reject the speculative efficiency hypothesis using longer data sets and more sophisticated statistical techniques.[26] In fact, they have provided such convincing evidence against speculative efficiency that researchers have turned their attention toward explaining deviations from uncovered interest parity in terms of risk premia (while maintaining the hypothesis that the exchange market is efficient).

Direct Evidence of Risk Premia

If investors are risk averse, the expected returns on securities denominated in different currencies will be separated by a risk premium which is a function of the relative supplies of foreign and domestic securities, domestic and foreign wealth, and other factors.[27] Investigators have searched for evidence of this risk premium without success. Rogoff (1984), for example, finds no evidence that the interest differential between U.S. and Canadian bonds is sensitive to the relative supply of these bonds. (So he finds no evidence that sterilized intervention in the Canadian dollar market, which would alter the relative supplies of U.S. and Canadian dollar bonds, could affect exchange rates.) Other investigators have used more elaborate models to investigate risk premia, and have reached conclusions similar to those of Rogoff.[28]

Interpreting the Conflicting Evidence

The two sets of evidence from speculative efficiency and portfolio balance studies seem to give conflicting results. The studies of speculative efficiency suggest the importance of a time-varying risk premium, but the portfolio balance studies are unable to explain that risk premium in terms of relative asset supplies. There are at least three ways to reconcile this evidence. First, an appeal can be made to market inefficiencies which would account for the ex post interest differentials without appealing to a risk premium. But to date no one has provided a convincing rationale for why traders would fail to eliminate any perceived profit opportunities in the foreign exchange market. Second, it may be the case that, even though a time-varying risk premium is important in explaining interest differentials, sterilized intervention (or any other change in relative bond supplies) has a negligible effect on that risk premium. Third, existing empirical methods may not be sophisticated enough to establish the effectiveness of sterilized intervention. Unfortunately, there is no basis for choosing between these last two alternatives. It is evident that the menu of assets available to investors is much larger than the choice between domestic and foreign bonds modeled in many studies. Portfolio decisions, moreover, have an intertemporal dimension in which consumption and investment decisions are made simultaneously, in contrast to the static models that form the basis of existing empirical estimates.[29] It is unclear whether or not more sophisticated empirical models, based on a larger menu of assets and incorporating intertemporal decisions, would confirm or refute existing empirical evidence. To date, however, there is no evidence that sterilized intervention can affect exchange rates, at least through conventional portfolio balance channels. On the basis of existing evidence, therefore, it is difficult to justify using sterilized intervention to carry out exchange rate policy.

If sterilized intervention is ineffective, a second conclusion follows: to pursue active exchange rate management, there is no substitute for monetary policy. Monetary policy can be pursued either with traditional domestic instruments or with nonsterilized foreign exchange intervention. Whether the latter is called monetary policy or not is of little importance.

Yet even if monetary policy is necessary for exchange rate management, there is still a potential role for sterilized intervention if such intervention provides a signal to the market about future monetary policy. Because of the very nature of announcement effects, however, it is difficult to find evidence of them using conventional statistical methods. Two successive intervention operations of equal size may provide different signals to the market, so they may have different effects on the exchange rate.

2.2.3 Two Episodes of Foreign Exchange Intervention

Because statistical evidence leaves the question of announcement effects unresolved, one might believe that the study of specific episodes of active foreign exchange intervention might help to resolve this question. Such episodes are difficult to interpret, but two particularly interesting episodes are singled out for study. These are the November 1, 1978, announcement of a dollar defense package by the Carter Administration and the G-5 intervention of September 1985.

1978 Dollar Defense Package

This episode bolsters the Jurgensen Report's view that intervention can have significant short-term effects. But the ultimate failure of the defense package, despite the fact that U.S. authorities assembled $30 billion for foreign exchange intervention, suggests that short-term intervention packages alone are not effective unless they are followed by longer term changes in monetary policy. The dollar defense package came at a time when the foreign exchange market was in disarray reflecting the growing loss of confidence in the policies of the Carter Administration. In her in-depth study of this crisis, Margaret Greene a senior official in the Federal Reserve Bank of New York, described the market as follows: "During the last week of October, the selling of dollars reached near-panic proportions, and dollar rates plummeted to record lows against several major currencies" (1984, 28). After the President announced an anti-inflation program on October 24, a program received with skepticism by the financial markets, the authorities sold almost $1 billion equivalent of marks. Yet the dollar dropped against the mark from DM1.81/$ to DM1.72/$ over the new four trading days. Similarly, the dollar dropped against the yen from ¥181/$ to ¥178/$.

The package announced on November 1, in contrast to the anti-inflation program, was an impressive one. First, monetary policy was tightened, with the discount rate raised by an "unprecedented" 1 percentage point to a (then) historic high of 9½ percent. (Thus the package had an important monetary policy component.) Second, a $30 billion package of foreign currency resources was assembled for future intervention consisting of $15 billion in swaps with foreign central banks, $5 billion in drawings on the IMF and sales of SDRs, and $10 billion in so-called Carter bonds, U.S. Treasury notes denominated in marks and Swiss francs to be sold abroad.

The market was obviously impressed with the scope of the package and the resolve about future policy which it seemed to represent. By 9:13 AM on November 1, the dollar had moved 7¼ percent above the previous day's low against the mark to DM1.83/$.[30] Within 23 minutes, the dollar had moved up another 1 percent against the mark while the Desk sold the equivalent of $69 million marks, to SF1.567/$ while the Desk sold $19 million of Swiss francs, and to ¥187.5/$ with the Desk selling $5 million. As figure 2.6 illustrates, by the time of the closing in London, the dollar had risen against the mark to DM1.85/$ and against the yen to ¥186.5/$. By the end of the (New York) day, the dollar had risen to DM1.879/$ and to ¥187.9/$, up 7–10 percent from its lows of the day before. The foreign exchange intervention undertaken by the Desk that day amounted to a little more than $600 million, over two-thirds of it consisting of intervention in the market for marks.

The U.S authorities, in cooperation with the Bundesbank, Swiss National Bank, and Bank of Japan, had to intervene repeatedly in the following weeks as the market tried to test official resolve. Figure 2.6 shows that the dollar stabilized at around DM1.90/$ and ¥190/$ through the first two weeks of November, then rose somewhat more in the following two weeks. By the end of November, U.S. intervention had totaled more than $3.5 billion. On December 1, the spot rates for the dollar were DM1.94/$ and ¥203.5/$, both rates being significantly above the October lows.

This episode illustrates the effectiveness of monetary and exchange market operations in halting a currency's slide. But it also illustrates the limitations of such action if not followed up by more fundamental changes in monetary policy and macroeconomic policy in general. The rise of the dollar stalled in early December as market participants became skeptical again about the Carter Administration's policies toward inflation. Then the dollar was hit by the shock of an OPEC price increase of 14.5 percent following the political upheavals in Iran. During the month of December, foreign exchange intervention was almost as sizable as in November, totaling more than $3.1 billion. Yet no new monetary policy initiatives were taken. By the end of the month the

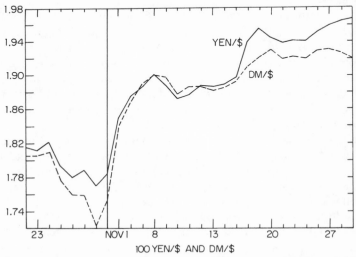

Fig. 2.6   November 1, 1978, Policy Shift. *Source: The Financial Times.*

dollar had fallen to DM1.828/$ and ¥194.60/$. The short-run impact of the November 1 package had faded, and the time afforded to make more fundamental adjustments in policy had been squandered. As Greene (1984) summarized the episode: "If this time is not put to productive use, then intervention alone, no matter how large or how well coordinated, will not be effective" (p. 40).

G-5 Intervention in September 1985

The dollar rose through most of the four years of the first Reagan Administration, peaking in February 1985. After falling from its February highs during the following spring and summer, the dollar began to rally in early September. That rally was cut short by the Group of 5 (G-5) meeting of finance ministers and central bank governors in New York on Sunday, September 22. According to the G-5 statement issued at the end of that day:

> The Ministers and Governors agreed that exchange rates should play a role in adjusting external imbalances. In order to do this, exchange rates should better reflect fundamental economic conditions than has been the case. They believe that agreed policy actions must be implemented and reinforced to improve the fundamentals further, and that in view of the present and prospective changes in fundamentals, *some further orderly appreciation of the main non-dollar currencies against the dollar is desirable.* They *stand ready to cooperate more closely to encourage this* when to do so would be helpful. (IMF *Survey,* October 7, 1985, p. 297; Emphasis added)

The statement had an immediate effect on exchange rates. As the Harris Bank *Foreign Exchange Weekly Review* later remarked: "Foreign exchange traders were taken by surprise, and the dollar dropped sharply following the announcement, even before any official intervention occurred" (February 7, 1986, p. 1). In figure 2.7, daily exchange rates for the yen are illustrated. The dollar fell against the yen from ¥240.1/$ to ¥231.7/$ by the close in London on Monday, September 23. It fell further to ¥219.5/$ by Friday of that week. The dollar also fell sharply against the mark from DM2.844/$ on Friday, September 20, to DM2.680/$ on the following Friday.

There is a puzzle in this dramatic movement. The exchange rates fell despite the fact that interest differentials were virtually constant. In the case of one-month Eurocurrency deposits, for example, the interest differential between dollar and yen deposits and between dollar and mark deposits remained roughly constant throughout the week. Indeed, both differentials remained constant until late October when the Japanese authorities tightened credit conditions in their market. The fall in spot rates in the absence of interest rate movements may be due to pure *announcement effects* of the G-5 communique. That is,

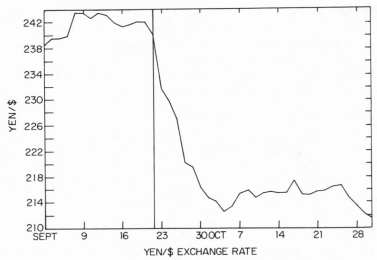

Fig. 2.7   G-5 intervention. *Source: The Financial Times.*

the exchange rates may have moved primarily because the G-5 announcement signaled future changes in policy rather than because of the foreign exchange intervention that followed the announcement. This interpretation is bolstered by the fact that, even though foreign exchange intervention following the G-5 announcement was not much greater than intervention in February and March of 1985, exchange rates moved much more after the G-5 announcement.[31]

What did the G-5 announcement signal? The Bank for International Settlements (BIS) *Annual Report* of 1986 cited two factors. First, the joint communique gave a "convincing demonstration of unanimity and common policy resolve, and . . . the subsequent intervention operations were fully coordinated and had the wholehearted support of nearly all the major industrial countries represented" (p. 149). The fact that the policy actions were coordinated was said to be of crucial importance both because of the potentially larger scale of any intervention operations and because there was more of an assurance that the authorities of different countries would not be working at cross-purposes. Second, the G-5 statement marked a major change in U.S. policy, which had shunned foreign exchange intervention since the beginning of the Reagan Administration. As the BIS *Annual Report* describes it:

[f]rom the point of view of credibility, it was of crucial importance that, for the first time, the US authorities, whose capacity to sell dollars is in principle unlimited, were seen to recognize the need for a further downward adjustment of the dollar. (p. 149)

Yet, given the evidence against sterilized intervention, one must remain skeptical about whether either factor, international coordination or the active participation of the United States, could have been decisive if the G-5 countries had simply announced a series of *sterilized* intervention operations. Instead, the G-5 announcement may have moved exchange rates because the market believed either that the intervention would be monetized or that the intervention, even though sterilized, signaled future changes in monetary policy.

In the case of the G-5 announcement, the evidence is unclear whether or not foreign exchange intervention was monetized. As indicated above, short-term interest differentials between the dollar and the mark or yen remained constant from September 22 through most of October. The first unambiguous sign of changes in monetary policy occurred in Japan in the last week of October. The dollar had begun to rally somewhat, so the Japanese authorities decided to tighten monetary conditions, sending short-term interest rates from 6.5 percent to 8 percent in only a few days. As a result, the yen resumed its upward rise.

Comparison of These Two Episodes

A comparison of these two episodes is quite instructive. The 1978 defense package bucked a downward trend of the dollar. If it had been the signal for a fundamental change in U.S. monetary policy toward a more restrictive stance, then the short-term gains in strengthening the dollar in November and December 1978 might have been consolidated and extended into 1979 and beyond. But since no such fundamental change was forthcoming, the dollar resumed its downward trend. The G-5 intervention, in contrast, was clearly reinforcing rather than bucking a trend. In fact, it is useful to ask whether the G-5 announcement and the actions that followed were on balance successful in driving the dollar down relative to its previous trend.

Figure 2.8 tries to answer that question by putting the period immediately following this announcement into a longer term perspective. This figure shows the weekly movement of the yen from January through December 1985, highlighting the G-5 announcement. The trend of the dollar against the yen is downward throughout, but in the period immediately following the announcement the dollar's fall accelerates. The same cannot be said of the dollar's fall relative to the mark. It is true that the G-5 announcement halts a temporary rise in the dollar, but it merely restores that mark to its previous trend. These figures lend support to Martin Feldstein's (1986) view that "for Germany and other G5 countries, the Plaza (New York) meeting was essentially a nonevent" (p. 6). Yet, even if Feldstein is right about currencies other than the yen, the G-5 period may provide evidence for announcement effects in the case of the yen. Under one interpretation, the dollar fell relative to the yen because the market perceived a greater degree of cooperation between Japan and the United States than in the previous four years, as well as a willingness on the part of the Japanese government to

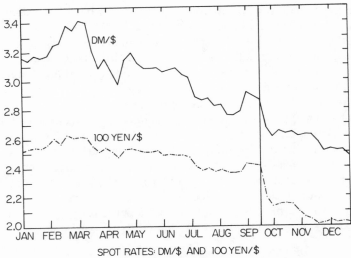

SPOT RATES: DM/$ AND 100 YEN/$

Fig. 2.8   Weekly spot rates in 1985. *Source:* Harris Bank, *Weekly Review.*

pursue a tighter monetary policy to drive the yen down, a policy not actually put into effect until late October.

This section has established the limits of foreign exchange intervention as a distinct exchange rate policy. If intervention is monetized, it can have powerful effects on exchange rates, but so also can conventional monetary policy. If intervention is sterilized, in contrast, then its effects on the exchange rate are thought to be minimal. The announcement of the intervention may be the occasion for a rally in the exchange market, but perhaps only if the market believes that the intervention signals broader changes in monetary policy.

Because the evidence implies that sterilized intervention is ineffective, the remainder of this paper assumes that monetary policy, broadly defined to encompass nonsterilized intervention, is the prime instrument of exchange rate policy.

Exchange rate policy could take a variety of forms. First, governments could reestablish a system of *fixed* exchange rates, perhaps with wider bands to accommodate greater variability of exchange rates. The fixed rates could be confined to regional groupings of countries, as in the European Monetary System, or they could encompass all industrial countries. Second, governments could retain the present system of flexible exchange rates, but institute stricter rules governing exchange rate management. Third, governments could establish a system of *target zones* for exchange rates with "soft margins" that leave governments with some discretion concerning intervention. All three alternatives, which involve *systemic* changes in the international monetary system, contrast sharply with ad hoc agreements like the G-5 intervention, which are designed to cope with specific exchange rate problems. Sections 2.3 and 2.4 will explore these alternatives.

2.3 Putting Humpty Dumpty Back Together Again: Restoring Fixed Exchange Rates

This section analyzes the case for returning to fixed exchange rates. The first part considers the general rationale for fixing exchange rates. The next two parts ask what lessons can be learned from two fixed exchange rate systems, the Bretton Woods system, which lasted until 1971, and the European Monetary System established in 1979.

2.3.1 Rationale for Fixed Exchange Rates

Although many rationales have been offered in support of fixing exchange rates, two are particularly prominent in most discussions. First, fixed exchange rates help to neutralize financial disturbances that might otherwise have an impact on the real side of the economy. Second, fixed rates provide discipline to governments that might otherwise follow inflationary policies. Each argument is considered in turn.

Sources of Disturbances

Economists analyzing exchange rate regimes have often posed the following question: Would fixed or flexible exchange rates be preferable in the presence of a particular disturbance? Fixed exchange rates can be shown to be superior when financial disturbances are predominant in an economy. A fall in the demand for money, for example, can be neutralized by a reduction in its supply leaving the exchange rate unaffected. If investors shift from domestic money to foreign securities, this can be neutralized by intervention in the foreign exchange market. In either case, the policy designed to keep the exchange rate fixed also helps to keep the disturbances confined to the financial sector, so that output and employment are left undisturbed. If disturbances originate in the real sector of the economy, however, it is difficult to make a case for preventing exchange rate movements since these movements generally facilitate the adjustment of relative prices that real disturbances require.[32] A rise in demand for exports, for example, leads to an appreciation of the domestic currency under flexible rates since the increase in demand raises domestic interest rates and attracts capital from abroad. The appreciation of the domestic currency, by shifting demand to foreign goods, helps to dampen the rise in domestic demand.[33] Thus fixed exchange rates (or target zones for exchange rates to be discussed below) are better designed for periods when financial disturbances are predominant.

Most economists analyzing the desirability of foreign exchange intervention have implicitly assumed that exchange rate fluctuations can be traced directly to a particular disturbance or group of disturbances. The case for foreign exchange intervention is much stronger if exchange rate fluctuations instead reflect excessive volatility due to market inefficiencies. If exchange rates are excessively volatile (as discussed in section 2.1), then fixed rates, or at least policies designed to limit exchange rate fluctuations, may be called for even in economies where disturbances are predominantly real in origin. Similarly, if exchange rates are driven by speculative "bubbles," self-fulfilling expectations that depart from market fundamentals, then exchange market intervention may be called for.

In the present context of the misaligned dollar, this characterization of real and financial disturbances takes a more specific form. As mentioned above, many economists trace the appreciation of the dollar during the first four years of the Reagan Administration to the expansionary fiscal policy of that administration. This fiscal expansion represents a "real" disturbance because the defense buildup has shifted expenditure toward U.S. domestic goods (both traded and nontraded). Branson (1986) points out that the appreciation of the dollar has moderated the effects of the fiscal expansion on domestic output and prices by switching domestic and foreign private consumption toward foreign goods. If that appreciation had been prevented through the monetary expansion required to keep exchange rates fixed, then the real appreciation of the dollar required for adjustment in the real sector would have been brought about by a rise in the U.S. price level rather than by a nominal appreciation of the dollar. Branson suggests that higher U.S. prices would not have been preferable to the nominal appreciation and consequent fall in the inflation rate that did occur.

If, instead of being caused by the fiscal expansion, the dollar's recent rise had been due to a speculative bubble or to a more conventional type of financial disturbance, then the case for fixing the exchange rate would have been stronger.[34] In the presence of financial disturbances, intervention to limit or halt the appreciation of the dollar would have helped to insulate the real sector from the disturbance. Presumably this intervention would have had to have been nonsterilized, in which case the intervention would have involved a significant change in monetary conditions. The question that has to be asked is whether governments are willing to tie their monetary policy to an exchange rate target in such circumstances.

Discipline

Proponents of fixed exchange rates often base their case on a second rationale: fixed rates impose discipline on national governments since inflationary policies soon run up against a balance of payments constraint. It is true that a government following inflationary policies under flexible exchange rates must contend with the depreciation of its currency, but that same government under fixed exchange rates is likely to have to contend with a highly visible balance of payments crisis. If the crisis results in a devaluation of the domestic currency, that change in currency value is likely to be much more politically damaging than a gradual change in currency value brought about "by the market." This discipline argument for fixed exchange rates might appear to be a persuasive one, especially after more than a decade of high inflation when governments were free to pursue "independent" monetary policies under flexible rates.

In practice, however, the discipline provided by fixed rates is less than complete for the following reasons:

1. Fixed exchange rates exert no discipline over expansionary fiscal policies, at least as long as capital flows are highly sensitive to interest differentials. Higher government spending financed by either taxes or bond issues induces an inflow of capital and a balance of payments surplus rather than deficit.[35]

2. The fixed rate system as a whole has no external constraint unless currencies are tied to an external standard. If $N-1$ currencies are tied to a reserve currency, as currencies were tied to the dollar under the Bretton Woods system, then there is discipline for the system as a whole only to the extent that the reserve currency country manages to discipline itself.[36] Under Bretton Woods, the United States maintained a relatively stable price level throughout the 1950s and early 1960s, but during the Vietnam War the Johnson and Nixon Administrations followed what were widely regarded as inflationary policies.

3. If, instead, all currencies are tied to a commodity like gold, then the increases of the world money supply are dependent on chance discoveries of gold and can be affected by political instability in the producing countries. If the gold supply does not increase rapidly enough to keep pace with real activity, then either the world price level must fall (accompanied, most likely, by a fall in real activity) or banking systems must develop alternative means of payment (as happened in the last half of the nineteenth century). In times of crisis, moreover, governments are unlikely to adhere to the external standard, since the stability of their banking systems is likely to be regarded as more important than the credibility of their external standard. During several banking panics of the nineteenth century, even the Bank of England, the stalwart defender of the gold standard system, suspended gold payments in an attempt to stabilize its banking system.

4. Whether or not the U.S. dollar (as the Nth currency) is tied to an external standard, par values for all N currencies can be changed.

Once a par value is changed, future commitments to a fixed rate system are less credible than before, so countries must weigh the benefits of a change in parity against the loss of credibility. A general lesson to be learned from past exchange rate systems is that governments will abandon fixed pegs, even if only temporarily, if exchange rate flexibility will help to ease the adjustment of their economies to a major shock. This was as true of Britain in the nineteenth century, despite its pivotal role under the gold standard, as it was of France and later Britain in the interwar period, and a host of countries in the Bretton Woods period. If governments are likely to abandon pegs in a crisis, then it is necessary to ask, what is the value of the discipline afforded by fixed rates? The answer must be that the value of the discipline is highly dependent on how participants in the financial markets assess the commitment of the government to the par value and the likelihood of shocks large enough to alter that commitment. So the discipline argument is less decisive than it appears to be.

2.3.2 Weaknesses of the Bretton Woods System

The Bretton Woods system was the fixed rate system that tied most currencies together during the postwar period until 1971. After fifteen years of flexible exchange rates, many observers look back longingly at this period. As already noted, the macroeconomic performance under Bretton Woods compares favorably with that of the more recent period. Against this must be weighed some of the inherent weaknesses of the Bretton Woods system which observers of the time considered major drawbacks of this fixed rate system.

Lack of Monetary Independence

The Bretton Woods system was often criticized for providing no discipline for the reserve currency country (for the reasons discussed above). The United States, in effect, was too free to pursue an independent monetary policy to the detriment of the system as a whole. But an equally serious weakness of Bretton Woods was the lack of monetary independence afforded to other countries of the system. Bretton Woods imposed such an extreme form of discipline on these countries that independent monetary policies to deal with disturbances were severely handicapped.

If one country tried to increase its money supply by increasing domestic credit in the banking system, this led to an incipient decline in interest rates and an outflow of capital which offset, at least partially, the initial increase in the money supply.[37] This *offsetting effect* of capital flows is characteristic of any fixed exchange rate system with internationally mobile capital.

Capital Controls

If capital flows offset domestic monetary expansions or contractions, one solution is to restrict such flows with controls of one form or another. That solution was adopted widely under Bretton Woods. The recent period of exchange rate flexibility, by no coincidence, has witnessed the progressive dismantling of controls, beginning with controls in Germany and the United States in 1974, Britain in 1978, and Japan in several stages beginning in 1980. Of the major industrial countries during this period, Italy has maintained and France has enhanced their controls, but that is because they have had to defend exchange rate parities within the European Monetary System.[38]

The overall effectiveness of capital controls in stemming reserve flows is in some doubt since banks and other institutions go to some lengths to find ways to evade controls. But there is no doubt that controls distort investment and borrowing incentives, as two episodes from the Bretton Woods period will illustrate.

1. The Kennedy and Johnson Administrations constructed progressively more complex barricades in an attempt to stem outflows of capital from the United States during the 1960s. In 1963, the Kennedy Administration began with an interest equalization tax on securities issued by foreigners in the U.S. market. The Johnson Administration followed with its voluntary credit-restraint program in 1965, which limited the liquid foreign assets that U.S. banks and nonbank financial institutions could hold, and a direct investment program in that same year, which compelled U.S. corporations to finance overseas operations with funds raised outside the United States. U.S. banks responded by expanding their operations in London and other foreign centers, in part to serve the U.S. corporations driven abroad for financing. With the arbitrage link between the United States and foreign financial centers severed, large interest differentials developed that reflected the distortionary effects of the controls. At one point in 1969, the three-month Eurodollar deposit rate rose to 11.5 percent at a time when U.S. Treasury bill rates were at 7.7 percent and U.S. certificate of deposit rates (because of the Federal Reserve's Regulation Q) remained fixed at 6 percent. Such remarkably large differentials distorted financing decisions by U.S. and foreign corporations. The controls also had the unintended effect of giving infant industry protection to the Eurodollar and Eurobond markets in London.

2. Similar interest differentials developed between Germany and the Eurocurrency markets in response to a network of controls that the German authorities built beginning in 1971. The controls were progressively tightened in an attempt to close loopholes, finally extending

to nearly all claims by nonresidents to residents, until they were removed in early 1974. Figure 2.9 compares the internal German interest rate (on interbank loans) with the Euromark deposit rate (which is always approximately equal to the covered Eurodollar rate). The figure illustrates very clearly the effects of the controls, designed to limit *inflows* rather than outflows of funds, which led to a higher interest rate in Germany than in the market for mark deposits in London. At one point in early 1973, the differential between the internal and external markets reached the remarkably high level of 11 percent. That is, an interbank loan in Germany carried an interest rate 11 percent higher than a *mark-denominated* loan, perhaps made by the same bank, in the Eurocurrency markets. With differentials that large, there is no doubt that considerable managerial effort was expended in finding ways to evade such controls.

The U.S. and German controls were not isolated examples. In fact, controls were the norm during the Bretton Woods period. As discussed in section 2.3.3, they are also a prevalent feature of the European Monetary System.

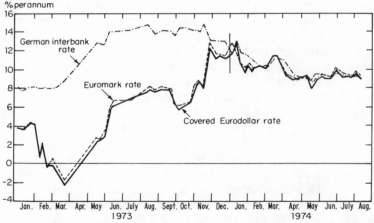

Fig. 2.9   The Euromark, covered Eurodollar, and German interbank rates, January 1973–August 1974. *Note:* Euromark rate— Wednesday quotations on three-month D-mark deposits in London; German rate—rate of interest in the Frankfurt interbank loan market for three-month funds; covered Eurodollar rate—the Wednesday quotations on the bid rate on three-month, U.S. dollar-denominated time deposits in London minus the Wednesday D-mark premium quoted in Frankfurt. *Source: Money Manager* for Euromark rate: Federal Reserve Board for all other interest and exchange rates; Herring and Marston (1976, 9).

Exchange Rate Crises

In the 1960s there was a tendency to blame private agents in the financial markets for the "speculation" that brought on balance of payments crises. Thus, for example, British Labor Government ministers characterized speculators who took positions against the pound as the "Gnomes of Zurich." More recently, however, international economists have formulated "balance of payments crisis" models whose central actors are these same Gnomes, now transformed into rational investors who speculate against governments. These governments, in turn, blindly follow domestic credit expansions that are unsustainable. The Gnomes help to accelerate the date of the crisis, a crisis that is in any event inevitable, but otherwise act like responsible citizens.

There is no doubt some truth in both views of balance of payments crises. As politicians of the 1960s knew only too well, increased capital mobility makes it more difficult for governments to sustain parities that are under attack by speculators. But, on the other hand, the decision to change parities is often dominated by political considerations because governments have committed themselves to defending parities. When parity adjustments justified by economic factors are postponed on political grounds, speculators attempt to force the government's hand. The government may respond by instituting restrictive macroeconomic policies simply to defend a parity value, policies it might be able to avoid under a flexible rate system. Or it may attempt to shield its reserves from attack by restricting capital movements. Whether the government successfully defends the parity or not, the country loses. If the parity holds, the economy is disrupted by the crisis and by the policies that have been adopted to defend the parity. If the parity collapses, speculators win capital gains at the expense of the central bank. We illustrate several of these features of exchange rate crises by describing the sterling crisis of the mid-1960s.

The Sterling Crisis

This crisis began building when Harold Wilson's Labor Government came to power in October 1964.[39] The Wilson Government chose not to devalue at that time despite a strong economic case that devaluation would help restore British competitiveness. One prominent reason given for the decision was the government's fear that it would be identified as the "devaluation party," the Labor Party having devalued the last time it was in power (in 1949). (This is a good example of the discipline provided by a fixed rate system, although in this case the discipline postponed needed adjustments.)

Having made the decision not to devalue, the Wilson Government had to face a series of balance of payments crises beginning soon after attaining office when it had to arrange a $3 billion international credit from foreign central banks. (This was at a time when British bank reserves totaled only $2.6 billion and the monetary base was $9.1 billion.) The government managed to surmount each crisis, in part by arranging foreign central bank financing but also by instituting restrictive macroeconomic policies, until the fall of 1967 when the speculative pressure became overwhelming. On the final day before devaluation— Friday, November 17—British foreign exchange reserves fell by $1 billion, in a country where capital controls were as tight as anywhere in Western Europe (Solomon 1977, 95). The next day sterling was devalued by 14.3 percent. Not only did the government have to succumb to the pressures of foreign exchange speculation, but in doing so it lost over £350 million as a result of intervention in the forward markets.[40]

In his assessment of the sterling crisis, Robert Solomon, a former senior adviser at the Federal Reserve Board, points out two lessons:

> It exhibited the potential for, and the impact of, speculative flows in the accounts of a major trading country. . . . It pointed up the weakness of an exchange rate system in which a change of parity of a major currency became a political issue of the highest order that engaged heads of state; in such a system a change in the exchange rate could be excessively delayed, permitting the buildup of a large imbalance which, when action was finally taken to correct it, required massive shifts of resources. (Solomon 1977, 99)

These same two lessons were consistent themes in the exchange rate crises of the Bretton Woods system until its demise in 1971.

These weaknesses of Bretton Woods turned opinion sharply against fixed exchange rates, especially after the failure of the Smithsonian Accord of December 1971 (to be discussed below). It was only after a near decade of floating that sentiment turned against flexible rates, at least in Western Europe where the European Monetary System was established in 1979.

2.3.3   The European Monetary System

The European Monetary System (EMS) was established on March 13, 1979, to tie together the currencies of member countries in a joint float against the dollar and other foreign currencies. The initial membership of the EMS consisted of all European Community members except the United Kingdom, which elected to float freely.[41] All members except Italy agreed to limit fluctuations of their currencies to 2¼ percent around a grid of central rates; Italy adopted a 6 percent margin. As stated by the European Council in its Resolution of December 1978, the main objective of the EMS was to create a "zone of stability in

Europe." The following evaluation of the EMS's success in achieving this objective is based primarily on an excellent statistical analysis by Rogoff (1985).[42]

Reducing the Variability of Exchange Rates

There is evidence that the variability of *bilateral* exchange rates has been significantly reduced in the EMS. Rogoff (1985) measures exchange rate variability by the variances of unanticipated changes in exchange rates.[43] For both nominal and real bilateral rates, the variances have fallen for exchange rates between the mark and the other two major currencies, the French franc and lira. In the case of the nominal franc/DM rate, the variance of monthly prediction errors has fallen by two-thirds, while in the case of the nominal lira/DM rate, the reduction has been by almost four-fifths. The results for real exchange rates are less dramatic, but still statistically significant. This is for a period when bilateral rates between the mark and dollar or yen were becoming more, not less, volatile.

Countries in the EMS, however, should be concerned about the variability of *effective* exchange rates as well as EMS bilateral rates. There is some reason to believe that the stability of intra-EMS bilateral rates is purchased at the price of greater variability in exchange rates between EMS currencies and those of other countries, so the EMS may not have stabilized effective exchange rates.[44] Rogoff shows that among the three major EMS currencies, only the lira has experienced a reduction in volatility for its nominal effective exchange rate. A similar pattern emerges for the real effective exchange rate, with the lira being the only currency among the three to experience a significant reduction in volatility. It should be pointed out that countries outside the EMS, including the United States, United Kingdom, and Japan, experienced statistically significant increases in the volatility of real effective rates, so the EMS may have helped to prevent the volatility of EMS currencies from rising even further.

Role of Capital Controls

Another set of evidence, also due to Rogoff (1985), provides an interesting perspective on how the EMS works. Rogoff examined real interest differentials within the EMS. If most disturbances are financial in nature, then foreign exchange intervention that stabilizes exchange rates should also stabilize interest rates. Yet, as Rogoff shows, the variability of real interest rate differentials has *increased* in the EMS, at least between the three largest countries.[45] There are two possible interpretations of this result, neither of them favorable to the EMS. First, disturbances may have been primarily real in nature. But if this is the case, then foreign exchange intervention within the EMS is undesirable (see the discussion of intervention policy in section 2.2). Or *capital controls* may have been a major factor contributing to the stability of EMS exchange rates. If the EMS is held together by extensive capital controls, it provides much less of a model for a world exchange rate system.

Giavazzi and Giovannini (1986) present an interesting analysis of the role of French and Italian capital controls within the EMS. Figure 2.10 reproduces their graphs of interest differentials between the (free) Eurocurrency markets and national markets in French franc and lira instruments. Large differentials between the free and regulated markets emerge at times of exchange rate crises. (In normal times, trade credits, which are largely exempt from the controls, are sufficiently large to

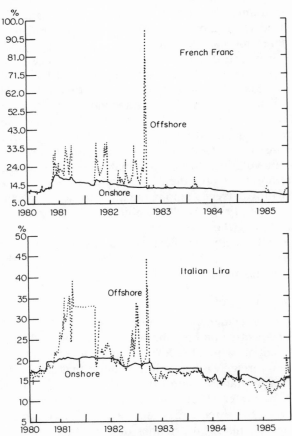

Fig. 2.10   Onshore and offshore interest rates on one-month deposits.
Source: Giovannini and Giovazzi (1986 468).

eliminate any differentials.) These interest differentials that emerge in times of crises show how binding the controls are on investment flows.[46] Nonetheless, the controls appear to be essential if the authorities are to defend weak currencies of the EMS from speculative attack. As Giavazzi and Giovannini conclude:

> In the present system weak currency countries have to choose between the welfare losses associated with capital controls and the losses arising from the volatility of short-term interest rates, and, as the evidence shows, overwhelmingly opt for the former. Thus capital controls appear to be an important feature of the EMS, which allows weak currency countries to take part in the exchange rate arrangement, without suffering from excessive domestic interest rate fluctuations. (p. 473)

Thus we have in the EMS an exchange rate system that has managed to stabilize bilateral exchange rates within Europe, but only by severely limiting capital flows between the countries of the EMS. Perhaps that is the only way to maintain fixed exchange rates in today's environment.

Other Features of the EMS

One reason that capital controls are so essential to the EMS is that the system has failed to bring about the convergence of inflation rates among its members, a key objective of the EMS.[47] Rogoff (1985) compares five-year-average inflation rates before and after the establishment of the EMS. He reaches the surprising conclusion that any convergence of inflation rates that did take place was between the inflation rates of Germany and two outside countries, Japan and the United Kingdom.

Because inflation rates have been so divergent, frequent parity changes have been necessary among EMS currencies. There have been eleven realignments since the inception of the EMS. The franc/DM parity alone has been changed six times, the latest realignment being in January 1987, for a cumulative depreciation of the franc relative to the mark of over 27 percent. Similarly, the lira/DM parity has been changed seven times for a cumulative depreciation of the lira of over 38 percent.

Some of the realignments have been quite large. The latest realignment on January 12, 1987, involved a revaluation of the mark and guilder by only 3 percent and the Belgian franc by 2 percent. But the April 1986 realignment lowered the franc relative to the mark by 6 percent, while in July 1985 the lira was devalued 7.8 percent against all other EMS currencies and in April 1986 fell 3 percent more relative to the mark and guilder when those currencies revalued by 3 percent. The frequency and magnitude of these realignments suggest how difficult it is to maintain a fixed rate system today.

2.4 Managed Floating

The alternative to fixed exchange rates would seem to be flexible exchange rates, but there are many shades of gray in between these two extremes. Present exchange rate arrangements are usually referred to as a system of managed flexibility. There are very few rules to this system, if indeed the term "system" is appropriate to a laissez-faire world. In its 1978 amendments to its Articles of Agreement, the IMF did specify certain guidelines for exchange rate intervention. This section begins by examining these guidelines then turns to several more specific rules for managed floating that have been proposed. Very different from these rules are the taxes on exchange market transactions, which will be considered next. Finally, "target zones" for exchange rates are analyzed in some detail because they have received so much attention recently.

2.4.1 Alternative Approaches to Managing Exchange Rates

In the 1978 amendments to its Articles of Agreement, the IMF specified three principles that should govern exchange rate policies:

Principle A: A member shall avoid manipulating exchange rates or the international monetary system in order to prevent effective balance of payments adjustment or to gain an unfair competitive advantage over other members.

Principle B: A member should intervene in the exchange market if necessary to counter disruptive conditions which may be characterized inter alia by disruptive short-term movements in the exchange value of its currency.

Principle C: Members should take into account in their intervention policies the interests of other members, including those of the countries in whose currencies they intervene. (IMF *Survey*, May 2, 1977, 131–2)

It is not easy for a group of governments with different agendas to achieve agreement on a set of policy rules. So it may not be surprising that the principles adopted in this agreement are not specific enough to be binding on any government. Unless there are objective criteria for determining whether or not a country is "manipulating" its exchange rate to gain unfair competitive advantages, for example, Principle A may not prevent such behavior. Even the definition of "disruptive short-term movements" may prove elusive once it is recognized that exchange rates naturally exhibit high volatility. To ensure that these principles are carried out, some have proposed more specific rules of exchange rate management.

Minimal Reform: The "Reference Rate" Proposal

One of the most interesting proposals was that made by Wilfred Ethier and Arthur Bloomfield (1975) in the Princeton Essay series. These economists, writing soon after the breakdown of Bretton Woods, recognized that a return to fixed exchange rates, whether desirable or not, was simply not feasible. So instead of specifying rules that mandated central bank intervention, as had been done in the Bretton Woods system, they proposed rules that prohibited certain types of central bank actions. But unlike the IMF principles later adopted, they offered objective criteria for evaluating central bank adherence to rules. The "reference rate" proposal formulated by Ethier and Bloomfield (1975, 10) had two rules:

1. No central bank shall sell its own currency at a price below its reference rate by more than a fixed percentage (possibly zero) or buy its own currency at a price exceeding its reference rate by more than a fixed percentage. This is the sole restriction imposed upon central-bank intervention.

2. The structure of reference rates shall be revised at periodic pre-specified intervals through some defined international procedure.

The aim of the first rule was to prohibit a central bank from driving its currency away from its reference level (thereby "manipulating" its exchange rate, in the language of the IMF's Principle A). For example, a central bank could not drive its currency down to gain competitive advantage for its export industry. At the same time, the proposal did not oblige the central bank to intervene at all. (It is in this sense a "minimal reform" proposal.) Nor did the proposal prevent the central bank from "leaning against the wind" to limit movements away from the reference rate.

The authors recognized that their proposal was limited in aim, but it did provide a means to limit the type of competitive depreciations that had plagued countries during the 1930s. In order for this proposal to be successfully implemented, however, countries would have to agree on the reference rates themselves "through some defined international procedure" (their second rule). The discussion of target zones below identifies some of the formidable problems involved in defining equilibrium exchange rates. It also points out how difficult it would be for different national governments to agree on equilibrium rates. Both of these problems carry over to any agreement on reference rates.

Rules for Leaning against the Wind

Because volatility itself is viewed as a major problem by some governments, policies of "leaning against the wind" have become common.

Such policies are designed to limit the "disruptive short-term movements" addressed by the IMF's Principle B. This form of intervention requires minimal knowledge of what factors may be moving the exchange rate and does not require that the authorities have superior knowledge about the long-run equilibrium exchange rate. It does presuppose that exchange rates are too volatile in general, and that intervention operations can be effective in reducing this volatility.

There is a danger, however, that central banks might lean against the wind more in one direction than the other, thus imparting a bias to exchange rate movements over time. To ensure against "manipulating" exchange rates in this way, central banks could be required to balance out their net purchases and sales of foreign exchange over a given period. Argy (1982, 27) cites one rule that "[n]et reserve changes in a given direction should not persist for more than a few consecutive months (except when reserve levels are excessive or deficient)." Argy, however, goes on to argue that such rules would be difficult to implement and might even provoke one-way speculation.

If governments wish to limit exchange rate volatility, there is a nonmarket alternative to foreign exchange intervention. This involves imposing a tax on exchange market transactions.

Tobin's Exchange Market Tax

This tax, proposed by James Tobin (1982), is imposed on each exchange market transaction at a uniform rate, perhaps 1 percent. The tax has the explicit aim of "throw[ing] some sand in the wheels of our excessively efficient international money market" (Tobin, 1982, 489). According to Tobin, a tax of this magnitude is unlikely to make much difference to merchandise trade transactions, since the tax represents such a small proportion of the value of the product and the profit on the transaction. But such a tax is likely to be a much more significant factor in a round-trip financial transaction, thus discouraging "hot money flows." It would make overnight or one-month round-trip investments in foreign currencies almost prohibitively expensive. Even in the case of a three-month investment, a 1 percent tax paid twice in the round-trip transaction could be overcome only by an 8 percent differential between interest rates in the two currencies involved.

For a tax of this nature to be successful, it must be uniformly imposed throughout the world, otherwise financial transactions will gravitate to tax-free zones. The experience of U.S. controls in the 1960s illustrates that point. If such a tax were somehow internationally coordinated, however, it is likely to have a significant impact on the volume of foreign exchange transactions, especially those associated with short-term investments. For that reason, the tax may reduce the volatility of exchange rates. But such a tax is unlikely to have a significant effect on the misalignment of exchange rates because longer term investments and trade transactions would remain largely unaffected. William Poole has drawn an analogy between Tobin's tax and real estate transfer tax.[48] The latter may reduce the volatility of real estate prices but surely does not affect the longer run level of prices. Nor would it prevent a speculative bubble from developing.

Like the exchange market tax, the reform proposals governing intervention outlined above offer no solution to the misalignment problem. They provide "rules of the game" for managed floating, but they provide little positive guidance for exchange rate policy. The first rule of the reference rate proposal does prohibit central banks from deliberately creating a misalignment through exchange market intervention, but none of the major misalignments experienced recently have been caused by central bank intervention. None of the rules prohibit other macroeconomic policies that can lead to misalignment. Nor do they require that central banks take positive action to prevent misalignments from developing.

2.4.2 Targets Zones for Exchange Rates

In the Bretton Woods system of fixed exchange rates, the national authorities were committed to intervening in the foreign exchange market whenever the exchange rate reached a 1 percent "band" on either side of its par value vis-à-vis the dollar. A "target zone" system of exchange rates also has bands for the exchange rate, but these bands are typically much farther apart, thus allowing considerable fluctuation in the exchange rate. More importantly, in a target zone system the authorities make no firm commitment to defend those margins. One of the leading advocates of target zones, John Williamson, has described the zone as "a range beyond which the authorities are unhappy to see the rate move, despite not being prepared to precommit themselves to prevent such movements" (Williamson 1985, 64).

Williamson's Proposal for Target Zones

Given Williamson's central role in the debate over target zones, it is useful to spell out his proposal more fully.[49] His target zones would involve five elements:

1. Soft margins, rather than a commitment to prevent the rate from straying outside the target zone;
2. A zone perhaps 20 percent wide (i.e., with 10 percent margins), outside of which rates would be considered "clearly wrong";
3. A crawling zone, with the crawl reflecting both differential inflation and any need for balance of payments adjustment;
4. Publication of the target zone; and
5. The partial direction of monetary policy, including foreign exchange intervention, to discourage the exchange rate from straying outside its target zone. (Williamson 1985, 72)

The target zone system thus would be a form of managed float with the targets well defined but with national authorities only tentatively committed to intervention or other policy actions.

Anatomy of Target Zones

Target zones share some of the characteristics of fixed exchange rates, but there are important differences that may be the source of both strengths and weaknesses for this proposed system. Some of the system's crucial characteristics are:

1. *Wide bands*. With margins permitting fluctuations of 20 percent, this system is not designed to limit the volatility of exchange rates. Thus hedging by corporations will be as important as in a flexible regime. But if the targets are adhered to and the margins hold, then the system can be regarded as a way of avoiding misalignments.

The wide margins permit those abrupt shifts in speculative sentiment that appear to characterize flexible regimes. Nonetheless, exchange rate crises cannot be ruled out, at least when exchange rates approach the margins.

2. *Analogy with national monetary targets*. Zones are more akin to national monetary targets than exchange rate parities under the Bretton Woods system. Like monetary growth targets, target zones for exchange rates single out one economic variable for special attention without firmly precommitting the national authorities to achieving a specific target for that variable.

Yet there are important differences between monetary growth targets and target zones for exchange rates. First, unlike the money growth targets, the target zones provide no continuous guide for policy since the targets are binding only when the exchange rate reaches one of its margins. It is true that in some countries monetary growth targets are set in terms of bands, but these bands are usually much narrower than those proposed for exchange rate targets. Second, the variable targeted, the exchange rate, is an endogenous variable normally determined by many factors other than economic policy. It is true that the money supply is also an endogenous variable affected by both bank and nonbank behavior, but the authorities have more direct control over the money supply than the exchange rate.

3. *Anchor for system?* One of the advantages of a fixed rate system is the anchor such a system provides for inflationary expectations. Target zones provide no such anchor since the zones are explicitly adjusted for differences in inflation rates. The zones may help to anchor expectations regarding *real* exchange rates, but only if governments are perceived as being willing to defend the margins.

4. *Commitment to defend margins*. Despite the wide margins around the targets, governments will eventually be faced with the choice be-

tween defending the targets or changing them. Economists advising a government faced with a speculative attack are likely to advocate defending the targets only if they view exchange rate movements as part of the problem. (Recall the discussion of economic disturbances in section 2.3 where exchange rate movements sometimes facilitate, rather than hinder, the adjustment of the economy.) Given a permanent shift in the demand for a country's exports, for example, the government would be well advised to change the exchange rate target rather than defend it. But if the change is temporary, then defense of the target might be warranted.

5. *The political economy of target zones.* The rationale for target zones is very different if governments are viewed as the principal source of economic disturbances. Target zones then might have a political rather than an economic role to play in stabilization. Proponents of target zones argue that announced exchange rate targets might constrain governments in their macroeconomic policies, much like multilateral tariff agreements constrain national trade policies.

In the specific context of the dollar's misalignment, it is argued that target zones might have encouraged the Reagan Administration to follow a less expansionary fiscal policy. This may be a difficult argument to sustain, however, since in order to pursue its fiscal policy, the Administration overcame much stronger domestic constraints than any international agreement could have imposed.

A better case for the political role of target zones can be made in the European context. A frequent argument in favor of the EMS is that it constrains member countries to pursue policies closely in line with its largest member, West Germany. The Mitterrand Government in France, for example, stayed within the EMS despite being severely constrained at times by the requirements of membership. One major exception to this European pattern is the United Kingdom, which has rejected joining the EMS exchange rate arrangements in favor of the free floating of the pound sterling.

Perhaps the best that can be said for this political justification for target zones is that it may be relevant to governments predisposed to the constraints or strongly committed to regional or global cooperation. For governments aiming to pursue policies significantly different from those of other industrial countries, target zones may be swiftly discarded if they become a major impediment to such policies.

6. *Objective criteria for modifying targets.* The problem of constraining government behavior would be less serious if the target zone proposal did not provide for the modification of targets. Here there is a direct conflict between the politics and economics of international agreements. In order to constrain governments to keep commitments, there should be no exceptions permitted except those clearly specified

at the time of an agreement. But the economic arguments for modifying targets in the face of real disturbances may be very compelling.

To complicate the problem, there is seldom a consensus among experts about the need for changes in real exchange rates. Instead, they may disagree about the nature and scope of a disturbance as well as about its effects on the real exchange rate. Without objective indicators dictating when targets should be changed, the changes made will be based at least partly on political considerations.

Consider the recent misalignment of the dollar. Although the appreciation lasted over four years, there is no clear-cut consensus about its causes. The appropriate policies to follow if the misalignment is due to the fiscal policies of the Reagan Administration are very different from those to follow if the dollar's appreciation is due to bubbles or to capital flows seeking a "safe haven" or to an investment boom triggered by tax changes.[50] Similarly, although sterling's appreciation lasted over four years, economists still dispute whether North Sea oil, tight monetary policies, or other factors caused the appreciation. When there is so much dispute about the causes of a misalignment, there is unlikely to be a consensus about modification of targets.

Defining Exchange Rate Targets

If economic conditions are favorable, governments might be willing to precommit themselves to a system of target zones. But formidable problems await the negotiators of such an agreement. Chief among these problems is that of finding (and agreeing upon) appropriate targets. It is useful to follow Williamson's (1985) description of how targets might be defined.

1. The first step in defining a target rate or target zone for the real exchange rate is to decide the appropriate equilibrium current account balance of each country (or equivalently, the "underlying capital flow" in Williamson's terminology, since the capital account must be the mirror image of the current account). The equilibrium current account of a developing country like Brazil or Thailand is very different from that of an industrial country like Germany or France. In estimates of his "fundamental equilibrium exchange rate," Williamson makes explicit allowances for such differences among countries. This is not to say that judgments about equilibrium current accounts are easy to make, as the experience of the Smithsonian meeting discussed below makes clear. Not least of the problems is that the negotiating governments will understand the close connection between the current account "equilibrium" agreed upon and the prospects for their leading export industries.

2. Once figures for equilibrium current accounts are agreed upon, then real exchange rates consistent with them can be calculated using

a trade model with its associated trade elasticities. To do so, it is first necessary to adjust the current account for cyclical factors, then to calculate the discrepancy between the equilibrium current account and the cyclically adjusted current account for a particular year. The trade model is then used to calculate the change in real exchange rates necessary to equilibrate the current account.[51] Since estimates of price elasticities range widely, this step in the calculation is fraught with difficulties. Cutting the elasticities in half, for example, requires twice as large a change in real exchange rates to achieve equilibrium.

3. The calculations so far only determine the equilibrium real exchange rate in a single year. It is then necessary to adjust that rate for real disturbances that occur through time. Among such real disturbances are the oil price shocks experienced twice during the 1970s, natural resource discoveries (such as North Sea oil for Britain), secular movements in demand, and secular movements in supply, including differential productivity growth rates. One issue that arises is whether to take into account changes in government policy if such changes are not just temporary measures but last for a number of years. In his study of exchange rates, Williamson explicitly excludes the shift in U.S. fiscal policy under the Reagan Administration because it is not sustainable in the long run. He also excludes variations in demand or supply over the business cycle from whatever source.

Most of these adjustments require that arbitrary judgments be made. Recall how difficult it was for analysts to evaluate the effects of the first OPEC price increase in 1973. Even the effects of productivity growth are difficult to assess. To illustrate some of the difficulties involved in determining equilibrium rates, the next section examines the Smithsonian agreement on exchange rates, an agreement reached by the major industrial countries in December 1971.

Multilateral Agreement on Exchange Rates: the Smithsonian Accord

The Smithsonian agreement provides one of the few examples of a multilateral exchange rate agreement, but the lessons to be learned from this agreement are none too encouraging about exchange rate agreements in general.

First, the agreement was reached only after prolonged and sometimes acrimonious negotiations stretching through the fall of 1971. One of the reasons why the negotiations were so difficult was that the objectives of the participants were inconsistent with one another, which is not surprising given the pivotal role played by exchange rates in each economy. The Nixon Administration wanted to achieve a turnabout of $13 billion in its current account through the realignment of currencies. The other major countries of the OECD envisaged, when their individual estimates were summed, a reduction of their current balances of only $3 billion (Solomon 1977, 199). That an agreement was at all possible in these circumstances is probably attributable to the heavy-handed actions of the Nixon Administration. In August 1971 that administration imposed an import surcharge of 10 percent in lieu of an agreement to realign the major currencies.

Second, the agreement set new exchange rates that were simply unsustainable in the long run, despite President Nixon's characterization of the accord as the "most significant monetary agreement in the history of the world" (*New York Times,* December 19, 1971, p. 1). It is interesting to compare the rates agreed upon at the Smithsonian meeting with those prevailing a little over a year later after the agreement had broken down and most rates were allowed to float. Table 2.5 presents the central rates agreed upon at the Smithsonian meeting as well as the market exchange rates prevailing in the second quarter of 1973. The market rates diverge from the Smithsonian central rates by more than 10 percent in three out of four instances, with the dollar weaker after the advent of floating than before (except in the case of the pound). The table also presents a comparison between the market rates in the second quarter of 1973 and the central rates adjusted for changes in prices in order to see if the divergence was caused by relative inflation rates during the interim period. (Wholesale prices in manufacturing are used to adjust the central rates.) In the case of the yen and pound, the market rates deviate more from the adjusted central rates than from the original central rates; for the other two currencies, the deviations are smaller, but are still about 10 percent off the mark. Thus an agreement reached only after prolonged negotiations resulted in an exchange rate realignment that did not go far enough in lowering the value of the dollar.

The obstacles to agreement and to successful implementation of target zones are formidable. As James Tobin, writing in 1978, expressed

Table 2.5   **Comparison of Smithsonian and 1973 2nd Quarter Spot Rates**

| | Smithsonian Parities | | | % Deviations | |
	Actual	Adjusted[a]	1973 II Actual	from Actual	from Adjusted
¥ $	308.00	309.72	264.98	−14.0	−14.4
$/£	2.6057	2.6886	2.5300	−2.9	−5.9
DM/$	3.2225	3.1119	2.736	−15.1	−12.1
FF/$	5.1157	4.8842	4.4288	−13.4	−9.3

Sources: Parities: Bank for International Settlements, *Annual Report,* 12 June 1972; Exchange rates: IMF, *International Financial Statistics;* WPI for manufacturing: unpublished IMF data.

[a]Smithsonian parities adjusted for changes in WPI for manufacturing from December 1971 to 1973 II.

it: "it is scarcely conceivable that the various OECD countries could individually project, much less agree on, much less convince skeptical markets of, a system of equilibrium or target exchange rates for 1980 or 1985" (Tobin 1982, 493).[52]

Some advocates of target zones acknowledge the economic arguments against such a system but nonetheless contend that targets have a role to play in fostering international economic cooperation. They argue that an agreement on target zones at least commits governments to regular consultations on exchange market developments. Even such regular consultations, however, may not induce governments to limit the divergences in macroeconomic policies that cause many misalignments. And if they do not, then this argument for targets loses much of its force.

2.5 Concluding Comments

This paper began by describing two distinct types of exchange rate variability—volatility and misalignment. Each type of variability imposes its own costs on an economy, and each presents a different challenge to exchange rate policy.

The volatility of exchange rates could be sharply curtailed if the industrial countries agreed to reinstitute a fixed rate system with narrow bands. The EEC has succeeded in fixing bilateral rates within Europe, although fixed rates within the EMS have been maintained only through frequent parity adjustments and through the imposition of extensive capital controls.

In contemplating such a move, however, countries should recall the lessons of Bretton Woods. Fixed rates cannot be maintained without extensive capital controls. This paper has analyzed the distortions to investment and borrowing incentives that are entailed by such measures. Balance of payments crises, moreover, will inevitably break out unless frequent parity changes are permitted. But if parity changes are permitted, one of the chief benefits of fixed rates, the credibility given to inflation targets, will be lost. Fixed rates, finally, will inhibit the adjustment to real shocks like the oil price increases experienced in the 1970s.

Short of fixing exchange rates, countries could pursue more active foreign exchange intervention policies. There might be a role for international agreements to ensure that intervention is confined to "leaning against the wind" operations or to prevent intervention from allowing countries to "manipulate" exchange rates to gain competitive advantages. The analysis of foreign exchange intervention policy above suggests that the intervention would have to be nonsterilized, so active intervention would require a compromise of monetary targets.

If misalignment is the most important problem, then the search for an ideal exchange rate policy may be too narrowly focused to be effective. A major source of misalignment in the last ten years has been the macroeconomic policies pursued by countries like the United States and Britain. It is not at all clear that the solution to major policy imbalances among the industrial countries lies in limiting exchange rate movements rather than changing the policies themselves.

The adoption of target zones for exchange rates, on the other hand, may play a useful role in inducing governments to modify their policies. At the very least, the breaching of target zones may call attention to the need for international consultations on macroeconomic policies. Whether target zones would be any more successful than the IMF agreements remains to be proven.

The Jurgensen Report concluded that exchange rate policy must consist of more than (sterilized) intervention to be successful. Countries must be willing to commit their macroeconomic policies to controlling exchange rates. In many circumstances, governments may find that limiting exchange rate variability is not worth this price.

Notes

The author would like to thank William Branson, Martin Feldstein, Dale Henderson, and Richard Herring for helpful comments on an earlier draft of this paper.

1. The passages are from Paris (1938, 166) and Harrod (1951, 582–84).

2. Productivity tends to rise in recovery periods, so the recent rise in productivity in these two countries may be partly a cyclical phenomenon.

3. Later sections discuss how measures of misalignment take into account real economic shocks (which usually require departures of exchange rates from relative price trends).

4. A useful survey of this literature is Frenkel and Mussa (1984).

5. Kenen and Rodrik (1984) show that other measures of volatility give roughly similar results.

6. Similar results are obtained for earlier periods by Frenkel and Mussa (1980) and Bergstrand (1983).

7. If R_t measures the real exchange rate of the dollar relative to the pound sterling, for example, then a rise in R_t reflects either a rise in U.S. relative to British prices (i.e., P_t/P_t^* rises) or a fall in the dollar price of the pound (X_t falls, reflecting a depreciation of the pound). In either case, a rise in R_t reflects a loss of competitiveness for U.S. exports.

8. Notice how much less variable the effective exchange rates, which represent a diversified basket of currencies, are compared with the bilateral rates (whether nominal or real).

9. Just because most movements in an exchange rate are unforecastable does not imply that the exchange rate is excessively volatile, although companies

engaged in international trade may regard the volatility as too high. Instead, the volatility of an exchange rate is "excessive" if it exceeds that of the factors which determine it.

10. Meese and Rogoff (1983) examine the out-of-sample performance of several well-known models of the exchange rate and conclude that a random walk model performs as well as any of these models.

11. Williamson's concept of the "underlying capital flow" is linked to current account targets (as discussed below in the subsection on "Defining Exchange Rate Targets" in section 2.4.2).

12. It is interesting to note that while the yen was more volatile than the dollar during the period 1973–85, the misalignments of the dollar were larger than those of the yen. This underscores the need to carefully distinguish between the two concepts.

13. Note that a rise in the real exchange rate represents a real appreciation of that currency.

14. For further discussion of adjustment costs associated with misalignments, see Branson (1981), Richardson (1984), and Williamson (1985).

15. As pointed out by Williamson (1985), it is interesting that Johnson (1966) saw misalignments arising from misguided intervention policy under fixed rates (maintaining unrealistic parities) rather than from market forces under flexible rates. Like most economists at that time, Johnson did not foresee the large misalignments that were to occur under flexible rates.

16. See Atkinson, Brooks, and Hall (1985). Note that the second round of OPEC price increases in 1978–79 raised the value of the North Sea discoveries.

17. If the real appreciation was equal to 45 percent, then 10 percent represents 2/9 of the entire loss of competitiveness. Forsyth and Kay (1980) attribute a larger proportion of the appreciation to North Sea oil.

18. These series are obtained from the IMF's *International Financial Statistics*. Because productivity growth is generally greater in the manufacturing sector than elsewhere in an advanced economy, real exchange rates based on general price indexes (which contain nontraded as well as traded goods) provide a less reliable index of relative competitiveness than real exchange rates based on manufacturing prices alone. For further discussion, see Marston (1986). For a discussion of the relative merits of value-added deflators and unit labor costs as measures of international competitiveness, see Artus (1978).

19. There is no evidence, for example, that interest rates charged on Eurodollar loans to Europeans rose relative to loans to American residents.

20. These figures, taken from the national income accounts, are smaller than the balance of payments figures widely quoted in the press, but they are more relevant for determining the effects of the misalignment on output and employment.

21. Philippe Jurgensen was Chairman of the Working Group. The countries represented in this group were the so-called Group of 7 (G-7) countries: Canada, France, Germany, Italy, Japan, United Kingdom, and United States.

22. Sterilized intervention effectively consists of swapping foreign bonds for domestic bonds, although the operation has several steps to it. Recall that central banks typically hold foreign exchange reserves in the form of interest-bearing, foreign-currency-denominated securities. When a central bank wants to intervene in the exchange market, it first sells the foreign securities, then uses the foreign currency so obtained to buy domestic currency from the private sector. If the intervention is to be sterilized, the sale of foreign currency is followed by an expansionary open-market operation (or an analogous monetary

operation in different institutional environments) involving the purchase of domestic bonds with the recently acquired domestic currency, thus restoring the monetary base to its initial level. For further discussion of such operations, see Girton and Henderson (1976) and Marston (1985).

23. This description of the three channels draws on Loopesko (1984).

24. Mussa (1981) emphasizes the importance of announcement effects in his study of foreign exchange intervention for the Group of 30. See also the recent analysis of announcement effects by Kenen (1986).

25. If i_t, i_t^* are the domestic and foreign interest rates, respectively, and s_t^e is the expected change in the spot exchange rate (the capital gain on the foreign currency), then uncovered interest parity implies that

$$i_t = i_t^* + s_t^e.$$

26. Hansen and Hodrick (1980), for example, adopt a generalized least-squares estimating procedure so that they can utilize overlapping observations, thus making it possible to use weekly data rather than the monthly or quarterly data typically employed in the past. Cumby and Obstfeld (1984) also use weekly data but adopt techniques to take into account the nonstationarity of the foreign exchange data. These studies and others that have followed are able to reject decisively the joint hypothesis of market efficiency and uncovered interest parity. Levich (1985) provides a comprehensive survey of recent studies.

27. Two recent surveys of the theoretical literature on risk premiums are Adler and Dumas (1983) and Branson and Henderson (1985).

28. See, for example, Obstfeld (1983), Frankel and Engel (1984), and Danker et al. (1985).

29. Studies of international asset pricing based on intertemporal utility functions include Stulz (1981) and Hansen and Hodrick (1983).

30. The following account relies heavily on Greene (1984).

31. For a similar view, see Ueda (1986). Intervention in the autumn of 1985 totaled $13 billion compared with $10 billion in February and March of 1985 (Bank for International Settlements, *Annual Report,* 1986, p. 149).

32. For a general analysis of foreign exchange intervention in the presence of different types of disturbances, see Henderson (1984).

33. A similar analysis applies to any aggregate demand disturbance. The effects of aggregate supply disturbances on the exchange rate, however, are ambiguous since an increase in aggregate supply lowers prices at the same time that output expands (so nominal output, and hence the demand for transaction balances, may rise or fall).

34. Among those investigating speculative bubbles as the source of the dollar's appreciation are Krugman (1985) and Frankel and Froot (1986).

35. If a government pursues an expansionary fiscal policy indefinitely, then eventually foreign investors will balk at further exposure to political risk. But until that point is reached, a country is free to expand through fiscal means.

36. If the reserve currency country follows an expansionary monetary policy, the resulting balance of payment deficits are automatically financed, since the country gaining reserves invests them in the securities of the reserve currency country. The monetary base of the reserve currency country, moreover, does not decline as a result of the deficit as long as other countries choose to hold their foreign exchange reserves in the form of securities rather than the monetary base of the reserve currency country. McKinnon (1974) has proposed that all foreign currency reserves be held in the form of central bank balances (bearing a market interest rate). If this were the case, foreign exchange intervention would affect the monetary bases of both reserve and nonreserve currency countries alike.

37. If domestic and foreign securities are perfect substitutes, the attempt by one country to increase its money supply through domestic credit expansion succeeds only to the extent that this one country manages to increase the money supply of the entire system. (The system would be like a set of reservoirs connected by open channels; an attempt to increase the water level in one would succeed only to the extent that the water levels of all were increased.) Formal models of the offset phenomenon are presented in Kouri and Porter (1974) and Herring and Marston (1977).

38. In 1986 both Italy and France relaxed some of their controls, but many transactions by residents remain restricted.

39. For an excellent account of this period, see chapter 5 of Solomon (1977).

40. Bank of England, *Quarterly Bulletin*, December 1969, table 18.

41. The members were Belgium, Denmark, France, Germany, Ireland, Italy, Luxembourg, and the Netherlands. The United Kingdom formally joined the EMS, but chose not to participate in the exchange rate mechanism. For a detailed discussion of the system, see Ungerer et al. (1983).

42. One of the successes of the EMS, which will not be discussed since it lies outside the scope of this paper, is the development of the European Currency Unit (or ECU) as a parallel currency. For an interesting discussion, see Padoa-Schioppa (1985).

43. He uses the forward rate as the predicted exchange rate in the case of nominal rates, and he uses forecasts of real exchange rates based on a random walk model or a vector autoregression (VAR) in the case of real exchange rates.

44. Canzoneri (1982) and Marston (1984) analyze this possibility in theoretical models of exchange rate unions.

45. The one exception is the real interest rate differential between Germany and Italy formed by using a VAR forecast.

46. The controls also lead to asymmetric responses of EMS currencies to outside disturbances, since among the three most important EMS currencies only the mark has open capital markets. When there is speculative pressure involving the dollar, for example, the mark takes the brunt of this pressure, thus causing strains within the EMS. See Marston (1984).

47. As Jacques van Ypersele, one of the architects of the EMS, has described it: "The objective was indeed that external stability be the result less of artificially imposed constraints than of a convergence of economic trends among member countries, in particular of prices and costs" (Ypersele 1985, 15).

48. See Brainard and Perry (1986, 234). Another tax that has been proposed by Liviatan (1980) is the "real interest rate equalization tax." This tax, by creating a wedge between domestic and foreign interest rates, tries to reduce the incentive for outflows (or inflows) of capital when a country abruptly changes its monetary policy. A country trying to stabilize its price level through monetary contraction, for example, would ordinarily have to contend with an appreciation caused by an inflow of capital. By creating a wedge between domestic and foreign returns, however, a country might be able to dampen the currency appreciation. Such a tax is probably best thought of as a supplement to national monetary policies, to be used when one country's policies depart sharply from those of other countries.

49. Earlier advocates of targets for exchange rates include the "Optica Group" of economists from EEC countries, see Commission of the European Communities (1975).

50. Branson (1986) underscores the confusion regarding the source of the dollar's rise by suggesting that misalignment is a "topic . . . for the National Science Foundation, not a new Bretton Woods" (p. 176).

51. For further discussion of this approach to estimating equilibrium exchange rates and the problems associated with it, see Artus (1978).

52. There is reason to believe that agreements on equilibrium rates would be even more difficult to achieve in the 1980s than in 1971. Experts differ widely in their estimates of equilibrium rates today, in large part because of the many structural changes which have occurred since the Smithsonian agreement. Consider the key bilateral rate between the yen and dollar. Before the dollar recently plunged from ¥250/$ to ¥160/$, estimates of the equilibrium value of this bilateral rate were as wide ranging as the market rates themselves. Williamson (1985), for example, cites six studies with estimates ranging from ¥131/$ to ¥209/$. Krause (1986) writes of a possible ¥100/$ rate. Changes in energy prices make all such calculations difficult. But another major reason why the yen/dollar rate is difficult to assess is the pattern of productivity growth in the United States and Japan which distorts simple purchasing power parity calculations. For further discussion, see Marston (1986).

References

Adler, Michael, and Bernard Dumas. 1983. International portfolio choice and corporation finance: A survey. *Journal of Finance* 38:925–84.

Akhtar, M. A., and R. Spence Hilton. 1984. Effects of exchange rate uncertainty on German and U.S. trade. *Federal Reserve Bank of New York Quarterly Review* (Spring):7–15.

Argy, Victor. 1982. *Exchange rate management in theory and practice*. Princeton Studies in International Finance, no. 50. Princeton, N.J.: International Finance Section, Princeton University.

Artus, Jacques R. 1978. Methods of assessing the long-run equilibrium value of an exchange rate. *Journal of International Economics* 8 (May):277–99.

Atkinson, F. J., S. J. Brooks, and S. G. F. Hall. 1985. The economic effects of North Sea oil. *National Institute Economic Review* November.

Baldwin, Richard, and Paul R. Krugman. 1986. Persistent effects of large exchange rate shocks. NBER Working Paper no. 2017. Cambridge, Mass.: National Bureau of Economic Research.

Bergsten, C. Fred. 1982. What to do about the U.S.-Japan economic problem. *Foreign Affairs* 60 (Summer):1059–75.

Bergstrand, Jeffrey H. 1983. Is exchange rate volatility "excessive"? *New England Economic Review* (September/October):5–14.

Brainard, William C., and George L. Perry, eds. 1986. Symposium on exchange rates, trade, and capital flows. *Brookings Papers on Economic Activity* 1:165–235.

Branson, William H. 1981. "Leaning against the wind" as exchange rate policy. Typescript.

———. 1985. Causes of appreciation and volatility of the dollar. In *The U.S. dollar—Recent developments, outlook, and policy options*, 33–52. Kansas City, Mo.: Federal Reserve Bank of Kansas City.

———. 1986. The limits of monetary coordination as exchange rate policy. *Brookings Papers on Economic Activity* 1:175–94.

Branson, William H., and Dale W. Henderson. 1985. The specification and influence of asset markets. In *Handbook of international economics*, vol. 2, ed. Ronald W. Jones and Peter B. Kenen, 749–805. Amsterdam: North-Holland.

Branson, W. H., and James P. Love. 1986. Dollar appreciation and manufacturing employment and output. NBER Working Paper no. 1972. Cambridge, Mass.: National Bureau of Economic Research.

Buiter, Willem H., and Marcus H. Miller. 1983. Changing the rules: Economic consequences of the Thatcher regime. *Brookings Papers on Economic Activity* 2:305–65.

Canzoneri, Matthew. 1982. Exchange intervention policy in a multiple country world. *Journal of International Economics* 13 (November):267–89.

Commission of the European Communities. 1975. Optica report 1975: Towards economic equilibrium and monetary unification in Europe. Brussels. Typescript.

Cumby, Robert E., and Maurice Obstfeld. 1984. International interest rate and price level linkages under flexible exchange rates: A review of recent evidence. In *Exchange rate theory and practice,* ed. John Bilson and Richard C. Marston, 121–51. Chicago: University of Chicago Press.

Cushman, David O. 1983. The effects of real exchange rate risk on international trade. *Journal of International Economics* 15 (August):45–63.

Danker, Deborah J., Richard A. Haas, Dale W. Henderson, Steven A. Symansky, and Ralph W. Tryon. 1985. Small empirical models of exchange market intervention: Applications to Germany, Japan, and Canada. Staff Studies no. 135. Washington: Board of Governors of the Federal Reserve Board.

Ethier, Wilfred, and Arthur I. Bloomfield. 1975. *Managing the managed float.* Essays in International Finance no. 112. Princeton, N.J.: International Finance Section, Princeton University.

Feldstein, Martin. 1986. The impact of economic policies on the outlook for world trade. Remarks delivered to the International Monetary Conference, Boston. Typescript.

Forsyth, J. P., and J. A. Kay. 1980. The economic implications of North Sea oil revenues. Working Paper no. 10. London: Institute for Fiscal Studies.

Frankel, Jeffrey A., and Charles M. Engel. 1984. Do asset-demand functions optimize over the mean and variance of real returns? A six-currency test. *Journal of International Economics* 17:309–23.

Frankel, Jeffrey A., and Kenneth Froot. 1986. The dollar as a speculative bubble: A tale of fundamentalists and chartists. NBER Working Paper no. 1854. Cambridge, Mass.: National Bureau of Economic Research.

Frenkel, Jacob. 1985. Commentary on "causes of appreciation and volatility of the dollar." In *The U.S. dollar—Recent developments, outlook, and policy options,* 53–63. Kansas City, Mo.: Federal Reserve Bank of Kansas City.

Frenkel, Jacob, and Michael Mussa. 1980. The efficiency of foreign exchange markets and measures of turbulence. *American Economic Review* 70:374–81.

————. 1984. Asset markets, exchange rates, and the balance of payments. In *Handbook of international economics,* vol 2, ed. Ronald W. Jones and Peter B. Kenen, 679–747. Amsterdam: North-Holland.

Giavazzi, Francesco, and Alberto Giovannini. 1986. The EMS and the dollar. *Economic Policy* 1(2):455–74.

Girton, Lance, and Dale W. Henderson. 1976. Central bank operations in foreign and domestic assets under fixed and flexible exchange rates. In *The effects of exchange rate adjustments,* ed. Peter B. Clark, Dennis E. Logue, and Richard J. Sweeney, 151–79. Washington, D.C.: Department of the Treasury.

Goldstein, Morris. 1984. *The exchange rate system: Lessons of the past and options for the future*. Occasional Paper no. 30. Washington, D.C.: International Monetary Fund.

Greene, Margaret L. 1984. U.S. experience with foreign exchange intervention: September 1977–December 1979. Staff Studies no. 128. Washington, D.C.: Board of Governors of the Federal Reserve System.

Hansen, Lars Peter, and Robert J. Hodrick. 1980. Forward exchange rates as optimal predictors of future spot rates: An econometric analysis. *Journal of Political Economy* 88(5):829–53.

⸻. 1983. Risk averse speculation in the forward foreign exchange market: An econometric analysis of linear models. In *Exchange Rates and International Macroeconomics*, ed. by Jacob Frenkel. Chicago: University of Chicago Press.

Harrod, R. F. 1951. *The life of John Maynard Keynes*. London: Macmillan.

Hause, J. C. 1966. The welfare costs of disequilibrium exchange rates. *Journal of Political Economy* 74 (August):333–52.

Henderson, Dale W. 1984. Exchange market intervention operations: Their role in financial policy and their effects. In *Exchange rate theory and practice*, ed. John F. O. Bilson and Richard C. Marston, 359–442. Chicago: University of Chicago Press.

Herring, Richard J., and Richard C. Marston, 1977. *National monetary policies and international financial Markets*. Amsterdam: North-Holland.

Hooper, Peter, and Steven W. Kohlhagen. 1978. The effect of exchange rate uncertainty on the prices and volume of international trade. *Journal of International Economics* 8 (November):483–511.

Huang, Roger D. 1981. The monetary approach to the exchange rate in an efficient foreign exchange market: Tests based on volatility. *Journal of Finance* 36(1):31–41.

Johnson, Harry G. 1966. The welfare costs of exchange rate stabilization. *Journal of Political Economy* 74 (August):512–18.

Kenen, Peter B. 1986. Exchange-rate management: What role for intervention? Paper presented at the American Economics Association meetings, December. Typescript.

Kenen, Peter B., and Dani Rodrik. 1984. Measuring and analyzing the effects of short-term volatility in real exchange rates. Working Papers in International Economics. Princeton, N.J.: International Finance Section, Princeton University.

Kouri, Pentti, and Michael Porter. 1974. International capital flows and portfolio equilibrium. *Journal of Political Economy* 82 (May/June):443–67.

Krause, Lawrence B. 1986. Does a yen valued at 100 per dollar make any sense? Typescript.

Krugman, Paul R. 1985. Is the strong dollar sustainable? In *The U.S. dollar— Recent developments, outlook, and policy options*, 103–32. Kansas City, Mo.: Federal Reserve Bank of Kansas City.

Lanyi, Anthony, and Esther C. Suss. 1982. Exchange rate variability: Alternative measures and interpretation. Staff Papers. Washington, D.C.: International Monetary Fund.

Levich, Richard M. 1985. Empirical studies of exchange rates: Price behavior, rate determination and market efficiency. In *Handbook of international eco-*

nomics, vol. 2, ed. Ronald W. Jones and Peter B. Kenen, 979–1040. Amsterdam: North-Holland.

Liviatan, N. 1980. Anti-inflationary monetary policy and the capital-import tax. Warwick Economic Research Paper no. 171.

Loopesko, Bonnie E. 1984. Relationships among exchange rates, intervention, and interest rates: An empirical investigation. *Journal of International Money and Finance* 3(3):257–77.

McKinnon, Ronald I. 1974. *A new tripartite monetary agreement or a limping dollar standard.* Princeton Studies in International Finance no. 106. Princeton, N.J.: International Finance Section, Princeton University.

Marston, Richard C. 1984. Financial disturbances and the effects of an exchange-rate union. In *Exchange rate management under uncertainty,* ed. Jagdeep Bhandari. Cambridge, Mass.: MIT Press.

———. 1985. Stabilization policies in open economies. In *Handbook of international economics,* vol 2, ed. Ronald W. Jones and Peter B. Kenen, 859–916. Amsterdam: North-Holland.

———. 1986. Real exchange rates and productivity growth in the United States and Japan. NBER Working Paper no. 1922. Cambridge, Mass.: National Bureau of Economic Research.

Meese, Richard A., and Kenneth Rogoff. 1983. Empirical exchange rate models of the seventies: Do they fit out of sample? *Journal of International Economics* 14 (February):3–24.

Mussa, Michael. 1979. Empirical regularities in the behavior of exchange rates and theories of the foreign exchange market. In *Policies for employment, prices, and exchange rates,* ed. Karl Brunner and Allan H. Meltzer, 9–57. Carnegie-Rochester Conference Series on Public Policy, vol 11. Amsterdam: North-Holland.

———. 1981. *The role of official intervention.* Occasional Paper no. 6. New York: Group of 30.

Obstfeld, Maurice. 1983. Exchange rates, inflation, and the sterilization problem: Germany, 1975–81. *European Economic Review* 21(1,2): 161–89.

———. 1985. Floating exchange rates: Experience and prospects. *Brookings Papers on Economic Activity* 2:369–450.

Padoa-Schioppa, Tomasso. 1985. Lessons from the European Monetary System. European University Institute, European Forum Lecture. Florence: Badia Fiesolana.

Paris, James Daniel. 1938. *Monetary policies of the United States: 1932–38.* New York: Columbia University Press.

Richardson, J. David. 1984. The new nexus among trade, industrial and exchange-rate policies. In *The Future of the International Monetary System,* ed. Tamir Agmon, Robert G. Hawkins, and Richard M. Levich, 253–79. Lexington, Mass.: Lexington Books.

Rogoff, Kenneth. 1984. On the effects of sterilized intervention: An analysis of weekly data. *Journal of Monetary Economics* 14(2):133–50.

———. 1985. Can exchange rate predictability be achieved without monetary convergence: Evidence from the EMS. *European Economic Review* 28(1,2):93–115.

Shiller, Robert J. 1979. The volatility of long-term interest rates and expectations models of the term structure. *Journal of Political Economy* 87 (December):1190–1219.

Solomon, Robert. 1977. *The international monetary system, 1945–76: An insider's view.* New York: Harper & Row.
Stulz, Rene. 1981. A model of international asset pricing. *Journal of Financial Economics* 9:383–406.
Tobin, James. 1982. A proposal for international monetary reform. In *Essays in economics: Theory and policy,* 488–94. Cambridge, Mass.: MIT Press.
Ueda, Kazuo. 1986. Japan-U.S. current accounts and exchange rates before and after the G5 agreement. New York University Working Paper no. 15.
Ungerer, Horst, Owen Evans, and Peter Nyberg. 1983. *The European Monetary System: The experience, 1979–82.* Occasional Paper no. 19. Washington, D.C.: International Monetary Fund.
Williamson, John. 1985. *The exchange rate system.* Policy Analyses in International Economics no. 5. Washington, D.C.: Institute for International Economics.
Working Group on Foreign Exchange Intervention. 1983. *Report.* Washington, D.C.: U.S. Treasury (the Jurgensen Report).
Ypersele, Jacques van. 1985. *The European Monetary System: Origins, operation and outlook.* Brussels: Commission of the European Communities.

2. Guido Carli

International Financial Policies

International Cooperation in a Fixed Exchange Rate System

My experience in the area of foreign exchanges goes back more than forty years. In 1945 the Italian Exchange Office was restructured and I became a member of the Board of Directors and the Executive Committee. In 1947 Italy became a member of the International Monetary Fund and I was elected Executive Director.

The Italian Exchange Office was reshaped to establish close links between the Bank of Italy and the Italian Exchange Office. During the 1930s the links had been severed and the exchange office was given full autonomy in managing the external positions related to trade and payments. In the framework of a policy aiming at autarchy, international trade and payments were regulated through export/import quotas, bilateral payment agreements, and multiple exchange practices.

The arrangements adopted immediately after the end of the war reflected the conviction of the Governor of the Bank of Italy, who later became the President of the Republic, that balance of payment surpluses and deficits have to be reversed by equivalent expansions or contractions of the currency circulation.

Between 1958 and 1968 the international monetary system designed at the Bretton Woods conference in 1944 went into full operation; it could be described as a gold exchange standard in the process of becoming a dollar standard; the international cooperation aimed at making the transition as gradual as possible. The establishment of external convertibility for the European currencies at the end of 1958 was expanded to other currencies, including the Japanese yen, and was followed by the elimination of exchange restrictions on current payments and to some extent on capital transfers; adjustments of parities were limited to "fundamental" disequilibrium in the balance of payments, in accordance with the objectives of the system created by the delegates to the conference.

The extent to which members of IMF cooperated to make the system work can be attributed to concomitant circumstances; I mention the hegemony of the United States and its acceptance by the rest of the countries of the Western world.

Japan, Germany, and Italy in particular were interested in integrating their respective economies in the international market; the economies of these countries were more or less to the same degree export-led and from the expansion of world trade received a major impulse to develop internally. In addition, political considerations played a role. The Germans considered the presence of American troops on German soil to defend the independence of their country a priority; the Italians saw the strengthening of the international cooperation as the most powerful barrier against the instauration of a collectivist economy advocated by the Communist Party.

The functioning of the Bretton Woods system depended on an adequate volume of international liquidity and on its composition being commensurate with the preferences of the major trading partners.

Because the United States resolutely opposed a change of the monetary price of gold, the balance of payments of the United States, on a liquidity basis, became the only source of additions to international liquidity. In order to reconcile the U.S. opposition to increasing the price of gold and the mounting resistance by some countries to accepting dollars as the main component of international liquidity, it was decided to begin studies within the IMF in order to develop an artificially created reserve asset to be adapted to the liquidity needs of expanding trade and to be made independent from the gyrations of the American balance of payments. It was a timid attempt to limit the American hegemony.

In February 1962 the Federal Reserve Bank of New York was authorized to buy or sell foreign currencies in spot and forward markets and to negotiate a network of swap facilities with the central banks of other countries. The swaps provided a specific amount of foreign currency in exchange for an equivalent dollar credit for foreign central banks, with each party protected against loss due to a change in the par value of the other parties' currencies. The Bundesbank and the Bank of Italy had accumulated large amounts of foreign exchange reserve because of balance of payment surpluses, had refrained from converting them into gold, and had collaborated very extensively.

Other collaborative efforts to defend the international monetary system, in spite of its weakness, became more and more evident with the institution in 1961 of the so-called gold pool. The central banks of France, Germany, Italy, Belgium, the Netherlands, Switzerland, and the United States along with the Bank of England intervened in the London market to hold the market price of gold at or close to the official price. In March 1968, it was decided to suspend the arrangements of the gold pool; during the period of its operation, the participants sold a net total of $2.5 billion of gold on the London market of which $1.6 billion was provided by the United States.

The decision to suspend the arrangements of the gold pool was taken in a meeting held in March 1968 at the headquarters of the Federal Reserve Board in Washington. I took an active part in the debate; it was recognized that:

(a) Given the fixed price of gold, on one side, and the rising national price levels, on the other side, gold had become an undervalued asset in short supply. To sell gold to the markets could bring about the complete depletion of gold reserves and their substitution with dollar assets. The transition to the dollar standard could become the unavoidable consequence and could have the effect of further deteriorating confidence in the dollar.

b) Public opinion outside the United States could not understand the sacrifice of the gold reserves in order to finance the dollar overhang created by an uninterrupted period of balance of payment deficits on a liquidity basis by the United States. Not only France, but most European countries had become more reluctant to keep an ancillary position vis-à-vis the United States.

After 1968 it became evident that the system of fixed exchange rates based de facto on a reserve asset inundating the market at the rhythm of $7.7 billion a year could not survive. Efforts were made by the central banks of Japan, Germany, and Italy to defend the system by resisting temptations to get out of dollars. The United Kingdom was in need of dollars to face the strong pressures on the sterling. When in August 1971 the gold convertibility of the dollar was suspended, the world was not taken by surprise; it was the end of an era.

Market Interventions in a Floating Exchange Rate System

"The Bretton Woods system might have been able to survive an end of gold convertibility. It could not survive inflationary policies of the center country that characterized the decade from the mid-sixties on," the report to the Congress of the Commission on the Role of Gold in Domestic and International Monetary Systems concluded. I fully agree with this statement.

The emergence of the floating rate, which left exchange rates to market forces, did not end concern about exchange rate policies. At the annual meeting of the IMF in September 1973 in Nairobi, Mr. Witteveen spoke of the need for governments to accept responsibility for exchange rates within a context of internationally agreed rules. He clearly had in mind that some degree of management of floating rates was needed.

At the annual meeting of the IMF in September 1974 in Washington, D.C., Mr. Simon stated, "Market forces must not be treated as enemies to be resisted at all costs, but as the necessary and helpful reflections of changing conditions in a highly interrelated world economy with wide freedom for international trade and capital flows."

The conflict between these two schools of thought opened in the second half of 1971 when exchange rates of industrial countries floated. Karl Schiller characterized some floating rates as "cleaner" than others. The terms "clean" and "dirty" have been commonly used by economists and occasionally by public officials to distinguish a situation in which a floating rate is left wholly to market forces from that in which the rate is influenced by buying and selling operations by central banks, by imposition of restrictions, surcharges, or advanced requirement deposits as a way to restrain purchases of foreign exchanges.

After more than fourteen years of generalized floating, the problem of establishing some degree of international cooperation in managing the floating rates remains unresolved.

Market intervention as an instrument of economic policy was rehabilitated at the Versailles meeting of the G-7 in May 1982. Although the final communiqué reiterated the articles of the IMF, according to which interventions to counter disorderly market conditions have to be limited, the G-7 agreed to conduct a study on exchange market intervention. On the basis of an impressive amount of econometric texts, the report of that study did *not* confirm the position that intervention would be ineffective and counterproductive, as maintained by the U.S. Treasury representatives in the study group.

In January 1985 finance ministers and central bank governors of the G-5 reaffirmed their commitment to undertake coordinated interventions. Notwithstanding official sales of $10 billion, there was little evidence of a broad coordinated intervention effort and markets remained unconvinced of official determination to curb the extraordinary strength of the dollar.

In September 1985 finance ministers and central bank governors of the G-5 met again, on the initiative of the United States, in New York to reassess their policies. The demonstrative show of official unanimity took the market by surprise. The day after this meeting the dollar registered its sharpest fall. Total concerted dollar sales were $13 billion; crucial to this success was the direct participation of the United States selling $3 billion.

The dollar exchange rate has since declined uninterruptedly; the balance of trade of the United States has shown little improvement, and the reactions in the United States have not been univocal.

The Chairman of the Board of the Federal Reserve System repeated that he did not consider it to be a sensible policy to declare "you drive the dollar down forever until you see an improvement in trade."

Uncertainties about the future of the dollar exchange rate could dampen the willingness of foreign investors to maintain funds in the United States. The Federal Reserve could be forced to raise interest rates.

The Chairman of the U.S. Council of Economic Advisers admitted that exchange rate stability is desirable, but he was not prepared to accept target zones; "The markets know best" appears to be his unshakeable faith.

President Reagan and the Secretary of the Treasury confirmed their determination of not allowing that dollar exchange rates to "cripple" American farmers and exporters again; they considered it harmful to speculate on what the appropriate level of the dollar should be; the fall of the dollar exchange rate was regarded as an alternative to protectionism; they strongly opposed protectionism.

The American Congress has increasingly received requests by the various pressure groups more adversely affected by the loss of competitiveness to take action to protect their interests. To argue about the length of time needed in order for the fall of the dollar's exchange rate to manifest its effects does not convince those who better understand the effectiveness of custom duties applied case by case.

The Adjustment Process in a Floating Exchange Rate System

The Chairman of the Board of the Federal Reserve System has described the present position of the United States and the possible corrections in the following terms:

> . . . We are drawing on the savings of others—in 1986, the net influx of foreign capital appears to have exceeded all the savings generated by individuals in the United States. That capital influx is the mirror image of the deficit in our current account—we cannot, at one and the same time, borrow abroad (net) to cover domestic investment-savings imbalances and run a balanced current account.
> . . . we are living beyond our means—individuals, businesses, and government have collectively been spending more than we produce.

That might be acceptable if we were matching the foreign borrowing with a surge in productive investment in the United States. That has been the case at all times in the distant past in the United States. . . . But we are not making that match now—it is consumption that has been leading the economic parade.

. . . to close our 150 billion dollar trade deficit by increasing the manufactures (and I do not see another practical avenue) implies a 15/20 percent increase in industrial output over the coming years above and beyond that required to support domestic growth. While a surge of that kind would be welcome in many respects, the challenge is to achieve it without renewing inflationary pressures in that sector.

[What is needed is] to increase our own savings or reduce others' demands on savings at home. The obvious candidate is a reduction in our federal budget deficit. Unless productivity in the economy as a whole is to dramatically increase above the recent trend of 1 percent or so—and unhappily there is no solid evidence for that—we will not be able to close the gap in trade without slowing the growth in domestic consumption well below the 4 percent pace it has averaged during the current expansion.

The strong appreciation of the U.S. dollar, followed by its equally strong depreciation, interacted with an economic recovery in the United States characterized by:

1) faster growth of GNP than in partner countries;
2) faster growth of domestic demand than GNP;
3) decline of exports to indebted LDCs;
4) excess demand of savings requiring capital inflows;
5) high interest rates which stimulated those inflows;
6) lower productivity growth and higher import propensity than the OECD average.

The above has resulted in an average growth of real imports that has been twice that of exports and has led to a level of nominal imports almost twice that of exports.

The position of the Japanese economy is the opposite:

1) slower growth of GNP than in the United States;
2) slower growth of domestic demand than GNP;
3) excess supply of savings requiring capital outflows;
4) lower import propensity than the OECD average.

The above has resulted in an average growth of real exports that has been twice that of imports and has led to a level of nominal imports two-thirds that of exports.

In Europe the reduction of fiscal deficits has been followed by deceleration of growth, domestic demand, inflation, and employment and has contributed to world trade imbalances.

To promote more balanced global growth, six countries (G-5 plus Canada) agreed that surplus countries should commit themselves to follow policies designed to strengthen domestic economy while maintaining price stability, and deficit countries should encourage steady, low inflation growth while reducing their domestic imbalances. Newly industrialized economies "should assume greater responsibility for pursuing policies that allow their currencies to reflect more fully underlying economic fundamentals." More explicitly, Germany and Japan pledged to follow monetary and fiscal policies geared toward expanding domestic demand, thus helping to reduce the external surplus.

To reduce existing imbalances, the adjustment process requires the rest of the world economies to receive impulses broadly symmetrical to those in the United States. Under the present circumstances I believe it doubtful that stimulative policies in Japan and Germany could create an expansion of private demand of the dimension needed to compensate for the withdrawal of public demand in the United States. To reestablish balanced growth I see no alternative solution except redirecting flows of international capital to developing countries to relieve the constraints to which they are submitted if they have to service foreign debt. The rescheduling of foreign debt is a necessary condition; it is not a sufficient condition.

If the United States succeeds in establishing equilibrium between savings, investments, and budget deficits, if it moves from a position of a net capital importer to a position of a net capital exporter and therefore the trade deficit disappears and possibly a trade surplus appears, an excess in savings, in Keynesian terms, becomes manifest worldwide. World demand is condemned to shrink and the ultimate consequence is stagnation. Not without justification all forecasters have already revised their forecasts for 1987 and onward: the EEC Commission in its latest report has finally admitted that the contraction of world markets necessarily influences negatively the prospects of growth.

Coming back to the earth from the empyrean of absolute rationality, it appears unlikely that a cheaper dollar will produce a dramatic recovery in the U.S. balance of trade; a substantive upsurge of American exports depends preponderantly on strong sales of capital goods and industrial supplies to sluggish Europe and debt-burdened Latin America, and it is not likely to happen. As long as the United States avoids recession and consumer goods demand continues growing, the trade deficit will shrink little if at all. As a result, protectionism—product by product, country by country—will intensify.

I have expressed doubts about the possibility that the easing of monetary policies in Japan and Germany would boost the world economy to the extent needed to reduce the balance of trade deficit of the United States. Expansionary policies, to be effective, need the United States to accelerate its expansion too; but it seems that the Federal Reserve could not take the risks of monetary expansion as long as it is worried by the combination of the falling dollar, large budget and trade deficits, higher oil prices, and government disarray. Nor does it appear likely that whenever the evil of recession looms near the Federal Reserve will refrain from reluctantly taking a more accommodating stance.

The financial market appears to be scarcely affected by balance of payment considerations; nor does it appear to be affected by fears of interest rate hikes. What the market feels is that the industrial world is awash in liquidity; in conditions in which productive factors and products are in large supply, liquidity does not start prices rocketing; it spills over into financial assets driving bonds higher, interest lower, stocks higher.

Foreigners seem to be more eager to buy American stocks than to buy American commodities, and this, to a certain extent, explains the contradictions of the coexistence of a sluggish economy, a balance of trade deficit, and a bull market fueled principally if not only by the decline in interest rates.

A tide of money is foreseen to flow into stocks: the main sources being pension funds, money market funds, companies that buy up their own shares to oppose takeovers. Acquisitions and buyouts in 1986 totaled $267 billion; statistics published by the *Federal Reserve Bulletin* show that funds raised by nonfinancial companies in the form of shares in the three years from 1984 to 1986 have been negative by an amount of $226.1 billion.

In 1986 in most industrial countries monetary growth overshot its targets. It occurred in the United States, in Britain, in Germany, in France; the only country where the targets were respected was Japan. In the OECD countries taken together broad money expanded in real terms by 7 percent; it was the fastest rise since the early 1970s.

In the same period, globalization of financial markets, deregulation, and innovation all accentuated the creation of financial instruments having a degree of liquidity similar to that of conventional money.

Reference Ranges in a Floating Exchange Rate System

In defining a correct pattern for the exchange rates of the U.S. dollar, the Japanese yen, and the German mark, the various objectives should be listed in order to establish the extent to which they are compatible with each other. To declare that the exchange rate of the dollar has to be fixed at a level that does not cripple American exporters implies that it should not be influenced by capital movements and that the United States does not need to import foreign capital to finance the excess of investment over disposable domestic savings after financing the general government deficit. If the capital account is in surplus, there must be an equivalent excess of imports of goods; somebody must be hurt.

Projections of the savings-investment balance for the United States and Japan in percentage of GNP show that in the United States in 1987 private savings are estimated at 16.4 percent of GNP, private investment at 16.5, general government deficit at 3.4 percent; the result is a deficit of savings of 3.5 percent of GNP that will be reverberated on an equivalent surplus of the capital account and on an equivalent deficit of the current account of the balance of payments; in money terms this is calculated to be $140 billion.

Compare this to the position of Japan: private savings 34.2 percent GNP; private investment 28.9 percent of GNP; excess of savings over investment 5.3 percent of GNP; general government deficit of 1.0 percent; surplus on current account 4.3 percent; in money terms: $79 billion.

Accepting the validity of such projections, decisions on the most appropriate exchange rate of the yen to the dollar should be made keeping in mind the limits of fluctuation that would offer Japanese investors the prospect of an appropriate income. To that aim, interest rate differentials play a major role; the greater the uncertainty about the exchange rates, the greater the interest rate differentials should be. The agreement between the United States and Japan to cooperate in keeping exchange rate variations within "reference ranges" could be interpreted as an offer to Japanese investors of greater protection against exchange losses.

If it is generally agreed that the U.S. current account deficit in 1987 will be between $140 billion and $130 billion, that in 1988 it will be reduced by $10–$20 billion, and that it will stabilize at around the $100 billion mark for the rest of the decade, the correct pattern of exchange rates to be aimed for should fit the conditions of a country in need of foreign capital.

Upper and lower limits chosen as "reference ranges" without adequate consideration of their credibility by private investors could produce the consequence that the function of providing funds to the country in deficit of savings, instead of being discharged by private investors, would be discharged by central banks forced to support the exchange rate within the limits of the "reference ranges" by selling their respective currencies in exchange for the currency of the nation in need of foreign capital. Alternatively, the full weight of the adjustment could be placed on interest rate differentials.

The practical objective in choosing "reference ranges" should be to restrict the risks of international investors generated by the exchange rate volatility. In recent years the markets have developed new instruments that transfer risks from one economic agent to another, but they do not eliminate the risks. By stabilizing the relationships between the major currencies, the monetary authorities take risks themselves that the markets are unable to bear; at the same time they accept a limitation of their monetary sovereignty.

At the meetings held in Paris, February 1986, the finance ministers and the central bank governors of the G-5 and Canada reached a major agreement to stabilize exchange rates around current levels.

The ministers agreed that the substantial exchange rate changes since the September 1985 agreement to depress the dollar have "brought their currencies within ranges broadly consistent with underlying economic fundamentals." They concluded that the dollar's sharp decline "will increasingly contribute to reduce external imbalances" and that "further substantial exchange rate shifts among their currencies could damage growth and adjustment prospects in their countries."

"Our agreement is a temporary one. This is not a transition to a new monetary order," stated the German Finance Minister.

During the fifteen years (1958–1973) in which the international monetary system was based on fixed exchange rates, international cooperation worked satisfactorily. Contributing to its effectiveness were:

a) De facto acceptance of the hegemony of the United States; willingness of countries like Germany and Italy to accumulate dollars in their foreign exchange reserves and to support the dollar exchange rate by taking active part in the establishment of a network of swap agreements among central banks.

b) Constant improvement of the terms of trade of the industrial nations; limited size of external imbalances; recourse to demand management policies; control of capital movements in order to make monetary policies more autonomous.

c) Greater correlation between variations of monetary aggregates and price levels; limited size of financial instruments created outside the control of the monetary authorities and having a high degree of substitution of money.

The imbalances that have developed in the three major industrial nations since 1982 have no precedent and it is unlikely that they can be corrected by exchange rate variations only. The globalization of financial markets has helped to transfer savings from countries where there is excess to the country where there is a deficit; at the same time profound structural changes have taken place making the external position of the United States weaker. In particular:

1) excess production of foodstuffs in Europe and its position as a major competitor of the United States as exporter of grains;

2) indebtedness of LDCs and the need of LDCs to attain trade surpluses to service the external debt;

3) loss of competitiveness of American manufactures and increase of international trade of high-quality products.

These factors will make the depreciation of the dollar less effective in bringing about the adjustment process of the U.S. balance of payments on current account. If the projections of the possible evolution of the trade deficit between now and the end of the decade prove to be correct, the U.S. external debt will probably amount to 20 percent of GNP. That could imply a heavy burden of interest payments to foreign creditors on the external account and could result in severe intermittent pressures on the dollar exchange rates and instability in the international financial markets.

To avoid these detrimental consequences, the external deficit of the United States needs to be put on a declining path, not one that turns up again after 1989. But depreciation alone will not produce the effect of rectifying the external deficit; it could prove to be highly inflationary for the U.S. economy; a resurgent U.S. inflation would make it almost impossible to bring the trade account into balance.

To make the adjustment process of the existing payment imbalances as orderly as possible, one important ingredient of international cooperation is the supervision of the activities of financial concerns (banks and nonbanks). I do not imply that capital movements around the world should be restricted as they were when fixed exchange rates operated. What seems desirable is a higher degree of coordinated supervision on the behavior of financial markets to strengthen the links between finance and the real economy.

The authors of the Bretton Woods agreements sought to make finance the servant and not the master of human desires in the international as well as in the domestic sphere. U.S. Secretary of the Treasury Morgenthau declared that he wanted to erect new institutions that would be "instrumentalities of sovereign governments and not of private financial interests"—in short, "to drive . . . the usurious money lenders from the temple of international finance."

Of course, the tide of global financial markets, financial innovation, and deregulation cannot be reversed; however, a higher degree of international cooperation could reduce the risks associated with them without throwing sand into the wheels of the markets.

Two problems concerning fundamentals cannot be solved by the financial authorities; namely:

1) the distribution of the burden of defense between the United States and Europe and its impact on central governments' expenditures; the extent to which Japan could devote a higher proportion of its resources to its own defense;

2) the indebtedness of LDCs and its consequences on the rate of growth inside these countries; here again the Western world is confronted with a major political problem that profoundly affects social and political stability around the world.

Last but not least, more attention should be devoted to the different ratios of population increase in the various parts of the world and their impact on the distribution of real resources. The demographic balance is likely to generate excess savings outside the United States and deficient savings inside until the early years of the next century. This means that the United States will be a net capital-importing country during this period.

These are reflections of an elder person who started his career as a member of the Board of Directors of the IMF forty years ago and who had to deal with the dismantling of bilateral payment agreements, the establishment of the European Payments Union, convertibility, fixed exchange rates, floating exchange rates, dollar scarcity, and dollar glut. I feel dazzled by the globalization of international markets, deregulation, innovation; but I cannot help questioning the ability of these changes to promote development, employment, monetary stability, and a more equitable distribution of wealth inside nations and among nations.

Note

This paper reflects the author's personal views on international cooperation in exchange rate management, how things are evolving and which directions should be taken in the future, based on personal past experience.

3. Jacques Attali

The Costs of Changing the International Monetary System

It is very hard to speak after Mr. Carli, because I agree with almost everything he said. Let me begin by addressing the issue of changing international financial institutions, the topic on which Mr. Carli concluded (see above).

I believe that we are now at the end of the second chapter in international finance since the Second World War. The conclusion of the first chapter was marked by the collapse of the Bretton Woods agreement, which in my view was terminated back in 1961, when it first became clear that the dollar/gold parity could not be changed. I will come back to this point later on, but for now let me say only that the high political costs of making needed adjustments in the parity signaled the real end of Bretton Woods. Today we stand at the end of the period of generalized floating exchange rates.

Mr. Carli has clearly explained the history of change from Williamsburg and Versailles. In the days following the Williamsburg agreement, we spent the nights writing memoranda and communiqués, formulating agreements on how we would keep the markets in check. Perhaps we were so satisfied by the prospect of a new era of coordination that we did not ask whether even coordinated intervention could be effective. Our governments could agree to the central banks expending several billion dollars, but in markets that saw a daily volume hundreds of times as large. Yet an extraordinarily long fight against the political and financial experts had to be fought before even these paltry sums could be agreed upon. A main part of my message today is that such political machinations—the meetings, the agreements, the press conferences— are really just a shadow in front of reality. They are nothing. They are really just to keep TV on the air and to let the public think that their leaders are actually dealing with the issue, when in fact they are not. Not at all.

Nevertheless, there is a little hope to be found in a consensus that seems to be emerging between the ideologues and the pragmatists. The theoreticians, such as John Williamson, have built the idea of reference zones, which would be something like a worldwide European Monetary System. These theoreticians now find real consensus with the pragmatists for three reasons that I can see.

The first reason for this unusual consensus comes from the fundamental idea of Bretton Woods, the real root of wisdom that was perhaps the only common ground shared by Harry Dexter White and John Maynard Keynes: that you cannot have both free trade and free exchange rates. Either you have fixed exchange rates and free trade, or you have protectionism with floating exchange rates. Today we see an emerging consensus on this proposition, that the lack of discipline in exchange rates is pushing the world toward increased protectionism. The second area of consensus is that floating exchange rates tend to channel finance toward speculation and away from long-term investments. I believe we will see more and more of this if the current system is to survive. Such unbridled speculation jeopardizes the whole worldwide economic system. The third area of consensus is that floating exchange rates do not move to correct trade imbalances. Although the theory held that exchange rates would fulfill such a function, they clearly have not.

Thus I think that now, among the supposed decision makers around the world, there is a consensus that something must change. Indeed, beginning with the agreements of the last year, we have evolved in the direction of a reference zone system. We now have the embryo of it.

That is, we have first an agreement between the G-7 countries to monitor the main barometers of the economies. One must, of course, ask what is on the list of barometers, and this is a very important question. Is it only GDP? Is it inflation rate, interest rates, budget deficit? I am sure that with time these will be better specified.

There also appears to be interest in choosing bands or target zones that would hold currencies within a reasonable range of values. While the analysis here is not as advanced as that on macroeconomic barometers, it is a start. Of course there are many issues that must be settled first. Which currencies shall we target? As far as Europe is concerned, will it be the Deutsche mark or the European Currency Unit? Will the targets be preannounced and public or implicit and secret? Will they be "hard" or "soft"? Another issue is how much money we should devote to intervention on the market.

But we do have this embryo. And I personally think that the next few months or the next year will decide whether or not this embryo develops. I believe this is the crucial time because we are facing the moment when we have to move the current parities among rates. When the parity must be changed, the question arises: Which is more costly politically, changing the parameters or breaking the system?

This to me was one of the main mistakes of Bretton Woods, that it was politically less costly to break the system than to change the parameters. The main asset of the European Monetary System, an asset that is integral to its construction, is the high cost politically for each government in Europe to break the system and the low cost of accepting a realignment or change in the parameters. No reference zone system can work if the political cost of breaking the system is not higher than the political cost of changing the parameters.

Meanwhile a substantial, coordinated realignment of the major currencies of the world would be very costly. It is clear now that for the German, Japanese, or American governments, the political costs of breaking the system is nothing—zero. And the political cost of changing the parameters is maybe higher because it has the appearance of a political defeat.

Why is this so? Popular political support for a multilateral system of target zones is simply very weak, especially in comparison with important domestic political issues. I believe that it is impossible to build a reference zone system without domestic political support. Such a system is viable only when political leaders have to pay with their own parochial popularity if they do not keep their word. An important issue for the future is whether we can build this kind of basic political support for target zones. As far as I am concerned, we have little chance in winning over the public if we are not bold enough first to make the agreements, which are now supposed to be secret, explicit. We must be willing to announce not only modifications to domestic economic policy that are made in the interest of coordination, but also the precise bounds of the zone in which we agree exchange rates must lie. There can be no political costs to breaking a reference zone agreement if the zone itself is secret. And we must stress that leaders stick by their word on international economic affairs. As it is, politicians find it costly to change their word on matters of defense or arms control but not on matters of international economic cooperation.

We have achieved a certain political foundation in Europe for the European Monetary System. This, I believe, is really the most important achievement of Europe in the past two decades. To bring this success to the global level, we must develop it as an open, public issue, an item of international debate. As far as the future is concerned, I think that we must make the issue public, which means we make public the fact that we need to have an increase in taxes in the United States and growth in Japan and Germany. If we do not take these steps, then the whole system will be broken. Whether exchange rates are better left within a generous band so that some semblance of floating still exists, or whether rates should be fixed outright and the floating rate system discarded altogether remains an open question, but I think it is a subsidiary one. If we succeed in raising these issues domestically, I am sure that there will be a clear path for the future.

One obvious step along this path is to abandon the G-5 and G-7 frameworks and go to the IMF. Let the IMF reinstate the surveillance process it followed in the 1960s and resume its duties in managing and coordinating parities. I have always been very skeptical of the idea that exchange rate coordination and targeting could be accomplished in such small forums as the G-5 and G-7. We have to institutionalize a move back to the larger multinational institutions, which were originally designed precisely for these purposes.

Second, we have to include both the Third World and Eastern Europe in our negotiations. Clearly, we need in each country a leadership that is penalized if it does not respect that kind of international agreement. It is obvious that any such international agreement today would have to address the fundamental imbalances directly and would therefore have to stress an increase in taxes in the United States. This policy is certainly risky, since it might trigger a recession in the United States and perhaps around the world. But I view this as an outcome preferable to the scenario under which the United States does nothing to correct its chronic fiscal deficits. This, I believe, would lead to crisis. The United States simply cannot continue accumulating a large external debt. We have already had one experience with this, and, as I have said, it marked the end of the first chapter in postwar international finance.

In sum, I believe that if the leadership in the United States fails to be bold enough, the costs of international economic linkages will be very high in the future. I hope we can avoid paying that price.

4. John R. Petty

National Interests and Global Obligations: A Call for Meaningful Dialogue

What we are talking about today is where economics and politics meet. The adjustment process, especially when anything more is involved than normal macro policies on a national basis, always probes and sometimes penetrates deep into the structure of local economic interests—and therefore deep into local political alignments.

The mechanisms of international financial cooperation can sometimes blur this fundamental reality. Its smooth functioning minimizes the pain. However, as balance of payments adjustment is delayed, new economic patterns develop. With this delay, economic expectations and political alignments quickly reflect these new circumstances. In surplus countries especially, long or protracted deviations from the norm in national accounts tend to compound resistance to adjustment. The beneficiaries of new gains come to expect its continuance as their economic birthright. Yet in a global sense, significant deviations from the norm can only be enjoyed temporarily.

How might this traditional, and very human, reaction to achieving economic advantage be countered? I will argue that for a starter what is needed is a broader appreciation of what world economic equilibrium requires. The intent is to encourage the development of expectations that focus on the norms inherent in such a theoretical equilibrium. In turn, this would help create a climate of understanding to support the political decisions necessary to move deviant national accounts back toward the norm.

Too often, however, discussion of international financial cooperation moves quickly beyond the presumption of support from political leadership to dwell upon the niceties of the technical financial aspects of one approach or another. The result is that the degree of political backing necessary for a well-functioning international financial system receives less attention than it deserves.

This is a serious shortcoming. Not only because it removes from the public debate discussion of the essential political ingredient to meaningful adjustment, but because it permits wishful thinking to prevail—the impression that adjustment can be low cost, even free, and financial coordination alone can do the trick.

Not surprisingly, politicians find it tempting to move quickly beyond the questions of necessary political endorsement and active support. Doing so allows them to sidestep issues. It tends to take them off the hook.

This inadequate level of top political involvement exists because such involvement has not been demanded except in crises, and leaders don't go looking for points of friction. Moreover, a broad conceptual base or framework is largely missing from the public debate on critical issues. And the discussion we do have lacks the degree of specificity necessary to get beyond generalities and into constructive dialogue.

For example, we seek a stable equilibrium with a constant variance. But how much effort is spent going into what that means in terms of national economies? We lack a consensus about where it is we want to go. We lack a common understanding of what it is we are trying to achieve and the compromises necessary to get there. Instead, too much of the dialogue is directed toward the coordination of official foreign exchange actions and exchange rate regimes.

The world lacks a commonly understood view of what constitutes, approximately, an equilibrium environment of the global economy. This means that not only does an underlying political consensus not exist to support sufficiently the work of economic and financial leaders, but it is unlikely to be developed.

This lack of a shared view of what is desirable globally—and necessary nationally—robs us of more progress toward a happier global economic environment. Advisers to presidents, prime ministers, and legislators speak mostly of national interest; too little is said of global obligations. And, of course, national interests prevail. True, more often than not *flagrant* excesses of national policy measured against the obligations of a multilateral system are avoided. But more than that is required. After all, we admit to being an interdependent world.

To begin the long process of shifting more emphasis of national governments toward explicitly recognizing and responding to global obligations, we should commence a deliberate program. Our first step should be to define, roughly, what constitutes a sustainable balance of payments equilibrium on a global basis. As the second step, a debate should be encouraged on the outcome. Our trading partners too must have their own internal debate. Clear recognition should be given to what would be involved for each nation to operate within the relevant constant variances.

I do not deceive myself that this will be easy. The illusion that it is possible to pursue independent monetary policy and decidedly national economic goals in an interdependent world does not disappear quickly.

Yet this conceptual framework, this global vision with reasonably compatible national economic expression, would provide credibility, encouragement, and assistance to advocates in national governments who seek to pursue national programs consistent with a sustainable global model.

It is a long road. And that is why we should start now.

The remainder of this paper will describe (1) how we might create this framework within our multilateral system; (2) how we might approach obtaining the political as well as the financial endorsements necessary to make the framework the lynchpin of our global adjustment mechanism; and (3) certain reinforcing rules designed to encourage good behavior.

Our first objective should be to define a reasonably sustainable equilibrium model in the world trade and payments. This would entail a technically executed, but increasingly politically led, multilateral effort to explore, and then attempt to define, what national accounts would look like in a global equilibrium movement. Never mind that such a condition among nations is more theoretical than real and that the quantification of trade balance and current accounts objectives by nations would be more illustrative than a national intention, certainly at first.

Such a recommended objective, for example, would tend to stir debate on what level of Japanese trade surplus is sustainable—sustainable, that is, in terms of multilateral equilibrium and compatible goals among nations. We can all agree that the Japanese trade surplus should be nowhere near 4–5 percent of GDP. But what number is most appropriate as a target? Current account composition and size would certainly also be part of the debate.

Think of the value of a comparable discussion about the United States which related the size and duration of the federal deficit and foreign capital flow to what is necessary in the trade balance of the future.

To illustrate: If the United States shifted to a trade surplus at the rate of 2 percent of GNP per year, starting in 1988, we would be in surplus in 1989; the external debt would peak at $440 billion.

If the shift took place at the rate of 1 percent of GNP per year, starting in 1988, we would be in surplus in 1991, and the external debt would peak at $580 billion.

If the shift was at the rate of ½ percent of GNP (a $22 billion annual improvement), starting in 1988, we would be in surplus in 1995, and the external debt would peak at almost $1,000 billion.

The interest cost of servicing the debt at 7 percent would be 0.6 percent, 0.7 percent, and 0.9 percent of GNP, or roughly 0.5–1.0 percent of GNP in the form of a trade surplus would be required to service the external debt (assuming a constant relative level of debt).

The implication of these numbers is profound and worthy of much discussion and understanding.

Creating a hypothetical global model would bring to the surface many such issues. A few such models do exist, and they no doubt generate subjects of discussion too.

To some extent, there is an interesting historical precedent to this approach, though the precedent was far more limited in the breadth of its exposure. At Working Party 3 of the OECD in the 1968–69 period, efforts were made to define national balance of trade and current account goals in the context of a global environment. Initially the United States was offered as the residual in the equation and LDCs were for the most part ignored. As the exercise was repeated every six weeks, and participants began to think of their goals in terms more compatible with a sustainable global framework, objectives were moderated somewhat. When the United States was presented on other than a residual basis (i.e., a nation that had objectives too) and the LDCs were given trade goals compatible with their debt service and growth needs, the exercise reached its practical limits at that time. But it was far from useless.

The disparity between what nations wanted and what the system ideally should have was so great that technical level discussions begged for political determinations. In a way, they got it. The real impact of the exercise may never have been noted: The death knell of the "adjustable peg" exchange rate system was tolled. The Working Party 3 work demonstrated to some in the U.S. Treasury that a discrete devaluation of the dollar against our trading partners was not going to happen normally. Analysis alone would not occasion other nations to accept the loss of their trade advantage to the dollar. This began the search for the time and the mechanism by which the United States could achieve a discrete devaluation, not simply a devaluation against gold with no trade advantage. In fact, this was the background to August 15, 1971.

Our task today of finding a mechanism is simpler. We have much increased flexibility in our exchange rate system. We have increased habits of financial cooperation, even coordination. And we have the Economic Summits which provide a critical cog in the multilateral machinery. These Summits are the avenue to obtaining over time the more explicit political endorsement necessary if national actions are to conform to international behavioral requirements. It may be several years before this point is reached, but the benefits of this type of intense consultation begin to accrue much sooner. The Tokyo Round declaration and the presumed work underway is a beginning. How much political will lies behind that effort remains to be seen.

Today the exploration, and then the description, of national trade and current account goals might initially be pursued through any of a number of forums. This would involve suggesting globally compatible constant variances on a national basis. Clearly, fundamental local and national economic interests are involved and I do not minimize the task.

This work should be brought together and given integrity and credibility under the auspices of the IMF. This would provide institutional support and, ideally, formal political endorsement in due course through becoming part of the five-year IMF Quota Review process. By tying the process in with the quota review negotiations, we get the necessary balance between continuity and adjustability in goals in a changing world.

The framework, which is an amalgam of reasonably compatible national goals, must be reinforced through the multilateral institutions with encouragement for good performance and a remedy for neglect.

It is necessary to stimulate again a most active discussion about enforcement mechanisms, pointed to the surplus countries equally as to the deficit countries. Good behavior will need to be encouraged, and negligent behavior—behavior that ignores responsible participation in the multilateral system—will have to be vulnerable to denials that will tend to induce cooperation.

Is adjustment too slow? Do all the dynamic new elements of modern-day trade and investment overwhelm the adjustment mechanism when achieved only, or primarily, through macroeconomic stimulants to wage and price levels? Do we allow political forces of protection too much time to gather? Are early warning systems enough?

Earlier involvement of political leadership has to be our objective. Righting imbalances sooner is the best way to expand support for the multilateral system. Too little study has been given to the impact of slow versus fast adjustment. There is not enough recognition of the threat of too slow a response. Has the academic community demonstrated to the politicians the cost of delayed action? Should they not be shown it is *not* cost free?

The scarce currency clause must be revisited and active consideration must be given to what is necessary to make it an effective tool of compliance. Respectable people should no longer avoid meaningful discussions about the "scarce economy" clause or its equivalent.

Besides the IMF, the GATT too has a little-used mechanism designed to pressure the surplus country: the quota privilege of the deficit country. While accepting the idea of negative inducements, an alternative to quotas must be found. Withholding tariff concessions previously granted might be the approach. This could be done selectively. The full discipline of multilateral machinery must assure both the reasonableness and the temporary nature of any such action. Discipline also requires multilateral bodies to assure that deficit countries do not shirk from their adjustment responsibilities. By making these denial mechanisms (scarce currency and withholding tariff concessions) meaningful possibilities, more symmetry would be brought to the system. They could deter or limit unsportsmanlike conduct just as deficit countries get credits if they play by the rules. As in all deterrents, their mere existence and credibility provide more value to the multilateral system than their usage.

Moreover, having these surplus country inducements only makes sense where national expectations are both understood and accepted. That is, where the framework—the constant variance vision of a stable world environment—identifies when responsible actions must be taken in conjunction with other off-variant nations. The IMF, the press, and the international financial community would help to communicate these instances, and the discussion I am looking for should help create a public understanding of what needs to be done.

Gaining clear political endorsements nationally of the implications of accepting a global economic framework will not be easy. It may not be fully possible. It certainly will not happen quickly. But the exercise has intrinsic merit:

It will educate the participants and many others.

It will stimulate discussions and tend to focus debate on the implications of adjustment.

It will influence policymakers in the right direction, even if they won't admit it.

All of these things will create an environment more hospitable to tough political decisions.

Of itself, the process will build further the framework of cooperation between nations and with the multilateral institutions. The coordination of monetary policy, intervention, and economic programs would be greatly facilitated by the process of building this framework *and* developing the consensus. As the relative size of the world economic pie forces more choices, the benefits of this cooperation will encourage the political determinations which ultimately are inescapable.

5. *Robert Solomon*

Exchange Rates, Macroeconomic Policies, and the Debt Problem

We have heard three very interesting talks. It's clear that the topic of international financial policy is not really distinguishable from macroeconomic policy, which was the subject of the first panel. All three speakers have talked about macro policies, understandably. The narrower definition of this panel might have seemed to refer to exchange rates in particular. The excellent background paper written by Dick Marston (see above) does focus on exchange rate policies. I'll start with that subject and then broaden out a bit to the more general.

On exchange rate policies in particular, I shall say a few words about the Paris agreement (or perhaps we should call it the Louvre agreement to maintain a certain parallelism with the Plaza). It was not long ago that the G-6 met in Paris and agreed to stabilize the exchange rates against the dollar, on the grounds that rates had somehow reached levels that reflect underlying fundamentals. Most economists would disagree with that judgment. Most economists, not all, believe that the exchange rate adjustment that's been going on since March 1985 needs to go further. One of the reasons it needs to go further is that if you look at the extent of the dollar depreciation in real terms against the other industrial countries and the developing countries (I'm using the Morgan Guarantee Index, which includes about eighteen developing countries and twenty-two industrial countries), the dollar has moved back only about three-fourths of the way to where it was in 1980. In other words only three-fourths of the appreciation of 1980–85 has been reversed. While there is nothing sacred about the year 1980 or any other base, the U.S. current account was more or less balanced in 1980. As a couple of speakers have already pointed out here, the string of current account deficits that the United States has incurred so far in this decade, and will continue to incur before the current account deficit disappears, will change the net investment position by $700–$800 billion. Using an interest rate of 7 percent, one comes out with a net increase in interest payments of something like $50 billion. If we want to get our current account back to where it was in 1980, we need an extra $50 billion of trade surplus. Now one could argue that the United States should have a surplus on current account, not just a balance, given the need for resource flows to the developing countries.

For these reasons, to put it all very briefly, there is a case for additional depreciation of the dollar beyond where it has gone so far. Yet we had this agreement in Paris to stabilize the exchange rates. The question: Why did those six sets of finance ministers and central bank governors make that agreement? Why in particular did the Americans agree to it?

The only explanation that I can come up with is that Secretary Baker and Chairman Volcker were worried about the shock to the economies of the other industrial countries of the exchange rate adjustment that has occurred so far. They're worried about too slow growth, if not recession, in Germany and Japan, and they came to the judgment that we need at least a breather, a pause, in this exchange rate adjustment to provide some time for the other countries to adopt domestic demand policies so that they can compensate for the contraction in aggregate demand resulting from the fall-off in their external surpluses. I therefore regard the Paris agreement as a temporary one providing only for a pause.

I'll now say a word or two about target zones if I may. Some people have interpreted the Paris agreement as being a first step toward a target zone system. Whether one agrees with that or not doesn't matter for present purposes. We could spend an entire session on target zones. I would just very briefly state what I regard as the nub of the objection to the target zone system in present-day circumstances.

The point is that fiscal policy is immobilized in the United States, and it's almost immobilized in the other major industrial countries. If we went to a target zone system, how would countries respect those target zones? We know, and Dick Marston's paper makes the point very well, that sterilized intervention is a rather weak instrument for regulating exchange rates. So it would have to be monetary policy. Unsterilized intervention, which is equivalent to monetary policy, would have to be used to hold exchange rates within the target zones.

Since we cannot at present flex fiscal policy very much in any of the industrial countries, we would be linking monetary policy to the exchange rate. Such a monetary policy would not always be the appropriate policy for domestic stabilization, therefore, we would be giving up domestic stability in order to try to achieve stability of exchange rates. And that does not seem to me to be a very sensible trade-off.

In my view the reform that we need before we try to reform the exchange rate system is a reform of fiscal policy in all the major industrial countries, which is desirable for its own sake.

Let me now talk a little bit about the macroeconomic interactions between developing countries and industrial countries. It seems to me this hasn't received quite enough attention, even in Jeff Sachs's paper (see above), if I read that paper properly. It is not well enough recognized that the weakness in the industrial countries in the past year, 1986, is partly the result of very weak import demand in the developing countries.

The developing countries suffered a severe terms of trade deterioration in 1985–86. Not only the oil-exporting countries, which we all know about, but the non-oil developing countries also suffered a very severe deterioration in their terms of trade and they all had to cut back on their imports. And that cutback in the imports of the developing countries reduced the GNP of the industrial countries. The OECD *Outlook* for December 1986 estimates that effect at 1 percent of the GNP of the OECD group of countries. That's a big impact! The economies of the industrial countries have weakened. Governor Carli (see above) has pointed out the latest assessment of the European Commission, which shows a fairly slow growth in Europe; they cut the estimate for 1986 back to 2.5 percent, and they estimate 1987 at 2.3 percent.

We have a situation where the developing countries cut their imports, weakening growth in the industrial countries. The weaker growth in the industrial countries makes conditions worse in developing countries. We have a vicious circle going on between the developing and the industrial countries. I don't think that point has received enough attention at this meeting so far.

There is a corollary to what I've said. We know that exports have slowed in Germany and Japan and maybe other industrial countries. This is usually attributed to the exchange rate change that has occurred in the last two years. It is just possible that some of that slowdown in export growth in industrial countries is not yet the reflection of the exchange rate, but it may be a reflection of the weak performance of the developing countries, and we may still have ahead of us the affects of the exchange rate adjustment. Consider that as a possibility. Some mixture of exchange rates and weakness in the developing countries is what's going on here.

The challenge is to convert this vicious circle into a virtuous circle. That leads me to two sorts of recommendations. Being the last speaker of this program, I will take advantage of that position to set out broad policy recommendations.

Number one: It's conventional wisdom that to correct the imbalance of international payments and current account positions in the world, the United States should be cutting back on its domestic demand and the countries in surplus should be speeding up the growth of their domestic demand. The United States should do it, of course, by cutting its budget deficit. How the other countries should speed up their domestic demand is usually not specified as clearly. The general principle is widely respected, though it hasn't been activated very much in practice. The U.S. budget deficit is going down this fiscal year by something like 1 percent of GNP. It's rather uncertain so far what will happen in the next fiscal year. Ideally, it would go down by 1 percent of GNP each year and it would be gone by 1990 or so.

What I would like to suggest is that while we all accept what has to be done on both sides, maybe the emphasis has to be shifted a little bit, given the weakness of total demand in the industrial world, and given this vicious circle that I was referring to. I would say we need to put more emphasis on increasing domestic demand in the surplus countries and a little bit less emphasis, not zero, but a little bit less emphasis on the need to cut demand in the United States. Just shift that emphasis a little bit and not put them on a par, simply because the world economy, and the outlook for the world economy, is so sluggish. If that were done and we did get a net increase in domestic demand in the industrial world as a whole—including the United States and Europe and Japan—that would be one step toward trying to convert this vicious circle into a virtuous circle.

There is one other measure that would be needed. We would have to find a way to increase the flow of capital from the industrial to the developing countries, because the developing countries need more than better terms of trade and a faster growth in their exports so that those that are potentially creditworthy will appear that way. The developing countries also need a net increase in capital inflow, or they need to reduce the net capital transfers that they are making to the rest of the world, so that they can increase their investment, which, as we all know, is too low.

If we could somehow find a financial technique for increasing the flow of capital to the developing countries so that the developing countries could increase their imports, that stimulus to demand in industrial countries would be much more welcome, somehow, than an increase in domestic demand that comes from cutting taxes. Fiscal policy is just not a very popular instrument of policy in those countries that are in surplus, and it's not usable in the United States in an expansionary way. But I have no doubt that an increase in exports would be quite welcome in Europe and Japan. One way to bring that about is to try to find a way to get a bigger flow of capital to the developing countries. I'm not going to suggest precisely how that can be done, because I don't know. But I would say that the routes that are worth exploring go beyond the commercial banks. I have great doubts that we can expect very much increase in lending—concerted lending, as it's called— to the developing countries in the present circumstances.

The thought that goes through my mind is that the way to try to encourage a flow of capital to those developing countries that are potentially creditworthy (I'm leaving out Africa here, talking about basically the Baker-15 countries) is through some form of partial guarantee that would encourage a flow of portfolio capital to the developing countries. That seems to me to be the one source that has some potential, since one has to rule out the banks, and direct investment itself can't do the trick. Part of the rationale for looking to portfolio capital as a way to get funds into the developing countries is that the United States has been absorbing portfolio capital from other countries with its current account deficit.

The U.S. current account deficit will go down in the next three or four years. It already started down in real terms in the fourth quarter. As the U.S. current account deficit goes down and the U.S. need for capital diminishes, perhaps the countries that have been exporting capital to the United States can be induced to shift portfolio capital to the developing countries, where it's obviously badly needed.

Summary of Discussion

Anthony Solomon began by expressing his pessimism about the long-term effectiveness of coordinated intervention. He agreed with Guido Carli that if both surplus and deficit countries acted in concert, the benefits would be large. But such coordination is unlikely, and, by default, the dollar will continue to fall. He argued that as financial markets become more integrated, shocks to the system will increasingly require capital controls. Failures in the ability to coordinate may imply the need for capital controls in the future. Solomon expressed a gloomy view of the outlook for the future. He felt that even with a further decline of the dollar, adjustments in the underlying balances would be slow. The falling U.S. terms of trade and the more restrictive monetary policy that would be required would also imply future constraints on U.S. growth.

Feldstein gave additional evidence on intervention by the Central Bank of Japan. Official accumulation of U.S. assets by the Bank of Japan was $15 billion and $16 billion in the second and third quarters of 1986, respectively. The total for 1986 was $36 billion, approximately half of Japan's current account surplus.

Marston asked if this intervention was monetized. If not, then he was skeptical that, even with figures this large, the intervention had much effect on the yen/dollar exchange rate. *Feldstein* agreed that sterilized intervention does not generally matter. He had offered these figures to demonstrate both the magnitude and duration of recent intervention by Japan. But if one believed that foreign governments were prepared to finance the U.S. current account deficit for a sustained period of time, it would seem likely that the dollar would fall more slowly. He pointed out that private investors would be able to swap out of dollar assets if the Bank of Japan were able to finance U.S. deficits indefinitely, however unlikely that possibility may be.

Marston noted that if we were to move to fixed rates, capital controls would be required. First, to reach agreed-upon targets, monetary policy would have to be used. Second, each country would be forced to subordinate its own domestic growth targets. It is unlikely either that the United States would persevere or that other countries would follow U.S. monetary policies in order to preserve the targets. Third, the choice would then be: scrap the reference rates altogether or adapt extensive capital controls. Indeed, even though the Europeans have broadly coordinated their monetary policies, the real secret of the EMS lies in the capital controls on France and Italy. To make target zones work, less financial integration is required.

Attali objected, saying that capital controls need not be so stringent if there is a credible agreement to adjust fundamental policies. Capital controls may not always be unappealing, especially when the alternative is a large increase in protectionism. One should not disregard the gains that accrue merely from putting a credible system of target zones in place. The EMS was built with capital controls and now is strong enough for their removal. An important feature of the EMS is that the cost of getting out of the system is currently higher than the cost of adjusting parities.

Marston noted that each time there is a crisis within the EMS, the Eurofranc interest differential reacts. Thus capital controls buy time to make the necessary adjustments of EMS parities, and in this sense they are essential to the functioning of the system. The reason the EMS cannot be generalized to the rest of the world without far more restrictive capital controls is that other central banks are unlikely to follow the Fed as closely as the Europeans follow the Bundesbank.

De Menil strongly disagreed with this point of view. The interest rate gaps to which Marston referred are temporary. The delay in adjustments is becoming even shorter as capital controls are relaxed. He emphasized that it was incorrect to point toward the EMS as a reason why exchange rate targets cannot work for the world. The EMS works because of the dominance and credibility of German monetary policy in Europe. The capital controls issue is a red herring. If target zones are not successful, it will be for political and not economic reasons.

Carli pointed out that we cannot expect foreign exchange markets to be more orderly unless a more serious attempt is made to regulate financial activities all over the world. If monetary coordination is going to be the centerpiece of a reference zone system, we must guarantee that the monetary authorities have controls over various financial institutions, banks and nonbanks.

Marston added that the EMS is far from a fixed rate system: the French franc has been cumulatively devalued by 38 percent against the Deutsche mark since the inception of the EMS. In his view the main issue is world policy coordination. Without such coordination, capital controls would be needed.

Sachs presented another view. Now, as in earlier episodes, we will get coordination, but this coordination will not be desirable. Most prior attempts at global policy coordination have failed. At the Genoa conference of 1922, there was general agreement about the return to the gold standard. But shortages of gold and poorly chosen parities led to a worldwide shortage of liquidity by the end of the 1920s and was a prelude to the Great Depression. Bretton Woods fared much better partly by historical accident and partly because of the dominance of the U.S. economy at the time. The Smithsonian agreement, however, lasted only fifteen months. During this period the greatest excess of world liquidity since the Potosi silver mine in the sixteenth century led to the collapse of fixed rates. The 1980–81 worldwide monetary tightening was initially hailed as the reversal of this tendency toward excess liquidity. In each of these cases, countries bought into a single set of undiversified monetary policies, and often the policies turned out to be either excessive or wrong. Floating rates provide diversification and can help stagger business cycles across countries. The relatively uneven growth record of the United States over the last decade can be compared with Japan's more even growth. For most of this period, the Japanese did not look to the United States to set their monetary policy. Thus, while there may be some gains to coordination in terms of reducing the volatility of exchange rates, the cost is that all countries must buy into a single set of beliefs, which are sure to be wrong some of the time.

Gains to coordination also depend crucially on the importance of transmission effects across countries. Sachs's research indicates that, under floating rates, monetary policy generates negligible transmission effects, whereas the effects of fiscal policy coordination are large. A monetary expansion depreciates the home currency while increasing income enough to fully offset any positive effects on the trade balance from the depreciation. Divergent monetary policies, therefore, do not require coordination. Given the current situation, Sachs also felt that we do not need coordinated fiscal policies; better fiscal policies would suffice.

Robert Solomon expressed the view that if West Germany joined a reference zone system with the United States in the 1980s, the Bundesbank would have to adapt its policy to the Fed. The German monetary authorities currently exercise great power within the EMS and, consequently, are not very enthusiastic about subordinating their present autonomy to a world target zone system.

With this, *Branson* disagreed. First, he argued that target zones would not have worked in the 1980s because of the U.S. fiscal position, not the reticence of German monetary authorities. If the United States had honored an exchange rate target, a large expansionary monetary policy would have been required in the early 1980s. Such a policy would have been politically unacceptable at that time. Second, target zones would also require coordination of fiscal policies. Branson thought that the literature on optimal currency areas could shed some light on the relative costs of abandoning a system of fixed rates versus changing the parities. There is an old and unresolved debate in economics over whether the whole world ought to be a single currency area. Charles Kindleberger, for example, has argued that the world should be a single area, while Max Corden wonders if Brittany is already too big for a single currency. In practice, however, the distinction is not so clear. A fixed rate system in which the parities are adjusted frequently and costlessly is not really a fixed rate system at all. Finally, Branson responded to a remark made earlier by Anthony Solomon, that many economists such as Paul Krugman and Charles Schultze have predicted that in five years the United States will have balanced merchandise trade, and that this seems to imply that the change will be both rapid and relatively painless. Branson stated that, while many economists are supportive of continued dollar depreciation, they do not believe that it will lead either to an abrupt or painless improvement in the trade balance.

Pratt was asked how multinationals would respond to capital controls. Would each subsidiary be forced to conduct its own financing separately? Pratt responded that this has long been Pfizer's policy. Even in the absence of capital controls, currency risks can most easily be hedged by issuing liabilities denominated in the host-country's currency. *Petty* agreed, adding that since most corporations now treat their financing arms as profit centers, capital controls would have little effect on direct investment. Capital controls are not new, and most multinationals long ago learned how to mitigate the costs such controls impose.

McNamar felt that the day that U.S. trade reaches balance is more than five years off. The capital inflows will persist, partly because institutional investors find little that is attractive in the EC or Japan. There are few new start-ups with prospects for high growth. Indeed, with the dollar depreciation and improving U.S. competitiveness, the U.S. market still looks most attractive. *Greenspan* added that portfolios are already skewed toward dollar-denominated assets, and that foreign residents will stop funding the U.S. current account deficit at some point. Only then will the current account reach balance.

Kunihiro admitted it is often said that the shortage of investment opportunities is responsible for the capital outflow from Japan to New York. There are attempts being made in Japan to resolve this, however, in addition to increasing fiscal spending on social investments. One of these attempts is in so-called third sector participation projects, such as the Konsai Airport, the Tokyo Bay Bridge, and building projects. The government is trying to siphon private money to these public projects, and this strategy is likely to become even more popular. Kunihiro also held that the ranges for exchange rates discussed at the G-7 agreement were in line with fundamentals. In Japan there is concern that further dollar depreciation will lead to inflation and higher interest rates in the United States.

Ruggiero suggested several ways to reduce the present imbalances while maintaining sufficient world growth. First, increases in aggregate demand in West Germany and Japan are needed, but they cannot alone be the solution. An adjustment by the newly industrialized countries would be helpful, but still not sufficient. Without an improvement in the U.S. saving/investment imbalance, we cannot solve our problems. Second, Ruggiero argued that more resources must be made available to LDCs. Third, exchange rates need to be made more stable. To do this, perhaps compatible rather than highly coordinated policies are necessary.

Richardson noted the underlying belief in the discussion so far that exchange rates matter in real economic decisions. He agreed, but recorded several facts that cast doubt on this view. Over several-year periods, exchange rates are not readily correlated with commodity prices, with trade volumes, with overall price levels, or with cross-border capital formation and investment. Perhaps these facts are consequences of the behavior of multinationals as described by Pratt and Blumenthal. Could it be that prudent financial management has made real economic decisions less sensitive to exchange rate fluctuations?

The discussion then turned to the lagging response of the trade balance to the depreciation of the dollar. *Greenspan* noted the very rapid changes in foreign exporter's profit margins. He speculated that more volatile profit margins could be responsible for the recent stubbornness of the trade deficit. *Branson* added that the J-curve is just now starting; during the six quarters following the dollar's peak, import quantities actually increased. *Schultze* commented that in its early stages a depreciation may affect profit margins on inelastic goods disproportionately, so that a small quantity response is observed.

Schultze also reflected on whether an exchange rate commitment could be expected to change policy behavior. He felt that this is a political proposition. To be successful, he argued, it is necessary to coordinate both monetary and fiscal policies. Schultze reiterated his view that the instruments of policy often become goals in themselves. The current U.S. fiscal stance is an excellent illustration. If instruments themselves become goals, a political willingness for and commitment to coordination is essential if coordination is ever to be successful.

Robert Solomon pointed out that our thinking about the J-curve is somewhat simplistic. When parities are fixed, it may be appropriate to ask how a single, discrete devaluation affects the trade balance over time. But the dollar has experienced a continuous two-year depreciation, so that the corresponding J-curve effect is an envelope of simple J-curves. Solomon admitted astonishment that so little had been said during the conference about European unemployment, which is one of the most costly problems confronting the industrialized countries today.

Attali projected into the future. He felt that if the world retains a floating rate system political disaster will result. If, on the other hand, exchange rate target zones are adapted, we will have a recession as the United States makes the necessary adjustment to its trade imbalance.

Carli reflected that global financial markets are outside the control of the authorities. In response, central banks must devise longer term cooperative strategies if sensible exchange rates are to be maintained. In the present circumstances, this will require leading central banks to finance the U.S. current account deficit and to accumulate U.S. assets. Otherwise, Carli felt, the system will collapse.

Feldstein was asked to summarize his views for the Sherpas in the upcoming Economic Summit. He stressed that the key challenge for this Summit meeting is to formulate a strategy that avoids the adverse effects of unwinding the U.S. trade balance deficit. Import quantities have begun to fall, so we have turned the corner. But he stressed that even with public sector support, sufficient funding for the current account deficit at the current level of the dollar will not be forthcoming. Instead, the dollar must depreciate enough to eliminate the trade deficit, and this will require a further 20 percent fall in its value. Feldstein noted that surplus countries, such as Japan, which has a current account surplus of over 3 percent of GNP, will sustain substantial damage unless domestic demand fills the void. With this situation as a background, he made three recommendations. First, the U.S. budget must be cut, and here not enough progress has been made. But regardless of the fiscal situation, the trade deficit will fall. In the not-so-distant future, the United States will have to run a trade balance surplus to service its external debt. Second, immediate steps must be taken to expand monetary and fiscal policy in West Germany and Japan. Governments need to anticipate the ultimate effects of the current exchange rate change. Third, expansion in West Germany and Japan is not an alternative to a decline of the dollar. Expansion is to maintain or increase employment in Europe and Japan, while the dollar must fall to achieve external balance. It would be a mistake if the Summit repeats the message from the Louvre agreement that the dollar has already reached an appropriate level. Such a message will encourage the wrong kinds of macro policies in the surplus countries. A falling dollar will help remind these countries that there will be further pain from current account adjustments in the absence of more stimulative macroeconomic policies.

3 Trade Policy

1. J. David Richardson
2. Robert S. Strauss
3. Michihiko Kunihiro
4. Edmund T. Pratt, Jr.

1. J. David Richardson
International Coordination of Trade Policy

3.1 Introduction and Overview

The post–World War II record of sovereign governments coordinating their international trade policies is really quite impressive. Yet it seems recently to have lost the luster that characterized its early life. Some recent initiatives have seemed to cartelize rather than liberalize. Others have failed to achieve coordination of any kind, dissolving in disarray. Fears cannot easily be calmed that the conventions and structures of postwar trade policy coordination are crumbling. Open hostility, military metaphors, and an air of frontier vigilantism are today quite common in trade policy discussions.

International trade policy coordination has clearly become more difficult. The postwar hegemonic environment has evolved into a more general strategic environment with several influential governments and blocs. New patterns of initiative and response have been slow to develop. New temptations have arisen for governments to abandon seemingly outdated conventions of cooperation, causing the system to retreat toward uncoordinated hostility. The growth of administered protection, aggressive reciprocity, and selectivity all illustrate this evolution.

International trade policy coordination is further complicated by economic developments. Some make a country's comparative advantage increasingly sensitive to sectoral predation by others, especially through subsidies and performance requirements aimed at multinational firms. Workers and others correspondingly bear the burdens of sharper adjustments and look to government to turn its trade policy narrowly inward in order to ease their load. Such "domestication" of trade policy is the antithesis of international coordination.

167

What changes might restore the liberalizing impetus of postwar trade policy coordination at its best? Several are considered in this paper. One is to extend the "Codes" approach to multilateral negotiations under the General Agreement on Tariffs and Trade (GATT). The Subsidies Code in particular seems ripe for refining, and ideas for development of a Safeguards Code are assessed. Standing GATT committees, with representative membership and regular meetings, are discussed, as are several ways that their independent leadership might be enhanced. A case is made that European and Japanese capacity to *initiate* coordinated liberalization is much greater and more promising than is generally acknowledged, as is that of even quite small countries in "minilateral" settings. Discreet preferential coordination is viewed as a way to rebuild trust and to write new rules and establish new precedents in administrative trade policy—rules and precedents that could eventually come to be accepted even by currently combative countries.

Many reflections in this paper are framed in categories from recent economic thinking about policy coordination in "strategic" environments—those with small numbers of self-consciously interdependent agents. I am hopeful that commentators on this paper will provide balancing admixtures of complementary perspective, institutional detail (e.g., beyond GATT), and operational feasibility. They will no doubt also provide important insights on other trade policy issues, not all of which concern coordination. Readers with limited interest in an introduction to strategic perspectives should find it easy to skim section 3.2 and read section 3.3 with more care.

At the cost of lengthening the discourse, I have tried to make it minimally "acronomyous." Thus I have resisted adopting IPC (eye-pick), ITPC (it-pick), and NITPC (nit-pick) as shorthand for international (trade) policy coordination or lack thereof. At the cost of exposing my ignorance, I have tried to draw a few insights from game theory, political science, history, and law. The nature of the topic seemed to compel it. I suspect I will be thanked for the first; I hope I can be forgiven for the second.

3.2   Postwar Trade Policy Coordination in Strategic Perspective

It seems quite natural to address a paper on economic coordination to international trade policy. It is a border policy that discriminates between foreign and domestic residents in goods and services transactions. Thus it always involves at least two countries and governments. There are many varieties of trade policy. Free trade is properly understood as the absence of any domestic/foreign discrimination (not the absence of government regulation), and national treatment as the absence of any added discrimination once border barriers have been "cleared." Most-favored-nation (MFN) treatment is the absence of discrimination among foreign residents of differing nationalities, and tariffs are discriminatory taxes.

Because trade policy always involves choices concerning international discrimination, it is fitting to ask about trade policy coordination, or its lack. Rules, aggression, unfair treatment, and similar terms all have natural usefulness in discussing trade policy.

At first blush, monetary and fiscal policies seem different from trade policy; they are really not. Monetary, fiscal, and trade policies all have discriminatory border effects that are quite similar. Monetary structure is a quintessential border policy, delineating regions of differing legal tender. Many taxes fall on residents of one country but not others. The ratio of government to private purchases can affect an economy's internal price ratio of domestic to foreign goods just like trade policy, because government purchases are usually concentrated on domestic goods. These similarities suggest that students of trade policy coordination and students of macroeconomic policy coordination have lessons to learn from each other.[1]

3.2.1 Retrospective Insights from a Simple Structure

The word "coordinate" is defined by Webster as "to bring into a common action, movement, or condition: regulate and combine in harmonious action: HARMONIZE." The key words in the definition suggest interdependence and mutuality. When applied to trade policy, the idea of coordination suggests both that each country's government fashions its policy conscious of its effect on other governments' trade policies and that the intended outcome is mutually advantageous to all.

Interdependence and mutuality are hardly revolutionary traits. They have permeated the past forty years of trade agreements among governments, most significantly under GATT. Interdependence and mutuality grew out of abhorrence of the consequences of world economic war followed by full-scale world war.[2]

Today there is a malaise that interdependence and mutuality are being abandoned world-wide, especially in the United States. Interdependent consciousness is on the defensive ("other countries be damned, we've got to *do something* about our trade deficit"), and mutuality is waning ("we've let ourselves passively be pushed around long enough; now it's time to teach those guys a lesson").

Are there good reasons for malaise? Is the future for trade policy coordination quite bleak? If so, is that so bad?

It is remarkable that the most familiar economic apparatus for analyzing trade policy is ill-suited for answering these questions because it applies to perfectly competitive environments with independent governments. Coordination questions arise only in "strategic environments." These insights were obscured in the early postwar period by the dominance of the United States in global trade. Yet even that period can be instructively described from strategic perspectives (see section 3.3.1).

Strategic environments are those in which the number of economic agents making interdependent decisions is relatively small. Each agent takes into account some counterresponse from rivals in calculating its best course of action. Actions include threats and promises, bluster and bluff, collaboration and commitment, all aimed at influencing the outcome of an endeavor toward one's own objectives. These are familiar features of games, war, and policy coordination. They have little place in the environment traditionally employed by economists to analyze trade policy.

In the perfectly competitive environment, each of many agents considers itself too small to influence market outcomes and, therefore, too small to be noticed. Each, therefore, makes choices assuming that all rivals' variables are given. Governments in the traditional framework are independent. They presume that their policies affect market equilibrium but do not account for the way that they may affect the behavior of other governments.[3] When agents take their rivals' actions to be immutable, strategic behavior plays no role, and coordination cannot even be characterized. Furthermore, there are only weak analytical defenses for trade policy of any sort except free trade.

Thus the analysis of policy coordination must begin in strategic environments.[4] The "prisoner's dilemma" model of table 3.1 is a primitive strategic environment from which to draw some simple first insights about historic trade policy coordination. One is that uncoordinated trade policy—policy that independently takes other countries' policy strategies as given—can lead to an outcome that, although rationally

Table 3.1   Gains and Losses from Alternative Trade Policies in a "Prisoner's Dilemma" Model

	"Their" Nation's Trade Policy	
"Our" Nation's Trade Policy	Cooperative Initiative (reciprocally liberalize)	Noncooperative Initiative (actively protect or promote)
Cooperative Initiative (reciprocally liberalize)	+ 1 for us + 1 for them	− 2 for us + 3 for them
Noncooperative Initiative (actively protect or promote)	+ 3 for us − 2 for them	− 1 for us − 1 for them

chosen, is unfortunate in the retrospective evaluation of each government. Each would prefer the cooperative outcome, but some form of coordination is necessary to attain and maintain it, specifically some communication and guarantee that each government will "play" the cooperative initiative and not "cheat." Without such a guarantee, uncoordinated national self-interest suggests that each government play noncooperatively. Each will be better off whether rival governments do the same ("we" would lose -1 instead of -2) or try to cooperate (we gain 3 instead of 1). Without coordination the grim outcome is trade war, well illustrated by the early 1930s.

The outcome of uncoordinated policy is less grim in a *succession* of encounters like that modeled in table 3.1. Experience and analysis show that a good uncoordinated trade policy strategy (called "tit for tat") is to play cooperatively unless cheated, then to retaliate (play noncooperatively), but only once until cheated again.[5] Nevertheless, it is obvious that a succession of coordinated cooperative outcomes would be even better for each country than "tit for tat," or certainly no worse. Thus coordination still looks desirable for the richer, dynamic version of this model.

The past forty years provide many illustrations of both the apparent desirability of coordination and what helps to attain it.

Coordination Compacts

GATT is a fine illustration of a compact in which governments coordinate by: (1) negotiating rules of cooperative play (e.g., "fair trade"), defining noncoordination (e.g., "nullification and impairment") and potential penalties for noncooperation (e.g., compensation, retaliation); and (2) exchanging pledges of cooperative behavior (by becoming signatories) and agreeing thereby to consult and ultimately to accept the stipulated penalties if they violate their pledge. Penalties for noncoop-

Table 3.2	**"Gains" and "Losses" from Alternative Trade Policies with a Hostile Opponent for the *Same* Prisoner's Dilemma Model**	
	"Their" Nation's Trade Policy	
"Our" Nation's Trade Policy	Cooperative Initiative (reciprocally liberalize)	Noncooperative Initiative (actively protect or promote)
Cooperative Initiative (reciprocally liberalize)	+ 1 for us 0 for them	− 2 for us + 5 for them
Noncooperative Initiative (actively protect or promote)	+ 3 for us − 5 for them	− 1 for us 0 for them

eration are complemented by rewards for cooperation, often involving redistribution (side payments) of the collective gains. In GATT such redistribution is reflected in the principle of reciprocity introduced in its Preamble (in practice, the value of concessions offered and advantages received should be approximately equal) and also in the major exception to that principle (developing countries are freed from strict reciprocity in order to redistribute gains toward them—implicitly the side payment for their continued cooperation).

In brief, GATT is a compact that establishes communication and conventions to facilitate coordination. A tighter compact might also have established an institution that monitors and/or polices trade policy, with independent power to reward cooperation and penalize noncooperation. This GATT is *not*, except for very limited monitoring. It contrasts with the International Monetary Fund (IMF), which is a quasi-independent (yet representative) institution with greater ability to monitor (surveillance)[6] and limited powers to police (quota requirements, interest charges and payments, conditionality, limits on cumulative access). Had the International Trade Organization (ITO) not been aborted in 1950 (see Diebold 1952), the institutional support for trade policy coordination might be closer today to that for monetary coordination. (Whether this would necessarily be a "good" thing is another question entirely and will be addressed below.)

Common Objectives

Communication, conventions, compacts, and coordinating institutions come about only if there is enough mutual agreement among governments on objectives. Such agreement might be said to be a primordial condition for coordination devices to be attractive (see Cooper 1986, 1987) and was quite influential in the postwar design of GATT. Governments were nearly unanimous in their attraction to cooperative outcomes.[7]

This impetus for coordination can vanish, however, if mutuality of objectives is undermined, as may be happening today. The structure of table 3.1 provides a simple illustration. Suppose "their" government were to become determinedly hostile to "ours," even to the point of valuing our loss as much as their gain.[8] The implied objective for them would become the difference in their payoff and ours in table 3.1: $+3 - (-2)$, $-1 - (-1)$, $-2 - (+3)$, and $+1 - (+1)$, moving clockwise from the northeast quadrant. The new payoff matrix is given in table 3.2. Its innovation is that there is no longer any attraction for the hostile government to choose cooperative trade over trade war. Perceived gains are 0 in either case. Coordination may be infeasible because it takes two to make peace, but only one to break it.

The difference-in-objectives problem obviously grows worse if both governments are hostile toward each other.[9] Then goals are inconsistent, and neither government sees any attraction in coordinating. Trade wars like the 1930s are more enduring than under simple uncoordinated policy because they cannot be shaken by any mere provision of information, institutional reform, encouragement, or exhortation. What is needed before these devices can be used is stabilization of hostility (cease-fire), then reconciliation if possible—ideas that are reflected in the GATT principles of "standstill" and "rollback." Without genuine standstill and rollback, coordination for mutual gain is as impossible among hostile trade negotiators as it was between the Hatfields and McCoys![10]

One general lesson of postwar coordination is that it is very tough among agents with different objectives and may be impossible among agents with inconsistent objectives. A corollary is that momentum toward coordination can be maintained by limiting the scope for cooperative initiative to like-minded trading partners, thereby isolating hostile ones.[11] Correspondingly, an organization of sufficiently hostile governments can easily become paralyzed with an inadequate constituency for any attempt to reclaim or enhance coordination. The view that GATT has reached this point is evaluated below.

Common Structural Understanding

Agreement on objectives is, in turn, possible only if there is sufficient common understanding among governments on the payoffs to alternative trade policy initiatives and, therefore, on the structure of world trade that links policy to payoffs. Such common understanding might be said to be a "pre-primordial" condition for coordination devices to be attractive.

In this regard, it is sobering to consider how ill-developed is professional consensus on empirical models of global trade patterns and the effects of trade policy—ill-developed even in comparison to empirical models of global macroeconomics (e.g., the IMF's multilateral exchange rate model), which are widely acknowledged to have their own distinct problems. It is arresting to learn from macroeconomic research, such as Frankel (1986) and Frankel and Rockett (1986), that when models differ across participants, policy coordination *fails* to improve macroeconomic performance almost as often as it succeeds. Similarly arresting is Baldwin and Clarke's (1985) finding that *non*cooperative solutions to conflict over alternative Tokyo Round tariff-cutting formulae seemed superior for all protagonists to the compromise formula that actually emerged from coordinated negotiation.[12]

3.2.2 Deeper Dimensions of Postwar Trade Policy Coordination

Trade policy coordination is, of course, much more subtle and complex than suggested in the preceding account. There are at least four deeper dimensions: scope, virtue, instrument, and motive force.

Scope

Prospects for trade policy coordination and its outcome depend very much on its scope. Scope has three important variants. *Geographical* scope determines which governments are involved, whether coordination is multilateral, "minilateral," or bilateral—involving all trading partners, some, or only one.

Mutuality/hostility, as described above, is one criterion for determining the most promising geographical scope for coordination efforts. It also influences the choice of *substantive* scope and *sectoral* scope— what issues are to be covered, and for what sectors. Postwar trade policy coordination has emphasized trade in manufactured commodities, in part because trade in agriculture, services, corporate capital (e.g., investment, rights of establishment), and labor effort (e.g., immigration, guest workers) were inflammatory by comparison. Coordination was pursued on substance and in sectors where mutuality was feasible; substance and sectors where hostility reigned were isolated. By comparison to postwar trends, mutuality seems more feasible today for trade in some services, some corporate capital, and perhaps certain agricultural sectors. But international hostility seems to have grown in standardized labor-intensive manufactures such as textiles/apparel and basic metals.

Another criterion for determining the most promising scope for coordination is the "fluidity of side payments," how easy it is to exchange concessions on one issue with one trading partner for advantages on another issue with another trading partner. Recent trade policy coordination has employed two principles to enhance fluidity. One is across-the-board bargaining, with limited exceptions lists, which allows for concessions and advantages to be exchanged fluidly from sector to sector. An older principle is nondiscrimination (as defined by MFN, concessions must be offered to *all* trading partners, not just some), which allows for "inequities" in some bilateral tally of concessions and advantages to be offset fluidly by "windfalls" in some other.[13] It is obvious how important it is for fluid side payments to have common understanding among governments on payoffs and the underlying structure (model) of trade, as described above. Otherwise measures of concessions and advantages are wildly different among participants.

There is unavoidable tension between these criteria for scope. Caution to avoid hostile undermining of coordination encourages narrow scope; concern to lubricate the distribution of benefits from coordination encourages wide scope. Deep pockets capable of making lots of change sometime disintegrate from its weight.[14]

Virtue

Policy coordination by itself may have little value independent of its "virtue." The case for coordination is probably strongest where the case for policy intervention itself is strongest and weaker elsewhere. Thus, in public health (Cooper 1986), where externalities and international spillovers are clear and even quantifiable, the case for coordination is strong. In influencing the sectoral/industrial structure, however, where the case for government policy is less universally acknowledged, the case for coordination is weaker. This perspective may help to explain why the IMF found readier approval in the United States after World War II than did the ITO; there was readier approval at that time of an active role for government in macroeconomics than in microeconomics.

This lesson has been blurred in recent commentary on trade policy. There is an unwarranted tendency to believe that international policy coordination is by its very nature "good" and to neglect the possibility that uncoordinated unilateral policy may be "better." Virtue and coordination do not necessarily go hand in hand.[15] Language alone provides a way to appreciate this. Almost any outcome described as coordinated or cooperative could also be described as collusive. Almost any outcome described as uncoordinated (or chaotic!) could be described as competitive. Exactly the same formal structure supports types of coordination of very different timbre: coordination that signals harmonious forums full of respectful give-and-take in the mutual pursuit of noble goals; and collusion that sounds like closed, mean-spirited cartels which victims deride as vicious old-boy networks. It is all too easy to slip into the benign belief that the objective of government is the "public good," so that coordinated pursuit of that good is good in itself and to be desired. It is all too easy to forget public choice and other grounds for skepticism that government's objectives are prima facie good, on which coordinated pursuit of dubious objectives becomes doubly dubious.[16]

Postwar trade policy provides many illustrations. A traditional defense of MFN treatment is that it constrains the formation of predatory and other "bad" coalitions (coordinations) of trading partners; legitimate customs unions and free trade areas are, however, excused from MFN because these coalitions are on balance "good" (liberalizing). It is arguable that international policy coordination has been just as thorough and strong in the recent cartelization of global steel trade and the market-sharing negotiated under successive Multi-Fiber Arrangements as it was in the Toyko, Kennedy, and earlier rounds of GATT-sponsored trade negotiations. Voluntary export restraints are bilateral examples of deliberalizing coordination. Their ambiguous name has merit, though; they do involve a side payment (compensation) to the "offending" parties in order to maintain coordination—the implicit "quota rents" (Deardorff 1986). Although deliberalizing, they are nevertheless cooperative and thus not as hostile as a unilateral protective counter against an import surge.

Concerns about virtue would be mere fretting if the size of the gains or losses from coordination were small.[17] Some empirical research seems to suggest that these gains and losses are indeed small. Deardorff and Stern (1984) find that the economic welfare gains from the elimination of all post–Tokyo Round tariffs are infinitesimal. Whalley (1985, 180–84) finds that the gains from elimination of tariffs and all other deliberalizing post–Tokyo Round trade barriers are less than 0.5 percent of world income. Kreinin (1974, chap. 3) estimates the gains to the original six members of the European Economic Community (EEC) as around 1.5 percent of their 1970 national income, but MacBean and Snowden (1981, chap. 8) find the estimate diminished as the EEC expanded to nine members due to losses from the Common Agricultural Policy (itself arguably an example of deliberalizing coordination).

These calculations are misleadingly small estimates, however, of the gains from *maintaining* the status-quo level of coordination relative to trade war. They estimate instead the difference between the status quo and free trade. If the real status quo is far to the right along a continuum running from "trade war" to "free trade," then the measured gains to further "virtuous" coordination will be small, but the potential losses from failure of existing coordination or from extreme deliberalizing coordination might be huge. In the famous (infamous?) bicycle metaphor of trade policy coordination, there may be little additional momentum to squeeze into a bicycle cruising reasonably close to its maximum speed, but a great deal of momentum to lose if the bicycle were to fall down. Or, it's a long way down the slippery slope to the valley when you're close to the peak.

Whalley (1985), in fact, estimates both kinds of gains and losses. His very rough calculations of the losses from trade war relative to status-quo coordination appear in table 3.3. They are surprisingly large, especially for Europe and Japan; five to ten times larger than the gains to be achieved from further "virtuous" coordination.

For reasons described in section 3.3, *preserving* the virtue of current coordination is the modern trade policy challenge, not *perfecting* it. Table 3.3 suggests that this challenge does indeed have quantitative importance for the entire world.

Instrument

Another deeper dimension of trade policy coordination is the choice of instruments relied on to encourage it. Here the most important

Table 3.3   **Percent of GNP Lost due to Multilateral Trade Wars**[a]

	All Trading Areas Adopt	
	60% Tariff[b]	"First Step" Optimal Tariff[b,c]
United States	0.4	2.3
European Community	2.2	5.9
Japan	2.2	5.9
Rest of World	0.1	1.5

Source: Whalley (1985, 248).

[a]Average of compensating variations (CV) and equivalent variations (EV).

[b]Rates assessed to all imports in presence of existing nontariff barriers and factor taxes.

[c]Apparent optimal tariff against the aggregate of all other trading regions assuming no retaliation.

distinction is between rules and discretion. At one extreme the compacts of coordination may attempt to legislate meticulous rules that the institutions of coordination correspondingly adjudicate. At the other extreme, the compacts may simply specify regular meetings for communication that the institutions convene and inform. Policy coordination via the Bank for International Settlements and the June summit meetings have the latter spirit; GATT historically has the former.

Reliance on rules makes most sense when issues and policies can be reasonably defined and measured. Otherwise rules require immense resources to draft and monitor and can easily appear arbitrary and inequitable. Discretion, discussion, diplomacy, and entreaty are often more productive and cost-effective when issues and policies are hard to define and measure.[18] In this light one can interpret GATT's historic rules-centeredness as fitting the historic reliance of the world on objectively measurable tariffs and quotas. GATT tariff bindings are in fact an excellent example of a rule aimed at avoiding surreptitious cheating on the compacts of coordination. (Such rules are known as "credible precommitments" in the language of strategic policy coordination.) One can correspondingly defend the more consultative flavor of the Tokyo Round's codes for nontariff measures as fitting the world's relative shift toward administrative policy instruments (see table 3.7 and the surrounding discussion).

It is instructive along these lines to wonder if the Toyko Round code dealing with the most measurable nontariff measure, subsidies, has been generally regarded as the least successful code precisely because it could have gone further toward definition, measurement, and rules. The problems of common objectives and structural understanding, discussed above, are admittedly severe in coordinating rules on subsidies. Yet in the absence of coordination, unilateral attempts to define, measure, and countervail them seem inevitable (Shuman and Verrill 1984). The idea of a coordinated defining and "binding" of subsidies, much as tariffs are "bound" in the GATT, is considered below.

Motive Force

Impetus is another aspect of policy coordination not captured in simple accounts. Coordination can be imposed, agreed, or implicitly chosen, with varying implications along a continuum that joins them. Coordination is *imposed* when weaker, smaller, or less-skilled agents harmonize their policies with those of a strong, large, or skilled agent, which tailors its policy to elicit policy response among the followers that furthers its own goals. Coordination is *agreed* when enough consensus exists on objectives and structure among agents of comparable strength that they negotiate a compact. Coordination can be *implicitly chosen* even in the absence of a compact (or with an ineffective one) when agents recognize at least some gain from mutually cooperative outcomes and some penalty from cheating, as in the concept of implicit collusion among oligopolistic producers. In this light, early GATT coordination of trade policy might illustrate the imposing force of a hegemonic United States; Kennedy Round coordination might illustrate explicit agreement among equals; and current coordination might illustrate the kind of implicit impetus that is maintained solely by tenuous conjectures of gains "if we all keep cooperating" and penalties "if I defect." The stability of the coordination seems greatest when imposed and weakest when implicit. However, its "representativeness"—its reflection of the collective objectives of participants—may be greatest when it is agreed or negotiated among equals.

Among other things, this implies a potential opportunity in the future for atypical participants to initiate fruitful ideas for enhancing coordination. The United States may today be in a better position to respond to cooperating, coordinating ideas from abroad (e.g., from Israel, Canada, Japan, Mexico) than to initiate them itself. We turn in the next section to prospects such as this in the midst of changing environments for trade policy coordination.

3.3 Changing Environments and Prospects for Coordination of Trade Policy

The environment for trade policy coordination today is quite different than in the early post–World War II period when many enduring conventions of coordination were established under the GATT.

In the policy environment for coordination, the most significant changes have been the leveling out of influence among national governments relative to U.S. dominance in the early postwar period and the development of new administrative instruments of trade policy to replace the limitations that the GATT successfully coordinated for tariffs. In the economic environment for coordination, the most significant change has been the growth of large, mobile corporations that themselves practice coordination across borders. They are multinational in both operations and ownership. In the intellectual environment, these changes have been captured in the development of an analysis of trade policy coordination in strategic environments—those with small numbers of large rival firms and/or governments—that has challenged insights from the venerable competitive consensus.

These environmental changes interact with each other. Multinational corporations make it harder for any government to define and pursue its "own" national interest. Returns to the "capital endowment" that a country's residents own depend on revenue from far-flung foreign affiliates as well as revenue from home. Discriminatory border policies that increase revenue from one source at the expense of another have ambiguous effects on "our" multinational firms and their owners. Firms that are largely "ours" (majority-owned) may nevertheless pay significant fractions of their revenues to foreign shareholders. Strategic influence over the location and competitiveness of large, mobile multinationals is an understandably important objective of modern trade policy and leads to concerns about market access and administrative instruments such as performance requirements, tax incentives, and unitary tax systems. The sensitivity of firms to these policies aggravates the adjustment problems faced by owners of immobile factors of production—narrowly skilled workers, farmers, civil servants. Such groups are not internationally coordinated but may be large and coordinated internally (e.g., labor unions). Trade policies that protect and insure them, or that help them adjust to shifting sectoral prosperity, have a very different orientation than trade policies that expand markets abroad for exporting and multinational firms, insuring their right of establishment and fair competition. A country's own internal policy coordination can be undermined by a schizophrenia in which departments of commerce and ministries of industry promote "competitiveness"-enhancing trade policies while departments of agriculture and ministries of labor promote protectionist trade policies. International policy coordination is all the more difficult when large internal trade policy constituencies are uncoordinated or hostile.[19]

The following subsections describe these environmental changes in more detail and trace their implications for trade policy coordination.

3.3.1 Shifts in the Policy Environment

Policy environments have evolved (devolved?) since the 1950s and early 1960s. Strategic interaction among governments has come to reflect shifts in relative economic size and influence. New instruments, institutions, and principles of strategic policy interaction have emerged.

Relative National Strengths

For many reasons, dominant trade policy leadership fell to the United States early after World War II.[20] Its economy was least devastated by the war. Its military forces spearheaded resistance to Soviet expansion and played important roles in European and Japanese economic reconstruction. It vetoed the multilaterally planned ITO (Diebold 1952) in favor of a compact of its narrow commercial provisions, which became the GATT, more U.S.-patterned than the ITO would have been.

In strategic terms, this was a period of hegemonic interaction. Governments of relatively weak countries did not behave strategically. They tended to take U.S. trade policies as given and to adopt whatever trade policies seemed best for themselves without perceiving much scope for influencing the United States thereby. U.S. incentives were to act strategically, but in a unique way. The United States tended to choose trade initiatives mindful of collective foreign response, such as in its encouragement of European economic integration. But it could afford to be impassively obliging toward recalcitrance or provocation by single trading partners because the impacts were relatively small. This unusual combination of multilateral strategizing and bilateral impassiveness is similar to what one might expect from a large firm in an industry with a fringe of small perfect competitors. The large firm will be strategically calculating toward the aggregated collection of competitors but will appear unflappable toward isolated deviance.

Two things change if small agents in hegemonic environments grow significantly relative to the hegemon. They begin to act strategically toward the hegemon, seeking to press advantage and avoid its perceived "exploitation"; the hegemon no longer finds their provocations too minor to warrant response.

All this seems to have characterized the trade policy environment of the past forty years. First Europe and then Japan (and even several other countries) have grown relative to the United States in key indicators of economic influence. Patterns for two such indicators are illustrated in tables 3.4 and 3.5.[21] Such newly influential governments have begun to shape their trade policy strategically, attentive to U.S. response (e.g., Tokyo Round tariff-cutting initiatives by the EEC). And the U.S. government has become much more mindful of the domestic injury caused by "unfair" trade practices among its large trading partners and consequently has become much more active in legislating trade policy remedies. Figure 3.1 reveals the rise in unfair trade activity (bottom panel) relative to escape clause activity (top panel), which has actually fallen. Table 3.6 shows the recent acceleration of U.S. trade legislation, much of which is aimed at "redressing inequity."

Table 3.4   Ratio: National Real GDP per Capita[a] to the Equivalent for the Aggregate of the Ten Countries in the Table

Year	Brazil	Mexico	Korea	India	Japan	U.S.	Germany	France	U.K.	Italy
1953	0.416	0.691	0.309	0.220	0.619	2.963	1.464	1.473	1.751	0.961
1963	0.479	0.787	0.307	0.195	1.017	2.633	1.944	1.714	1.698	1.269
1973	0.570	0.825	0.454	0.156	1.703	2.543	2.059	1.969	1.630	1.343
1977	0.657	0.857	0.574	0.163	1.711	2.511	1.996	2.030	1.579	1.454
1983	0.595	0.955	0.956	0.158	2.009	2.560	1.835	1.867	2.010	1.583
1984	0.535	0.855	0.989	0.155	2.074	2.744	1.756	1.706	1.840	1.560

Sources: Real GDP per capita: 1953, 1963, 1973, 1977 from Kravis, Heston, and Summers (1982, 330–36); 1983, 1984 from World Bank (1985, 1986) with data spliced to Kravis, Heston, and Summers data in the following manner: table entry = $y^* \cdot k/p$,

where y^* = GNP per capita in 1983 or 1984 dollars (World Bank 1985, 1986);

  k = Ratio of Kravis, Heston, Summers figure for 1975

  $\dfrac{\text{real GDP per capita to World Bank figure for 1975}}{\text{GNP per capita}}$

  p = 1983 or 1984 deflator for U.S. GNP assuming 1975 = 1.00, from IMF, *International Financial Statistics Yearbook*, 1986, pp. 690–91.

Population: 1953[b], 1963, 1973 from U.S. Bureau of the Census (1980); 1977, 1983, 1984 from World Bank (1979, 1985, 1986).

[a]In 1975 dollar prices.
[b]Average 1950–1955.

Table 3.5   **Percent Share of Exports in Aggregate Exports of the Ten Countries in the Table**

Year	Brazil	Mexico	Korea	India	Japan	U.S.	Germany	France	U.K.	Italy
1953	4.1	1.6	0.1	2.9	3.4	41.8	11.7	10.6	19.9	4.0
1963	1.9	1.3	0.1	2.2	7.5	32.0	20.0	11.2	16.8	6.9
1973	2.2	0.8	1.1	1.0	13.2	25.4	24.1	13.1	11.1	7.9
1977	2.3	0.9	1.9	1.2	15.5	23.2	22.6	12.5	11.2	8.7
1983	2.6	2.5	2.9	1.1	17.5	23.4	19.8	11.1	10.7	8.5
1984	3.0	2.7	3.2	1.0	18.6	23.8	18.8	10.7	10.3	8.0

Source: IMF, *International Financial Statistics Yearbook,* 1981 and 1985 issues.

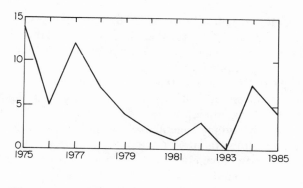

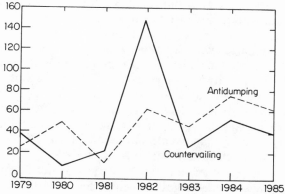

Fig. 3.1 Trends in U.S. import relief (Section 201) and unfair trade remedies. *Top panel:* Escape clause investigations, 1975–85. *Bottom panel:* Countervailing duty and antidumping investigations, 1979–85. *Source:* Destler (1986, 124, based on appendix B).

Table 3.6 **Number of Trade Bills Introduced in Various U.S. Congresses (percentage change over previous Congress)**

Congress (years)	Destler (1986) Count[a]		Ahearn (1986) Count[b]	
96th (1979–80)	62	—	1089	—
97th (1981–82)	56	(−10%)	1150	(−6%)
98th (1983–84)	57	(+2%)	1401	(+22%)
99th (1985–86)	93[c]	(+60%)	1758[d]	(+25%)

Sources: Destler (1986, 75–76), Ahearn (1986).

[a]Counts bills whose primary purpose was to restrict trade or benefit U.S. producers.

[b]Counts bills employing twenty trade-related terms, some to expand trade, some to protect, with various shades based on personal evaluation.

[c]Growth rate between January-September of 1985 and January-September of 1983 applied to number of bills introduced to 98th Congress: (49/30) × 57.

[d]1985 figure times 2.

Instead of being analogous to an industry with one large firm facing a fringe of small competitors, the trade policy environment today is closer to a genuine oligopoly with a small number of large "coequals."

This has many implications:

1. It suggests that trade policy coordination cannot feasibly be imposed but must be either explicitly negotiated ("agreed" in the language of section 3.2.2) or implicitly adhered to. The United States can no longer dictate the timing, agenda, or formulae for multilateral trade liberalization, as illustrated by comparing the outcomes of GATT ministerial meetings in November 1982 and September 1986 to those prior to the Kennedy Round in 1963 (Baldwin 1986a, 5–12).

2. It suggests that *any* of the coequal governments can initiate trade policy coordination, not just the historic "leader."[22] In fact, if the historic leader is nursing a sense of injustice and grievance over lost ("stolen") influence, with sporadic withdrawal and "lashing out" as in interpersonal conflict, then it might enhance the chance of success for coordinating initiative to be reversed. The United States may, today in particular, be better able to respond cooperatively to cooperative initiatives abroad than to defend taking cooperative initiative itself.[23] The posture implied for governments in Europe and Japan is more aggressively inviting than usual; that implied for the U.S. government is more "seductively responsive" than usual.[24]

3. It suggests that if trade policy leadership is not adequately forthcoming from newly coequal governments, there may be reason to invest "independent agents" with specified leadership functions. Such functions might include monitoring, reporting, and initiating meetings (and perhaps even complaints). Suggestions range from radical to mild. Some favor restructuring the GATT institutionally to resemble the IMF (Camps and Diebold 1983, 59–67).[25] Others suggest merely the creation of an Independent Trade Policy Committee ("serviced by the GATT Secretariat"; GATT Wisemen's Report 1985, 42) or a permanent negotiating committee (Aho and Aronson 1985, 48). The aim of all such suggestions is to facilitate leadership impetus and provision of accurate information, both crucial to maintaining policy coordination and avoiding devolution into disarray and possibly trade war.

4. It suggests the advent of discriminatory trade policy coalitions. A coalition is coordination of limited scope among a subset of trading partners over (perhaps) a subset of issues. It is a natural occurrence in strategic interaction among coequals and is by its nature discriminatory (*not* MFN). A hegemonic environment by its nature provides no motive for coalitions either for the large agent or for the many small ones. These insights seem little appreciated in recent discussions. Today's trade policy environment is *structurally* conducive to coalitions and hostile to MFN, whereas the postwar hegemonic environment was

the opposite. The difficult question is whether conservation efforts aimed at preserving the life of this endangered animal (MFN) are still worthwhile, or whether inevitable extinction should be hastened in an effort to breed species more at home in today's jungle!

5. It suggests that if implicit trade policy coordination is followed, (see section 3.2.2) then periods of cooperation may be punctuated by periods of "punishment" for perceived policy violation with, of course, counterretaliation and symptoms of trade war.[26] Difficult technical questions involve how the probability and duration of such periods vary with asymmetries in the size of the agents involved or with the size of the parties or coalitions being "punished,"[27] and what sort of dispute-settlement mechanisms most predictably restore the peace of implicit coordination.

New Instruments, Institutions, and Principles

Administered intervention. Every coordination compact is at risk because of the constant temptation for each rival to try surreptitiously to avoid the constraints on behavior, that is, to "cheat" secretly on one's partner-rivals.

This instability can be seen in the growth of "administered intervention" aimed surreptitiously at undoing the effects of GATT-coordinated reductions in tariff bindings. Administered intervention is flexible, discretionary decision-making toward opaque nontax instruments of import protection and export promotion. It includes voluntary export restraints, orderly marketing agreements, standards, licensing, and internal distribution barriers to imports, as well as performance requirements, tax forgiveness, credit guarantees, and implicit subsidies of many types for exports.

Whalley (1985) provides a striking way to illustrate the significance of administered intervention. In estimating the welfare effects of complete removal of both tariffs and nontariff barriers to imports, he finds the latter to account for more than half of the estimated effects. His calculations are summarized in table 3.7.[28] According to them, administered intervention affects the exports and imports of Japan the most and the United States the least.

One implication of the greater use of administered intervention is intricacy. It becomes harder to identify foreign policies, much less measure their effects. It also becomes harder to implement one's own trade objectives. Intricacy raises the resource cost of estimating and monitoring, and slows down trade policymaking. In the United States, administrative intervention in trade, unlike tariffs, invades the turfs of regulatory agencies, congressional oversight committees, and sometimes even the judiciary.

Table 3.7	Nontariff Barrier Share of Own-Country Welfare Effect from Unilateral Abolition of all Protection[a] (post–Tokyo Round)	
	Four-Region Model	Seven-Region Model
United States	42 to 57 percent	40 to 47 percent
European Community	52 to 62 percent	56 to 62 percent
Japan	58 to 75 percent	53 to 69 percent

Source: Whalley (1985, 181–82).

[a]Low number in each cell assigns *none* of the interaction effect from removing both tariffs and nontariff barriers together to nontariff barriers; high number assigns *all* the interaction effect to nontariff barriers.

Intricacy increases allegations of unfairness and discrimination because administered intervention is inherently opaque. Opaqueness heightens suspicions that something discriminatory and unfair is going on below surface appearances. Information about administered intervention can become so costly for noninsiders to obtain that extraordinary mechanisms are needful to obtain it, such as "protection balance sheets" and "surveillance reports" (GATT Wisemen's Report 1985, 35, 42). The value of information for maintaining coordinated cooperation is higher in environments with administered intervention than in those with more transparent trade policy instruments like tariffs, quotas, and export subsidies. Economists who applaud the benefits of price competition but are chary of nonprice competition (advertising and so on) might consider the trade policy analog. There may be much clearer benefits to "tariff competition"—negotiating coordinated concessions in the traditional way, threatening tax-based retaliation, and so on—than to competition and coordination among governments in administered intervention. All the features that make prices effective and efficient signals in private resource allocation make tariffs and other trade taxes effective and efficient signals in policy coordination. Among other things, this supports the recommendation sometimes heard for "re-tariffication" (e.g., Hufbauer and Rosen 1986).

Another implication of administered intervention is heightened "preemptive consciousness." Anticipations of a brave new world of coordinated (voluntary) export restraints, with market shares allotted according to the historical status quo, creates a race among large firms, and maybe entire industries, to "stake out claims" by penetrating and expanding quickly. Administered intervention may thus bring import surges upon itself. They are the rational response to expectations that a government will soon decide to vest the import "rights" of existing large suppliers in a set of "fair shares." Steel firms and automakers abroad observe that it happened in apparel and anticipate it for themselves; machine toolmakers abroad observe that it happened in steel and autos and anticipate it for themselves; and so on.[29] Tariffs and other transparent policy instruments have not historically created the same preemptive surges because both levels and changes were transparently bound into the GATT.

"Minilateralism." Allegations of unfair and injurious behavior on the part of large trading partners who have "caught up" with the United States have made it more vigilant about unfair trade from any source. Even small trading partners come under scrutiny. All developed countries view the catch-up growth of newly industrializing countries (visible most clearly for Brazil, Mexico, and Korea in table 3.4) with alarm and similar suspicions. (Indeed there *are* legitimate grounds for such suspicions as the economic environment includes more and more internationally coordinated multinational firms, as discussed in section 3.3.2). Although negotiation with dynamic small competitors may not seem worthwhile, exclusion of them from multilateral trade policy initiatives is easy and quite tempting. Isolation of "offenders" is a seemingly cheaper alternative to coordinated dispute settlement.

Thus the apparent growth of unfair trade becomes one of the forces behind "minilateralism," the tendency to circle the wagons, to reduce the number of participants involved in trade policy coordination.[30] This has virtue (section 3.2.2) to the extent that international catch-up pressures really do depend importantly on unfair practices. But to the extent that these are just fair and normal competitive pressures for new entrants, coordinated "minilateralism" is synonymous with barriers to entry and cartelization, and has little economic merit.

A closely related force behind minilateralism is the disparity of market dependence among GATT countries. Degrees of regulation vary, as does reliance on private rather than state-owned and state-supported firms (see below). Multilateral negotiations of a traditional kind have become increasingly cumbersome because of differences of objective and structural understanding.

These differences lead naturally to initiatives that narrow the geographical and sectoral scope of negotiations in order to make any progress at all. The 1986 report of the United States Trade Representative (USTR 1986, 61–62) is remarkably blunt:

> Nevertheless, multilateral negotiations are not an end in themselves. . . .
>
> America has decided to pursue *trade liberalization* opportunities *wherever* and *whenever* they exist, whether in a multilateral, plurilateral or bilateral context.
>
> Although the United States would prefer pursuing trade liberalization through multilateral negotiations, it is deeply concerned that

the process may now be *too cumbersome* to achieve meaningful and timely results. Indeed, the increasing number of GATT Contracting Parties and growing divergence of their viewpoints guarantee ever more awkward and prolonged negotiations. . . .

If the United States cannot reach timely trade agreements on a multilateral basis, it is prepared to progress on trade issues by negotiating on a bilateral or plurilateral basis with like-minded nations. . . .

It is time to recognize that across-the-board discussions among all GATT members may not be the best way to promote GATT goals. There is a greater need for a variety of arrangements under the GATT umbrella so trade liberalization can progress on at least some fronts without waiting for *all* issues to be settled to *all* parties' satisfaction. When a group of countries can negotiate a trade liberalizing agreement, provision should be made for its acceptance under the GATT.

Consistent with this intent, the United States has in the past few years negotiated: a quite inclusive free trade agreement with Israel and sectoral liberalization with Japan (Market-Oriented Sector Specific initiatives) and Caribbean trading partners. Negotiations continue with Canada toward sectoral free trade. The EEC, of course, continues to expand the boundaries of its own preferential liberalization. And forty-eight of the largest developing countries agreed in May 1986 to begin trade negotiations among themselves under a Global System of Trade Preferences.

A worrisome implication of these minilateral trends is, of course, that the world may become fragmented into hostile trading blocs, Uruguay Round notwithstanding. There is a more promising perspective, however. It is that in today's policy environment only minilateral liberalizing coordination is feasible. More than that, it is an ideal crucible in which to experiment with new coordination techniques: new definitions, rules, monitoring arrangements, and dispute settlement procedures. Minilateral coordination within the EEC, for example, is almost surely going to involve important progress on coordinating trade policy in services, such as in telecommunications. Minilateral coordination between Canada and the United States is almost surely going to make progress on unfair trade rules and procedures. In the longer run, multilateral negotiations over new GATT codes and among "blocs" (a pejorative term in this context) may be usefully informed by the precedents and experiments of minilateralism.

It is undeniable that these minilateral and bilateral movements are retreats from multilateral coordination of the historic kind, resting on the MFN principle (unconditional in principle, but in the practice of nearly every country, quite conditioned). Strategic "retreats" may, however, allow trade policy coordination to regroup beneficially just as they do an army. They may furthermore be wise if increasing parity among countries in economic influence undermines MFN and enhances the idea of optimal coalition-building (see point 4 of "Relative National Strengths" in this section). In this light, it might be better not to call this a retreat from multilateralism based on MFN but, for example, to call it a "new" multilateralism based on a "*More*-Favored-Nation principle"![31] The GATT codes of the Tokyo Round can in fact be seen as an innovative vehicle for the new multilateralism.

GATT codes. GATT codes are an innovative device for adopting the best aspects of coordinated minilateralism, controlling the worst aspects of administered intervention, and maintaining the many GATT mechanisms that continue to be relevant to liberalizing coordination.

Five important codes were negotiated during the Tokyo Round of GATT negotiations: on subsidies, procurement, standards, import licensing, and customs valuation. Each was negotiated by a subset of GATT members, each on a trade policy issue of narrow scope. Each forms a supplement to the GATT, with five independent lists of signatories that do not include all GATT members. By restricting participation and focusing on narrow issues, the codes reduced the potential for hostile undermining of coordination. Their provisions are, however, applied in principle on an MFN basis (except by the United States whose application of the first three codes was conditional).[32] Each is administered by a Committee of Signatories serviced by the GATT Secretariat, and each has its own dispute settlement mechanism.

In general, the Tokyo Round codes aimed at rules and procedures for harmonization and transparency rather than at significant liberalization. This is one reason for not according undue weight to assessments of their "only modest" success, or to the general agreement among commentators that the subsidies code in particular has not worked well. They might be judged more optimistically as successful "standstill" agreements, strategic defenses against decoordination rather than catalysts of coordination.[33] They might also be judged successful for creating strategically ambiguous[34] GATT-consistent minilateralism. And they are commendable attempts to cope with administered intervention in a realistic way.

The Tokyo Round attempt to negotiate a safeguards code failed, however, and the subsidies code has room for considerable improvement, comments above notwithstanding. Acceptable codes on subsidies and safeguards are, in fact, especially needful because of important changes in the economic environment.

3.3.2 Shifts in the Economic Environment

Modern trade policy issues arise in economic environments that seem increasingly strategic and do not fit the orthodox competitive paradigm.

Mobile Multinational Firms

One essential aspect of a firm is coordination within itself; as firms have grown multinationally over the past few decades, corporate international coordination has grown apace. There are many reasons for this growth. The EEC, communications innovation, capital-market integration, and ambitious development plans all have encouraged coproduction, joint ventures, mergers, and global identity. In some global markets, the same few firms compete everywhere. In some national markets, a small number of firms vie for a "prize" that is essentially control of the whole national industry. The growth of trade has been more rapid in manufactures—with potential for firm-focused economies of scale, technological gaps, product differentiation, and taste for variety—than in agricultural and mineral products, as shown in figure 3.2. Within manufactures, the growth of trade has been more rapid in industries with a concentrated, oligopolistic market structure than in those with a competitive structure; trade in aircraft, electronic machinery, chemicals, and petrochemicals grew much faster between 1973 and 1983 than trade in wood, paper, and foods, as shown in table 3.8. Table 3.9 shows further that U.S. multinational firms maintained their shares of world exports over the past thirty years, even as the U.S. geographical share declined, and have grown in their shares of U.S. trade.

In concentrated strategic environments, firms clearly recognize the effect that their actions have on the behavior of other firms, and often

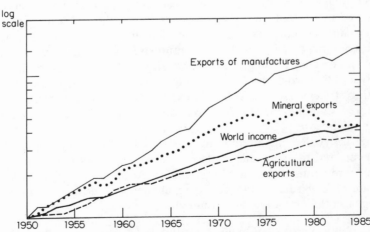

Fig. 3.2   Changing commodity composition of world exports, 1950–85 (broad categories; volume indices, 1950 = 100). *Source:* GATT (1986a, 12).

Table 3.8 **Changing Commodity Composition of World Imports, 1973–1983 (narrow categories)**

1983 Rank	1973 Rank	Product categories	Percentage shares in value of world trade 1983	Percentage shares in value of world trade 1973	Percentage shares in value of world trade excluding fuels 1983	Percentage shares in value of world trade excluding fuels 1973
1	1	Crude petroleum	12.4	7.6	..	..
2	7	Petroleum products	4.9	2.4	..	..
3	4	Passenger motor cars	3.8	3.8	4.7	4.2
4	2	Iron and steel	2.8	4.6	3.5	5.1
5	3	Textile yarn, fabrics, made-up articles	2.6	4.1	3.2	4.6
6	9	Clothing	2.2	2.2	2.8	2.5
7	20	Office machines, data processing equipment, parts	2.2	1.4	2.8	1.5
8	8	Parts and accessories of motor vehicles	2.0	2.2	2.5	2.5
9	45	Gas, natural and manufactured	2.0	0.3	..	..
10	15	Artificial resins, plastic materials, articles of plastic	2.0	1.9	2.4	2.1
11	18	Organic chemicals	1.9	1.6	2.4	1.8
12	6	Wood manufactures, paper	1.9	2.4	2.3	2.7
13	5	Cereals and preparations	1.8	2.7	2.2	3.0
14	10	Fruits and vegetables	1.5	2.2	1.9	2.4
15	11	Oilseeds, vegetable oils, oil cakes	1.5	2.2	1.8	2.4
16	24	Aircraft	1.2	0.9	1.5	1.0
17	17	Telecommunication equipment, parts, accessories	1.2	1.6	1.5	1.7
18	37	Transistors, etc. (electronic components)	1.2	0.7	1.5	0.8
19	27	Coffee, tea, cocoa, spices	1.1	0.9	1.4	1.0
20	26	Lorries, special vehicles	1.1	0.9	1.4	1.0
		Total of above	51.3	46.6	..	..
		World trade (market economies)	100.0	100.0	..	..

Source: GATT (1985, 17).

Table 3.9   U.S. Multinational Corporate Presence in International Trade

| Year | Percentage Share of World Exports | | Percentage Share of U.S. Geographical Trade | |
	from geographical U.S.	from multinational firms[a]	Exports[b]	Imports[b]
1957	22.7[c]	n.a.	n.a.	n.a.
1966	17.5	17.7	17.6	11.0
1977	13.3	17.6	26.7	21.7
1982	14.3	17.7	n.a.	n.a.
1983	13.9	17.7	n.a.	n.a.

Sources: Lipsey and Karvis (1986, 29) for columns 1 and 2; Little (1986, 44) for columns 3 and 4.

[a]Including majority-owned foreign affiliates.

[b]Trade between U.S. multinational firms and their foreign affiliates, majority-owned only, it would seem.

[c]1957A figure x (1966B figure/1966A figure), where A and B are different classification systems.

of governments. Governments recognize this, too. They have turned to firm-focused performance requirements for which firm-focused favors, such as tax incentives, are returned. Each firm or government conjectures how rivals and other agents will react to its own decisions. Governments, furthermore, are sometimes the owners and indirect managers of firms and may strategically "game" among themselves.

Large multinational firms might seem at first impression to be a force against discriminatory border policy and encouraging to coordinated liberalization of world trade—as influential constituents of many different governments simultaneously, whose flexibility and mobility would be enhanced most by free trade. This can be true but need not be in strategic environments. The Ford Motor Company supports protectionist initiatives in the United States, and Airbus Industries has depended on its sponsoring governments for support; Toyota and Nissan have not clearly suffered from auto voluntary export restraints, especially not in their competition with smaller Japanese automakers. Large firms will sometimes have the potential for influencing (exploiting?) groups without strategic size or power. Krishna (1983), for example, has shown how oligopolistic domestic *and* foreign firms may welcome voluntary export or import quotas. These quotas can facilitate implicit collusion among them, reducing competitive cheating by stabilizing market shares, at the expense of customers. Or, for another example, oligopolistic national firms wanting to avoid potential entry from abroad may be able to convince governments correctly that national economic welfare would indeed be higher with import barriers that protect their market power (Dixit and Kyle 1985). Oligopolistic national firms wishing to initiate entry into some unpenetrated market may be similarly correct to make a national-welfare case for export subsidies.[35]

Mobility of multinational firms and their professional work force also internationalizes ostensibly domestic policies,[36] accentuating their spillovers abroad and provoking foreign pressure for international policy coordination. There is, of course, always *some* tendency for a country's sectoral policies to spill over abroad in mirror-image fashion. But the size of these spillovers is much larger when corporate capital resources are mobile. Most countries' industrial policies, for example, entail corporate taxes and subsidies that encourage some domestic sectors at the expense of other domestic sectors, but also at the expense of the same favored sectors abroad. Alert multinationals may decide that their expansion can be shifted to whichever of their affiliates enjoys the most favorable sectoral policy incentives. Domestic subsidies and taxes can thus easily become instruments of strategic sectoral predation among countries.

It is no surprise, as multinational corporations have increased in size and strategic influence, that domestic subsidies, performance requirements, and unfair trade have become hard bones of contention in the policy environment.[37] The recent claim that strategically calculating policy can shape ("create," "destroy") a country's comparative advantage is correct, after all, where that same policy is capable of moving capital endowments from one place to another, using the mediating facilities of internationally coordinated firms, leaving labor and immobile endowments behind. One country's strategically active sectoral policy in that world can also deter another's from its beggar-thy-neighbor attempts to shift comparative advantage and desirable employment. Passive (more exactly impassive) policy does not have this capability for defensive deterrence. Policy coordination in such a world is an attempt to establish a peaceful equilibrium that may nonetheless be backed up by arsenals of strategic policy weapons!

It is for these reasons easy to endorse the idea that there is unique importance to the Uruguay Round negotiations on subsidies, including revision of the existing subsidies code.[38] At the very least, such negotiations will likely generate sharper definitions of spillovers and agreement on procedural rules (Hufbauer and Shelton-Erb 1984). And it may be timely for substantive rules and full-fledged attempts to exchange request-and-offer lists for reciprocal reductions of specified subsidies that would then be "bound" like tariffs.[39]

The more fundamental question this prospect raises is whether policy should be just as coordinated among governments as corporate planning is among national affiliates. Skeptics about the merits of markets, especially internationally integrated markets, tend to respond "yes." Skeptics about the merits of industrial regulation, especially when centralized on a global (coordinated) scale, tend to respond "no."[40]

Adjustment

Adjustment problems in the economic environment have become arguably more severe in the past fifteen years. Average unemployment rates and excess capacity are higher. Burgeoning, globally integrated, financial markets have created volatile changes in exchange rates, international competitiveness, and goods trade. These changes and the strategic sensitivity of multinational firms to governments and each other have aggravated the stimuli facing workers, farmers, and other owners of immobile resources. Their adjustment problems are made even worse by the potential for substitutability between goods trade and mobile corporate capital. When goods and firms are both internationally mobile, then only slight changes in the economic or policy environment can bring about striking changes in exports, imports, and the livelihood of immobile factors that are tied closely to them (Mundell 1957). To a large multinational firm, moving the goods and moving the plant across borders are close substitutes; they are not to its immobile workers and their unions. Displaced workers and mid-level managers who are unable to acquire or transfer skills useful to alternative sectors face long periods of unemployment and below-average earnings.

Table 3.10 hints at the size of the adjustment problem that might face immobile workers from trade liberalization in today's economic environment. Sector-by-sector employment changes are quite large, even though their aggregate (sum) may be small. They are much larger than similar estimates prepared for the Tokyo Round negotiations in the late 1970s by Baldwin, Mutti, and Richardson (1980, 419).

In brief, immobile workers seem to be saddled with sharper and more frequent unanticipated shocks from international forces than in the past (Grossman and Richardson 1985, 20–23). Some of the agents who represent them are strategically large within countries, although uncoordinated across them, such as unions, regional governments, and Departments (Ministries) of Agriculture. Strategic interaction between them and their own government can lead to indefinite protection—a kind of strategic paralysis of unproductivity.

In this environment the challenge to all policy, national and internationally coordinated, is formidable. Adjustment burdens can be reduced if national policy minimizes the economic hardship to immobile segments of the population, and sensible policy may include temporary and degressive protection (Diamond 1982). But commitment to eventual adjustment seems a necessity, since rational strategic agents will forecast future government action when contemplating a specialized investment. Government commitment to "preservation" makes no pri-

Table 3.10   **Percentage Change in Japanese and U.S. Employment by Sector under Trade Liberalization**

ISIC #	Sector	% of Change in Total Japanese Employment with Removal of U.S. and Japanese Tariffs and NTB's by Sector	% of Change in Total U.S. Employment with Removal of Japanese Tariffs and NTB's by Sector
1	Agric, Forestry & Fisheries	−50.2%	+96.6%
310	Food, Beverages & Tobacco	+9.4	−4.9
321	Textiles	+18.8	−24.1
322	Wearing Apparel	−1.3	−0.6
323	Leather Products	+0.3	−1.7
324	Footwear	+0.1	−0.1
331	Wood Product	−0.7	−1.3
332	Furniture and Fixtures	+0.2	−0.1
341	Paper and Paper Products	+2.9	−2.0
342	Printing and Publishing	+0.4	−0.7
35A	Chemicals	+4.7	−3.7
35B	Petroleum and Rel. Prod.	−9.5	+0.2
355	Rubber Products	+1.7	−2.2
36A	Nonmetal Min. Products	+2.3	−1.0
362	Glass and Glass Products	+0.4	−0.5
371	Iron and Steel	+26.0	−7.8
372	Nonferrous Metals	+1.3	−1.4
381	Metal Products	+1.9	−2.5
382	Nonelectric Machinery	+5.0	−2.8
383	Electric Machinery	+3.4	−2.8
384	Transport Equipment	+4.2	+1.0
38A	Miscellaneous Manuf.	+13.3	−14.9
2	Mining and Quarrying	+4.3	−2.8
4	Electric, Gas & Water	+2.7	−1.2
5	Construction	−3.2	0.0
6	Wholesale and Retail Trade	−9.3	−12.6
7	Transportation, Storage and Communication	+1.1	−3.3
8	Finance, Ins. & Real Est.	−2.6	−3.4
9	Commercial, Social and Personal Services	−18.7	−2.2

Source: Saxonhouse (1986, 242), combining estimates in Deardorff and Stern (1986) and Staiger, Deardorff and Stern (1986).

vate adjustment the strategic and equilibrium response. Government commitment to unspecified "eventual" adjustment makes waiting the strategic and equilibrium response. Only credible commitment to adjustment makes it possible for anticipations of government reaction to alter ex ante location and allocation decisions.

Yet it is hard for a national government on its own to guarantee credibly that protection is only temporary or degressive. If the conditions that justified the protection continue to exist, the incentives are nearly irresistable for the government to repeat its "temporary" dose at similar intensity, and to repeat it again and again. If strategic agents sense how irresistible this pattern is, they will refuse to believe in the proclaimed temporariness of the trade policy and will remain active in the protected sector rather than exiting. Their continued activity keeps conditions the same as those that warranted the trade policy in the first place and seduces the government to repeat its temporary protection. The sequence then repeats. It should be clear that this cycle represents a strategic equilibrium, a position of rest in which temporary or degressive trade policy is impossible (that is, not sustained by the postulated strategic behavior).[41]

Strategic policy coordination among governments can help alleviate this problem. Under GATT rules, trading-partner governments can already request consultation and compensation when a temporary trade policy becomes permanent. If the consultation/compensation mechanism were working well, then the first government's pledge of transience would become more credible. Private agents would be more likely to exit. Such consultation and compensation have been largely abandoned, however, as have other safeguard procedures under Article XIX of the GATT. This heightens the urgency of safeguard revisions in the Uruguay Round negotiations and explains the possible appeal of a standing "adjustment committee" (GATT Wisemen's Report 1985, 43–44) that would monitor temporary, degressive protection and facilitate international pressure on a government to keep its degressivity credible to domestic constituents. A standing committee with this charge illustrates how an "independent agent" can sometimes help strategic rivals to achieve coordination by making their promises credible, as discussed in section 3.3.1 above.[42]

There are reasons, of course, why trade policy may not be the ideal insulator of an economy from unforeseen shocks, nor the most desirable catalyst for adjustment. A less wasteful alternative for achieving the same goal might be a loan and insurance scheme for worker experience and investment in human capital (Grossman and Richardson 1985, 26), providing benefits (contingent on payment of premiums) dependent on the state of competition from abroad. Under such a program, countries would continue to enjoy the benefits of low-priced imports, and incentives for factor reallocation might be preserved.

Strategic policy coordination could have a role to play here as well, in that some of the beneficiaries from "our" smoother adjustment are "their" firms, workers, and unions who take over the market. These agents might therefore fairly be expected to contribute to the insurance premiums that help fund our adjustment. More exactly, since successful adjustment creates *favorable* foreign spillovers, coordinated international loan and insurance schemes may some day be worth consideration, perhaps financed most easily by a small tax on all international transactions (capital movements as well as trade), or possibly by a more targeted but larger tax on trade surpluses, administered by a GATT standing adjustment committee as described above. Coordinated international loan and insurance programs might also be more resistant than national schemes to moral hazard problems and to "capture" by political forces (e.g., the U.S. government's use of trade adjustment assistance to assuage autoworkers in the late 1970s).

Notes

This paper has benefited immeasurably from the detailed comments of Robert E. Baldwin and Geoffrey Carliner on an earlier draft. It was written as part of the NBER's research program in international studies, but the opinions expressed are my own.

1. So, too, might students of other kinds of international policy coordination; see Cooper (1986) for an instructive linking of public health to macroeconomic coordination.

2. See Cooper (1987, 299–301) or Baldwin (1984b, 5–9) for an account along these lines of the growth of the U.S. Trade Agreements Program. It is easy to forget that the genesis of those agreements was the burden of trade repression during the hostile trade wars of the early 1930s. For the United States, which legislated the infamous Smoot-Hawley tariffs in 1930, the constant-dollar value of trade (exports plus imports) fell 35 percent between 1929 and 1934, almost half again further than real GNP, which fell 24 percent (U.S. Department of Commerce 1976, 324). Overall world trade volume declined 25 percent (GATT 1986a, 31) during the same period.

3. Framers of trade policy are always quite mindful of other governments, as are a few analyses as well, most notably Johnson (1954). Otherwise brief mentions of retaliation, but little analysis, appears in traditional economic commentary.

4. There *are* fundamental insights about policy coordination from analysis of competitive environments, but such analysis nevertheless begs the central question. Traditional competitive analysis can generate the ideas that open international trade is a global public good, that some governments may be tempted therefore to "free ride," and that a country's trade barriers create impacts abroad of the same character as externalities (spillovers). Some sort of mechanism would be desirable to alleviate the public good/free rider/externality problems and seems on the face of it to require international policy coordination. The crucial question being begged, though, is what incentive motivates any one of a large number of competitive governments to create and maintain coordination with others. What "internalizes the externalities"? Perfectly competitive assumptions rule out much of the motivational impetus for policy coordination from the start. If someone protests that in reality a number

of governments are large, not atomistic, then such a protestor has implicitly accepted the need for strategic analysis, perhaps without realizing it, and has also pointed to the kind of strategic bargaining (pricing) that *does* internalize the externalities in the fashion of Coase (1960).

5. See Brander's (1986, 36–43) or Richardson's (1986, 270–74) account, each of which applies to trade policy the extensive research of political scientist Robert Axelrod (1983) on repeated prisoner's dilemma games.

6. The word "surveillance" in GATT parlance entails each signatory's obligations to publish all trade measures, to consult, and if necessary, to participate in dispute settlement procedures. In essence, each member thereby monitors all the others; no central institution does so.

7. In the primitive model of table 3.1, each government agrees that the objective is to maximize its own country's feasible gains without regard to what the other country achieves. Since $+3$ is infeasible without luck, foolishness, or coercion (a kind of coordination by force), each government prefers $+1$ to -1 and is attracted to proposals to create coordination devices.

8. The obvious characterization of this objective is "cutting off one's nose to spite one's face." It is an all-too-familiar posture for agents in hostile conflict. Trade embargoes are a good example.

9. Objectives might then seem to be common again, but they are not. "My" goal is the distance between me and you; "yours" is the distance between you and me.

10. See, for example, the Uruguay Round invocation of these principles in GATT (1986b, 3). Camps and Diebold (1983, 55) remark that:

> The approach we suggest is based on reason. . . . But governments are apt to be driven by more immediate aims, by a sense of damage and a wish to rectify matters.

11. The sheer number of participants can matter, too, for reasons described in note 4. Having too many potential participants makes the negotiating environment more competitive, less strategic, and reduces the motivational incentives for each government to contribute toward cooperative initiative. Thus to limit the scope by limiting the number of participants enhances coordination in its own right; choosing like-minded participants enhances coordination further. It is in this light that one can understand why each of the Tokyo Round "codes" for nontariff measures was negotiated by an interested subgroup within the GATT, and why each maintains its own list of signatories—with implicit discrimination against nonsigners. See further discussion in section 3.3.1.

12. The issue of common understanding of payoffs and behavior is discussed further in Cooper (1986) and Holtham (1986).

13. Baldwin (1987) gives a useful account of both principles.

14. Camps and Diebold (1983, 29–30) illustrate this tension nicely:

> The goal is . . . to improve the conditions of international agricultural trade. . . . But there is also a need to protect the rest of the GATT system from the impact of fierce disputes about agriculture . . . [which] can hinder progress on other subjects.

So does the Uruguay Round declaration (GATT 1986b, 2), albeit with the appearance of doublespeak:

> Balanced concessions should be sought within broad trading areas and subjects to be negotiated in order to avoid unwarranted cross-sectoral demands.

15. See Keohane (1984) for an extensive discussion.

16. One might think of this as the "bad-ideas-are-better-botched" principle.

17. See Oudiz and Sachs (1984) for an approach to this question for macroeconomic policy coordination.

18. Parenting offers many illustrations. So does the discussion of how "constitutions" come about and what they contain, as applied to trade policy notably by the late Jan Tumlir (1985) and Banks and Tumlir (1986).

19. Proponents of free trade and skeptics about the virtue of coordination of course argue that this schizophrenia is "good." See Price (1986) and Goldstein (1986) for descriptions of these different constituencies and their influence on U.S. trade policy. Destler (1986) contains an excellent up-to-date evaluation of U.S. internal coordination of trade policy.

20. Baldwin (1986a) and Destler (1986, 42–47) provide informative perspectives on the material in this subsection.

21. Again environmental changes can be seen to interact with each other. The convergence in per capita income among the countries in table 3.4 encourages especially the growth of intraindustry trade, based on product differentiation, variety, and scale. These characteristics often engender imperfectly competitive market structures and significant reshufflings of narrow product "niches" among firms as technological change and other shocks occur, with consequent volatility for immobile factors (see section 3.3.2 below).

22. Baldwin and Richardson (1987, 143) list several reasons why trade policy coordination among coequal governments might be just as stable as hegemonic coordination. They also mention, however, that it suggests different "styles" or "tactics" of trade policy for all the participants.

23. See the discussion of hostile environments in section 3.2.1.

24. See Richardson (1987a, 289; 1986, 97). See also Destler (1986, 48–49), who remarks that

. . . [S]ince the new competitors were slow to assert leadership in multilateral trade negotiations, there was a growing divergence between the loci of trade-political activism and trade-economic power.

A similar reasoning underlies the observation that the United States still has strong leadership to *preserve* present trade policy coordination by refraining from hostile and/or uncoordinated initiatives, yet has lost leadership power to *advance* coordination. See Baldwin and Richardson (1987, 123–24), for example.

25. The GATT has never technically "been" an "institution" at all—only a "compact with signatories"—unlike the IMF with its executive directors, standing committees, rules of order, and representation of membership.

26. For descriptions of implicit coordination in the context of oligopoly and trade policy, see Friedman (1977), Jensen and Thursby (1983), Rotemberg and Saloner (1986), and Lambson and Richardson (1987).

27. On an industrial counterpart to these issues, see Lambson and Richardson (1987). One among several conclusions they draw for the case of price-setting supergames is that symmetry among firms stabilizes implicit collusion, making "punishment" shorter and less likely, compared to slightly asymmetric configurations of firms.

28. They seem to be a more meaningful way to measure the relative importance of administered intervention than alternatives, such as tabulations of the share of trade affected in some fashion by nontariff barriers. See Balassa and Balassa (1984) and Nogues, Olechowski, and Winters (1986a, b).

29. Each is playing a rational strategy for an "end game," as illustrated, for example, by Lawrence and Lawrence (1985). An end game is one in which a future equilibrium is known, in this case cartelized industrial structure, and agents choose optimal strategies for approaching it over time.

30. Curzon and Curzon (1985), for example, recommend that the (fair) traders within the GATT form a coalition that aims at a free trade area that would "eventually" cover "substantially all" trade, thereby attaining consistency with Article XXIV, and isolate the non (unfair) traders.

31. "New" multilateralism is the term used by Camps and Diebold (1983). "More-Favored-Nation" treatment is a term suggested by Thomas O. Bayard.

32. See Stern, Jackson, and Hoekman (1986, 6). This paper is a thorough evaluation of the operational features of the codes, although not their economic effects or legal standing.

33. Liberalizing coordination is, however, a logical future step, involving probably "trade in concessions across Codes"—accession by one country to one code in return for accession to another by another, forgoing insistence on some provision in one code for a rival's concession in another code, and so on.

34. Ambiguity can sometimes be a bargaining strength. See, for example, Dixit (1987, 274).

35. See Brander's and Spencer's contributions to Krugman (1986) and other work referenced there. These examples are from the new analytical thinking on trade policy in strategic environments, also surveyed by Grossman and Richardson (1985) and Richardson (1987b).

36. This is the twin of the observation that trade policy has become increasingly "domesticated," drawn, for example, by Ahearn and Reifman (1984).

37. Camps and Diebold (1983, 22) illustrate this when they write that:
one of the basic principles that we think should guide the new multilateralism . . . [is] that the international community has a legitimate concern with domestic actions when they have important external effects.

38. Camps and Diebold (1983, 39) comment that:
It is no exaggeration to say that the damage will ultimately lead to the collapse of the system of cooperation unless better ways are found to deal with the conflicts among national industrial policies.
Policy coordination on subsidies and countervailing duties is also near the top of Canada's list of reasons for pursuing bilateral trade liberalization with the United States.

39. Baldwin (1986b, 28–34, among other places) outlines a detailed plan for such negotiations in which modalities from historic rounds of tariff liberalization are adapted to subsidies. One reason this makes sense is the inherent (admittedly complex) measurability of subsidies as compared to more administrative intervention, hence their susceptibility to coordination by rules (see section 3.2.2 above).

40. Many economists believe that policy competition among governments exercises a healthy discipline on costly abuses of their regulatory powers. The framers of the United States Constitution ambiguously reserved to Congress the power "to regulate . . . commerce among the several states" (Article I, Section 8.3), implicitly excluding state governments from coordinating interstate trade policy, yet nevertheless reserving the authority to do so for a centralized body.

41. This policy problem is known technically as time inconsistency—this year's optimal value for next year's policy intensity will no longer look optimal when next year rolls around. The same problem can afflict all temporary policy. See Staiger and Tabellini (1986) and Feenstra (1986) for further applications of the idea to trade policy.

42. The same reasoning underlies the independence of a central bank from political forces and accords the IMF, or a new intermediary, an independent role in helping debtors' promises appear credible to creditors.

References

Ahearn, Raymond J. 1986. Protectionist legislation in 1985. Typescript.
Ahearn, Raymond J., and Alfred Reifman. 1984. Trade policymaking in the Congress. In Baldwin (1984a).
Aho, C. Michael, and Jonathan David Aronson. 1985. *Trade talks, America better listen.* New York: Council on Foreign Relations.
Axelrod, Robert. 1983. *The evolution of cooperation.* New York: Basic Books.
Balassa, B., and C. Balassa. 1984. Industrial protection in the developed countries. *World Economy* 7 (June): 179–96.
Baldwin, Robert E., ed. 1984a. *Recent issues and initiatives in U.S. trade policy.* National Bureau of Economic Research Conference Report. Cambridge, Mass.: NBER.
———. 1984b. The changing nature of U.S. trade policy since World War II. In Baldwin and Krueger (1984).
———. 1986a. The new protectionism: A response to shifts in national economic power. National Bureau of Economic Research Working Paper no. 1826. Cambridge, Mass.: NBER.
———. 1986b. Alternative liberalization strategies. National Bureau of Economic Research Working Paper no. 2045. Cambridge, Mass.: NBER.
———. 1986c. GATT reform: Selected issues. In *Protection and competition in international trade: Essays in honor of Max Corden,* ed. Henry K. Kierzkowski. London: Basil Blackwell.
———. 1987. The multilateral approach to liberalization. Typescript.
Baldwin, Robert E., and Richard N. Clarke. 1985. Game modeling the Tokyo Round of tariff negotiations. National Bureau of Economic Research Working Paper no. 1588. Cambridge, Mass.: NBER.
Baldwin, Robert E., and Anne O. Krueger, eds. 1984. *The structure and evolution of recent U.S. trade policy.* Chicago: University of Chicago Press.
Baldwin, Robert E., John H. Mutti, and J. David Richardson. 1980. Welfare effects on the United States of a significant multilateral tariff reduction. *Journal of International Economics* 10 (August): 405–23.
Baldwin, Robert E., and J. David Richardson, eds. 1986. *Current U.S. trade policy: Analysis, agenda, and administration.* National Bureau of Economic Research Conference Report. Cambridge, Mass.: NBER.
———. 1987. Recent U.S. trade policy and its global implications. In *Trade and structural change in Pacific Asia,* ed. Colin I. Bradford, Jr., and William H. Branson. Chicago: University of Chicago Press.
Banks, Gary, and Jan Tumlir. 1986. The political problem of adjustment. *The World Economy* 9 (June): 141–52.
Brander, James A. 1986. Rationales for strategic trade and industrial policy. In Krugman (1986).
Camps, Miriam, and William Diebold, Jr. 1983. *The new multilateralism: Can the world trading system be saved?* New York: Council on Foreign Relations.

Carmichael, W. B. 1986. National interest and international trade negotiations. *The World Economy* 9 (December): 341–58.

Coase, Ronald H. 1960. The problem of social cost. *Journal of Law and Economics* 3 (October): 1–44.

Cooper, Richard N. 1986. International cooperation in public health as a prologue to macroeconomic cooperation. Brookings Discussion Papers in International Economics, no. 44.

———. 1987. Trade policy as foreign policy. In Stern (1987).

Curzon, Gerard, and Victoria Curzon. 1985. Defusing conflict between traders and non-traders. *The World Economy* 9 (March): 19–35.

Deardorff, Alan V. 1986. Why do governments prefer nontariff barriers? University of Michigan Research Seminar in International Economics Seminar, Discussion Paper no. 186.

Deardorff, Alan V., and Robert M. Stern. 1984. The effects of the Tokyo Round on the structure of protection. In Baldwin and Krueger (1984).

———. 1986. *The Michigan model of world production and trade: Theory and application.* Cambridge, Mass.: MIT Press.

Destler, I. M. 1986. *American trade politics: System under stress.* Washington, D.C. Institute for International Economics; New York: The Twentieth Century Fund.

Diamond, Peter A. 1982. Protection, trade adjustment assistance, and income distribution. In *Import competition and response,* ed. Jagdish N. Bhagwati. Chicago: University of Chicago Press.

Diebold, William, Jr. 1952. *The end of the I.T.O.* Princeton University Essays in International Finance.

Dixit, Avinash. 1987. How should the United States respond to other countries' trade policies? In Stern (1987).

Dixit, Avinash, and Albert S. Kyle. 1985. The use of protection and subsidies for entry promotion and deterrence. *American Economic Review* 75 (March): 139–52.

Feenstra, Robert. 1986. Incentive compatible trade policies. Typescript.

Frankel, Jeffrey A. 1986. The sources of disagreement among the international macro models and implications for policy coordination. National Bureau of Economic Research Working Paper no. 1925. Cambridge, Mass.: NBER.

Frankel, Jeffrey A., and Katharine Rockett. 1986. International macroeconomic policy coordination when policy-makers disagree on the model. National Bureau of Economic Research Working Paper no. 2059. Cambridge, Mass.: NBER.

Friedman, J. 1977. *Oligopoly and the theory of games.* Amsterdam: North-Holland.

GATT (General Agreement on Tariffs and Trade). 1985. *International trade 1984/85.* Geneva.

———. 1986a. *International trade 1985/86.* Geneva.

———. 1986b. Ministerial declaration on the Uruguay Round. *GATT Focus* 41 (October): 2–5.

GATT Wisemen's Report. 1985. *Trade policies for a better future: Proposals for action* (by Fritz Leutwiler, Bill Bradley, Sumitro Djojohadikusumo, Pehr G. Gyllenhammar, Guy Ladreit de Lacharriére, I. G. Patel, and Mario H. Simonsen). Geneva.

Goldstein, Judith. 1986. Ideas, institutions, and American trade policy. Typescript.

Grossman, Gene M., and J. David Richardson. 1985. Strategic trade policy: A survey of issues and early analysis. Princeton University, Special Papers in International Economics, no. 15.

Holtham, Gerald. 1986. International policy coordination: How much consensus is there? Brookings Institution Discussion Papers in International Economics no. 50.

Hufbauer, Gary Clyde, and Joanna Shelton-Erb. 1984. *Subsidies in international trade*. Washington, D.C.: Institute for International Economics.

Hufbauer, Gary Clyde, and Howard F. Rosen. 1986. *Trade policy for troubled industries*. Policy Analysis in International Economics no. 15. Washington, D.C.: Institute for International Economics.

Jensen, Richard, and Marie Thursby. 1983. Free trade: Two noncooperative equilibrium approaches. Typescript.

Johnson, Harry G. 1954. Optimum tariffs and retaliation. *Review of Economic Studies* 21:142–53.

Keohane, Robert O. 1984. *After hegemony: Cooperation and discord in the world political economy*. Princeton, N.J.: Princeton University Press.

Kravis, Irving B., Alan Heston, and Robert Summers. 1982. *World product and income: International comparisons of real gross product*. Baltimore: Johns Hopkins University Press.

Kreinin, Mordechai E. 1974. *Trade relations of the EEC: An empirical investigation*. New York: Praeger.

Krishna, Kala. 1983. Trade restrictions as facilitating practices. Princeton University, Woodrow Wilson School Discussion Paper in Economics no. 55.

Krugman, Paul R., ed. 1986. *Strategic trade policy and the new international economics*. Cambridge, Mass.: MIT Press.

Ladreit de Lacharrière, Guy. 1985. Case for a tribunal to assist in settling trade disputes. *The World Economy* 8 (December): 339–52.

Lambson, Val Eugene, and J. David Richardson. 1987. Tacit collusion and voluntary restraint arrangements in the U.S. auto market. Typescript.

Lawrence, Colin, and Robert Z. Lawrence. 1985. The dispersion in manufacturing wages: An end game interpretation. *Brookings Papers on Economic Activity*, no. 1.

Lipsey, Robert E., and Irving B. Kravis. 1986. The competitiveness and comparative advantage of U.S. multinationals, 1957–1983. National Bureau of Economic Research Working paper no. 2051. Cambridge, Mass.: NBER.

Little, Jane Sneddon. 1986. Intra-firm trade and U.S. protectionism: Thoughts based on a small survey. *New England Economic Review* (January/February): 42–51.

MacBean, A. I., and P. N. Snowden. 1981. *International institutions in trade and finance*. London: Allen and Unwin.

Mundell, Robert A. 1957. International trade and factor mobility. *American Economic Review* 47 (June): 321–35.

Nogues, Julio J., Andrzej Olechowski, and L. Alan Winters. 1986a. The extent of nontariff barriers to imports of industrial countries. World Bank Staff Working Paper no. 789, Washington, D.C.

————. 1986b. The extent of nontariff barriers to industrial countries' imports. *The World Bank Economic Review* 1 (September): 181–99.

Oudiz, Gilles, and Jeffrey Sachs. 1984. Macroeconomic policy coordination among the industrial economies. *Brookings Papers on Economic Activity* 1:1–64.

Price, Lee. 1986. Trade problems and policy from a U.S labor perspective. In Baldwin and Richardson (1986).

Ray, John E. 1986. The OECD "Consensus" on export credits. *The World Economy* 9 (September): 295–309.

Richardson, J. David. 1986. The new political economy of trade policy. In Krugman (1986).

_____. 1987a. "Comment" on Dixit 1987. In Stern (1987).

_____. 1987b. "Strategic" trade policy: Research and practice in the United States. In *Shaping comparative advantage,* ed. Richard G. Lipsey and Wendy Dobson. Toronto: C. D. Howe Institute Policy Study no. 2.

Rotemberg, Julio J., and Garth Saloner. 1986. Quotas and the stability of implicit collusion. National Bureau of Economic Research Working Paper no. 1948. Cambridge, Mass.: NBER.

Saxonhouse, Gary R. 1986. Japan's intractable trade surpluses in a new era. *The World Economy* 9 (September): 239–58.

Shuman, Shannon Stock, and Charles O. Verrill, Jr. 1984. Recent developments in countervailing duty law and policy. In Baldwin (1984a).

Staiger, Robert W., Alan V. Deardorff, and Robert M. Stern. 1986. The effects of Japanese and American protection. In *The new protectionist threat to world welfare,* ed. Dominick Salvatore. Amsterdam: North Holland.

Staiger, Robert, and Guido Tabellini. 1986. Discretionary trade policy and excessive protection. Typescript.

Stern, Robert M., ed. 1987. *U.S. trade policies in a changing world economy.* Cambridge, Mass.: MIT Press.

Stern, Robert M., John H. Jackson, and Bernard Hoekman. 1986. An assessment of the implementation and operation of the Tokyo Round codes. University of Michigan Research Seminar in International Economics, Discussion Paper no. 174.

Tumlir, Jan. 1985. International trade policy and other constitutional issues. Typescript.

U.S. Bureau of the Census. 1980. *World population 1979—Recent demographic estimates for the countries and regions of the world.* Washington, D.C.: U.S. Department of Commerce.

U.S. Department of Commerce. 1976. *The national income and product accounts of the United States, 1929–74: Statistical tables.* Washington, D.C.: Government Printing Office.

USTR (United States Trade Representative). 1986. *Annual report of the President of the United States on the trade agreements program, 1984–85.* Washington, D.C.: Government Printing Office.

Whalley, John. 1985. *Trade liberalization among major world trading areas.* Cambridge, Mass.: MIT Press.

World Bank, *World development report.* Various issues.

2. Robert S. Strauss

Current Issues in U.S. Trade Policy

In response to the comment about the Europeans not being fully represented, after listening to Helmut Schmidt yesterday, I would say that the Europeans were in fact a bit overrepresented. As was to be expected, Helmut was impressive enough and strong enough to last for two days and thoroughly presented the European position.

This morning, when I was thinking about addressing this group on the subject of trade and economic issues which each of you know so much about, I was reminded of an incident that happened to me several years ago when I was testifying before the Senate on trade issues. In the question-and-answer session, one senator was not only addressing me but also perhaps lecturing me a bit on negotiations, in particular on how to negotiate with the Japanese. Senator Hollings interrupted and told this story, which is a bit crude but also relevant and amusing, and you will forgive me if I relate it to you.

Senator Hollings noted that our colloquy reminded him of a story about Jesse James, the old bank robber. As Jesse and his gang held up a Texas bank, they got everyone out and put the men on one side of the room and the women on the other, and Jesse said to them, "Now, if you'll just behave, nobody's going to get killed. We're going to take the valuables, the guns, and the money from the men, and then we're going to ravish the women, and we're going to leave quietly. No one will be killed." And with that, one of the men spoke up and said, "Now wait a minute, Mr. James, you can have our money and our valuables, and you can have our guns, but you can't put a hand on our women." In response, a woman over on the other side spoke up and said, "Now, Fred, don't go telling Jesse how to rob a bank." In speaking to this group on trade and economics, I feel as if I'm telling Jesse how to rob a bank.

But let me get started.

I've been asked to cover a number of things, including an overview of where we are and where we're going in the current round of trade negotiations, and to talk a little bit about the Tokyo Round of trade negotiations and relate that to the real political world and what's currently going on in the United States with respect to trade.

It occurred to me while I was making my notes for this talk that I could open and close by saying that trade relations today are characterized by a great deal less multilateralism, more bilateralism, some minilateralism, and a great deal of ill-thought-through unilateralism. That would just about summarize what I have to say on the issue of trade. More seriously, however, let me begin by talking about trade negotiation.

To be honest, when President Carter asked me to take the position of Trade Ambassador, I wasn't sure whether this was a good decision. Did it make sense to ask a fellow who had absolutely no background in international trade matters, but whose background was in law, politics, and negotiation, to be Trade Ambassador? At the time, I thought it was a questionable decision and, frankly, I was concerned when I accepted the responsibility because of my lack of expertise in the field of trade. I might add, of course, that a great many others were also concerned.

In retrospect, I believe it was a very good decision in terms of the type of person he chose. And I'm not talking specifically about myself, Bob Strauss, but rather about the type of person that the job really requires. Because as I became involved in the Tokyo Round negotiations, it became readily apparent that someone who had skills in moving the political process was needed a great deal more than a specialist in international trade issues and problems. And frankly, the skills that were necessary in that particular negotiation, insofar as the political process was concerned, just couldn't have been acquired or mastered in time to get through a very troubled Congress. With the help of a first-rate staff, I was able to deal with the substantive issues.

Protectionism in 1977–78, you will recall, while not in the shape it is today, was serious and the fires were raging. We were talking about protectionism in terms that we had not talked about since the days of Smoot-Hawley. The country's trade policy was under some attack, and I can assure you that good trade policy can only exist where there is a political consensus to support it. When I came on the job, there was no political consensus for the Tokyo Round or for a progressive, sensible trade policy for the United States. Therefore, the first thing we really went about doing was to fashion a consensus on the importance and goals of U.S. trade policy.

My first months on the job were spent in doing two things: one, trying to learn the trade issues; and two, going around the country, personally and with members of my staff, to hundreds of congressional districts and media centers, telling the story of America's self-interest. That's what trade really boils down to in the United States. What really drives the political process on trade and what we had to get across was the self-interest that people around the country—politicians, labor leaders, businessmen, farmers—really had in the trade negotiations.

It took that same kind of approach to entice our trading partners back to the table in a real negotiating posture. The Japanese, particularly Prime Minister Fukuda, were committed and supportive of the Tokyo Round negotiations, but the Prime Minister wasn't prepared to really get in front and lead the charge. The Europeans were reticent and hesitant, with the French openly hostile to many of the positions and goals we had outlined, as they are today. They were particularly concerned with what might happen to the common agricultural policy and other programs. But after much work, we were able to get everybody to the negotiating table and begin the process.

The key in moving the negotiating process forward was the strong leadership exercised by the various heads of state. I am deeply concerned that one thing that was present throughout the Tokyo Round, that is not present today as we begin the Uruguay Round, was a deep commitment by the leaders in each country to the trade negotiations.

During the Tokyo Round, Fukuda, Schmidt, Callaghan, and Carter were each committed to an aggressive trade negotiation. Moreover, these leaders also understood the issues thoroughly and were able to talk about these issues among themselves and were comfortable in discussing them with their various constituencies.

Let me just give you an example based on my relationship with President Carter. As far as President Carter was concerned, within an hour after a phone call I could get into the Oval Office and tell him that he needed to speak with Fukuda or with Schmidt, for example, on an intractable problem that we just couldn't move the negotiators on. His ability and willingness to pick up the phone, again within a very short time period, and have a responsible, in-depth, substantive conversation with the Prime Minister or Chancellor or whoever, was a tremendous help and we never would have been successful without that. I would also add that Mike Blumenthal, who was deeply involved in the Kennedy Round as Secretary of the Treasury, was committed to the negotiations and was a strong force in the Carter Administration as were Cy Vance and Richard Cooper at State.

Unfortunately, we don't have that type of strong network right now. Clayton Yeutter doesn't have that kind of support, and I see no reason to expect that his successor, whether he be a Democrat or a Republican, will have that support. I am also not certain that the support that Chancellor Kohl or Prime Minister Thatcher has given, or might give, is in any way comparable to what their predecessors gave. And that is unfortunate because, if nothing else, to complete a meaningful multi-lateral negotiation with all the attendant problems, you must have strong leadership and support for that leadership in each of the main countries. You cannot successfully complete trade negotiations with ministers or cabinet officers nibbling around the edges of the problem. In today's climate, the world needs heads of government who understand the issues in depth and who are willing to break them down and put their muscle and their political power behind efforts to solve seemingly intractable problems.

On a positive note with respect to the Uruguay Round, let me say that I think a great many people sold Ambassador Yeutter short. His predecessor, Bill Brock, commanded respect on the Hill, in the press, and with our allies and trading partners. I think Brock could have had a trade policy for this country had he had an Administration that focused on one. Yeutter came in with a good deal less going for him, and the outlook was pessimistic. I can assure you, however, that he has his hands on the controls. You can agree or disagree with certain actions, but he has launched the Uruguay Round much better than most observers ever dreamed he would be able to do. He deserves great credit for it, and I know his colleagues around the world have been cooperative and respect him. Within the government, he has had good support from Secretary of Commerce Baldrige and Secretary of Agriculture Lyng, but really little else to lean on.

As for specifics, I think the Uruguay Round has a very good chance of making progress in some very needed areas. For example, Yeutter and company have done a splendid job of kicking off the process in the area of services. He has gotten countries that I never thought would be interested, such as Brazil, involved in the process. With respect to agriculture, the problems are intense, but I think there is reason to believe they can make some progress. During the Tokyo Round we just couldn't move any further on agricultural subsidies or very far on subsidies in general, because the time wasn't right and the only thing I could say when we signed off was that we'll be back another day. Agriculture still needs a lot of work, but I think they can now make some progress in the area of subsidies generally because the timing has improved. All in all, I think we have reason to hope that over the next three to five years something positive will come out of the Uruguay Round.

Moving on to the issue of the U.S.-Canada Free Trade Arrangement, I think it's worth noting that everyone in Canada, as some of you know, is well aware of the negotiations. It's a key political issue. In the United States, however, I don't think anyone knows that the negotiations are going on, including two-thirds of the members of Congress. The fact that we're engaged in these negotiations really has been one of the few things that hasn't leaked out of this Administration.

For Prime Minister Mulroney, the successful conclusion of these negotiations is essential to his political career. Mulroney has staked a substantial portion of his political prestige on the fact that we told him that a U.S.-Canada trade agreement was a wonderful thing. And then we promptly lost interest in it on this side. In the United States, much of the burden of sustaining and supporting the negotiations has shifted to the private sector. Fortunately, important members of the American business community, such as Ed Pratt and Jim Robinson, have stepped in and initiated a private sector effort to try to build a bit more of a fire under the public sector, especially the Congress, to see if we can build a political consensus in favor of a balanced agreement.

Let me now talk a bit about the impact of the political process on trade issues. In my opinion, if we can make the political process begin to function again effectively between the Congress and the Executive Branch, then we can begin to grapple seriously with some of this country's trade and monetary problems. Otherwise, we will be unable to cope effectively with the problems facing us in international trade and the forces that continue to erode our competitive position in the world.

Unfortunately, over the past few years the political process hasn't worked at either the domestic or international levels. Without effective coordination between the political parties in this country or between our government and the governments of our main trading partners, there cannot be any public support for good trade policy. In the absence of public support, there is a void, and the result more often than not is bad trade policy. I'm sorry to say that we've seen more and more of that in recent years.

For example, while the Administration has been strong and effective in many areas, the White House has been a nonplayer in the field of trade despite the efforts of Brock, Yeutter, and Baldrige. Policy vacuums don't last for long in Washington, and the House of Representatives moved quickly in 1986 and passed a bad piece of legislation. Fortunately, nothing came of it. In 1987, the Administration has continued to resist protectionist legislation but has resorted to a series of ad hoc measures which have done little to remedy the country's trade position and even less to improve trade relations with our allies.

With respect to the political climate, and I mean no offense to my Japanese friends, I'm afraid the Japanese share much of the blame for their inability, not altogether their unwillingness, but their inability and unwillingness to deal with some of the problems their trade practices and trade surplus create in this country. I think Japan's inability to stem the trade costs borne by the United States has led directly to the sharp erosion in this country's support for a good trade policy. In my opinion, we've gone overboard on Japan bashing and retaliation, but the Japanese have responded poorly to the problem. I am seriously concerned that what we are dealing with today is far bigger than beef, citrus, autos, or semiconductors, because what we are talking about is the basic Japanese-American relationship. This relationship is precious and important to both of us.

Given this setting, it is essential that the West's leaders take charge, consult regularly, and work together to resolve the principal conflicts that threaten to seriously undermine world trade. On the domestic front, it is essential that the U.S. government articulate effectively to the American public the importance of the Uruguay Round. Trade must be emphasized as a top priority. That means, of course, that the United States must face up to the underlying economic fundamentals that lead to trade crises. The only real way to address Japanese procurement problems and European agricultural problems is for the United States to candidly recognize that a principal culprit of the country's trade problems is our own domestic economic policy. While it may be politically very pleasant to blame the trade deficit on foreigners because foreigners don't vote, we're not going to solve the trade problems until we've come to grips with our macroeconomic policies. Foreign unfair trade practices may be a part of the U.S. trade deficit, but they are certainly not the major cause.

So how do we come to grips with these macroeconomic policies? Those of you here today understand the problems better than I do, but in my opinion we're not going to deal with them until the public is ready to, and I don't know when that's going to happen. U.S. politicians of both parties are guilty of not keeping the American people fully informed of the difficult choices that face us. It's easy to talk about dealing with the budget deficit and how we can go about reducing it. Unfortunately, our meager efforts have generally stopped there. When the leadership of the country goes to the American public with an honest assessment of where we are, what our problems really are, and a sensible strategy to deal with them, they will find support. Until then, there will never be a political consensus to deal with the subject.

The White House and the Congress must level with the American people on the economic steps that must be taken to restore a semblance of balance to the country's fiscal policies. The budget deficit remains an intractable issue, largely because there is a lack of political will to deal with it firmly. With Congress distracted by trade issues and the Iran-Contra affair and the White House trying to salvage a presidency, there is little hope for action on the federal deficit in 1987. There is even less likelihood of decisive action being initiated in 1988 in the middle of what should be a hotly contested presidential election campaign.

Unfortunately, neither the U.S. economy nor the world economy can afford to wait for the American political system to sort itself out. The United States cannot afford to go on being dependent on foreign capital to finance our excessive spending. Any moves to cut this dependence, however, must be made very carefully, as the world economy cannot afford a U.S. austerity program. The problems we face today simply will not go away without firm leadership and decisive policies.

Without being overly pessimistic, it is worth recalling that the U.S. deficit has continued to grow during a period of near record economic growth. If U.S. policymakers cannot manage the budget when things are going well, what will happen when the cycle turns down? In my opinion, it is absolutely essential that policymakers stand tall and put the country back on a sound economic footing. Not only is a large federal deficit unhealthy in economic terms, but in political terms it reflects a weakness in leadership that is equally damaging. Therefore, it is important that we not squander opportunities to make real progress in dealing with the broad range of interrelated economic and trade issues.

That is why I strongly believe that it is important for the Uruguay Round to be successful. The world cannot afford to pass up this golden opportunity to deal with the serious trade problems confronting us.

In summary, I would like to relate a few of the broader lessons I have learned from my experience in the public and private sectors.

One: On trade and other international economic issues, the Executive Branch must speak with one voice. International economic policymaking must receive the personal attention of the President and his White House advisors. I can't emphasize this point enough. No foreign nation will take our policies and negotiations seriously unless they believe that the President is personally involved in the process.

Two: The search for new ideas is a phrase that has become meaningless. The search for new policy ideas or clever strategies is not a substitute for effective action. Trade policy in particular has been the focus of significant study and great rhetoric during the past few years. The country's trade position, however, has continued to deteriorate. We must no longer postpone action.

Three: Neither the Congress nor the Administration can make good trade policy or economic policy on their own.

And four: Partisan policy generally equals bad policy. I've addressed the need of forging a political consensus on trade. As Trade Representative, I worked closely and constructively with leaders of both parties. Broad bipartisan support was essential to the drafting and almost unanimous passage of the 1979 Trade Agreements Act in both the House and Senate.

In conclusion, it is vital that politicians and governments recognize that the way out of the present trade morass begins with a commitment to deal honestly, and, I might add, bluntly, with the political and economic realities faced by each country. No country can go it alone, and no country can solve its own problems without an understanding of the problems faced by others in the world. Further, to deal with trade disputes requires that the political process at both the domestic and international levels function effectively, leading to political consensus. In democracies, it is only through the political process that successful and lasting compromises can be achieved and, once achieved, maintained. Our problems were not created overnight, and there are no overnight quick fixes. But we can succeed over time with persistence. The people in this room today have a responsibility to lead that effort.

3. Michihiko Kunihiro

International Trade Policy and Trade Negotiations

International trade today is confronted with three major problems. They are: (1) inordinate trade imbalances between major trade partners, (2) instability in exchange rates, and (3) growing debts of developing countries.

International trade has provided incentives for economic growth, but it may now function to hamper economic growth if we fail to address these problems effectively.

Inordinate Trade Imbalances between Major Trade Partners

The huge trade imbalance between Japan and the United States is now called "intolerable" and is even described as a "threat" to the free trade system. We can mention a number of factors that have brought about such a huge trade imbalance. Among them, I believe, the insufficient coordination in macroeconomic policies between the two countries is most responsible.

The Ushiba-Strauss Communiqué of 1979 dealt with this aspect, but the U.S. negotiators in the present Administration showed little interest in discussing macroeconomic policy implications until recently. Perhaps they were not inclined to be involved in demand management, or perhaps they were wary that the Japanese negotiators might divert the issue from market barriers.

The U.S. Congress now seems serious about reducing the budget deficit, even if the Gramm-Rudman-Hollings requirement seems increasingly unattainable. It would be helpful if Congress succeeded in convincing the world that further budget deficit reduction would be in train for years after fiscal year 1988.

Japan has for some years been engaged in a historic task of restructuring its government system. It was expected to reinvigorate the private sector by deregulations, cuts in subsidies, slimming the government agencies, and so on. But the resources made available as a result of these endeavors have been absorbed by another urgent national endeavor: the reduction of the government debt. Under these circumstances, the Japanese trade negotiators were not in a very convenient position to launch macroeconomic arguments forcefully. The deflationary effect caused by the recent yen appreciation is now prompting Japanese policymakers to try more seriously to expand domestic demand. The Paris meeting of G-7 last February helped to change the current. The immediate question is what measures Japan will be able to announce after the 1987 budget bill has passed the Diet.

The EEC has been more consistent in bringing up macroeconomic issues to Japan, although I am not well informed about how the issue has been addressed between the EEC and the United States.

Instability of Exchange Rates

Since the Plaza agreement, we have learned something more than the classic J-curve effect; the rampant fluctuations of exchange rates paralyzes business by making planning and decision-making extremely difficult.

A sizable appreciation of the currency forces structural adjustment to the economy. But, the repeated fluctuations hamper necessary investment decisions, precipitating the deflationary effect caused by the currency appreciation.

On the other hand, an excessive depreciation of the currency delays industrial adjustments, entailing much greater difficulties when industry eventually faces the need for the structural changes necessary to remain competitive.

The flexible exchange rate very often produces overshooting, but we have not found a feasible, better alternative.

It is agreed that better coordination of economic policies among major countries provides a base on which the stability of exchange rates can be sought. The policy coordination efforts envisaged in the Tokyo Summit declaration led to the Baker-Miyazawa talks in October 1986 and the Paris talks in February 1987, but it is yet to be seen how much each country will be prepared to bend its domestic policies for the sake of exchange rate stabilities.

The Growing Debt of Developing Countries

The retreat of heavily indebted developing countries from international trade is causing serious difficulties not only to those countries themselves but also to industrial countries, particularly the United States. The most urgent need is to alleviate the debt service burden of the most heavily indebted countries, but they must undergo growth-oriented structural adjustment at the same time to diversify export income resources and to strengthen domestic supply bases. We should not forget that the real key to the solution is to increase their export capabilities.

On the part of the industrial countries, they should aggressively promote structural adjustments so that they can provide more markets for products from developing countries. Here again, better coordination between domestic economic policies and trade policies bears particular importance.

The Erosion of the GATT System

As reviewed so far, the measures required to deal with the three basic problems in today's international trade are closely related to, and require adjustments in, domestic economic policies. But, in addition, international trade policies must assume their own responsibilities.

The basic framework of the postwar international trade policies has been the GATT. Indeed, it has been instrumental in bringing about the development of international trade, which has helped the world economic growth. But the function of GATT has eroded over the years. While not an exhaustive list, here are some examples of what I mean:

a) frequent resort to the so-called gray measures, such as voluntary export restraint agreements;

b) diminishing effectiveness of the dispute settlement mechanisms;

c) recourse to countertrade, requirements by developing countries;

d) inability to deal with agricultural issues;

e) lack of authority in dealing with services and other "new" issues.

These matters are of vital importance and warrant an early start of the Uruguay Round.

Worrisome Trend in Bilateral Trade Negotiations

The Uruguay Round, however, will take a few years to conclude, and a major trade bill will, it seems, pass the U.S. Congress in a few months. Perhaps it is too early to predict the final shape of the trade legislation, but we are concerned that whatever may happen in trade statistics and trade negotiations in the coming weeks and months will affect congressional decisions on U.S. trade policy. It is a right moment, indeed, to look back on what has been happening in trade negotiations in recent years.

Fair Trade

I shall start with the "fair trade" issue. In my memory, it was during the course of the 1984 election campaign that the U.S. Administration began to juxtapose "fair" with "free" in pronouncing its trade policy. The policy sharpened its edge on September 23, 1985, when President Reagan announced his new trade initiatives. There should be no objection to seeking fairness in international trade. But the basic problem of the U.S. approach is the fact that the USTR who negotiates to correct "unfairness" is also authorized to determine if "fairness" is achieved or not. He is even authorized to determine how much countermeasure will be necessary to restore "fairness." In the eyes of foreign trade partners, this procedure is "unfair" in itself. They insist, therefore, that the issue should be dealt with in accordance with the GATT.

The U.S. negotiators complain that the GATT procedure takes too much time. It is true. We should strengthen the dispute settlement function of the GATT. By nature, the countermeasure to restitute "unfairness" will not offer compensation. This makes it all the more necessary to place the whole procedure under the GATT discipline. As the U.S. Administration frequently wields Section 301 against almost all major trading partners, the American public gets the impression that everybody around the United States is unfair and develops an antagonistic attitude toward major trading partners. Another concern is that Section 301, especially if its retaliatory threshold is further lowered, will become "Cheap 201" or "backdoors to protectionism." Section 301 will then serve purposes for which it was not designed.

Voluntary Export Restraints

Another method used to circumvent the GATT scrutiny and the burden of compensation has been the "voluntary export restraint" (VER). At an early stage, it had the merit of limiting the damage of trade restriction to one or two exporting countries, rather than subjugating all trade partners to a nondiscriminatory import restriction that might otherwise have been applied. The VER is also a quick fix, isolating the restriction in a particular sector, avoiding a general protectionist policy. On the part of the exporting countries, the VER has the merit of cartelizing exporters to their own benefit.

Since then, the VER has proliferated in terms of both products and countries involved. Although it always starts as a temporary or even an emergency measure, the VER has an intrinsic nature of perpetuation. The textile agreement does have reluctant GATT blessing and is subject to GATT discipline, if only nominally, but almost all other VERs are short of transparency and GATT discipline. As the VER become a mainstream type of trade restriction, rather than an exception, third-party countries become concerned about its adverse effects on them.

The automobile is a case in point. The U.S. Administration maintains the position that it no longer asks for the restraint, but the congressional reaction will be more than obvious if Japan terminates the VER on autos. Under the present circumstances, Japan has no other choice, and yet the Japanese auto industry is blamed for opting for restraint to maintain higher prices. The fact is that the industry wants to discontinue the restraint because the industry is keenly aware that idling on the quota system erodes its vitality. The EEC, on the other hand, claims that Japan's VER agreement with the United States is shifting Japan's auto exports to the EEC market. Actually, in the U.S. market, Japanese auto exports may have reached a saturation point in view of the increased supply from Japanese factories inside the United States and the price effect of the yen appreciation. But it is the political heat in the Congress that is preventing Japan from terminating the VER at this juncture.

At any rate, the VER needs a thorough review, and it also calls for a review of the GATT safeguard mechanism.

Industrial Overproduction

It seems GATT is confronted with the new situation of industrial overproduction as a result of the worldwide industrialization helped by technological development. We see such a trend in textiles, steel, shipbuilding, semiconductors, and so on. To cope with the textile overproduction, the Multi-Fibers Agreement was introduced, but there is a growing discontent about it on the part of the developing countries.

For steel, both the United States and the EEC formed de facto international cartels on their own. As regards shipbuilding, the OECD has been trying for an informal coordination whose effect is not altogether clear. Perhaps the waning of traditional shipyards in countries, including Japan, may be the inevitable eventuality as far as export is concerned.

At one stage, a U.S. official suggested that we should refrain from extending the EX-IM credit to finance a new steel mill in Korea because the whole world is suffering from excess capacity. Was it a right approach? Even if it were, what should we do about other industries where the catching up of newly industrialized countries is bringing about excess facilities?

The semiconductor gives us a very perplexing problem. For the moment, Japan concluded an ad hoc agreement with the United States to deal with today's singular situation, causing a great deal of displeasure in other countries, particularly the EEC. It seems that much of the problem derives from the fact that Japan invested too much in the new chip facilities. Whether the estimate of the Japanese industry on the future demand was right or not, the fact remains that the increased production of more efficient semiconductors at very low prices will be possible by means of a comparatively small amount of investment and with relatively simple skilled labor, probably in many countries other than Japan. Can we stop it? Should we?

Other high-tech products may follow suit. A few highly educated scientists and gifted entrepreneurs in developing countries can start a business, possibly in joint venture with foreign firms, with facilities purchased at a relatively low cost and with standardized labor locally available, and produce products that will be able to compete well with those from industrial countries. Isn't it a dream-come-true story for many developing countries?

Yes, but the industrial countries don't know for sure yet what to do with this new situation. One orthodox answer is for the developed countries not to do anything but endeavor toward higher technological progress. A pragmatic approach might be to authorize importing countries to limit imports of that kind of product to a certain level, for example, 25 percent of the domestic consumption, while prohibiting any restrictive measures below that level. Of course, I support the former approach, but one might argue that the latter may be better than all the mutual recriminations and threats of destroying the world trading system that we are experiencing these days.

In any event, we should always bear in mind that the whole purpose of international trade policy is economic growth of *all* countries. The trade policy advocated by leading industrialized countries should not have the effect of denying industrial growth to developing countries.

Agriculture

Another situation of overproduction with which international trade policy is confronted is in agriculture.

It is mainly the product of heavy subsidies in developed countries, particularly the EEC and the United States, although technological progress also accounts for it. The increasingly heavy agricultural subsidy is imposing an unbearable budgetary burden in both the EEC and the United States. It is rendering damage to farmers in countries like Australia, New Zealand, and Canada. It is also causing distortion in agriculture in developing countries. We should urgently discuss some concerted actions, first to freeze the subsidy level and then to reduce it progressively.

The budgetary constraint will work as leverage for reducing subsidies, but our attempt should go further than overcoming the budgetary difficulties, because otherwise we would not achieve much more than a standstill.

The immediate problem in the agricultural trade policy is the export subsidy, but it may be difficult to discuss the export subsidy entirely separately from agricultural subsidy in general.

It is often said that, in agricultural policy, every country is a sinner. It may be that, all for political reasons, none of us will be able to save ourselves completely from this sin for a long time. For all practical purposes, we may have to work out agricultural trade policy on that premise. If so, we had better admit it and try to agree on a common rule that is different, to the extent necessary, from the one applied to industrial goods. In the particular case of agricultural trade, I am personally inclined to lean to the "minimum access" approach as suggested in the GATT study.

Reciprocity

Finally, we should touch upon the reciprocity issue. It is natural that we insist on reciprocity as a general guiding principle in trade negotiations. But what we should go after is reciprocity in opportunity for overall trade benefit. If we demand reciprocity on a sectoral basis and retaliate when the sectoral reciprocity is not given, the spiral of retaliation will lead to contraction in the total trade.

The so-called aggressive reciprocity on a sectoral basis is advocated for the reason that otherwise the importing country that maintains trade barriers would not feel compelled to eliminate them. But the recent argument pronounced by U.S. negotiators on some of the issues sounds more emphatic on countermeasures than mutually opening the market. The remedy, if necessary, should be sought in accordance with Article XXIII of the GATT.

International trade is experiencing its most crucial year in the postwar era. In my view, the realignment of exchange rates has already produced a definite change in trend, only it does not show up in statistics in U.S. dollars. Japan's real GNP growth last year was sustained by the contribution of domestic demand making up for the negative contribution of external demand. It will be a matter of another few months when we will see a marked improvement in the international trade balance also in U.S. dollar figures.

What I am very much worried about is the growing impatience in the Congress and the irritated attitude of the U.S. trade negotiators. On the part of the Japanese, many are feeling they are being penalized with the appreciation of the yen because their industry is suffering from heavy loss of profit and increasing unemployment. But they should take it to heart that just enduring the yen appreciation is not enough. I think the experience in the past year and a half has made the Japanese realize that, unless they import more, they will have to face a stronger yen which will inflict damage on Japanese industry.

And yet the U.S. Congress appears to be intent on "tough" legislative actions and urging the Administration to take further "tough" actions on Japan, and perhaps on a number of other countries with which it has a large trade deficit as well. The rhetoric used is even assuming the sound of vengeance. Policies like this will in the end have an effect of antagonizing America's trade partners who are, in fact, time-honored customers of American products. Indeed, we are at a very crucial moment when we all should see the whole problem in its true perspective.

Note

Opinions expressed in this paper are the personal opinions of the writer.

4. Edmund T. Pratt, Jr.

Changing Realities: The Need for Business-Government Cooperation

When Marty called me a number of months ago and asked me to come down here, my first reaction was that he probably had the wrong Pratt. Plain old businessmen like myself are not usually invited to august sessions of economists and former government leaders and the like. As a matter of fact, I haven't even been to a summit meeting!

And it's a little strange, when you stop to think about it from the businessman's point of view, that you don't find more of us represented at sessions like this. We could argue that the macroeconomic policies, debt concerns, and financial arrangements that are under consideration are primarily concerned with creating an atmosphere in which business can flourish or fail to flourish.

Therefore, after a little thought, I agreed to come—with some trepidation. And I have to say, I'm much appreciative for the invitation. I thought the debates and discussions yesterday were very, very revealing and interesting and, therefore, very helpful and important to me.

As I thought about it though, the idea of getting more businessmen involved in these discussions, although it's rational, may not be as good as our old policy. Under that policy we left issues like those discussed during this conference to the academics, governments, and bankers and then complained like heck when they blew it.

As a matter of fact though, I think it is fair to say that the business community has come a long way from earlier days when we relied on that strategy. The Business Roundtable, the NAM, the Chamber of Commerce, and all the various business organizations over recent years have made landmark changes in the way the business community approaches our relationship with other policymaking members of society. Perhaps one of the most critical things that has happened in the business community during my membership is our realization that all members need to be more involved in policy issues that impact us. If there is anything more critical to our country during an age of keen world competition, it is the fact that our competitiveness depends on better integration and cooperation with academia, government, and other elements of our society. We in the business community have the resources now to join in these debates and have been trying to influence policy.

I would like to follow up on Mike Blumenthal's comments and provide another businessman's perspective on how major U.S. companies like ours approach discussions on such policy issues as trade and investment. A little bit of background may be interesting and necessary to help understand how we approach the current debates.

Most of the major U.S. companies, indeed, I guess, in the world these days, are multinational companies. I've been a part of two of them. I spent the first half of my career with IBM and the second half with Pfizer. Our company, like Mike's, could well be considered a classic multinational company. Two-thirds of our employees are located outside the United States. We have about 160 manufacturing plants, two-thirds of those are outside the United States. Roughly half of our sales and somewhat less than half of our profits come from operations outside the United States.

And why is that? Why did companies like Pfizer and IBM over the last thirty or forty years aggressively go abroad and become part of the local communities rather than staying at home and exporting, which really would have been much simpler. We try to explain this to our tax people, and they say we did it for tax reasons. As a matter of fact, we did it for a very simple reason—it was the only way we could do business. We had currency problems in those days, and we had balance of trade problems, too. Almost every country in the world, when we started strongly going abroad from America in the years after World War II, had inadequate dollars to pay for our products. We would have been nowhere had we not found a way to solve that problem, not by negotiation but by unilateral reaction to the conditions from the businessman's point of view.

As a result of that, we now find ourselves with operations in nearly every country, in nearly every currency in the world. And we are therefore affected in a different way than those organizations that depend on trade and the relative balance of exchange rates to determine whether they can sell their products or not. We have effects from changing currency values, but they are more accounting effects than "ability to sell" effects.

An interesting figure that opens most Congressmen's eyes is that approximately 80 percent of all manufactured American export goods are done by multinational companies. And approximately 40 percent of all U.S. manufactured goods actually are exported to the foreign-owned subsidiaries of American companies.

These figures begin to give you the feeling of what the "trade" situation really is for many of us and for our country in general. We believe that the argument can well be made, as it has always been made, for freer trade, but it is just as important to have freer economic relationships. International economic cooperation, the subject of this conference, comes closer to describing what it is we have now. We don't have just international trade, we have international economic relationships.

Given the emergence of this new environment, the American business community has recognized that the GATT of the past really is inadequately focused to handle the problems we have relative to international business. Tariffs and trade barriers are important to us, but they're not the critical issues today.

Investments are now much more important to most of us; that is, the ability to continue to invest and to operate in other countries without being discriminated against. We've spent a lot of time in the last few years explaining this to our own government and our own Congress.

Services, investment rules, protection of intellectual property rights are for most of us the key issues of the day, not barriers and tariffs.

Certainly the importance of all of these things, international trade as well as international investment, we believe, is a win-win situation. Again, our discussion yesterday came to the rather obvious conclusion that a different kind of investment is needed in debt-ridden countries where traditional sources of money to relieve debt burdens in the future are less available. Strangely enough, in spite of the problems of their balance sheets, most of us in business are still willing to take the required risks and to invest sizable funds in these countries, given halfway reasonable rules in order to make those investments worthwhile.

Although macroeconomic policies play a more significant role in creating a favorable business environment today, trade policies do remain important to us. We continue to work in those vineyards, as we have for many years.

After World War II, the first really serious signs of protectionism began to emerge in the United States about twenty years ago. Certain industries began to be severely impacted by the industrial revival of major foreign competitors of the past and the emergence of the lesser developed countries. Those of us in the companies that had gone abroad years earlier, and to whom foreign markets were a critical part of our operation, formed an organization called the Emergency Committee for American Trade (ECAT). It included about sixty-five of the major American companies, a very large chunk of our industrial capacity.

It was created as an "emergency committee" to lobby Congress and the government as they began to consider the first protectionist activities that we had seen in a number of years. The ECAT companies recognized that somebody was going to pay for protectionist moves (very likely the sixty-five of us) and that it was in America's own interest, and certainly in ours, that we do something about it.

Interestingly enough, that committee was formed and we all put up some funds to create it with the agreement that we would get in there, do the job, and self-destruct. I've been Chairman of ECAT for the last twelve years. It still keeps going, and after over twenty years, we've wondered whether we should rename it, since the Emergency Committee for American Trade perhaps is not descriptive of a twenty-year-old situation. We've concluded, however, that we've had a continuing emergency for all that time. ECAT continues to be extremely involved today and, I believe, has played a major role in holding off many undesirable protectionist activities.

The U.S. private-public sector advisory network also plays an important role in the development of U.S. trade policy. Created by the Congress, the growing advisory network provides private sector input to the government on trade matters, including negotiations. This makes a lot of sense since the trade negotiators are negotiating *our* rules for international economic relationships. This advisory group embraces more than a thousand people who are actively involved in the process—labor leaders, lawyers, agricultural people, academics, business leaders, and so on. Representatives of this advisory network attend major international meetings, such as the Punta del Este meeting.

American business has generally always supported GATT—the obvious logic of what GATT is trying to achieve is clear to us. Having said that, it would be unfair not to tell you that the general feeling of the U.S. business community is that GATT, in general, has not been particularly good for America. In every negotiation, no matter how relatively successful, our country gave up more than it got. I realize that people in every country probably feel that way, but the facts suggest that in the aggregate our country has freer conditions than just about any other.

During the days of previous trade negotiations, our conceding more than we got was viewed as a reasonable outcome. It could almost be visualized as part of the Marshall Plan syndrome of the time. It was in our long-term interest to reach out to the countries that needed more help. But the situation has changed. Now many businesses in *this* country are in trouble. There is a growing concern that any further negotiations *not* proceed along that same path.

When the idea of the current Uruguay Round came up, members of the government's advisory network were canvassed on their reactions to a new round. You won't be surprised to hear that what we got, at best, was lukewarm agreement that another round was a good thing. Why? Because everyone was concerned that we were likely to lose more than we gained out of such a negotiation, if past history is any guide.

Indeed, the same reaction is what's behind the seemingly unconcerned attitude of American business leaders about the negotiations for a U.S.-Canada Free Trade Agreement. To our credit, even with the doubts that we have, American business has never opposed trying to promote trade agreements. But here again, when asked for our views, there was very lukewarm enthusiasm for such talks. The business community in general does not believe that the Canadians are likely to go very far in giving up things that they would have to give up to make such a negotiation of interest to us and in order for us to give up whatever we must in return.

Given the lukewarm support among American business for a new GATT round, we told our Administration we would support it only with certain provisions. In addition to the normal discussion items of the functioning of the GATT system itself, agriculture clearly is a critical item that needs serious attention in a multilateral framework. Second, in the manufacturing area, unless we included services, investment rules, and intellectual property, we would not support a new round of negotiations. The U.S. government did agree to those conditions and, in fact, has been particularly responsive in these critical areas that are new to GATT.

On investment, for example, we were never before able to get an American Administration to do more than say they weren't against direct foreign investment by U.S companies. Yet, we got a strong statement of support from the Reagan Administration, not only on the importance of investment but also on services and intellectual property protection. In a country whose competitiveness has been threatened by recent events, certainly our strongest suit is our innovation and technical competence.

The business community has also received increasing support from this Administration on bilateral trade actions against countries that disregard intellectual property rights and condone unfair trade and investment practices. While I strongly believe in the multilateral approach, it is also very clear to me that many of the major gains in the short run will continue to be on a bilateral basis.

However, some believe the Congress is trying to take U.S. trade policy too far on a bilateral basis, to the detriment of our multilateral obligations. The business community still has a moderating influence with respect to Congress and potential trade legislation. Nevertheless, we are in a much more aggressive mood concerning the role the Executive Branch should have in carrying out the existing rules and regulations relative to fair trade and, indeed, to critical economic policies. We don't understand, for example, why we should continue to sustain intolerable deficits with strong countries, particularly with Japan. We don't understand why we should continue to tolerate discrimination against us, even in the developing countries, which undoubtedly need special concessions from us in some areas. But the argument can be made, I think rightfully, that conditions leading to freer investment and trade flows with the developing countries are good for both sides. We should not continue to tolerate their closing us out.

After years of blaming the government for any problems U.S. industry had, now government leaders and others are pointing the finger more and more at the "competitiveness" of U.S. industry and arguing that it's really the main issue. A recent NBER study showed that American multinational companies have sustained their competitiveness in terms of holding onto their market share of world trade exports. This suggests that American management per se has not gone down for the count. It also suggests that there are some special problems related to our country and its ability to compete in today's world markets that are perhaps more significant than American management itself.

The business community understands that the key problems today are macroeconomic. It has for the last three or four years been demanding as strongly as it could from all of its organizations that the government get its act together on fiscal policy.

Finally, as far as American competitiveness is concerned, there is a whole list of domestic items that are critical to making us more competitive that have nothing to do with foreign trade. For instance, our export administration laws, where we regularly shoot ourselves in the foot to try to achieve some unachievable issue of human relations or security, have been proven over the years not to work and have been a sizable detriment to our operations. We have antitrust laws that tend to make us less competitive. Our tax policy has never put its effect on international competitiveness as a high priority, and our last tax bill was basically anticompetitive.

One of the critical issues we face which alone can end up making us noncompetitive in the world is the issue of tort reform. We have a huge number of lawyers in my company now, and it's not really that big a company. The millions of dollars and huge amount of time that is spent fighting off the growing hoards of ambulance-chasing lawyers is enough by itself to make you noncompetitive.

We probably need law changes, as much as we hate to say it, relative to the abusive takeover situation. In general, the extreme cases are negative to our economy and a diversion of resources in the American business community.

In summary, the U.S. multinational business community has recognized the new global economic environment in which it operates. We are responding to the challenging new policy issues facing us. Trade policy and competitiveness in American business need to also claim a higher priority in our government's action than they ever have before. The cooperation of policymakers in all segments of our society is a key factor to our continued economic vitality and competitiveness.

Summary of Discussion

Blumenthal once asked former Secretary of State Christian Herder why he came to the USTR from the State Department. Herder responded that he liked politics best, and that in his experience there are more politics wrapped up in trade issues than anywhere else. Trade, Blumenthal stated, is a political issue. Blumenthal argued that to make meaningful progress on trade problems it is important to have relative economic stability and growth, but that it is essential to have both domestic and international political consensus. In the current international environment, LDC debts, large current account imbalances, and exchange rate swings make successful trade negotiations much harder to achieve. Blumenthal felt that the last truly successful trade negotiations were the Kennedy Round because the key form of protection under negotiation was still tariffs. Much of the early postwar success with trade negotiations followed from the willingness of the United States to give up more than it would extract. This was true throughout the 1950s and early 1960s.

To this, *Anthony Solomon* added an anecdote of his own. As the Kennedy Round negotiations were concluded, Lyndon Johnson held a cabinet meeting in which several advisers discouraged him from signing. Many of the prospective trade flow numbers presented at the meeting showed the United States would not be getting as much as it was giving. At one point, Solomon mentioned to the President that the assumptions behind the numbers were very arbitrary and that minor modifications would easily yield a different bottom line. Johnson said nothing, but at the end of the meeting announced his decision: he would approve the Kennedy Round on the condition that Solomon "fix up the numbers."

Blumenthal also noted that at the time tariffs were the major form of protection. Governments held to the letter of the agreement but found new ways, which are far more difficult to regulate, to protect the industries of their choice. The protectionism typified by the agricultural policies of the United States and the Common Market has turned out to be more costly than ever imagined. Blumenthal was skeptical but did not rule out the possibility for progress at the Uruguay Round. He felt that any meaningful pact would require specificity and new enforcement machinery. The best that can happen until 1989 is that nothing happen.

Strauss assured Blumenthal that the nastiest provisions of the Gephardt bill, such as legal recourse to treble damages for industries injured by imports, would be dropped in conference. The modified Gephardt bill, which is likely to get through the House of Representatives and the conference committee, will focus primarily on countries that have large bilateral surpluses vis-à-vis the United States. Gephardt's presidential ambitions have allowed the unpopularity of an aggressively protectionist stance to soften the bill. He wants to finesse this bill without looking like a hawkish protectionist, but at the same time he needs to look good in Iowa. *Richardson* added that the bill had the positive and important feature that it would extend the negotiating authority for trade talks beyond December.

Blumenthal defended recognizing in the bill the question of bilateral imbalances. He argued that older concepts, such as reciprocity, were no longer as relevant as before. Even assuming that Japan's trading behavior is perfectly fair, large bilateral imbalances are *politically* unsustainable. Reciprocity and fairness are important in their own right, but, ultimately, trade is a political issue.

Schultze was less sanguine about the trade bill, even though its most monstrous features have been removed. Schultze believed that provisions of trade legislation that require the President to impose penalties unless he declares that doing so would be contrary to the national interest are not a good thing. Each time the President refuses to take the hardline position, he will expend some political capital. Eventually, it will become necessary for him to make an example out of a case in order to demonstrate that he is willing to act. This loophole is not without costs. Schultze pointed out that seemingly innocuous details of a bill often turn out to be costly. The definition of dumping in the 1974 Trade Act as sales below full cost has become a big problem.

Strauss responded that concerns about the Gephardt bill voiced by Schultze and Blumenthal were justified. The United States will now pay a price for the Administration's refusal to reverse the budget deficit and the rise of the dollar. But one must confront reality: there is going to be trade legislation. The only question that remains is what kind of bill we will have. He thought that the Administration will get involved when the bill is in conference. Waiting until such a late stage may prove to be a mistake.

Branson seconded the notion that this bill is moderate. The shift in emphasis to an active trade policy based on opening foreign markets, away from a reactive policy of closing domestic markets, is desirable. A likely outcome, one more important for politicians than for economists, is that the U.S./Japan bilateral balance will be improved.

Richardson was more optimistic about the medium-run outlook for trade policy coordination. He felt that there is a growing emphasis in trade policy on multinational interests, labor interests, and GATT codes instead of MTNs over tariffs. There is interest in a safeguards code that would alleviate back-door escape-clause proceedings via unfair-trade remedies. We therefore need not be so bleak about the medium-run possibilities for improved trade coordination, which would include the Japanese.

Sachs emphasized that large trade imbalances are ultimately a macroeconomic problem. Both the U.S. and Japanese current accounts have changed dramatically over the past five years, while commercial policies have remained virtually the same. Japanese savings as a percentage of GNP has not changed over the past six years. Instead, private and public investment have fallen by 1 and 3 percent of GNP, respectively. If Japanese macro policies are to blame, what can be done to reverse them? First, Sachs suggested that Japan reverse the drive for domestic financial market liberalization. Most of the controls that have been removed previously acted to keep Japanese savings within

Japan. Second, Japan has room for fiscal expansion. Third, the Miyakawa reforms could be explored more actively. There is no serious work being undertaken in Japan to ascertain the effects that tax changes and land use changes might have on the interest rate or savings. While Japan is confused about a course of action, the United States continues to pound the table over trade issues which do not speak to the heart of the problem. Several participants agreed that the trade problem was really a macroeconomic issue.

Feldstein added that the Japanese capital outflow was not only private: about one half of the net outflow from the second quarter of 1986 to the first quarter of 1987 was generated by purchases of U.S. assets by the Bank of Japan. Indeed, net purchases of dollar assets by the Bank of Japan in January 1987 were $9 billion, a figure larger than Japan's trade surplus in that month.

Strauss felt that in spite of the furor over trade, Congress had not overreacted. The United States may be frustrated by Japan, but the Japanese feel equally put upon. Each day C-span carries the speeches of congressmen trying to please their constituents. Their rhetoric rarely finds its way into policy, but audiences in Japan rightly think that the United States is nuts. Such TV diplomacy is becoming a serious problem.

Kunihiro asserted that Japan regarded as vital their relations with the United States, and that they were willing to make sacrifices to maintain a good relationship. Japan has no intention of undermining U.S. industry: they want the United States to be strong. Kunihiro felt that Section 301 tends to be counterproductive because it generates moral accusations which are often unfair in the eyes of the trade partners and that the Japanese would better understand if the recourse were made to the 201 cases filed in the United States, the avenue open to U.S. industries damaged by imports. He wondered, however, if justice had been done in the U.S. retaliation for alleged Japanese noncompliance with the semiconductor agreement.

Kunihiro also offered his comments on the semiconductor agreement. He acknowledged that the 100 percent tariff placed on $300 million of imports is a reaction to a growing frustration with Japan and that semiconductors themselves are not the only issue. The timing is unfortunate, in that considerable changes are already taking place in Japan. He felt that Japanese negotiators interpreted the semiconductor agreement as offering more latitude than the United States was comfortable with, particularly in third-country markets. The United States did warn Japan that a time limit for compliance had elapsed, but the Japanese were not convinced that all avenues had been pursued. Kunihiro was not optimistic about the future.

Blumenthal felt that the United States would have to pound the table in order to get results from Japan. When dealing with the Japanese on trade matters it seems that logic is useless and facts are irrelevant. He felt that Japan's confusion is a political reality and must be confronted. The fact is that the bilateral imbalance is egregious, and Japan must be convinced of this. What the Japanese choose to do to eliminate the current account surplus is their problem; they will act when it is in their interest to act.

Strauss suggested that Blumenthal had overstated his case. First, the Japanese need not bring their current account into balance; their surplus could be sent, for instance, to the LDCs. Second, bilateral balances do not really matter as much as some seem to perceive. *De Menil* concurred that the situation with Japan should not be viewed as a bilateral problem. He speculated that if the dollar fell to 120 yen by the summer, we might expect to see a significant reduction in Japan's current account. *Blumenthal* agreed with Strauss that a Japanese current account of zero is not required, but reiterated his view that bilateral imbalances of such magnitude were politically untenable.

Fischer commented that the rising yen helps ease the disparity between savings and investment, not only by increasing Japanese demand for foreign products but also by reducing income in Japan relative to its trading partners. A reduction in income forces an increase in government spending and lowers savings more than proportionately, thereby helping to reduce the current account surplus. Fischer also made the point that while bilateral balances are not important in principle, the United States is a good candidate to be close to bilateral balance with Japan. Japan is a major importer of goods, such as raw materials, oil, and agricultural goods, which we export. *Feldstein* added that if the United States were to drop its restriction on shipping oil from Alaska the perception of the bilateral balance problem would be reduced.

Rosett spoke as a U.S. consumer who has bought, and bought cheaply, many Japanese products. He wondered whether any politicians would capitalize on the support from consumers to continue the availability of cheap imports. *Greenspan* underscored the fact that it is very hard to hit Japan without hitting the U.S. consumer where it hurts. There may be a big backlash when the prices of these products double.

Attali shared Blumenthal's view that the imbalances are so large as to be a predominantly political problem. In the coming months the solution will be found more through a continued depreciation of the dollar than through any changes in commercial policy. He went on to say that the trade issue for the United States is the tip of the iceberg and that underlying economic reforms must be made. He compared the current situation of the United States with that of the United Kingdom in the early twentieth century. Perhaps a kind of reverse Miyazawa report should be written for the United States, detailing desirable changes in incentives, where profits are made, and where youth and the elite are going. In any event, solutions to trade issues will not be found in trade legislation.

Marston was encouraged to hear the blame for trade imbalances placed primarily on macroeconomic matters. Suppose, he suggested, that the macroeconomic problems were solved and that exchange rates were stabilized at an appropriate level. He was curious whether Ed Pratt thought the United States would be able to compete in high-tech areas. Research by Paul Krugman indicates that U.S. firms were blocked from competing in the Japanese market for 16K semiconductor chips. This strategy gave Japan a foothold and allowed them to overtake the United States in subsequent chip designs.

Pratt responded by saying that the United States continues to retain its advantages in many high-tech areas and that it spends more on research and development than does Japan. A policy of blocking foreign products is not new there. Unlike most of the rest of East Asia, there are no U.S. automobiles in Japan. On the other hand, his company, Pfizer, has been successful in getting into Japanese markets by investing there instead of trying to only export to Japan. Nevertheless, the outcome of Japan's protectionist policies has been to keep imports out once they have capacity in place. We have mistakenly allowed Japan to do this. *Blumenthal* added that the Japanese really have not been so successful in computers. Unisys is one of the largest producers in Japan. But for the difficulty in reaching Japanese markets, Unisys would have been even bigger.

Ruggiero agreed with Blumenthal that it will be hard to sign any trade agreement whose intention is to expand the scope of the system at a time of such worldwide economic uncertainty. Nevertheless, one need not be uniformly pessimistic. For example, great progress can be made on the Common Market agricultural program. There is a consensus building that the current situation is unsustainable, and the ECC is already beginning to tackle the problem.

De Menil felt that trade issues can also spill over to affect investment. An example would be Fujitsu's failed attempt to acquire Fairchild Semiconductor from Schlumberger. The intimidation of Fujitsu was a mistake for the United States; a revitalized Fairchild would have been good for employment here. He felt that Fairchild's competitors created enough emotion about the transaction that it was no longer a business decision.

McNamar said that once an issue had reached a kind of bumper-sticker mentality, it was hard to control. Hence, the unwarranted focus on the bilateral imbalance with Japan or the Schlumberger-Fairchild affair. He thought that the current U.S. strategy of using a bilateral agreement between the United States and Canada on services as a model for the Uruguay Round was not a good one. A better approach would have also involved Mexico in a North American free trade zone.

He pointed out the contradiction between the current U.S. negotiating emphasis on open investment rules and the U.S. reaction to the proposed Schlumberger sale of Fairchild to the Japanese.

Gergen asked Strauss what kind of leadership we could expect in 1988. He was doubtful that in two years we will have solved the budget problem; candidates seem willing to make too many campaign promises for lower taxes and higher agricultural subsidies. The United States needs leadership, and those running are not inspiring.

Strauss agreed that there will be excessive bidding for the protectionist vote and that tax commitments will be made which shouldn't be fulfilled. He regretted that, their importance notwithstanding, economic issues will take a backseat. The next presidential election and foregoing primaries will be decided by issues such as abortion, ERA, Aids, and even whether the U.S. embassy should be located in Tel Aviv or Jerusalem. When these are the issues of the day, it is hard to get the best people to seek office and win. He felt that neither the Republicans nor the Democrats had put up their best candidates for 1988.

The thought of letting Iowa and New Hampshire narrow the field is crazy, and the incentives to make campaign promises that should not be kept are overwhelming. While the unknown candidate needs the early primary as a means of gaining notoriety, Strauss felt that the loss of the dark horse candidate is a worthy sacrifice for making the entire process more rational. He suggested that Sam Nunn is possibly the most capable man the Democrats could nominate, but that Nunn couldn't get votes in Iowa. Perhaps it would not be long before a frontrunner adopted the strategy of not going to Iowa at all. Perhaps this is why Cuomo dropped out.

Kunihiro said that he had listened to the criticisms, warnings, and advice of the conference participants. He realized that the political clock was running faster than the economic clock. The Miyazawa report has been and would be influential in changing the Japanese way of thinking. It would raise awareness that 40,000 steel workers, shipping workers, etc., will be unemployed in the years to come if nothing is done. Kunihiro stressed the effects of the high yen: an exodus of production from Japan, reductions in employment, an increase in imports of manufactured products beginning in the fourth quarter of 1986. All of these are working as a strong lever for structural adjustment. While manufacturing imports from the United States have not increased substantially, imports from other countries have. There is no reason why the United States shouldn't do as well if U.S. firms take the Japanese market seriously. He agreed that the current bilateral imbalance with the United States was unsustainable and stated that Japan would act to reduce it. The overall surplus of Japan, however, is partly due to the reduction in mineral fuel prices, which alone improved the current account by $19 billion last year.

Pratt, in closing, reiterated his admiration for Japan. He looked forward to the opportunity of solving the problems together.

4 Developing Country Debt

1. Jeffrey D. Sachs
2. Anthony M. Solomon
3. William S. Ogden
4. Eduardo Wiesner
5. R. T. McNamar

1. Jeffrey D. Sachs

International Policy Coordination: The Case
of the Developing Country Debt Crisis

4.1 Introduction

The LDC debt crisis has differed from other problems in the world
economy in an important and fascinating way. From the beginning of
the crisis, all leading governments have acknowledged the need for an
activist and internationally coordinated policy response. Even the ostensibly laissez-faire Reagan Administration went swiftly into action
in August 1982 when the global debt crisis exploded with Mexico's
announcement that it would be unable to meet its international debt
service obligations. Within days, the U.S. government arranged for
billions of dollars of emergency financing for Mexico. Since then, the
U.S. government has taken the lead in managing the international response to the crisis, a response that has called for the coordinated
actions of the leading creditor governments, the debtor governments,
the international banks, and the multilateral financial institutions.

The management of the crisis has been only a partial success. On
the positive side, the dire predictions of pessimists in 1982 have not
come to pass: the countries with the largest debts have serviced their
debts and not defaulted; the international commercial banks have remained solvent; the international capital markets have continued to
function and, indeed except for the debtor countries, have expanded
in their scope and functions; and the world has not fallen into a default-
induced depression. These favorable outcomes resulted in significant

part from the actions of policymakers at key junctures in the past five years.

On the other hand, the economic results for most of the debtor countries have been poor. Economic development for hundreds of millions of people has been halted or partially reversed. The long-term adequacy of the current debt strategy therefore remains very much in doubt, despite the success to date in avoiding a financial crisis. Contrary to the forecasts of the IMF, the creditor governments, and the commercial banks, the debtor countries have enjoyed neither sustained recovery nor renewed access to market lending under the current rules of the game. In some countries, the economic situation has become so desperate that governments have been forced into unilateral moratorium on debt servicing, even at the cost of a serious rupture of international financial relations.

This mix of success and failure is related to the kind of international policy coordination advocated and managed by the United States in recent years. The U.S. government and the other leading creditor governments (including the United Kingdom, Japan, and Germany) have worried more about continued debt servicing to the commercial banks than about the pace of economic development in the debtor countries. By opting to use their political and economic influence to bolster their banks' positions, the creditor governments have been able to sustain the flow of debt payments from the debtor countries, but often at very high economic and political costs to the debtor countries themselves.

The policy emphasis on debt servicing to the commercial banks is not surprising and was certainly not inappropriate in the first couple of years of the debt crisis. The threat of insolvency of the world's largest commercial banks was the most serious problem raised by the debt crisis at its inception. As shown in the data of table 4.1, the LDC exposure of the largest U.S. commercial banks greatly exceeded 100 percent of bank capital at the end of 1982. The same is apparently true of the largest banks in Europe and Japan, although data on bank exposures and bank capital are not generally available outside of the United States. Widespread debt repudiations could have easily triggered a global banking crisis, and it was not unreasonable for policymakers to fear that such a crisis could have pushed the world from a deep recession into a deep depression.

Moreover, various analyses suggested that if the short-term problems of the debt crisis could be contained, then most of the debtor countries had the longer term capacity to resume debt servicing and to restore economic growth, a viewpoint which has been bolstered by the continuing decline in world interest rates. Most of these analyses also stressed, however, the need for a continuing flow of new capital into

Table 4.1   **U.S. Bank Assets in the Debtor Countries (nine major banks)**

	End-1982	Mid-1984	March 1986
Total Exposure ($ billion)			
All LDCs	83.4	84.0	75.6
Latin America	51.2	53.8	52.2
Africa	5.6	4.9	3.6
Exposure as Percent of Bank Capital			
All LDCs	287.7	246.3	173.2
Latin America	176.5	157.8	119.7
Sub-Saharan Africa	19.3	14.3	8.1

Source: Federal Financial Institutions Examination Council, "Country Exposure Lending Survey." End-1982 figures from statistical release of October 15, 1984; March 1986 figures from release of August 1, 1986. Exposures are calculated using data for "total amounts owed to U.S. banks after adjustments for guarantees and external borrowing." Total exposures are calculated for all LDCs (OPEC, non-oil Latin America, non-oil Asia, non-oil Africa); Latin America (non-oil Latin America plus Ecuador and Venezuela); and Africa (non-oil Africa plus Algeria, Gabon, Libya, and Nigeria).

the debtor countries, a need which was widely recognized by policy-makers but which has not been satisfactorily satisfied.

In the past two years, the nature of the debt management has provoked increasing opposition in the debtor countries, since the debtor countries have been making large sacrifices but without renewed growth, and since the spectre of a global banking crisis has lessened. Moreover, the worldwide drop in commodities prices since 1985 worsened the economic situation in many of the debtor countries, as did a further drying up of bank lending. Several smaller debtor countries have recently rejected the international rules of the game and have unilaterally restricted debt servicing, Peru being the best-known case. The threat of a breakdown in continued debt servicing led U.S. Treasury Secretary James Baker III to propose the "Baker Plan" in October 1985, which called for increased inflows of private and official capital into the debtor countries in return for internationally supervised policy adjustments in those countries. However, more than a year after the announcement of the Baker Plan, there is little evidence of a renewed flow of private foreign capital into the debtor countries.

This paper reviews the management of the debt crisis to date and considers several possible alternative approaches for international cooperation in the future. Section 4.2 briefly reviews the scope of the crisis and some of the reasons for its onset. Section 4.3 describes the internationally coordinated policy responses to the crisis. Section 4.4 describes the conceptual underpinnings of this coordinated response, and section 4.5 then describes some of the reasons for the incomplete success of the policy response. Section 4.6 discusses several alternative measures for the future. Conclusions from the paper are summarized in section 4.7.

4.2   The Scope and Origins of the LDC Debt Crisis

The basic outlines of the LDC debt crisis are by now very well known, so only a brief summary of the onset of the crisis will be needed here.[1] Spokesmen in the developing countries sometimes insist that the debt crisis arose solely because of global economic dislocations, while creditor country policymakers sometimes suggest that mismanagement by the debtor countries is entirely to blame for the crisis. The truth is of course somewhere in the middle. The fact that more than forty countries simultaneously succumbed to crisis suggests that global factors were crucial to the onset of the crisis. But the fact that many countries affected by global shocks avoided a crisis (e.g., most of the debtor nations in East Asia) highlights the importance of country-specific factors, often involving important policy mistakes, in the onset of the crisis. We turn first to the global factors in the crisis, then to the mistakes of economic management in the debtor countries themselves.

4.2.1   Global Factors in the Onset of the Crisis

After the bond defaults of the Great Depression, international commercial lending to the developing countries virtually disappeared until the development of cross-border commercial bank lending in Eurodollars in the late 1960s.[2] During the period 1950 to 1970, foreign direct investment provided the bulk of international private capital flows, and private capital flows as a whole were smaller in magnitude than official flows from the multilateral institutions and from individual creditor governments. In the early 1970s, private capital flows to the developing countries began to exceed official flows, as private bank lending rose to become the dominant form of international capital flow. The sharp rise in world liquidity during 1971–73, related to overly expansionary U.S. monetary policies and the demise of the fixed exchange rate system, contributed to the expansion of the Eurodollar market and to an increase in bank funds available for lending to developing countries. Thus the rise in international bank lending predated the first OPEC oil shock of late 1973.

The first OPEC shock in 1973 dramatically increased the pace of LDC bank lending, as the new savings of the Persian Gulf countries were channeled to the international commercial banks, which lent (or "recycled") these savings to the developing countries. This burst of lending was not simply the result of oil-importing countries trying to maintain their real consumption levels after the rise in oil prices, as is sometimes suggested. Indeed, many oil *exporting* LDCs outside of the Persian Gulf (i.e., countries such as Mexico and Nigeria) borrowed substantially from the international banks, so that by 1983, after the enormous rise in real oil prices during the previous decade, the top ten developing country debtors, as a group, were oil exporters.[3]

Most of the international lending during this period was undertaken by *official* borrowers (i.e., central governments, public sector development banks, parastatals, etc.) rather than by the private sector, though the proportion of public and private borrowing differed by country. In many cases, the borrowing was used to finance ambitious public sector investment programs that could now be funded with readily available international bank credits at low real interest rates. The strategy of a rapid growth takeoff, based on foreign financing of large-scale public investments, has been termed "indebted industrialization" by Friedan (1981), who has studied the politics of this strategy in some detail in the cases of Brazil, Korea, and Mexico.

An idea of the share of public and private borrowing can be gleaned from the *World Bank Debt Tables,* which separates public sector and publicly guaranteed borrowing from private sector borrowing (the World Bank data refer only to medium-term and long-term debt, since the data do not provide a breakdown of the short-term debt by kind of borrowing). For Latin America as a whole, about three-fourths of all long-term borrowing at the end of 1978 and also at the end of 1983 was public or publicly guaranteed. Note that this ratio might be biased upward to some extent because debts contracted by the public sector are probably more completely covered by the World Bank Debt Reporting Service than are debts contracted by the private sector.

The fact that the external debt is heavily concentrated in the public sector has had profound implications for adjustment to the debt crisis by the debtor countries. As I stress later, these countries have two fundamental problems to overcome. The first, and most widely recognized, is that of transferring national income (via trade surpluses) to the foreign creditors. The second problem, which is perhaps as difficult, is that of transferring income from the *private* sector of the debtor country to the *public* sector so that the public sector may service its debts. In many countries, the nation as a whole does not lack the resources to pay the foreign creditors, but rather the public sector is unable or unwilling to tax the private sector sufficiently to generate an adequate debt-servicing capacity.

As of 1979 the pace of international lending did not seem to pose a particular danger to the banks or to the world economy. Various debt indicators, such as the popular debt-export ratio, gave very few signs of danger. Exports from the borrowing countries were booming, so that debt-export ratios (table 4.2[d]) actually fell between 1973 and

Table 4.2   Trade, Interest Rate, and Debt Indicators for the Developing Countries

	1978	1979	1980	1981	1982	1983	1984	1985
(a)								
Interest Rates[a]								
Nominal	8.2	11.2	13.1	18.3	14.4	9.5	11.3	9.6
Inflation	7.3	8.8	9.1	9.6	6.5	3.8	4.1	3.3
Real	0.9	2.4	4.0	8.7	7.9	5.7	7.2	6.3
(b) Trade Volumes and Values (annual change for nonfuel exporters)								
Exports:								
Volume	9.4	8.4	9.1	6.5	0.7	8.3	11.7	3.4
Price	5.5	17.3	13.5	−2.6	−5.9	−4.4	0.5	−3.3
Earnings	15.4	27.1	23.8	3.7	−5.2	3.5	12.2	0.0
Imports:								
Volume	8.9	9.3	6.5	1.5	−5.5	1.6	5.2	3.3
Price	9.8	18.7	20.6	2.8	−3.3	−4.6	−1.0	−2.1
Earnings	19.5	29.8	28.4	4.4	−8.7	−3.1	4.2	1.1
Trade Balance								
($ billion)	−34.8	−50.1	−75.0	−80.2	−62.7	−41.9	−19.9	−23.7
(c) Trade Volumes (annual change) and Trade Balance for Western Hemisphere LDCs								
Export Vol.	9.6	7.5	1.2	6.1	−2.2	7.1	7.3	−1.2
Import Vol.	5.5	8.0	9.3	2.6	−17.7	−22.2	2.9	−1.3
Trade Balance								
($ billion)	−4.0	−0.8	−1.9	−3.2	7.2	28.7	37.0	33.6

	1973	1978	1979	1980	1981	1982
(d)	Debt Indicators for Non-Oil Developing Countries (ratios in percent)					
Debt ($ billion)	130.1	336.3	396.9	474.0	555.0	612.4
Debt/Exports	115.4	130.2	119.2	112.9	124.9	143.3
Debt Service/ Exports	15.9	19.0	19.0	17.6	20.4	23.9
(e)	Debt Indicators for Western Hemisphere LDCs					
Debt ($ billion)	44.4	114.3	135.1	154.7	192.6	208.9
Debt/Exports	176.2	211.5	192.9	178.4	207.9	245.6
Debt Service/ Exports	29.3	41.7	40.9	35.6	41.7	54.0

Source: IMF, *World Economic Outlook*, April 1986.

[a]Nominal interest rate is a three-month U.S. interest rate. Inflation is the annual change in the GDP deflator. The real interest rate is the nominal rate minus inflation.

1980 despite the jump in total debt of the non-oil developing countries (hereafter NOLDC's) from $130.1 billion in 1973 to $474 billion in 1980. With this happy state of affairs, international financial specialists, academics, and policymakers welcomed the continued "recycling" of OPEC money and worried little about a debt crisis.

The key to this happy state of affairs was that nominal interest rates on dollar loans were consistently below the rate of growth of dollar export earnings of the borrowing countries (or, to put it another way, real interest rates were consistently below the rate of growth of *real* export earnings). In 1979, for example, as shown in table 4.2(a) and (b), nominal U.S. interest rates averaged 11.2 percent, while the export earnings of the LDC nonfuel exporters grew by 27.1 percent. In these circumstances, a debtor country can borrow all the money that it needs for debt servicing (i.e., all of the interest and amortization due) without experiencing a rise in its debt-export ratio.[4]

However, if nominal interest rates exceed the growth of nominal export earnings, then a country that borrows all the money it needs for debt servicing will experience an ever-increasing debt-export ratio. Sooner or later, the country will be cut off from new borrowing, and it will have to pay for its debt servicing out of its own resources (i.e., by running trade surpluses). With nominal interest rates in the mid-to-late 1970s at 10 percent or so, and with LDC export earnings growing at more than 15 percent per year in dollar terms, debt-export ratios were easily kept under control. Very few observers suspected that in the near future the debtor countries would suddenly have to shift from *new borrowing* to *trade surpluses* as the way to meet their debt-servicing needs.

The second, devastating phase of international borrowing took place in 1980–82, after the heady and highly profitable experience of 1973–79. Almost none of the relevant actors, neither borrowers nor lenders (nor, it should be said, academic observers) understood quickly enough that the success of the first period was built squarely on the temporary condition of low interest rates and high growth in export earnings. Prudent debtors and bankers should surely have expected that within a few years interest rates might rise to exceed growth rates, but few could have anticipated the sudden and dramatic turnaround in the interest rate/earnings growth relation after 1980, which is shown in figure 4.1 and in the data of table 4.1.

The debt crisis followed relentlessly upon the rise in interest rates and the collapse in export earnings. Once this reversal took place, all of the debt warning signs started to fly off of the charts, as seen by the rapid increase in the debt-export and debt-service ratios after 1979 (table 4.2[d] and [e]). Bank lending itself dropped off, with gross Bank for International Settlements (BIS) claims on the NOLDCs rising at

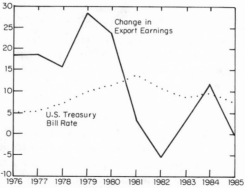

Fig. 4.1   Interest rates and annual percentage change in non-oil LDC export earnings. *Source:* 1976–79 "non-oil" LDCs export value growth, year over year, from IMF, *World Economic Outlook,* June 1981; 1980–85 "non-fuel exporter" LDCs export value growth, year over year, from the IMF, *World Economic Outlook,* April 1986. Interest rates are U.S. Treasury bills, 3-month.

the rate of 24 percent in 1980, 18 percent in 1981, and 7 percent in 1982, but the growth in export values declined even more sharply, from 26 percent in 1980, to 5 percent in 1981, and −4 percent in 1982. Consequently, the debt-export ratio rose quickly.

As is well known, the rise in interest rates had an especially pronounced effect because of the nature of the LDC debt to the commercial banks, most of which was in the form of medium-term (generally three to seven years) rollover credits, with interest rates at a fixed spread over a short-term reference rate (such as the London Interbank Offered Rate [LIBOR], or the U.S. prime rate). Thus, just as soon as short-term interest rates rose at the end of 1979, the interest rates charged on the existing syndicated bank loans to the LDCs rose by the same amount. Also, since the great bulk of the debt was dollar denominated, the rise in the dollar exchange rate (and the consequent fall in dollar prices of internationally traded commodities) was especially painful.

The reasons for the rise in interest rates and fall in the dollar value of trade have been widely discussed. After the second OPEC price shock, the leading industrial countries embarked on a widely endorsed policy of rapid disinflation, based on very tight monetary policies which raised interest rates around the world. No international organization, not the IMF nor the World Bank nor the OECD, gave any hint at the time that the suddenness and sharpness of the monetary tightening would be problematic. To the contrary, international officials everywhere applauded the seriousness of purpose of the anti-inflation fight.

The rise in interest rates was particularly large in the United States in 1981 and after, because in addition to tight monetary policies there was the prospect of many years of large budget deficits caused by the tax cuts of 1981. As is now well understood, the especially high U.S. interest rates created a capital inflow into the United States and a sharp appreciation of the dollar.

4.2.2   The Role of Domestic Policies in the Onset of the Crisis

Without the global shocks, the debt crisis would not have occurred. However, in almost all countries that succumbed to an external debt crisis, domestic policy mistakes also played an important role, a point which makes commercial bank lending (especially after 1979) harder to understand, since the banks should have seen some of the policy disarray in these countries. Some economies that faced severe external disturbances, such as South Korea and Thailand, were able to surmount the shocks and maintain international creditworthiness and growth, at least after a short interval. Other economies, which actually could have benefited on balance from the external events, such as the oil-exporters Mexico, Nigeria, and Venezuela, collapsed under the weight of higher world interest rates. What were the crucial differences that led to successful adjustment in some cases but not in others?

In a recent paper (Sachs 1985), I explored some of the possible differences by looking at the experiences of the Latin American and the East Asian debtor countries. Among the major Latin American countries, all but Colombia succumbed to a foreign debt crisis (as indicated by the need for a commercial bank debt rescheduling and by the exclusion from continued borrowing on normal market terms), while in Asia all of the countries avoided the need for a bank rescheduling with the exception of the Philippines. Interestingly, the differences in experience were not fundamentally due to the differences in the *size* of the external shocks hitting the two regions. As an example, Mexico's debt crisis arose despite a nearly fourfold increase in export earnings (due to oil) during 1978 to 1982, so that Mexico benefited rather than suffered from the commodity price movements in the years preceding the debt crisis. Rather, as stressed also by Balassa (1984) among others, the orientation of trade policy and exchange rate policy was vital. Countries with export-promoting trade policies were far more successful in surmounting the external shocks. And, not sufficiently stressed in the 1985 paper, the short-run policy responses after 1979 were vital: a quick reaction to the change in the international environment was necessary for a successful adjustment.

The key economic difference in the two regions is the rapid export growth in Asia, which kept down that region's debt-export ratios. The export-orientation of the Asian economies, in contrast to the import-substitution strategy in Latin America, is well known and well documented. It should be stressed that the export orientation of the Asian countries is decidedly a matter of policy choice rather than inherent structure, since two of the leading examples of export-led growth (South Korea and Indonesia) went through a Latin-American-styled, import-substitution phase in the late 1950s and early 1960s, with the result that exports were stifled and growth was retarded. Incredibly, South Korean exports were a mere 3 percent of GNP in 1960, compared with 37 percent of GNP in 1983. Indonesian exports rose from 5 percent of GNP in 1965 to 23 percent of GNP in 1983!

In addition to the question of long-term economic policy orientation, the external shocks imposed serious challenges for short-run policy after 1979. The rise in world interest rates placed direct and significant pressures on government budgets because of the rise in debt-servicing costs on both foreign and domestic debt (domestic debt in most countries experienced a rise in interest rates in response to the rise in world rates). It also provoked capital outflows and reserve losses in countries with fixed exchange rates (virtually all of the developing countries at the time). Exports dropped as world trade slowed, and investments fell in response to higher interest rates. Thus aggregate demand and employment tended to fall, at the same time that deficits were rising and foreign reserves were falling. The freedom of action for both monetary and fiscal policy was therefore extremely limited.

In Asia, budget deficits were kept under control and exchange rates were devalued after 1979 in response to these shocks (remarkably, Indonesia took a preventative devaluation to spur non-oil exports in 1978, in the belief that oil exports would remain weak). Starting from a diversified export base, these policy changes in Asia caused a fairly quick rise in the region's export volumes. Also, both policies helped these countries to avoid the problem of capital flight, which tends to occur in anticipation of a currency devaluation, an anticipation that in turn is naturally raised by large budget deficits.

In Latin America, the story is almost the opposite. In almost all of the countries concerned (certainly including Argentina, Bolivia, Chile, Mexico, Uruguay, and Venezuela) the exchange rate was allowed to become substantially overvalued during 1979 to 1981, with the result that export growth in the early 1980s was meagre. Brazil was the important exception to the exchange rate overvaluation, and it alone enjoyed an export boom between 1981 and 1984. To the extent that the Latin American governments endeavoured to maintain economic growth, they did so mainly through expansionary fiscal policy, which exacerbated the budget deficits that were already bulging because of higher interest payments on home and foreign debt. Money financing of the budget deficits increased in many countries, with the result of enormous capital outflows and reserve losses during 1981 and 1982. After the reserves and access to borrowing ran out in 1982, the continuation of money-financed deficits led to sharp currency depreciations and an explosion of inflation (with triple-digit inflations in Argentina, Bolivia, Brazil, Peru, and now, in 1986, Mexico).

The data in table 4.3 show the differences in real exchange rates of the two regions (vis-à-vis the U.S.) during the years building up to the crisis. The real exchange rate is measured here as the country's consumer price level relative to the U.S. consumer price level, adjusted for exchange rate changes. A value above 100 signifies a real appreciation after 1978, implying that the country's goods and labor became relatively expensive in international markets. The results of these exchange rate policies are reflected in the superior export performance of the Asian economies, as shown by the annual changes in export volumes during 1980–84 (IMF, *World Economic Outlook*, 1986, p. 205):

	1980–84 (Avg.)	1980	1981	1982	1983	1984
Latin America	3.9	1.2	6.1	−2.2	7.1	7.3
Asia	8.6	9.2	9.3	0.5	10.1	14.0

4.2.3 The Collapse of Bank Lending in 1982

The warning signs of impending crisis were everywhere in 1981 but were virtually ignored. World interest rates were at historic highs and international trade was stagnant. Several countries, including Bolivia, Jamaica, Peru, Poland, and Turkey were already in serious debt difficulties by the end of 1980. By the end of 1981, massive capital flight

Table 4.3   **Real Exchange Rate Behavior, Selected Countries (1978 = 100)**

Year	1978	1979	1980	1981	1982	Average (1980–81)
Latin America						
Argentina	100	141	179	138	59	159
Brazil	100	92	76	80	77	78
Chile	100	102	116	126	100	121
Mexico	100	106	117	127	85	122
Venezuela		101	108	114	118	112
	100					
East Asia						
Indonesia	100	78	81	81	80	81
Malaysia	100	99	93	87	86	90
South Korea	100	106	96	94	89	95
Thailand	100	101	104	99	93	102

Source: IMF, *International Financial Statistics.*

Note: The real exchange rate is calculated as P/EP^*, where P is the CPI, E is the exchange rate in units of currency per \$US, and P^* is the U.S. CPI. A rise in the index signifies a currency appreciation.

was occurring in Argentina, Mexico, and Venezuela as unrealistic exchange rates came under attack, and as large domestic budget deficits (particularly in Argentina and Mexico) fed a rapid increase in the money supply. According to one estimate, by the end of 1983, cumulative capital flight accounted for 61 percent of Argentina's gross external debt, 44 percent of Mexico's debt, and 77 percent of Venezuela's debt.[5]

If the banks could be excused for their lending during 1973–79, it is much harder to justify a veritable explosion of bank lending to Latin America in the circumstances of 1980–82. Latin Americans by the thousands were lining up at their local banks to take money out of their countries during 1981 and 1982 at the same time the commercial banks were shoveling the money in. High-ranking Mexican officials have recounted, off the record, that at the end of 1981 Mexico had decided to undertake a desperately needed devaluation, but was discouraged from doing so by a leading New York bank, which assured the Mexican government that a large line of credit would be available to the government to continue to defend the prevailing parity.

Thus, as shown in table 4.4, the net claims of international banks on Mexico virtually doubled in the two years between the end of 1979 and the end of 1981, and the net claims more than doubled for Argentina. The combined claims on the three large debtors—Argentina, Brazil, and Mexico—almost doubled in the two-year period, increasing by $48 billion. In Asia, only the net claims on South Korea increased markedly, and then from a much lower level than in Latin America.

By early 1982, the international commercial banks began to understand the longer term implications of the rise in world interest rates and the fall in export growth rates. Projections of debt-export ratios prepared in these new international circumstances showed that the debt-export ratios of the developing countries would rise rapidly in the near future unless these countries shifted toward a trade surplus,

Table 4.4   **Net Liabilities of Countries to International Banks in the BIS Reporting Area ($ billion)**

Country	December 1979	December 1981
Argentina	5.3	16.3
Brazil	28.8	44.8
Mexico	22.5	43.4
Subtotal	56.6	104.5
Indonesia	− 0.1	− 1.5
Malaysia	− 1.3	0.2
South Korea	7.2	13.7
Thailand	1.6	1.8
Subtotal	7.4	14.2

Source: BIS.

something that was hard to imagine at the time. Bank jitters were increased by the growing number of countries with "special" problems, such as Poland in 1981, and Argentina (at war in the Falklands) in the spring of 1982. Banks also came to appreciate the possibility of a classic liquidity squeeze. Given the buildup of debt and the large share that was short term, the total debt servicing due in 1982 (including all short-term debt as well as amortizations and interest on medium-term and long-term debt) came to exceed 100 percent of exports in 1982 for several Latin countries, though not for the Asian countries. Taking the average debt service to export ratios for 1980–83 for the two regions, we see the difference in table 4.5. Thus, a cessation of new lending (including an inability to roll over short-term debts) would inevitably force the Latin countries into a moratorium on debt servicing, even if *all* of their exports were to be used for that purpose!

Mexico, of course, set off the global shock in 1982. In the beginning of 1982, Mexico finally devalued its grossly overvalued currency, but then almost immediately lost international confidence by giving a large public sector wage increase as compensation for the devaluation. The budget deficit remained enormous (an estimated 17.6 percent of GDP in 1982), meaning that even the new pegged level would soon become unsustainable. In the spring of 1982, Mexico canvassed the banking community for a new large international loan, but received a cool response. International reserves fell sharply throughout the spring and summer, and the Mexican public speculated against the new exchange rate. Unable to win bank confidence under these unsettled circumstances, the Mexican government took several remarkable steps in August, including: a freezing of dollar accounts in Mexican banks; a renewed depreciation of the currency under a new dual-rate system; an imposition of new exchange controls; and most important, a declaration of a temporary suspension of debt-service payments. Soon thereafter, in a parting shot, outgoing Mexican President Lopez Portillo nationalized the Mexican banks.

Table 4.5   Debt Service to Export Ratio, Average 1980–83

Latin America	
Argentina	214.9
Brazil	132.6
Mexico	161.8
Venezuela	117.8
East Asia	
Indonesia	n.a.
Malaysia	16.9
South Korea	90.1
Thailand	58.1

Source: Sachs (1985, table 4, p. 533).

These events of course stopped all new lending to Mexico, and the drop in lending rapidly spread to the other debtor countries, especially in Latin America. In quick response, more than a dozen debtor countries began negotiations with the banks and the official bilateral creditors on rescheduling debt payments for 1982 and 1983. The list of reschedulers eventually ran up to more than forty countries.

4.3   The Creditor Response to the Debt Crisis

So far we have established, in rough terms, how the debt crisis arose. Now we turn to the international policy response to the crisis itself. The theme of this section is that a credit crisis poses certain key and identifiable needs for international coordination and that, to an important extent, such needs were fulfilled by international policy coordination. The style of international management was set first in the Mexican bailout of 1982.

4.3.1   The 1982 Mexican Bailout

The events in Mexico prompted strong and almost immediate actions in support of Mexico from the official international financial community, under the leadership of the U.S. government, especially the U.S. Treasury and the Federal Reserve Board. Within days of Mexico's announcement of a suspension in debt servicing, the following actions were taken: (1) the U.S. government committed nearly $3 billion to Mexico, including $1 billion in prepayments for oil purchases for the strategic petroleum reserve, $1 billion in finance of agricultural exports to Mexico from the Commodity Credit Corporation, and a $925 million bridge loan from the Federal Reserve Board; (2) the Bank for International Settlements extended a bridge loan to Mexico of nearly $1 billion; (3) the export credit agencies of the leading creditor countries agreed to increase their lending to Mexico by $2 billion; and (4) talks got underway for a large IMF loan. By November 1982, the IMF agreement was reached, providing for $3.7 billion of lending over three years. The IMF agreement called for budget and monetary austerity in Mexico in view of the country's reduced access to foreign borrowing. In the following year, Mexico rescheduled it debts with its official creditors in the Paris Club forum.

The great novelty of the IMF agreement was to link the IMF financing to new lending from Mexico's bank creditors. The IMF declared that it would put new money into Mexico only if the existing bank creditors also increased their loan exposure. The requisite agreement with the commercial banks took effect in early 1983. The bank agreement called for a rescheduling of Mexico's existing debts falling due between August 1982 and December 1984 (the term of the IMF program), as well as a new loan of $5 billion, to be extended by the existing banks in proportion to their existing exposure. The rescheduling provided for continued and timely payments of interest on market terms on Mexico's existing debts, and in fact the spread over LIBOR on Mexican debt was increased in the agreement. Thus, in present value terms there was no sacrifice made by the banks in the debt rescheduling or in the new loan, assuming that both would continue to be serviced.

Moreover, under prevailing accounting conventions, the U.S. banks would not have to show any loss at all under the rescheduling agreement, since what is crucial for income accounting for the banks is the continued and timely servicing of interest on the loan, not principal. Indeed, the rise in spreads on Mexico's rescheduled debts meant that the banks would report higher, not lower, income as a result of the rescheduling operation. This concern of U.S. bank accounting with the interest flow on bank claims, rather than with changes in the underlying values of the claims, helps to explain the single-minded concern in the bank agreements with a continued and timely servicing of interest: no interest relief, then no loss of short-term profits.

In the discussion that follows, I will use the terms "debt relief" or "debt forgiveness" for arrangements that reduce in present value terms the contractual obligations on debt repayments. The term "debt rescheduling" will be taken to imply (as in the Mexican program) a postponement of repayments, but one that maintains the present value of contractual debt-servicing obligations.

4.3.2   Generalizing the Mexican Example

The Mexican program was rather quickly improvised, but it nevertheless became the norm for the dozens of reschedulings that followed. Like the Mexican program, virtually all of the debt restructurings have had the following characteristics:

- The IMF has made high-conditionality loans to the debtor government, always contingent on a rescheduling agreement being reached between the country and the commercial banks;
- The commercial banks have rescheduled existing claims by stretching out principal repayments, but without reducing the contractual present value of repayments;
- The debtor countries have agreed to maintain timely servicing of interest payments on all commercial bank loans;
- The banks have made their reschedulings contingent on an IMF agreement being in place;
- The official creditors have rescheduled their claims in the Paris Club setting, and have also made such reschedulings contingent on an IMF agreement.

While it has been true that all bank reschedulings have preserved the contractual present value of the bank's claims, only some of the rescheduling agreements have involved concerted lending. The amounts involved in the concerted lending dropped significantly in 1985 and revived only partially in 1986, entirely on the basis of a new loan to Mexico, as shown by the data in table 4.6. The fall off in concerted lending occurred not because of diminished needs for such loans, but because the banks have strongly resisted new lending in the past two years except in cases when default appeared to be a plausible alternative for the country in question (such as Mexico in 1986).

In cases with concerted lending, the packages have followed the initial Mexican pattern:

- Explicit backing for the loan by the IMF and U.S. government, often with pressure exerted on the banks by the U.S. Treasury and the IMF Managing Director;
- A pro rata allocation of the new loan among the existing banks, with a possible proviso excluding the smallest of the bank creditors;
- A linkage of the bank loan to the debtor country's compliance with an IMF agreement.

In addition to orchestrating the relationship between the debtor countries and the banks, via the IMF, the creditor governments also confront the debtor countries directly as official bilateral creditors, mainly through export credit agencies. For the most heavily indebted countries, most external debt (about three-fourths of the total) is owed to commercial banks and other private creditors, but for many of the smaller debtors, especially those with lower per capita income levels, much more than half of the debt has been extended by official creditors, often at concessional terms.[6] In general, official lending to the heavily indebted countries did not decline in the years after 1982, though there is some hint in the data of a slowdown of official bilateral lending in 1985 and after.

Official bilateral debt (but not the debt of the multilateral institutions) is rescheduled in the Paris Club setting. Paris Club reschedulings differ from commercial bank reschedulings in two important ways. First, reschedulings of debt in the Paris Club often represent a form of forgiveness, since some of the debt in question is already set at a concessional interest rate. Second, the Paris Club does not object as a rule to rescheduling part or all of the interest payments due, something that is an anathema to the commercial banks. This discrepancy is consistent with the overall strategy of the creditor country governments, which is not to maximize debt-service payments by the debtor countries but rather to protect the servicing of interest on the *bank* debt.

The World Bank and the multilateral development banks (MDBs) are the other major actors in the international management of the debt crisis, and their role has been growing under pressure from the United States since 1985. The World Bank has recently increased its lending to the heavily indebted countries, with many loans now coming as part

Table 4.6   Concerted Lending: Commitments and Disbursements, 1983–Third Quarter, 1986[a] (in millions of U.S. dollars; classified by year of agreement in principle)

	1983		1984		1985		1st–3rd Qtr., 1986	
	Commit-ments	Disburse-ments	Commit-ments	Disburse-ments	Commit-ments	Disburse-ments	Commit-ments	Disburse-ments
Argentina								
Medium-term loan	1,500	500	3,700	—	—	2,500	—	1,200
Trade deposit facility	—	—	500	—	—	500	—	—
Brazil								
Medium-term loan	4,400	4,400	6,500	6,500	—	—	—	—
Chile								
Medium-term loan	1,300	1,300	780	780	785	520	—	216
Cofinancing agreement with World Bank	—	—	—	—	300[b]	194	—	106
Colombia								
Medium-term loan	—	—	—	—	1,000	—	—	—
Costa Rica								
Revolving trade facilities	202	202	—	—	75	75	—	—
Ivory Coast								
Medium-term loan	—	—	104	—	—	104	—	—
Ecuador								
Medium-term loan	431	431	200	—	—	200	—	—

Mexico								
Medium-term loan	5,000	5,000	3,800	2,850	—	950	5,000	—
Cofinancing arrangement with World Bank	—	—	—	—	—	—	1,000[b]	—
Contingent investment support facility	—	—	—	—	—	—	1,200	—
Growth contingency co-financing with World Bank	—	—	—	—	—	—	500[b]	—
Panama								
Medium-term loan	—	—	—	—	—	—	—	—
Peru								
Medium-term loan	278	131	—	147	60	—	—	21
Philippines								
Medium-term loan	450	250	—	100	—	—	—	—
Uruguay								
Medium-term loan	240	240	925	—	—	400	—	175
Yugoslavia								
Medium-term loan	600	600	—	—	—	—	—	—
Total	14,401	13,054	16,509	10,377	2,220	5,443	7,700	1,718

Source: IMF, *International Capital Markets*, December 1986, table 45, p. 121.

[a]These data exclude bridging loans.

[b]These loans have an associated guarantee given by the World Bank in the later maturities equivalent to 50 percent of the nominal amount disbursed.

of an elaborate package including IMF, commercial bank, and creditor government loans (as in the 1986 Mexican package). The role for the World Bank is expanding under two pressures. First, the direct lending of the IMF is somewhat constrained, as many of the important debtor countries are near their ceilings on drawings from the IMF and, in fact, will be net repayers to the IMF in the next three years. Second, as the problems of the debtor countries are increasingly seen as structural and medium term (rather than simply reflecting a short-run liquidity squeeze), the long-term development finance of the World Bank is seen as increasingly relevant.

One substantive change in World Bank lending since the onset of the debt crisis is the shift from project lending to so-called policy-based lending. In policy-based lending, money is made available to facilitate policy changes on a sectoral or national level, mainly involving the liberalization of internal and external markets. In March 1986, the World Bank Executive Directors expressed support for a rise in policy-based lending to between 15 and 20 percent of all World Bank lending during 1986–88, up from around 10 percent in the early 1980s. For the heavily indebted developing countries, policy-based lending accounted for as much as 35 percent of all lending by the World Bank to the countries during 1986. A second substantive change in World Bank lending is the increasing resort to cofinancing arrangements with private sector creditors as a way to stimulate new private lending via new public lending.

The regional multilateral development banks (Asian Development Bank, African Development Bank, Inter-American Development Bank) are also attempting to increase their lending to the heavily indebted countries in conjunction with increased World Bank lending. In fact, these MDBs have had great difficulty in disbursing more loans in the past two years because MDB lending generally requires counterpart funding from the developing country itself, much of which has been dropped from austerity budgets. In fact, despite the extensive talk of increased public lending in recent years, the combined loans of the World Bank and the MDBs have grown rather slowly since 1980. To the fifteen largest debtor countries, the net disbursements per year have risen from $2.1 billion in 1980 to $3.7 billion in 1985, a rather meagre increase of $1.6 billion.[7]

4.4   The Conceptual Basis of the Debt Management Strategy

An interesting aspect of the management of the debt crisis is one thing that did *not* happen: no leading official in the Reagan Administration or in other leading creditor governments said that the crisis was a matter for the private markets only, with no role for government intervention. From the very first days of Mexico's August 1982 crisis until now, the U.S. government has been deeply involved in managing the crisis. One reason for this involvement was gut fear. At the end of 1982, the LDC exposure of the nine U.S. money-center banks was $83.4 billion, or 287.7 percent of bank capital (see table 4.1). In Latin America alone, the exposure was 176.5 percent of bank capital, and more than 70 percent of that was to Brazil and Mexico alone. It seemed obvious that if the largest debtor countries unilaterally repudiated their debt, then the largest U.S. banks could fail, with dire consequences for the U.S. and world economies. The creditor governments therefore recognized the importance of continued debt servicing and were willing to provide official financing for that purpose. But the motivation for official management of the crisis went deeper than fear, and that was the widely shared assumption, anchored in the experience of the Great Depression, that one can't simply "leave it to the markets" in the case of a financial crisis.

The policymakers took the view that the debt crisis reflected a short-term to medium-term liquidity squeeze, rather than a fundamental problem of solvency. It was felt from the beginning that if the debtor countries could be nursed along for a few years without a breakdown of the system, they would enjoy an economic recovery and be able to resume normal debt servicing and normal borrowing from the international capital markets. This conclusion, which must be tested on a country-by-country basis (since there are clearly some countries where solvency is really at stake), has been reached by a number of analysts, including Cline (1984), Cohen (1985), and Feldstein (1986).

For all of these analysts, the basic point is the same. Since the debt of a typical Latin American debtor country stands at about 70 percent of GNP, the interest charges on that debt represent approximately 5–7 percent of GNP (with an interest rate of 8–10 percent per year). This is a heavy, but not insurmountable, burden for a debtor country, particularly for a growing debtor country. With growth, the debt-GNP ratio of the country can be stabilized, even if the country does not pay the full interest burden but only the interest burden net of the growth rate of the economy. For an economy growing in dollar terms at 5 percent per year, the annual net interest burden is reduced to perhaps 2–4 percent of GNP, with the country borrowing approximately 2 percent of GNP in new loans each year.

While calculations such as these oversimplify the problems facing the debtor countries, they do highlight the potential for a long-term successful resolution of the crisis.[8] As viewed from the perspective of the creditor governments and the IMF, the problem is one of surmounting the short-term emergency problems without an economic collapse in the debtor countries and without a breakdown in debtor-creditor relations.

In this regard, the policymakers of the creditor countries recognized three distinct areas for international policy coordination. First, it was well understood that international loan agreements are difficult to enforce, so official pressures would be needed in order to keep countries from repudiating their debts. Second, if left on their own, the private international lenders would tend to withdraw too abruptly from the debtor countries, to the detriment of both the borrowers and the lenders. Third, the increased lending would have to be conditioned on better macroeconomic policies in the debtor countries. Only official institutions, rather than the private market, could arrange, monitor, and enforce such conditionality. The creditor governments did not of course always recognize the precise implications of these problems. There are good reasons to believe that enforcement of debt servicing has been too strict; that new lending has been inadequate; and that conditionality has lacked finesse. But to give due praise, the United States and other creditor country governments quickly recognized the need for official action and usually for the right reasons.

In any event, let us turn to a more detailed discussion of these three areas of public policy intervention.

4.4.1 Enforcement of International Loan Agreements

The creditor governments have played a major role in recent years in raising the costs of debt default for the debtor countries. The leading governments have steadfastly opposed all forms of debt forgiveness or moratoriums on debt payments, no matter how dire the situation in a debtor country. The IMF, pushed no doubt by the U.S. Treasury, has insisted that all IMF programs be based on the commitment of debtor countries to *complete servicing*, at market rates, of the interest on their commercial bank debts. Countries refusing to abide by this dictate risk forfeiting an IMF program, which is in turn the admission ticket for bank debt reschedulings, Paris Club reschedulings, and new lending from other multilateral lenders. They also risk the foreign policy displeasure of the creditor nations, and they fear the adverse reaction on private sector investors of stirring up that displeasure. It should be noted that such foreign policy "displeasure" can jeopardize the country's foreign relations with the creditor governments in a wide variety of areas, including military support, arms sales, trade policies, technology transfers, and foreign aid.

Later in the paper I question whether the creditor governments have pushed too far in support of full debt servicing. This is not easy to answer since two competing objectives are at stake. The higher the penalty of default, the safer international lending will be in general, and the easier it will be for debtor governments to obtain loans. On the other hand, when a debtor gets into trouble, a lower penalty is important as a kind of insurance or safety valve, to prevent too large a collapse of debtor country living standards. The opposition of the U.S. government to a debt moratorium in any of the major debtor countries was probably crucial to avoidance of a banking crisis in 1982 and 1983. Moreover, the fact that loans are still being serviced today is important for the future viability of the international loan market (which could hardly exist if loans became unenforceable). On the other hand, for some countries the enforcement has gone too far: the absence of the safety valve has forced some countries into situations of extreme economic misery and social instability.

4.4.2 Encouragement of International Lending

The creditor governments also recognized a second role: encouraging new lending from the private markets and from official sources. When a debtor is in financial distress, individual creditors have an incentive to withdraw credits even when collectively it is in the creditors' interests to continue to make loans. The collective withdrawal of credits can even provoke a default, with all of the attendant inefficiencies and costs, just as a panicked withdrawal of bank deposits can cause a healthy bank to fall victim to a run (see Sachs 1984 for a more formal discussion of this point). This kind of behavior is well recognized in the context of domestic bankruptcy law (especially in corporate reorganization), which stops individual creditors from collecting on their claims and thereby enforces collective decision-making by the creditors. In this sense, the IMF pressure for concerted lending played some of the role of the bankruptcy code in a corporate reorganization.

The possibility that banks might cause a "run" on a country, just as bank depositors might cause a run on a bank, was heightened by a fact that we noted earlier: debt service to export ratios exceeded 100 percent in 1982 for many of the Latin American countries. This meant that a freezing up in lending by any substantial group of banks would force these countries into a unilateral suspension of debt servicing. This vulnerability by itself became a good reason not to lend to the region after mid-1982. Even if an individual bank felt that Mexico's long-term prospects were good, it would not make sense to lend if the bank felt that *other banks* might soon be withdrawing their credits. Moreover, many of the traditional risk indicators (e.g., the debt-export ratio) began to flash red in 1982, so it was rational for any lender to fear that other lenders would soon stop lending.

This reasoning has been central to the IMF's insistence on concerted lending by the commercial banks. The IMF has insisted that the debtor countries have the *long-term* capacity to repay their loans and are just stuck in a short-term credit squeeze. The IMF also recognized correctly that even if each bank agreed with such reasoning, there is no guarantee that the loan market on its own would spontaneously provide sufficient capital to the debtor countries.

Concerted lending takes place without legal compulsion, as individual banks have to agree to sign on to the cooperative agreement. Economic theory predicts, and experience confirms, that such a situation gives enormous bargaining power to the smaller banks, who know that their small contribution of money will not make an economic difference to the debtor country, and who can therefore threaten to "free ride" on the lending decisions of the bigger banks. Indeed, it has been hard to keep the smaller regional banks in the concerted lending game. In some cases, the large banks have agreed to contribute the share of some of the smaller banks to make an agreement sail. In other cases, the initial concerted lending package is designed solely for the largest creditor banks. An illustration of the "exploitation of the large by the small" is shown in figure 4.2, reproduced from Sachs (1984), which shows the contributions of large and small banks to a concerted loan package to Brazil in 1983. As seen in the figure, the smaller banks were able and eager to escape from new lending.

The same kind of need for coordination of the creditors arises, even more acutely, when the debtor is truly insolvent. In that case there will again be a natural scramble of creditors to get out of the country, even if the resulting decapitalization of the country depresses the overall debt-servicing capacity of the country to the detriment of the creditors collectively. Assets will be removed from the country even if they earn more than the market return, because the individual creditor knows that he will not receive the asset's full return in any event, since it will have to be shared with the other creditors (and perhaps on a "first come, first serve" basis). Unless the creditors find some consensual

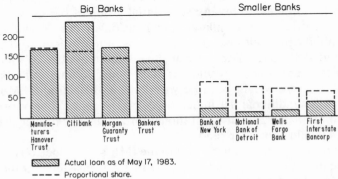

Fig. 4.2   Rescheduling package of interbank loans to Brazil in 1983 (in $ millions). *Source: Fortune Magazine,* July 11, 1983.

way to reduce the value of the debt or to convert it to equity, as in a bankruptcy proceeding, the debtor will inevitably be forced into an involuntary default, with the attendant inefficiencies of lawsuits and restrictions on international trade, and the absence of new financing for worthwhile new investment projects.

Note that merely because a debtor government has a negative net worth does not mean that it doesn't have many worthwhile *new* investment projects, each of which individually would meet the market test. These projects simply cannot be financed until the existing overhang of debt is resolved, which can occur in one of three ways: (1) the existing creditors can agree to write down some of the debt, perhaps taking an equity position in the debtor; (2) the existing creditors could agree jointly to finance the new project and share in the net returns; or (3) the existing creditors could agree to give senior status to a new creditor, who would finance the project on the basis that the *new* loan would be repaid in advance of the previous debt. In any of these cases (which are all familiar from bankruptcy law), official intervention will probably be needed to help the creditors arrive at a consensual agreement that will allow the investment to go forward.

4.4.3 The Conditionality Problem

The creditor governments recognized a third reason for joint action: the fact that the new lending would, at least to some extent, have to be predicated on improved macroeconomic performance in the debtor countries. To illustrate this role for policy intervention (in this case intervention by the IMF and to a lesser extent the World Bank), consider a country that would be in default in the absence of a new loan. Suppose that the new loan will be repaid only if it is used for investment purposes, not for consumption purposes. The country would prefer to receive the loan and to invest rather than simply to default. However, best of all, it would like to get the new loan, use it for consumption, and *then* default. If the creditors know this preference ranking and have no way to constrain the manner in which the country uses a new loan, the creditors would see clearly that the country would use any new loan for consumption rather than for investment, and the creditors would choose not to lend to the country. The market result would be one of no lending and subsequent default.

Now, suppose that an outside institution can impose performance terms on the debtor, forcing the debtor to use the loan for the purposes of investment. In this case, both the debtor and the creditors will be able to reach a better outcome, since the debtor will willingly submit to the conditionality and end up with the loan, the new investment, and the avoidance of default. This is a simple explanation of the role for IMF conditionality on loans to debtor countries. The debtor countries *willingly* tie their own hands in order to convince creditors that they are indeed worthy of new loans.

Such an argument for the IMF and World Bank role in conditionality supposes that the enforcement of conditionality is a kind of public good that can only be carried out effectively by a centralized public institution and not by hundreds of independent and competing banks. It also supposes that the IMF is effective in enforcing its conditionality and, most important, that the conditionality terms provide a plausible basis for raising debtor country welfare and for making it safe to lend new money to the debtor country. These assumptions are of course controversial, as I discuss in the next section.

4.5 The Mixed Success of the Debt Management Strategy

The strategy of the creditor governments has surely been successful to date in keeping the foreign debts serviced. A good measure of this success is the net resource transfer to the debtor countries, which measures the net flow of new capital into the debtor countries minus the repayment of interest and profits on foreign investment. Since 1982, the net transfer has been negative, since the debtors have paid back in interest much more than they have received in new loans. For Latin America, the negative net resource transfer between 1982 and 1985 totaled more than $95 billion (see Sachs 1986, table 1).

Moreover, the long-term prospects for the debtor countries has brightened with the recent decline in world interest rates, which will tilt the balance to the benefit of the debtor countries in the future. Indeed, export growth rates of the debtor countries might soon again exceed nominal interest rates on debt, thus giving rise to a significant restoration of confidence in the long-term debt-servicing capacity of the debtor countries and thereby easing the flow of new lending to these countries.

On the other hand, as mentioned in the introduction, the years under the debt crisis and IMF-managed austerity programs have been ones of extreme economic hardship and declining living standards in most of the debtor countries. The prospects in the next couple of years also appear bleak. In some of the worst cases, the declines are shocking, with real output per capita down by over 20 percent since 1980. The stunning declines in Latin American per capita output are shown in table 4.7. Also worrisome is the fact that investment in the debtor countries has declined sharply, so the underpinnings for renewed growth in the coming years are not now being put in place. Table 4.8 shows the large decline in national investment as a percent of GDP. Private savings in the debtor countries is today spilling over into capital flight rather than new domestic investments.

Table 4.7   **Changes in Per Capita GDP in Latin America**

Country	Cumulative Change in Per Capita GDP, 1981–85
Argentina	− 18.5
Brazil	− 2.0
Bolivia	− 28.4
Colombia	− 0.1
Costa Rica	− 11.2
Chile	− 8.7
Ecuador	− 3.9
El Salvador	− 24.0
Guatemala	− 18.3
Jamaica	− 2.2[a]
Mexico	− 4.3
Panama	0.7
Peru	− 14.8
Uruguay	− 18.6
Venezuela	− 21.6

Source: Economic Commission for Latin America and the Caribbean, ''The Economic Crisis: Policies for Adjustment, Stabilization, and Growth,'' April 1986, Santiago, Chile.

Table 4.8   **Ratios of Gross Investment to GDP, Debtor Nations, Various Years, 1980–85 (percent)**

Category	1980	1983	1984	1985
Countries with debt-servicing problems	25.4	19.1	18.0	18.0
Countries without debt-servicing problems	28.1	26.5	26.4	26.6
Western Hemisphere	23.4	17.4	17.2	17.9
Sub-Saharan Africa	19.9	17.7	16.5	17.2

Source: IMF, *World Economic Outlook,* April 1986, table A7, p. 186.

These declines in investment and output are intrinsic characteristics of economies responding to a sharp cutoff in new lending, combined with a sharp increase in interest servicing costs on existing debt. The immediate result of the credit crisis was a remarkably sharp drop in imports in the debtor countries. Import volumes in Latin America fell by about 40 percent in the two years 1981 to 1983, as shown in table 4.2(c), producing a swing in the Latin American trade balance from a deficit of $3.2 billion in 1981 to a surplus of $28.7 billion in 1983. Since the improvement in the trade balance resulted from a cutoff of imports rather than a rise in exports, the shock had a deeply contractionary effect on the debtor economies.

The question for policymakers is clearly posed by these facts. Is there a better way to manage the crisis that would prevent a financial collapse but at the same time encourage more growth? The answer would seem to be yes. Several concrete suggestions for reform have been broached, some of which are discussed in the following section. Before those suggestions are discussed, however, I will outline some of the main problems with the current strategy.

4.5.1   Problem 1: The Overemphasis on the Large Debtors

To a remarkable extent, the debt crisis has been managed with just a few of the largest debtor countries in mind, specifically those few countries that pose a real risk to the international banking system. The commercial bank debt is remarkably concentrated. Mexico and Brazil account for 40 percent of all U.S. money-center bank exposure in the Third World. Mexico, Brazil, Argentina, and Venezuela account for 56 percent. None of the other troubled debtor countries has enough bank debt to pose a serious risk by itself to the banking system. A detailed breakdown of U.S. bank exposure in the developing countries shown in table 4.9 clearly illustrates the high concentration of debt.

The current management of the debt crisis has been viewed as successful to the extent that these four major debtors are sustained politically and economically and continue to pay their debts. But at the same time, many other debtor countries are collapsing, and an adequate strategy should handle these cases as well. Indeed, with more than forty countries in crisis, it is inevitable that some extreme cases will need special help. Yet to date all countries have been required to play by the same rules as Brazil and Mexico.

A concrete example illustrates the problems of the current situation. Because of extreme political instability and economic mismanagement under several military regimes, as well as the devastating external shocks of the early 1980s, Bolivia fell into a deep debt crisis by 1982. When international lending to Bolivia dried up in 1981, the net transfer of resources to Bolivia shifted from large net inflow to large net outflow as a percent of Bolivian GNP (see Sachs 1986 for details). Since the foreign borrowing had been supporting government expenditures, the loss in foreign funds created a fiscal crisis. A new, weak democracy, which had come to power at the end of 1982, presided over this fiscal crisis and ended up creating one of the worst hyperinflations of this century. By mid-1985, the inflation rate had hit a 50,000 percent annual rate.

During mid-1985 to mid-1986, even after a new democratic government came to power committed to ending the hyperinflation, the IMF never relented from its position that Bolivia must settle with the commercial banks on normal rescheduling terms. Fierce battles were fought between a desperate government and the IMF staff, with the IMF

Table 4.9   **Exposure to U.S. Banks to the Debtor Countries, March 1986**

Region	9 Money-Center Banks			All Other U.S. Banks		
	$b	% of Capital	% of Lending to LDCs	$b	% of Capital	% of Lending to LDCs
Large Four Debtors (Argentina, Brazil, Mexico, Venezuela)	42.7	97.5	56.5	23.4	36.2	59.5
Latin America	52.20	119.7	69.0	28.4	43.0	70.5
Africa	3.6	8.1	4.8	1.0	1.5	2.5
All LDCs	75.6	173.2	100.0	40.3	61.0	100.0
Individual Countries in Debt Crisis:						
Brazil	16.0	36.7	21.2	7.7	11.6	19.1
Mexico	13.8	31.2	18.3	10.4	15.7	25.8
Venezuela	6.9	15.8	9.1	3.4	5.1	8.4
Argentina	6.0	13.8	7.9	2.5	3.8	6.2
Chile	8.0	9.2	5.3	2.3	3.5	5.7
Philippines	3.6	8.2	4.8	1.4	2.1	3.5
Yugoslavia	1.3	3.0	1.7	0.7	1.1	1.7
Ecuador	1.2	2.8	1.6	0.8	1.2	2.0
Peru	0.8	1.8	1.1	0.6	0.9	1.5
Uruguay	0.7	1.6	0.9	0.2	0.3	0.5
Panama	0.7	1.6	0.9	0.3	0.4	0.7
Nigeria	0.6	1.4	0.8	0.2	0.3	0.5
Morocco	0.6	1.4	0.8	0.2	0.3	0.5
Ivory Coast	0.3	0.7	0.4	0.1	0.2	0.2
Dominican Republic	0.3	0.7	0.4	0.1	0.2	0.2
Costa Rica	0.2	0.4	0.3	0.2	0.3	0.5
Jamaica	0.1	0.2	0.1	0.03	0.0	0.0
Romania	0.1	0.2	0.1	0.04	0.0	0.0
Zambia	0.08	0.2	0.1	0.00	0.0	0.0
Honduras	0.06	0.1	0.1	0.05	0.0	0.0
Malawi	0.05	0.1	0.1	0.05	0.0	0.0
Liberia	0.05	0.1	0.1	0.03	0.0	0.0
Senegal	0.05	0.1	0.1	0.01	0.0	0.0
Nicaragua	0.04	0.1	0.1	0.04	0.0	0.0
Sudan	0.03	0.1	0.0	0.00	0.0	0.0
Zaire	0.01	0.0	0.0	0.00	0.0	0.0

Source: Same as table 4.1.

insisting that it would support no program that did not include an adequate amount of bank debt servicing. The IMF program was vital to Bolivia's interests, both directly for the IMF loan and as a prelude to the Paris Club and a normalization of relations with the outside world. In the end, the government maintained a unilateral moratorium on bank debt servicing at whatever cost to its IMF program. The IMF finally backed down from its threats to block the program, though it continued to pressure the government to resume debt servicing.

The IMF advice to Bolivia in 1986, in the midst of a hyperinflation, is problematic. Bolivia was a clear case of a country crumbling under the weight of foreign debt pressures. Safety valves, such as internationally sanctioned debt-servicing moratoria, should be provided in such cases. Note that a cessation of interest on Bolivia's bank debt probably involved an income loss of about $40 million per year to all U.S. banks, or less than one-twentieth percent of U.S. bank capital.

4.5.2 Problem 2: The Overemphasis on the U.S. Money-Center Banks

Just as four countries represent "the debtor nations" in the minds of many policymakers, so too do nine U.S. banks represent the "world financial system." The U.S. bank debt is concentrated not only among countries but also among banks, with the money-center banks holding the great bulk of the LDC claims. At the end of March 1986, for example, the nine top U.S. banks held 65 percent of the LDC debt held by all U.S. banks, although the money-center banks accounted for only 40 percent of U.S. bank capital. The money-center bank exposure in Latin America was 119.7 percent of capital, while for the rest of U.S. banks the exposure was only 43 percent of bank capital. Thus, the risks to the U.S. banking system from the debt crisis can be isolated among a handful of banks, a fact that is often not appreciated in thinking about the debt crisis.

Note that even for the heavily exposed U.S. money-center banks, the risks of the debt crisis have diminished. Exposure in the LDCs relative to capital has declined significantly. The 119.7 percent of capital exposure in Latin America, for example, is down from a level of 176.5 percent at the end of 1982. Thus, even the big U.S. banks have some breathing room now, though the capital data probably overstate the cushion for the big banks, since measured bank capital includes subordinated bank debt in addition to true equity capital.

In the United States, bank regulators have required write-downs of loans in only the very worst cases, such as the Sudan, Bolivia, Peru, North Korea, and Nicaragua. This treatment of course postpones a realistic adjustment by the banks to cushion their positions, and it seems to be much more generous to the banks (and shortsighted) than comparable policies in other countries. The banks can report high earnings and pay large dividends on the basis of their LDC exposure even though future debt servicing is in question. The U.S. taxpayers thereby bear much of LDC risk (via potential claims on the FDIC in the event of bank failures), while the banks continue to make dividend payments. In other countries, the regulatory treatment of the debt seems to be much more realistic. In Canada, for example, there have been forced partial write-downs for thirty-two developing countries. In Europe, write-downs of debt are encouraged by a system of hidden reserves, which are given favorable tax treatment. By all reports, which admittedly are difficult to verify in view of the lack of published European data, the European banks have written off far more of their LDC debts than have the U.S. banks and are therefore in a stronger position to handle any new shocks or any program of debt relief.

The U.S. money-center banks have sought, and obtained, by far the greatest influence of the international commercial banks in designing banking policy vis-à-vis the problem debtor countries. The policy influence is felt most directly in the bank steering committees that negotiate with the debtor countries. As shown in table 4.10, U.S. money-center banks chair the bank negotiating committees for *all* of the largest debtor countries, including Argentina, Brazil, Chile, Mexico, the Philippines (Bank of Tokyo co-chair), and Venezuela (Lloyds Bank co-chair), and the U.S. banks have a plurality of votes in the case of every debtor country shown in the table except for Cuba, Madagascar, Morocco, Poland, and Romania. No doubt the European and Japanese banks find the hard-line position of the U.S. banks a convenient one, since it has produced years of complete debt servicing by the largest debtors. But it should be recognized that the European banks could readily accept a debt strategy that is more generous to the debtor countries.

One of the ironies of the current situation is that while the U.S. banks have vociferously opposed write-downs of LDC debt and all plans involving debt forgiveness, the market value of these banks has already declined in anticipation of future debt write-offs. The stock market puts a value on the commercial banks according to the values of the underlying assets and liabilities of those banks. Not surprisingly, the market appears to value the banks' claims on the problem debtor countries at much less than the face value of those claims, as seen by a decline in bank stock prices relative to the book values of the banks (see Kyle and Sachs 1984). Evidence of depressed stock prices is fully consistent with the discounts on LDC debt that trade among the banks is a secondary market. Recent quotations (Salomon Brothers, December 1986) on LDC debt show the following bid prices (per $100 of face value):

Argentina	66	Mexico	56
Bolivia	7	Peru	18
Brazil	75	Venezuela	74
Chile	67		

Thus, in a sense, a market write-down of LDC claims has already occurred. However, *the debtor countries have enjoyed no benefit from*

Table 4.10   Composition of Bank Advisory Committees

	Total	USA	Canada	Europe	U.K.	Japan	Others	Chair
Argentina	11	5	1	3	1	1	—	Citibank
Bolivia	9	7	1	1	—	1	—	Bank of America
Brazil	14	7	1	3	1	1	1	Citibank (Deputy: Lloyds Bank International/ Morgan)
Costa Rica	11	6	2	1	1	1	—	Bank of America
Chile	12	7	1	2	1	1	—	Manufacturers Hanover
Cuba	9	—	1	6	1	1	—	Credit Lyonnais
Dominican Republic	9	7	2	—	—	—	—	Royal Bank of Canada
Ecuador	12	8	1	1	1	1	—	Lloyds Bank International
Jamaica	10	5	3	1	—	1	—	Nova Scotia
Liberia	3	3	—	—	—	—	—	Chase
Madagascar	7	2	—	4	—	—	1	Chase
Malawi	5	1	1	—	3	—	—	National Westminster

Country								Lead bank(s)
Mexico	13	7	1	3	1	1	—	Citibank
Morocco	10	3	—	4	1	1	1	Citibank
Nicaragua	17	9	2	3	1	1	1	Deutsche Süd-amerikanische/ Bank of America*
Panama	11	4	1	2	1	3	—	Bank of America
Peru	12	6	1	3	1	1	—	Citibank
Philippines	12	6	1	2	1	2	—	Manufacturers Hanover (Deputy: Bank of Toyko)
Poland	14	1	1	7	2	1	2	Dresdner
Romania	9	2	—	5	2	—	—	Bank of America
Uruguay	6	3	1	1	1	—	—	Citibank
Venezuela	13	6	1	4	1	1	—	Chase Manhattan/ Lloyds Bank International/ Bank of America*
Yugoslavia	16	8	1	5	1	1	—	Manufacturers Hanover
Zaire	4	2	—	1	1	—	—	Citibank/Bankers Trust*
Zambia	7	3	—	—	3	—	1	Citibank

Source: Lomax (1986).
*Co-chairman.

this write-down (since it has not been matched by actual debt forgiveness), and the regulators have not forced the banks to bring reported earnings and dividends into line with these more realistic asset values.

4.5.3   Problem 3: The Instability of New Private Lending

The bargain between debtors and creditors since 1982 has been clear: the debtor countries are to continue servicing the interest on their bank debts in return for a postponement of principal repayments, easy terms on official credits (both old and new), and new concerted lending from the commercial banks. The third leg of this strategy has been shaky in the past two years, despite the stated support for new lending from the U.S. government in the context of the Baker Plan.

Three things have happened. First, for reasons described earlier, the U.S. regional banks have been able to avoid their pro rata share of new lending, as have many European and Japanese banks. The burden of new debt servicing has (predictably) been left to those banks that are already most deeply exposed, since the lesser exposed banks are able to free ride. Second, the willingness of the large U.S. banks to engage in concerted lending has also waned. As was shown in table 4.6, the amounts of money provided in concerted lending declined in 1985 and 1986 relative to the two previous years. In 1986, concerted lending rebounded somewhat over 1985, but only because of loans to a single country, Mexico, and only after a bitter fight between the banks and the U.S. Treasury (a battle not yet completely over at the time of writing this paper). Third, while the concerted lending has provided some new money to the public sectors of the debtor countries, the private sectors have been net debt repayers, so that the banks are reducing their total exposures in the debtor countries even while their loans outstanding to the debtor country governments are rising.

The result is an enormous breach between rhetoric and reality. During the year since the Baker Plan was unveiled, banking exposure has declined sharply. A recent report of the IMF contained the stunning news that, in the first half of 1986, the developing countries repaid $7.1 billion (in addition to making interest payments!), in contrast to a net borrowing of $9 billion in 1985, $15 billion in 1984, and $35 billion in 1983. (IMF *Survey,* December 15, 1986). Among the fifteen countries singled out by Baker for special attention under the Baker Plan, bank exposure fell by $3.4 billion. Data showing the decline in bank lending, by region of LDC borrower, are shown in table 4.11.

The 1986 bank settlement with Mexico, which included $6 billion of new financing for Mexico over an 18-month period, might be seen as revitalizing the process of concerted lending, but it is just as likely to cause a backlash against concerted lending, since many of the banks deeply resented the pressures to lend more to a collapsing Mexican

Table 4.11   **Bank Lending to Developing Countries, 1984–First Half 1986**
                    ($ billion)

	1984	1985	1st Half 1986
Developing Countries	15.0	9.1	−7.1
Africa	−0.3	1.4	−1.2
Asia	8.2	6.9	−1.3
Europe	2.1	3.2	0.5
Middle East	0.6	−0.2	0.0
Western Hemisphere	6.0	−0.1	−4.1
15 Heavily Indebted Countries	5.4	−1.9	−3.4

Source: IMF, *International Capital Markets*, December 1986, table 7, p. 46.

economy in which inflation was surging above 100 percent per year. As evidence for this resistance, countries such as the Philippines, which followed Mexico in the "queue" for bank rescheduling, hit a stone wall at the banks, who were particularly fearful of making the Mexican program a precedent for other countries.

Overall, the current method of involuntary lending is unsatisfactory for two reasons. First, the amounts involved appear to be insufficient to finance renewed growth in most of the debtor countries. Second, the amounts are unstable year to year. Whenever an economy looks like it can survive a year without new funds, the banks vociferously resist new lending. The lending resumes only in the context of a renewed balance of payments crisis. This kind of on-again, off-again lending greatly discourages investments in the debtor countries, since investors recognize that the debtor country will be prone to balance of payments crises for the foreseeable future.

4.5.4   Problem 4: Macroeconomic Oversimplifications in Conditionality

Even under the best of circumstances, the return of a debtor country from the financial brink is difficult. Lenders and investors are wary of an economy until a new and successful track record is established. New industries must be developed to replace the declining sectors that were previously fed by domestic demand or that have suffered from the collapse of international commodities prices. These difficulties usually require significant time and luck (a resource discovery, a terms of trade improvement, a rise in foreign demand), and any progress can come unhinged from domestic political unrest that follows in the wake of economic austerity. Moreover, the growth of new sectors often requires substantial public sector investment to provide the infrastructure (e.g., roads, energy, irrigation, etc.) to make the new industries viable.

One of the lesser recognized problems mentioned earlier is the fact that the bulk of the external debt is heavily concentrated in the public sector, so that the fiscal situation in many debtor countries has remained devastated even after the country's trade balance has improved. Thus, the debtor economies have remained the victims of very high interest rates (when the government deficit is bond financed), very high inflation (when money financed), or very inadequate public sector investments (when expenditures are cut to make room for debt servicing), or a combination of all of these afflictions. Higher tax revenues in many of the debtor countries will be a part of a realistic solution to the continuing fiscal crisis. Remarkably, however, the United States has recently opposed tax increases in the debtor countries as a matter of supply-side principle, almost regardless of the realities in the countries themselves. It is also true that, politically and economically, raising tax revenues during a recession is very hard, especially since the contractionary effects of a tax increase may intensify the recession.

The "official view" of the creditor community (with the United States, the IMF, and the World Bank in the lead) has simplified the macroeconomic picture by arguing that drastic liberalization of trade and domestic markets will solve the problem of economic recovery. These pronouncements ignore the problems just raised and are also ahistorical. The great successes of liberalization, such as in Japan or Korea, have been affairs over the course of decades, not months. Rapid liberalizations, as in the Southern Cone at the end of the 1970s, have more often than not failed. Moreover, strong government intervention in the Asian miracle economies of Japan, Korea, and Taiwan appears to have fostered, rather than hindered, economic growth.

4.5.5   Problem 5: Underemphasizing the Creditor Country Responsibilities

The creditors have made much of the policy mistakes of the debtor countries and have stressed that recovery from the debt crisis will require a change of behavior in those countries. This emphasis has some merit, we have seen, since most of the debtor countries made serious policy mistakes in the past decade. But the focus is also seriously misleading, since it reduces the much-needed scrutiny of the behavior of creditor countries as well. As noted earlier, forty countries did not simultaneously fall into crisis because of a virulent epidemic of bad behavior; rather, the shocks of macroeconomic policies of the creditor governments also played a key role. Similarly, the worsening of the debtor situation since 1985 is not a result of debtor country behavior but rather the collapse of commodities prices, which is a global macroeconomic phenomenon.

The leading governments have only recently begun to coordinate macroeconomic policies in ways conducive to recovery from the debt crisis. The Reagan Administration spent its first five years denying any responsibility for high world interest rates and renouncing any intention of coordinating macroeconomic policies. That is beginning to change, though the enormous U.S. fiscal deficit, which continues to hold world interest rates at unusually high levels (to the debtor country detriment), is only fitfully being brought under control.

Moreover, the United States and other creditor governments have successfully divorced discussions about the debt strategy from discussions about their own trade policies. It is an elementary proposition that rising LDC exports are a key to a successful resolution of the debt crisis, and yet with increasing frequency, trade actions by the United States and the Europeans work directly against this imperative. As an example, the United States recently (January 2, 1987) cut the benefits under the generalized system of preferences for eight developing countries, including the debtor countries Brazil, Mexico, South Korea, and Yugoslavia. Similarly, voluntary restraints on steel exports into the United States instituted in 1984 resulted in a restriction on steel exports from many debtor countries, most importantly Brazil and South Korea. In general, with worldwide trade in agriculture, textiles, steel, and increasingly electronics subject to extensive protectionism and controls, it is extremely difficult and risky for a debtor country to embark on an aggressive export push as a way to climb out of a debt crisis.

4.5.6   Problem 6: The Failure of Diplomacy

The final problem that I shall raise is one of political style rather than economic substance: the diplomatic manner in which the debtor countries have been dealt with in recent years, and the role of these countries in the formulation of their debt management strategies. My point of reference is the Marshall Plan, which had as one of its major ambitions the development of political, as well as economic, stability in Europe after World War II. One of the key aspects of the Marshall Plan was that the European nations were required to work out a recovery plan on their own and then to submit that plan to the United States for review and financing. After much debate, the Senate rejected imposing strict conditionality in the program, arguing that it would not be conducive to developing European support for and dedication to their own recovery program. In fact, the only specific condition imposed in the program was the establishment of a joint and continuous European organization to oversee the recovery effort (Wexler 1983, 48–49).

In the case of the debt crisis, the developing countries have not been treated with such dignity, but rather as if they needed constant scolding from superior developed country brothers. This has been an extremely harmful aspect of the recovery process, with much time spent on fights between the debtor countries and the IMF, which has rather autocratically attempted to impose its views on stabilization programs. The bad will also spilled over into the Baker Plan, which dictates a radical free market solution as the remedy for all of the debtor countries' problems.

This attitude of the creditor countries is particularly hard to understand in view of the fact that the debt crisis arose in most cases in South America under autocratic military dictatorships that have since been replaced by legitimate and responsible democratic governments. Democracies have replaced military dictatorships in Argentina, Bolivia, Brazil, Ecuador, Peru, and Uruguay, and in every one of those cases, the debt problem emerged under the previous military regime. In Asia, the same can be said about the Philippines. In other words, the most important step toward better government has already been taken.

4.6 Some New Steps in Managing the Debt Crisis

The earlier discussion in this paper suggests that the debt management has leaned too far in the direction of protecting the commercial banks and not far enough in promoting economic growth in the debtor countries. Several innovations in debt management could be effective in promoting debtor country growth, seemingly without posting major risks to the financial system. I will discuss three kinds of innovations, many of which have been debated in policy circles in the past couple of years. First, it has been suggested that there is a case for providing partial debt relief for countries in the most extreme difficulties. The present value of the country's obligations could be reduced through one of a number of mechanisms mentioned later. Second, for most other debtor countries, there may be a case for increasing and stabilizing the inflows of new capital, particularly in view of the fact that the concerted lending process seems to be functioning poorly. Third, some of the risks now faced by debtor countries could be shifted onto the international capital markets to allow the debtor governments a greater ability to meet the uncertainties of interest rates, the terms of trade, protectionism, and growth in the industrial countries.

These changes, which I will discuss at greater length in a moment, could be combined with other changes responsive to the problems identified in the previous section. Bank regulators might force a greater capitalization of U.S. banks, and more write-offs, to cushion them against losses on LDC debts in the future. International macroeconomic coordination could focus on the trade and interest rate linkages needed to overcome the crisis. Diplomacy could enhance, rather than diminish, the stature of the new democracies of Latin America.

4.6.1   Partial and Selective Debt Relief

Twenty years ago, policymakers would have been much more enthusiastic about the case for selective debt forgiveness. In the generation after World War II, policymakers in the creditor governments knew that the failure to grant timely relief on international debt had severely weakened U.S. allies in the case of interallied war debts after World War I; had contributed to the rise of Hitler in the case of German reparations; and had contributed to the attractiveness of Perón's demagoguery in Argentina in the 1940s and 1950s. These considerations led the creditor governments to grant debt forgiveness to Indonesia as recently as 1970.

Policymakers today fear debt relief because of its potential impact on the commercial banks. However, relief could be granted *selectively* and *partially* to a restricted group of debtor countries in a way that would pose only minimal risks to the international financial system. One proposal, suggested in Sachs (1986), would grant relief according to a formula that gives relief to the countries that have experienced the largest declines in per capita income in recent years (other criteria could be applied, such as granting relief only to the poorest countries, or those that have experienced the greatest terms of trade shocks, etc.). In order to minimize moral hazard problems, it is recommended that the relief be granted only as part of an internationally supervised program of stabilization and reform.

In the specific illustration in Sachs (1986), relief is given in the form of five years of complete forgiveness of interest payments from debtor countries that have suffered a drop in per capita GDP of 15 percent or more since 1980. In Latin America, this criterion includes most of the debtor countries, but importantly *excludes* Brazil and Mexico, whose GDP decline has been less severe. The suspension is to apply to all debts currently subject to rescheduling by the commercial banks and by the official creditors in the Paris Club. It turns out that the overall relief provided by U.S. banks to five major Latin debtor countries (Argentina, Bolivia, Peru, Uruguay, Venezuela) would total $6.6 billion in present value, and by all BIS banks, $19.1 billion. The forgiveness by U.S. banks would represent approximately 6.2 percent of bank capital. This 6.2 percent of bank capital is much less than the market write-downs of bank stocks that have already occurred!

How could relief by the banks actually be effectuated? One way would be through moral suasion of the creditor governments and the IMF, or even through legislation. A different and interesting way, suggested by Kenen (1983) and others would be through the intermediation of a financial institution (either an existing institution, such as the World Bank, or a new one created for this purpose). In the Kenen-Hatori plan, the international entity would issue a bond that is guaranteed by participating creditor governments and swap the bond with the commercial banks for their LDC claims. The new guaranteed bonds would have an interest rate somewhat *below* the market rate, and that lower rate would be passed along to the debtor countries. As in the previous example, the reduction in interest rates could be tied to the extent of deterioration of the debtor economy.

This plan has two key desirable features. First, the banks would be relinquishing a risky income stream with a positive spread over LIBOR for a safe asset with a negative spread. The improvement in the quality of the banks' portfolios would be enough to justify such a swap to bank shareholders, who might otherwise object to a straightforward write-down of debt. Shareholder objections would be moot, since it is clear that the market is already heavily discounting the value of LDC assets in the secondary market. Second, the plan would offer debt relief with no direct cost to the creditor governments (or their taxpayers). It would be self-financing, in the sense that the commercial bank shareholders would effectively be supplying the relief.

4.6.2   Increasing Net Capital Flows to the Debtor Countries

Many countries do not need explicit relief. Rather, they require increased and steadier inflows of public and private capital. The question here is how to generate the increased and steadier inflows in view of the fact that the commercial banks are *reducing,* rather than increasing, their exposures. Most proposals for vast amounts of new official lending are nonstarters, particularly in this period of budget austerity in the major industrial countries. There will have to be a continued reliance on private market lending to provide the needed capital, and the key to such lending is to make new private lending safer, in one way or another, than the existing stock of debt. There are several ways to do this. One common suggestion is for more cofinancing of projects between the World Bank and the private sector, thereby allowing the private lenders to piggyback on the seniority of World Bank loans (which by convention are never rescheduled). A related method would be to strengthen the insurance system for international investments (such as the MIGA).

A different way that leads to the same outcome, but without the need for any new official money, is proposed in Sachs (1986). In the proposal, an explicit agreement among the existing creditors would allow the debtor country to borrow a predetermined level of new funds that would be earmarked as senior to the existing debt. In other words, all creditors would agree that the specified new debt would be serviced in entirety before any of the existing debt is serviced. The new lenders under this arrangement would not have to be banks. Senior lending could be made on the basis of marketable securities purchased by asset funds, corporations, or private wealthholders. As with the relief proposal, eligibility for seniority borrowing should be limited to countries with poor economic performance, but not so poor as to trigger debt relief. For example, eligibility might be given to countries that have suffered a decline in per capita GDP during the 1980s.

The multilateral institutions would have several functions in this proposal. First, the IMF would reach an agreement with the country on the amounts of incremental lending that will be raised on a senior basis. Unlimited new borrowing would not be allowed. Rather, the amount of senior debt would be linked to growth targets in the debtor country and the quality of investment opportunities. The IMF would record and monitor the new senior borrowing and help to verify the senior treatment of the new debt. The World Bank and the MDBs would continue to play their existing roles of defining and monitoring the investment programs of the country to support the effective utilization of the new borrowing.

The proposed arrangement would have the virtue that new capital could be provided to the debtor countries without having to make a judgment about the eventual fate of the existing debt. If the debtor country resumes its growth, both old and new debts will be serviced. If growth does not resume, the old debts will be written off, which presumably would have happened anyway under the current system of concerted lending. The proposal has both pluses and minuses for the existing creditors. By agreeing to such a program, the banks could suffer a reduction in value of their existing claims, but at the same time they would be freed from the obligation of involuntary lending, which now puts the burden for new lending precisely on those banks whose portfolios are already filled with the largest exposure in the debtor country. Additionally, the value of the existing debt would be raised by this plan, not lowered, to the extent that the new borrowing enhances the debt-servicing capacity of the country by more than the interest cost of the new loans.

The amounts of new senior borrowing might represent 6 or 7 percent of the existing stock of debt each year for the next few years. This level would eliminate the net resource transfers currently made by the debtor countries to the creditors. At this rate, for example, Mexico would accumulate approximately $35 billion of new senior debt over the next five years, an amount that could readily be raised by new market borrowing, since $35 billion of debt could be easily serviced by Mexico in the future, as long as that $35 billion is serviced before any of the existing $100 billion of Mexican debt.

4.6.3   Shifting Risks to the International Capital Markets

So far, the international capital markets have done little to diversify the profound economic risks facing the debtor countries. Loan agreements have few contingencies, for example, linking the level of repayments to the state of the borrowing economy, its terms of trade, or any other indicators of the borrowing country's economic well-being. Commodity-linked bonds have never gotten off the ground for reasons that are not well understood by financial specialists. Interest rate risk is borne entirely by the borrower, since almost all debt is in the form of variable interest securities. The borrowers also face the risks of credit cutoffs, with little possibility of obtaining credit commitments for future borrowing.

It would seem that many of the risks facing the debtor countries could be more efficiently diversified through more complex loan agreements. An initial example is the Mexican accord reached in 1986, which contained two important innovations. First, there was a link of new financing (and of IMF performance criteria) to the price of oil: a drop in the price of oil raised the level of funds to be made available to Mexico, and a rise did the reverse. In either direction, the change in funding is gradually phased out over several quarters, so that eventually Mexico has to adjust to, and not simply finance, the changes in its terms of trade. The second special facility is a growth contingency loan, which allows Mexico to draw on more official and private funding for increased government spending if for any reason its growth does not meet the program targets during a fixed period. Given the complexity of the determinants of growth in the short term, negotiators felt that it was impossible to write an even more elaborate contract which linked the "growth" lending to changes in underlying conditions, even though the agreed terms suffer from the moral hazard problem that self-inflicted growth slowdowns are also rewarded by new lending.

There are several additional proposals that have been made in recent years of a similar nature. Interest rate capping was widely discussed in 1984 before being dropped, but it remains a promising way for shielding the debtor countries from some market risks. The debt-equity swap mechanism is also partly a way to shed risks (and also partly a hidden mechanism for partial debt forgiveness) by making the creditor take an equity position in the debtor economy. Finally, the mechanism of linking debt-servicing payments to the level of exports, as unilaterally adopted by Peru in its ceiling of debt servicing to 10 percent of exports, or to GNP (as proposed by Feldstein 1986) is yet another way for shedding some of the risks of debt servicing. Brazil, in a more consensual manner, is adopting the Peruvian position in its current debt negotiations by seeking to limit net resource transfers to its creditors to 2.5 percent of GNP. Such a rule would automatically alter the amounts of debt servicing according to market interest rates and according to GNP growth in Brazil.

4.7 Conclusions

The management of the LDC debt crisis since 1982 has been an important example of successful international policy coordination. At the time of the outbreak of the Mexican debt crisis in the summer of 1982, many observers feared that the crisis would provoke an international banking crisis and a global depression. Those fears have not come to pass in large part because of the active involvement of policymakers from the creditor countries, the debtor countries, and the multilateral financial institutions.

The origins of the debt crisis can be found both in the shift in the global macroeconomic environment in the early 1980s and in major policy mistakes in many debtor countries. From a macroeconomic perspective, the fundamental change in the global economy was the rise in interest rates to levels exceeding the growth rate of exports of the debtor countries. Once this rise in interest rates occurred, the debt-export ratios of the debtor countries could be stabilized only by a shift to trade balance surpluses, a shift which required deep and often painful macroeconomic adjustments. Moreover, since most of the foreign borrowing had been undertaken by the public sectors of the debtor countries, the shift in interest rates also required sharp budget cuts in the public sector. For most debtor countries, the long-term debt-servicing prospects are not bleak, and it is realistic to expect over the long term that needed adjustments to the trade balance and the budgets can be made in most countries. The recent declines in global interest rates greatly enhance the long-term prospects for a successful resolution of the crisis. Nonetheless, short-term difficulties could still easily derail a successful resolution of the crisis.

Policymakers recognized three distinct roles for public intervention in managing the debt crisis. First, public authorities recognized that the marketplace itself could not provide adequate enforcement of the existing debt contracts. A complete hands-off attitude of the public authorities would likely have resulted in widespread defaults by the debtor governments with adverse consequences for all parties concerned. Second, the policymakers recognized that if left by itself, the loan market would likely provide insufficient levels of new funding for the debtor countries. There is an inherent gap between the self-interest of individual banks, who want to pull out willy-nilly from new lending, and the collective interest of all creditors, who are best served by continuing to make new loans to the problem debtor countries. Third, the policymakers recognized that there is a role for the IMF to impose conditionality on debtor countries in return for new lending, particularly in cases where misguided policies contributed to the onset of the debt crisis.

The public role was conceived with these problems in mind. Led by the U.S. government, the creditor governments coalesced around a strategy that included: (1) pressure on the debtor countries to maintain debt servicing; (2) pressure on the commercial banks to continue lending in "involuntary" lending packages; and (3) IMF conditionality as the cornerstone of new lending agreements. To a significant extent, this package has forestalled widespread defaults and has prevented the worst fears of 1982 from coming to pass.

There continue to be serious problems, however, with the implementation of this strategy. First, the pressure to maintain debt-servicing payments has been carried to a point of absurdity, so that even countries in the midst of 50,000 percent hyperinflations, or free falls of income, have been pressed to maintain debt servicing. Second, the pressure on commercial banks to continue lending has waxed and waned. Involuntary lending has proved to be too little and too unstable a financial basis for economic recovery in most of the debtor countries. Third, the contents of conditionality have been oversimplified, with the IMF and the World Bank pressing for immediate liberalization as the key to recovery in the debtor countries, contrary to logic and historical experience. This has led to a backlash from the debtor countries that strongly resists such simple and politically dangerous prescriptions.

Several recommendations were discussed in this paper as possible remedies to these shortcomings. The recommendations revolved around three areas: partial debt relief; stabilized capital inflows; and a shifting of risks now borne by the debtor countries to the international capital markets. It was suggested that partial debt relief would not have to pose profound risks for the international system, and that such relief could be targeted to the countries most in need. With respect to new capital inflows, a proposal for new *senior* lending to the debtor countries was broached, with the aim of stabilizing and increasing the size of capital inflows into the debtor countries. Finally, various proposals were discussed that aim at shifting risks from the debtor countries to the international financial markets, such as interest rate capping and commodity-linked lending.

Notes

1. Detailed accounts of the crisis can be found in several recent books, including Cline (1984), Lever and Huhne (1986), Lomax (1986), Makin (1984), and Nunnenkamp (1986).

2. See Sachs (1982), Eichengreen and Portes (1986), and Fishlow (1985) for descriptions of the ups and downs of international lending during the past century.

3. The top ten debtor countries in 1983 ranked by gross external debt to BIS banks were Mexico, Brazil, Argentina, Korea, Venezuela, Philippines, Yugoslavia, Indonesia, Egypt, and Chile, of which Mexico, Venezuela, Indonesia, and Egypt are oil exporters, and Argentina is approximately self-sufficient. Oil exports exceed oil imports for this group of countries as a whole.

4. A country that borrows the money it needs to make its debt service payments will have its debt grow at the rate of interest (e.g., with interest rates at 10 percent, a country that borrows its debt-servicing bill will see its total debt grow by 10 percent per year). As long as that interest rate is equal to or less than the growth rate of export earnings, then the debt-export ratio will be stable or falling.

5. See M. P. Dooley, "Country-Specific Risk Premiums, Capital Flight and Net Investment Income Payments in Selected Developing Countries," IMF Research Department, DM/86/17, March 1986.

6. For a breakdown of the debt by creditor for different groups of borrowers, see IMF, *World Economic Outlook,* April 1986, table A48, pp. 244–46.

7. See IMF, *International Capital Markets,* December 1986, pp. 74–81.

8. The analytical oversimplifications tend to come in several places, as mentioned later in the text. First, in order to service the country's debts, GNP must be in an acceptable form—specifically, in the form of export earnings. However, as economies shift from domestic production to exports, measured GNP may well decline in the short run to intermediate run. Second, since the debts are generally owed by the public sectors of the debtor countries, debtor governments must raise taxes or cut spending in order to service the debts. Such fiscal actions will tend to exacerbate many macroeconomic problems, such as unemployment and recession. Third, private investors are likely to shun economies suffering from debt crises, thus undermining the economic growth that is counted on to facilitate future debt servicing.

References

Balassa, Bela. 1984. Adjustment policies in developing countries: A reassessment. *World Development* 12:955–72.

Bergsten, C. Fred, William R. Cline, and John Williamson. 1985. Bank lending to developing countries: The policy alternatives. Washington, D.C.: Institute for International Economics.

Cline, William R. 1984. *International debt: Systematic risk and policy response.* Washington, D.C.: Institute for International Economics.

Cohen, D. 1985. How to evaluate the solvency of an indebted nation. *Economic Policy* 1 (November):139–67.

Diaz-Alejandro, Carlos F. 1984. Latin American debt: I don't think we are in Kansas anymore. *Brookings Papers on Economic Activity* 2:335–89.

Dornbusch, Rudiger R. 1985a. Policy and performance links between LDC debtors and industrial nations. *Brookings Papers on Economic Activity* 2:303–56.

————. 1985b. External debt, budget deficits and disequilibrium exchange rates. In *International debt and the developing countries*, ed. Gordon Smith and John Cuddington. Washington, D.C.: The World Bank.

————. 1986. International debt and economic instability. Paper presented at the Federal Reserve Bank of Kansas City Conference on Debts, Financial Stability, and Public Policy.

Eichengreen, B., and R. Portes. 1986. Debt and default in the 1930s: Causes and consequences. *European Economic Review* 30:599–640.

Feldstein, M. 1986. International debt service and ecomonic growth: Some simple analytics. NBER Working Paper no. 2076. Cambridge, Mass.: National Bureau of Economic Research.

Fishlow, A. 1985. Lessons from the past: Capital markets during the 19th century and the interwar period. *International Organization*, Summer.

Frieden, J. 1981. Third World indebted industrialization. *International Organization* 35 (3):407–31.

International Monetary Fund. 1986. *International Capital Markets*. December.

————. *World Economic Outlook*. Various issues.

Kahler, M., ed. 1986. *The politics of international debt*. Ithaca, N.Y.: Cornell University Press.

Kenen, P. 1983. A bailout plan for the banks. *New York Times*, March 6.

Kyle, S., and J. Sachs. 1984. Developing country debt and the market value of large commercial banks. NBER Working Paper no. 1470. Cambridge, Mass.: National Bureau of Economic Research.

Lever, H., and C. Huhne. 1986. *Debt and danger*. Boston: Atlantic Monthly Press.

Lomax, David F. 1986. *The developing country debt crisis*. London: Macmillan.

Makin, John. 1984. *The global debt crisis*. New York: Basic Books.

Morgan Guarantee Trust Company. 1983. *World Financial Markets*. New York.

Nunnenkamp, Peter. 1986. *The international debt crisis of the Third World*. Sussex: Harvester Press.

Sachs, Jeffrey. 1982. LDC debt in the 1980s: Problems and prospects. In *Crises in the economic and financial structure*, ed. P. Wachtel. Lexington, Mass.: Lexington Books.

————. 1984. Theoretical issues in international borrowing. Princeton Studies in International Finance, no. 54. Princeton University.

————. 1985. External debt and macroeconomic performance in Latin America and East Asia. *Brookings Papers on Economic Activity* 2:523–64.

————. 1986. Managing the LDC debt crisis. *Brookings Papers on Economic Activity* 2:397–440.

Wexler, Immanuel. 1983. *The Marshall Plan revisited. Westport, Conn.: Greenwood Press*.

World Bank. 1986. *World Bank debt tables, 1985–86*. Washington, D.C.

2. Anthony M. Solomon

Prospects for the LDC Debt Problem

A couple of weeks ago I was in San Francisco when Marty Feldstein and his European and Japanese colleagues in a study group presented a very big paper on the debt question. I was struck by the careful analytic way in which they took all this myriad of debt management proposals, that we've been hearing for four and a half years, and categorized them, broke them down into three basic categories, and then did some evaluation of them.

I'm not going to do any of that today, because basically I think it's almost irrelevant to the process of dynamic action that is going on among the players. I believe that the banks—the creditor banks—are incapable of taking a concerted initiative to choose and push forward an alternative debt strategy. There are just too many differences among them—small banks versus large banks; European banks, Japanese banks, and American banks who have different regulatory, different supervisory, different accounting, and different tax policies. And even among the U.S. money-center banks there are some differences.

What I am going to try to do today is give you my feeling for what the new factors are and how this situation is likely to play out as a matter of reality. And believe me I have a lot of question marks in my mind because I have a cloudy crystal ball too.

But this is the way I like to approach it, because I just think it's too complicated to expect anything but the day-to-day evolving situation and the interplay among all these different players to determine the final outcome. Some people will say that, even though the banks may be incapable of a concerted initiative, you can have a forcing action by sovereign debtor governments, who will simply declare moratoria.

But I find myself very, very confused in this area. Look at the actual situation. Peru declared in effect a moratorium on commercial bank debt service, medium term and long term. Many of the bankers said they were going to get tough with Peru. Peru was small enough; their exposure to Peru was small enough to get tough and therefore teach a lesson. I have yet to see any retaliation against Peru by the banks.

Please don't misunderstand me. I'm not making any kind of judgments that they should or should not be retaliating. I'm trying to talk about the facts of this situation.

Mexico went for continuation of the existing conventional strategy, although in its Baker Plan form there is more emphasis on growth. Brazil has declared a moratorium, but I hear increasing talk that the Brazilian industrialists are bringing enormous pressure on the Brazilian president to dump his finance minister, to call off the moratorium, to make some conciliatory gestures, and to begin negotiating, because the industrialists are afraid that the financing for imports and exports will seriously hurt their businesses.

This is notwithstanding the freeze in short-term credits that the Brazilian government announced. I'm sure that Bill Ogden can enlighten us in greater detail, but I assume the reason why the freeze doesn't protect the Brazilian industrialists is that as particular letters of credit expire, that money returns to the Brazilian government if its frozen, and they have no confidence in the Brazilian government that it will make those funds available again to the Brazilian industrialists. I don't know if that's correct or not, but I assume that's why the freeze is not calming the fears of the Brazilian industrialists.

Argentina is talking about settling, if it can get Mexican terms. Now can you imagine that two-eighths of a point difference above LIBOR is going to make this kind of difference between confrontation and no confrontation? I find myself very confused by this, because so far the facts are that there has been no retaliation. There are certain countries that could probably continue a substantial part of their foreign trade (although in a much more inconvenient form) without the credit extended by the banks, but they are still reluctant to go down that road.

I also hear reports that what the Brazilians are really afraid of is a trade boycott by the U.S. government if they were to default. Again, I find that hard to believe. If they were to formally repudiate the debt, possibly. But that's not likely. They're not going to do it that way. They'll simply have a moratorium and, while they're negotiating, not pay interest for debt service, and this will drag on and on. But I cannot see the U.S. Congress imposing a trade boycott on Brazil. In fact, on the contrary, any consensus that may exist is to promote more U.S. exports to Latin America, and certainly a trade boycott on imports would not lead in that direction.

So I find myself thoroughly confused by the play and the players. I don't see that there is any clear trend yet whereby the sovereign governments are going to force moratoria. But I'll come back to this toward the close of my remarks.

I think there have been some changing factors in the last year or two that are important enough to comment on. One is that there is a much greater intellectual consensus and concern for growth in the LDCs than there was before. I think there is very little sympathy for what are called, I think erroneously so, IMF austerity programs. There is very little sympathy for LDCs being pressured to pay full interest by compressing their imports in order to have a large enough trade surplus. This is important because it changed the tone of the debate; it changed the bargaining power of the different players.

Another factor that is important, I think, is that there has been much more erosion of the ability of banks to get together to put up money. The smaller banks are falling by the wayside more and more, and the big banks are getting very desperate about this problem. Also, as more and more big banks write off or write down part of their loans (it's not entirely a rational action), it makes them more resistant than ever to putting up their share of new money. So you have a lot of fatigue, an erosion developing on the side of the banks' willingness to put up new money.

Another factor of course is that there is fatigue on the part of the LDC debtor countries willingness to do these austerity-type programs. There is this intellectual consensus on growth that's been made respectable by the Baker Plan, and all the talk goes in that direction.

So it seems pretty clear that the priorities are going to be such that any debt strategy has to be consistent with more adequate growth for the LDCs. This leaves everybody in confusion. What is really being looked at by the key players? I think it's fair to say, as I see the situation, that a lot of attention is on developing an exit vehicle for the smaller banks. There's not only a Reserve Bankers' Committee, but there are also certain high echelons in the World Bank that are studying this. It's not obviously a World Bank proposal by any means, and it would take the consent of creditor governments who are powerful in the Bank. But the proposal goes along the lines of a partial guarantee to a sovereign debtor government putting out a ten-to-fifteen-year bond issue, the money to be used to buy debt paper from the smaller banks, or up to a certain amount from all the banks, at the discount in the secondary market. That would have a double advantage. First, it would reduce the debt service of the debtor countries, because now when the paper is sold in the secondary market, that's no help to the debtor country. And second, of course, it would help clean up this problem of eliminating the nuisance of the small banks' refusal to put up their share of the new money.

There are different forms in which this can be done, and there's been talk—not in the World Bank, but outside the World Bank—by bankers about setting up another institution, a subsidiary to the World Bank which would be an intermediary in buying up debt paper at the secondary market discount. This is less practical politically.

Parenthetically, I'm not so sure that under any of these arrangements the small banks will rush to sell their paper at the discount of the secondary market. I can see the discount of the secondary market shrinking the minute they see anything really being done in this area.

It's an enormously complicated problem. The trouble with all of these debt proposals is that they sound nice sometimes, but they are incredibly complicated to implement in a way that would achieve the results intended.

I think it is worth saying that what we are seeing is that the public-sector component of these support packages for the debt-ridden LDCs is creeping up. In the Mexican package, the public sector has gotten up to 50 percent when you include the World Bank, the IMF, the official export credits, et cetera.

Now even if this exit vehicle instrument is devised, where does that leave us? Stepping back and looking at the whole picture . . . even if this proposal is successfully implemented . . . where does it leave us?

It seems to me it doesn't really affect the bottom line that much, even though it would be a help. The bottom line is still going to be that, in my opinion, without adequate economic growth in the industrialized countries, I see no way for the heavily indebted LDC countries to begin to get the adequate growth that there is now a consensus they must have. How else can they develop the resource flow they must have to get that growth while also, incidentally, although an important factor of course, methodically servicing their debt in an orderly and conventional way?

I think that all these debt strategy proposals basically boil down to ways of alleviating or mitigating the situation somewhat and buying time for the banks. There's talk now among the banks about developing what's called a menu of options, whereby each bank can choose the particular form of support that it wants to give. That's easier said, again, than put into practice. To develop equivalencies of sacrifice or of support or of whatever you want to call it is very, very difficult. The most obvious one support option has been talked about for many years: the capitalization of interest to an amount equivalent to the new money that other banks are putting up. In practice, capitalization is difficult because the banks fear that if the debtor governments see that 40 percent of the interest can be capitalized and stretched out, then they might unilaterally push for 60 percent or 80 percent or ultimately 100 percent.

So I feel that the problems are enormous without adequate OECD growth. That brings us back to the discussion this morning about policy coordination, and I won't go into that.

What happens if we don't have adequate growth and sufficient resource flow? I think that's by far the most likely scenario over the next couple of years. What's going to happen in the debt situation?

It seems to me, even if the Brazil moratorium gets cleared up, that we will see a recurrence of more random moratoria from time to time, and some of these will then get patched up in new agreements after a while. For example, I cannot see the next president of Mexico coming in and calmly continuing the conventional strategy that has been followed. I think both the political and economic situation in Mexico make that almost impossible. We will see confrontations from time to time. I doubt that the banks will be able to come up with a concerted bank compromise strategy package that could be successfully negotiated with the sovereign debtor governments. I think that there will be individual deals struck and many deals not struck. There will be confusion. I would assume that at some point the situation will force governments, particularly the U.S. government, to take the initiative and try to hammer out some compromise packages. That will probably involve more public support as a component, although I don't see a full bailout for the banks. It seems to me that the difficulty we will be getting into as the situation becomes more confused will be one where the U.S. government ultimately will have no alternative. Over the years as this process goes on, the banks will build significant reserves (or write-downs) against their exposure. My guess is that the history books will finally say that the larger part of the sovereign country commercial bank debt was never repaid (nor did they return to good-credit standing with the commercial banks), but the process of absorbing some substantial part of this debt as loss was successfully and gradually stretched out by all the parties.

---

3. William S. Ogden

The Need for Change in Managing LDC Debt

This August will mark the fifth anniversary of Finance Minister Silva-Herzog's visit to New York and Washington to inform governments and banks that Mexico could not service its external debt. His announcement, and the subsequent realization that many other countries were in similar circumstances, led to an abrupt halt in commercial bank lending to developing countries. At the peak of this truly worldwide crisis, over forty countries were affected.

I gave a talk on this subject in the fall of 1982 in New York. At that time, many observers perceived the causes of the crisis, and research has helped us understand them better today. I identified four principal players in the debt crisis: debtor countries, creditor country governments, multinational institutions, and commercial banks. Each shared responsibility for the onset of the problem and each currently has a critical role to play in its resolution. Within this context, I would like to comment briefly upon the policies pursued over the last five years, and then turn to the future.

Let me begin by saying that, with hindsight, it is easy enough to be critical of the initial responses of these players. We should remind ourselves, however, that in spite of their mistakes, the response to date has been largely successful. In this regard, I have special praise for Jacques De la Rosier and the role he played throughout this period. While designing an active role for the IMF, he managed to remind others that the IMF was actually filling a gap left by its member governments.

These players helped us avoid the threat to the economic system the debt crisis posed. Indeed, over the last five years some countries have seen major improvements. Many countries now enjoy access to international financial markets that they either did not have five years ago, or were in real danger of losing in 1982. The global economy has grown. World trade did not continue to decline. Protectionism, or at least protectionsim with a vengeance, has been held at bay. Even the banks are stronger, as their capital has grown and their income stream has become more diversified. Let us, therefore, not lose sight of our achievements as we examine the need for change in the process. Let us also remember that in 1982 we rejected many of the more radical solutions so easily set forth by others. Let us also continue to look with great skepticism on proposals for easy solutions which claim to make the problem go away.

Having said this, the need for change in the process has become increasingly apparent. It is more than a liquidity crisis arising from a sudden loss of confidence in almost all debtor countries. True enough, in some countries such as Korea, Columbia, and Thailand, it was an issue of confidence and they have regained market access. We have even forgotten now that Korea was affected in those early months of the crisis. But for a number of LDCs, the problem turned out to be more intractable, truly a debt problem. Unfortunately, some of the countries with the very largest external indebtedness fall into this group. For example, the five largest Latin American debtor countries have seen their foreign debt grow steadily, from $276 billion at the end of 1982, to $319 billion at the end of last year. As a result, the debt burden of this group, relative to its economic size, has remained substantially unchanged.

There were three events over the last year which represented both a greater recognition of the need for change in the process, and the beginning of a new chapter. The Baker initiative was one of them. It recognized the long-term nature of the problem. It also acknowledged the political impossibility and economic undesirability of strategies that are perceived as calling only for further sacrifice and slow growth well beyond the time horizon of a few years. Such policies are unpalatable in any context, but particularly in countries with rapid population growth and in those struggling to legitimate new democratic institutions. A third, but to my mind no less important, element of the Baker initiative was its explicit recognition that some countries are so deeply mired in underdevelopment, poverty, precious misallocation of resources, and social ills, that their problems cannot be solved through the coordinated efforts of the four principal players. Instead, these countries must work directly with creditor governments and multinational institutions. Nevertheless, the Baker initiative had important flaws. It was not a policy response with much in the way of specificity behind it. Nor did it provide leadership behind which the major players could rally, or even debate. Charitably, it was more than a speech, but not a policy.

The second event signalling a clear need for change occurred in the efforts this year to provide refinancing for Mexico. Concerns arose about the way it was done. Concerns over the system of allocating fair shares among the participants and the unwillingness of smaller creditor banks to participate at all. The coyness with which governments of major creditor countries attempted to position themselves in their dual role as both regulators and interested parties, and the different treatment of banks within each of the creditor countries was not helpful. All in all a host of frustrations made it extremely difficult to put the financing together.

Some of the difficulties, as Tony Solomon has already pointed out, just represented weariness on the part of the players. The fatigue was compounded by the slowness of mulitnational institutions to formulate a program that was consistent with the spirit of the Baker initiative. Even more fundamentally, there were doubts that Mexico, even with the best of intentions, could carry out its end of the program.

The third and complete turning of the page that made it clear the strategies of the last five years had finally become unworkable was the confrontational negotiating tactic adopted by Brazil in their most recent rescheduling. Such a strategy might be explained and even justified by some, while it would be condemned by many others. But, regardless of one's position, such behavior signals the close of the chapter on debt which began in 1982, and crystallizes the need for change. In my opinion, however, the need for change does not mean radical change or radical solutions. As weary as we are, and as desirous as we are to make the problem go away, instant gratification for all four players is just not feasible. It is also not desirable in terms of future access to international financial markets, or growth in the debtor countries, world trade and the world economy.

Now, I would like to turn to the kind of changes that I believe are necessary. First and foremost, it seems to me that we must stop dealing with debtor countries as though they are a homogenous group. Each country is unique, with a unique set of financial and development problems. Each should be encouraged to work out its own programs, recognizing both that growth must be a priority and that creditor concessions made to particularly troubled countries cannot automatically become the common denominator to be applied in all cases. For example, it is just as ridiculous to say to the Bolivians that they should look to Argentina for proof that the process is working rather than at their own suffocating economy, as it is to insist that concessions made to Bolivia must be applied to all countries across the board. Indeed, as a high Brazilian official pointed out to me recently, it certainly was not lost on finance ministers in debtor countries that a finance minister in Mexico was replaced ostensibly for not being tough enough on the banks.

A second element of needed change lies in that sore subject of conditionality. No country likes conditionality applied to it. Years ago I saw a number of countries in Europe take offense at the idea of conditionality being applied to them. Nevertheless, I firmly believe that cooperative efforts tied to highly questionable economic programs and short-sighted political windfalls not only cannot be part of such a process, but are self-destructive. Such efforts not only fail, their failure undermines the viability of cooperative solutions.

While it might sound naive, my own experience leads me to believe that if we can agree on a vision for growth with some mutual sacrifice and resistance to protectionism, a responsible conditionality, tailored to each individual country, could be achieved. To reach such an understanding, the creditor and debtor country governments would have to take the lead. They will need, however, to negotiate a lot less coyly than they have in the past. Put simply, we need leadership. Conditionality is too important a subject to be left to the IMF and other multinational institutions without strong political leadership from the major creditor countries.

The third area in which change is badly needed is in achieving growth in trade and income. Naturally, I refer to the frequently mentioned need for resistance to further protectionism in the creditor countries and for economic growth in the debtor countries. But I also believe that economic growth in the creditor countries and resistance to protectionism in the debtor countries are equally important. As far as creditor-country growth is concerned, I refer most particularly to creditor countries other than the United States. From 1982 to 1985, *all* of the net increase in Latin American exports to the industrial countries was accounted for by the United States. Over that time the share of that troubled region's exports bound for the U.S. rose from 33 to 41 percent. By contrast, Japan's imports from Latin America remained unchanged and Germany's registered only a modest gain.

Continued protectionism practiced by the debtor countries should also be questioned. This issue should be raised particularly with the emerging industrial countries that never lost market access. In general, creditor countries ought not condone highly discriminatory practices by debtor governments, regardless of whether or not the debtors have access to international financial markets or are members of the GATT.

I would like to put forward three other elements of change that focus on the role of the commercial banks. First, we must expect that adverse shocks to debtor countries, such as a precipitous drop in export prices or an earthquake, will require additional financing. I recognize that this goes against traditional precepts in that it implies increased lending when circumstances worsen. But there is both a precedent and a need for this. I think, however, that creditor governments should play a bigger role in reacting to the vagaries of external forces, both in terms of the financial commitments they are willing to make and in terms of their willingness to exert leadership roles.

Second, I believe that the private sector can play a more helpful role in developing both debt-for-equity swaps and the so-called secondary market for sovereign debt. These market-related responses are not a panacea and cannot solve the whole problem. They can be an important element, however, not only by helping to share and transform the risk, but by signalling that debtors prefer investment to debt. This signal becomes particularly clear when combined with sensible economic policies that encourage investment in the first place. In addition, such policies make possible the return of flight capital, which has made external financing much more difficult in many of the countries. It is appalling that some debtor countries have such tight restrictions on debt-for-equity swaps and yet complain of their inability to service foreign debt and of their need for growth.

Third, it is sometimes said that banks have not yet taken any losses in sovereign risk-lending. The truth is that many have, and that all will over time. This does not imply, however, that the debt should be for-given, nor that any rote formula should be applied across the board. Debt-for-equity swaps, for example, may lead to greater risk and fre-quently will involve write-down of the debt swapped.

As far as the secondary market for sovereign debt is concerned, it is developing. I think this is a healthy sign, and I can see considerable growth for it in the future. Nevertheless, it is important to remember that these secondary market transactions cannot by themselves solve either the problem of the current debt "overhang" or the problem of future lending. I also think that the accounting profession ought to stop quibbling over whether this so-called market establishes a price for debt instruments of a particular country. In additon, I think finance ministers in the debtor countries should not use the secondary market discount as a vehicle for clubbing the banks by arguing that, since the market has already written off a percentage of this debt, only a smaller amount needs to be serviced.

Next, let me come to two even thornier issues, as far as the banks are concerned. The first has to do with the negotiating process, which by its very nature requires that leadership be provided by a committee representing all bank creditors. This is a problem specific to the Amer-ican banks, simply because there are so many of us involved. I believe that communications have flowed smoothly from these creditor bank committees to creditor banks in other countries, where there are fewer syndicated banks and where confidentiality is more easily maintained. Frankly, there is also more confidence that the interests of all of the banks in countries other than the United States are being represented. It is not for lack of trying, and to be completely fair, also not for a lack of good will. This communication issue among the American banks is, nevertheless, a very nettlesome one. I applaud the efforts among the American banks, or at least some of them, to address this problem. It is critically important as we go forward.

The second issue that applies to all banks, but particularly to the American banks by virtue of the sheer number involved, is that some banks have a considerably smaller commitment to international banking. They not only wish the problem would go away, but have lost any willingness to participate. This is very understandable, particularly if a bank never had any genuine interest in international business, got into it in a burst of enthusiasm in the 1970s, and now has gotten burned. Such banks have little knowledge of how negotiations are proceeding and learn more from newspapers than they hear from the negotiating banks. They are constantly trying to explain their involvement to their boards of directors who share the view that the bank should never have gotten into the international business in the first place. Combine that with opportunities for profitable domestic business and with regulators who must already carry water on both shoulders, but view it as essential to continue reinforcing bank directors' responsibilities in the management of their banks, and you have an enormous amount of pressure to drop out of refinancing. We must find a solution to this problem. There have been many proposals made, ranging from the idea that no bank should be allowed to drop out to the idea that if a bank drops out it cannot have a free ride on everyone else. The central issue is, of course, who will make up the difference if some are permitted to drop out.

A further complication is that a number of banks have sold or swapped loans to other parties. In these instances, the problem of defining the size of a fair share becomes even more complicated. The purchaser of debt in the secondary market, or the holder of equity from a swap often does not intend to put up any new money for additional debt accumulation. As a result, in some cases a bank that has sold or swapped the debt of a particular country has been asked to put up a share of new money based on what it held formerly. This has already become a problem. As the market for loan sales and swaps increases, it will become an even bigger problem.

I think we have to find a way to address the issue of the smaller banks, especially those smaller American banks that want out. Tony Solomon has already alluded to some of the proposals that are being discussed. I would suggest we begin to develop a mechanism to encourage their participation rather than continue to ignore the dropout problem. One such approach might be a government program to guarantee partially the first x-million dollars or its equivalent of developing country debt held by each of the commercial banks. Because this would be an absolute amount, invariant to the amount of a bank's capital or the size of a bank's portfolio, it would represent a much larger percentage of the total amount held by any of the smaller banks. To qualify, the bank would have to set aside reserves of, say, a third of the guaranteed amount, or a fourth of the program amount. The same percentage would apply to any new funds that would have to be provided in the future. This scheme would recognize that, in voluntarily accepting the guarantee, a bank would also have to be willing to establish such a reserve. This would mean a reduction in defined primary capital by that amount, but would not be a write-off of the debt.

As an illustration, let me give you a sense of how this might have worked in the recent Mexican financing. If we assume that the government through some mechanism would provide a 75 percent guarantee for the first $25 million from each bank, we estimated that approximately 50 of the 101 U.S. banks that had committed by the end of March would have been fully covered by such a program. These banks, however, would be required to participate in future refinancing and would have to write down the 25 percent of the debt not insured. The U.S. government would therefore be guaranteeing about $1.3 billion of debt if all 101 U.S. banks chose to participate. For their part, the banks would have to increase reserves by about $435 million. These calculations exclude about 50 American banks which did not participate in the 1984 rescheduling negotiations. In other words, last time a third dropped out.

I would also like to suggest that the commercial banks, the accounting profession, and the Securities and Exchange Commission begin to explore a possible change in accounting conventions. One positive change would permit banks to set up allocated reserves of narrowly defined exposure in such a way that the charges could flow directly to their capital accounts, rather than through their income statements and then into their capital accounts. Before we all throw up our hands at this heresy, let me say that there are ample precedents in the way that we have treated some of the problems of the savings and loan industry, in the way that the country debt restructurings have not automatically meant loans were reclassified as nonperforming, and in the way that all corporations have been permitted to take exchange rate fluctuations, under certain carefully defined rules, directly to their capital accounts, rather than through their income statements.

It was not that long ago when every chief executive officer of a major multinational corporation in America was explaining how his earnings in any particular quarter were affected by foreign exchange fluctuations.

I would guess that a lot of chief executive officers are not even aware how this affected their capital accounts in this last quarter. I have not been asked by a bank-stock analyst in years about the impact of exchange rate fluctuations on our capital accounts, whereas I used to be quizzed regularly on the income statement.

I know there are problems with suggesting that loan write-offs be passed through to capital. But I think the idea should be explored, as it would allow increased flexibility and make it easier to take a longer view. This emphasis on quarter-to-quarter performance is a criticism of American corporate management we have all heard. Perhaps it is true, but it is partly a result of the unnecessary emphasis in our financial markets on short-term earnings.

In summary, the developing country negotiations seem to be well into a new stage. It seems likely, however, that current negotiations will require even more coordination than the substantial amount that has been seen in the last five years. I think a change in the process is urgently needed.

But it is also becoming increasingly apparent that the major players— the debtor countries, creditor-country governments, multinational institutions, and commercial banks—will have to begin to play significantly different roles, and that the political leadership has to come from government.

---

4. Eduardo Wiesner

Latin America's Policy Response to the Debt Crisis: Learning from Adversity

> It is notable that many advances in economic analysis have arisen from efforts to understand and cope with adversity. (Stanley W. Black, 1985)

I am most grateful to Dr. Martin Feldstein for having honored me with his invitation to participate in this Conference on International Cooperation. As we enter into the fifth year of dealing with the debt problem, this conference offers an excellent opportunity to take stock of what has been achieved and to reflect on the issues that still remain unsettled. More generally, this is a good occasion, I think, to look at Latin America's broad policy response to the debt crisis. I deeply believe that an examination of that response is the best way to determine the long-term significance of the debt crisis. What really matters is policies. So one must look at events and developments but always in terms of their relationship with policy change. I have organized my presentation in four parts. First, I will provide a brief background on the origins of the debt crisis. Second, I will review developments in the period 1983–86 and comment on what appears to be the major policy accomplishments of the region to date. Third, I will examine the current situation and the pending issues at this juncture. Finally, I will try to outline the directions that Latin America's policy response may take in the years ahead.

At the outset, let me underline that for reasons of brevity I will have to summarize and simplify very complex matters.

Origins of Latin America's Debt Crisis

The debt crisis was the combined result of three sets of interdependent causes: (a) inadequate economic policies followed by a large number of countries; (b) imprudent lending policies on the part of the commercial banks; and (c) adverse global economic conditions at the time.

On their part, the debtor countries incurred large fiscal deficits[1] which led to growing current account deficits and to excessive external indebtedness. The high absorption of external resources was not accompanied by a corresponding increase in investment but by increased consumption and by lower ratios of domestic savings. In brief, the accumulation of external liabilities was not accompanied by a significant increase in assets within the debtor country. In these circumstances a debt crisis became a question of time, which proved to be very short as external disturbances arose in 1982.

On the part of the creditors, there were imprudent lending policies, particularly by the large international commercial banks which offered ample and easy credit especially to the public sectors of the borrowing countries. They engaged in what Hirschman (1987) has called "vigorous loan pushing." These loans were made on the—mistaken—assumption that sovereign lending involved little if any risk.

Global international economic conditions changed abruptly in the early 1980s when real interest rates rose from about 0.6 percent in 1979 to more than 7 percent in 1982. An aggravating factor at the time was the deterioration of the terms of trade for most of the Latin American countries. Finally, when in 1982 the world economy, and with it world trade, entered into a severe recession, the debt crisis erupted.

In brief, the debt crisis came about because there was overborrowing and overlending. Without the imprudent policies of lenders and borrowers it is not certain that the adverse world economic conditions would have created, by themselves alone, a debt crisis.[2] These disturbances simply precipitated the crisis; they did not create it. The debt crisis came because both lenders and borrowers made mistakes.

One can then conclude that they both share the responsibility for the debt crisis.

Of course, one cannot assign proportions to this responsibility. Perhaps an implicit distribution can be found in the choices that were made at the outbreak of the crisis. The banks had to choose between (a) large and immediate losses if they were to turn their backs on their debtors, or (b) to provide some additional new money to protect their existing claims. The debtor countries had to choose between (a) abrupt and probably inefficient adjustment, if they were to declare formal moratoria; or (b) to make a serious effort to service their obligations in exchange for a relatively less onerous adjustment. As we know, both the banks and the countries chose negotiation over confrontation. They both saw a net gain in such a strategy.

Developments and Accomplishments, 1983–86

The strategy that was put into place in late 1982 and early 1983 worked well. Indebted countries adopted strong adjustment programs, commercial banks provided new money, and both official and multilateral creditors also substantially increased their disbursements. The results were prompt and positive. Between 1982 and 1984, Argentina, Brazil, Mexico, and other countries more than halved their nonfinancial public-sector deficit in relation to GDP. This strengthening of the fiscal position contributed to a very substantial improvement in the current account of the balance of payments of the region. For Latin America as a whole, the current account deficit was reduced from an average of $43 billion a year in 1981–82 to less than $3 billion a year in 1984.[3] Although this adjustment was achieved mainly through a sharp reduction in imports, it is worth noting that import volumes did increase in 1984 and 1985.

The policy corrections adopted by the debtor countries, besides being supported by additional concerted money from the banks, were helped by a more auspicious world economic climate in 1983 and 1984. During those years, growth resumed in the industrial countries and real interest rates declined. These factors contributed to a return of growth in Latin America, and the region as a whole grew by 3.2 percent in 1984 and by 3.7 percent in 1985 (see table 4.12).

The gains in adjustment made in 1983 and 1984 were not sustained in their entirety in 1985. Several factors contributed to that situation. There were slippages in economic policies in the debtor countries and inflation accelerated. Also, growth in the industrialized countries returned to a more moderate level of 3 percent. Lastly, oil prices began to come down at the end of 1985. These factors, together with the virtual cessation of commercial bank lending, resulted in renewed pressures on Latin American countries.

Table 4.12   **Real GDP Growth in Selected Latin American Countries, 1981–86**

Country	1981	1982	1983	1984	1985	1986
Argentina	−6.8	−4.6	2.8	2.6	−4.5	5.7
Brazil	−3.4	0.9	−2.5	5.7	8.3	8.2
Chile	5.5	−14.1	−0.7	6.4	2.4	5.7
Colombia	2.3	0.9	1.6	3.4	2.4	5.0
Ecuador	3.9	1.2	−2.8	4.0	3.8	1.7
Mexico	7.9	−0.5	−5.3	3.7	2.8	−3.8
Venezuela	−0.3	0.7	−5.6	−1.3	0.3	3.0

Source: International Monetary Fund.

The policy response was uneven. In some instances a frontal attack on inflation was launched, which was the case of Argentina with its Austral plan (June 14, 1985) and of Bolivia with its stabilization program (August 1985). In the case of Brazil, while the external sector remained strong, inflation accelerated to 235 percent in the twelve months ended in December 1985. Finally, in early 1986, the authorities adopted the Cruzado plan as a comprehensive monetary reform to eliminate inflation. In the case of Mexico policy, slippages led to higher inflation and to a real effective appreciation of the peso through the first half of 1985. Nevertheless, it can be said that, on the whole, the region continued to show relatively good performance in the external sector. Chile made considerable progress in reducing its current account deficit, and Venezuela, in spite of the drop in oil prices, maintained a current account surplus and reduced its overall public sector deficit.

This generally positive policy response contrasted sharply with the reluctance of the commercial banks to continue to bear their share of the costs. Although it was desirable for the banks to lower their exposure from the unsustainable rates of 1980 and 1981, the extent to which their lending contracted after 1984 created a very serious problem (table 4.13). Also, it was not clear how such a policy could have been in the best interests of the banks themselves.

With this setting, at the Annual Meetings of the International Monetary Fund and the World Bank in Seoul, Korea, in late 1985, the U.S. Secretary of the Treasury announced what became known as the Baker initiative. His proposal was aimed at revitalizing the debt strategy. It rightly stressed the three basic ingredients of the debt strategy: (a) a strengthening of policies on the part of the debtor countries; (b) additional financing from commercial banks; and (c) a greater technical and financial role by official creditors and by the multilateral institutions.

A key contribution of the Baker proposal was the emphasis it placed on the need for internal structural adjustment as a condition for sustainable growth. Underlying this initiative is the realization that a country

Table 4.13   Total Cross-Border Lending to Western Hemisphere Countries (in
                    billions of U.S. dollars: change in period)[a]

Year	U.S. billions
1981 (est.)	40.0
1982 (est.)	20.0
1983	14.9
1984	5.6
1985	1.0
1986 (Jan-Sept.)	−4.0

Source: IMF, International Financial Statistics; Bank for International Settlements, data
reported to the Fund on currency distribution of banks' external accounts; and Fund
staff estimates.
[a]As measured by differences in the outstanding liabilities of borrowing countries, defined
as cross-border interbank accounts by residence of borrowing banks plus cross-border
bank credits to nonbanks by residence of borrower. Adjusted for changes attributed to
exchange rate movements.

can register a large degree of external adjustment and still maintain
large internal imbalances (Wiesner 1986). In fact, we have seen that
many Latin American countries were able to improve substantially their
trade and current account positions but were unable to really suppress
inflation or to restore growth on a permanent basis.

This emphasis on structural change is correct, especially if it is seen
as the way to reconcile the constraints imposed by the other two possible alternatives to pursue growth. Since these countries already have
a heavy debt burden, they must minimize their external borrowings,
and since they cannot run the risk of higher inflation—or more depreciation—if they were to adopt expansionary fiscal and monetary policies to foster growth, they must look for the additional resources they
need in higher productivity and efficiency in the use of the *existing*
stock of capital.[4] This is the essence of structural change: extracting
additional resources from a more efficient resource use of existing
assets. It does not involve more indebtedness or the risk of higher
inflation or exchange rate depreciation.

I would like now to turn to the central theme of this paper, namely,
the policy response of Latin America to the debt crisis. In particular,
I will refer to the policy response in the area of external adjustment.

External Adjustment in Latin America

The long-term significance of Latin America's debt crisis will depend
on the effect it will have on the quality of the economic policies of the
region. If no basic improvement in policies were to emerge, then the
crisis would have been very costly indeed; but if some basic policy
lessons were to be distilled and were adopted as a permanent element

of economic management, then the debt crisis would not have been in vain and it could even prove to have had beneficial effects in the long term. Although it is still too soon to reach a final judgment on this matter, I believe it can already be said that in the process of adjustment one very basic lesson has been learned: Countries should not let their exchange rates become overvalued. This is what Fischer (1987, 32) has called "the most important commandment" of economic policy.

Before the debt crisis, Latin American countries had tended to allow their exchange rates to become overvalued and in some cases kept them in parity with the U.S. dollar in the face of rapidly declining international reserves and high rates of domestic inflation. As Cuddington (1986, 24) has pointed out, the consequences of this policy were capital flight, exchange rate instability, and stagnation of nontraditional exports. Well, it would seem that this is no longer the general case. It now appears as if Latin America's policymakers are determined not to be caught up again in a situation in which they do not have a minimum of international reserves to protect their trade and to meet their external obligations (table 4.14). Most policymakers seem committed not to let the history of 1982–83 repeat itself.

The results of this change are encouraging in terms of the growth on nontraditional exports. In the case of Mexico, nonpetroleum exports rose by close to 40 percent during 1986; agricultural exports in particular grew by almost 60 percent to $2.1 billion. In the case of Chile, noncopper exports have been growing at close to 10 percent a year since 1984. Nontraditional exports in Ecuador grew by 25 percent on average in 1985 and 1986, mostly on the strength of increased produc-

Table 4.14   **Real Effective Exchange Rate Changes in Selected Latin American Countries, 1980–86 (percentage change)**

Country	Dec. '86 Dec. '80	Dec. '86 Dec. '84	Dec. '86 Sept. '85
Argentina	−60.2	−6.1	15.7
Brazil	−14.4	−9.9	−2.5
Mexico	−48.2	−39.3	−30.8
Chile	−47.3	−25.3	−9.7
Colombia	−35.4	−37.4	−23.3
Costa Rica	−39.8	−20.8	−17.3
Ecuador	−34.9	−22.1	−24.3
Guatemala	−23.5	−28.9	5.1
Uruguay	−31.8	−2.3	1.6
Venezuela	−49.2	−44.7	−39.0

Source: IMF Information Notice System.
Note: Based on indexes 1980 = 100.

tion in agricultural, shrimp, and fish products. In general terms, one can see substantial gains in exports of nontraditional products in Colombia, Costa Rica, Venezuela, and others.

Behind these developments there is a remarkable degree of real effective exchange rate depreciation. From 1980 to 1986, Argentina has depreciated its currency by a little more than 60 percent, Venezuela, Mexico, and Chile by close to 50 percent, and Colombia by 35 percent.

In some cases, such as Mexico, Colombia, Ecuador, and Venezuela, there has been a very large real effective depreciation in the last two years. The particular situation of Mexico deserves to be underlined as the authorities have courageously maintained a realistic exchange rate policy even when there were calls to slow the pace of depreciation to, allegedly, moderate an already high rate of inflation. By following this policy, Mexico has been able to avoid a major crisis, even in the face of the sharp drop of the price of oil and the absence of the external financing expected from the commercial banks.

This more realistic and flexible exchange rate policy does not mean, of course, that the major problems of adjustment have been solved in Latin America. After all, current account deficits (tables 4.15 and 4.16) are still high, and it could be argued that the countries are just validating in the exchange rate the still high rates of domestic inflation (Fishlow 1986, 6). This may be true. Depreciating a currency in line with domestic inflation, or even with a differential with the rest of the world, does little to correct the internal imbalances that give rise to that inflation. It could also be argued that, under the so-called "real exchange rule, the authorities no longer control the price level and that inflation might become unstable" (Adams and Gros 1986, 439). This may be so but not in all cases. If the move toward a more realistic exchange rate does not result in a gain of international reserves, there is no reason to expect that the authorities will necessarily lose control of their domestic credit policy. But, even beyond this, my point is that it is better

Table 4.15   **BOP Current Account Surplus or Deficit (−) in Selected Latin American Countries, 1980–86 (as a percentage of GDP)**

Country	1980	1981	1982	1983	1984	1985	1986
Argentina	− 8.5	− 8.3	− 4.1	− 4.0	− 3.7	− 1.5	− 3.5
Brazil[1]	− 5.0	− 4.3	− 5.8	− 3.3	—	—	− 1.2
Chile	− 7.1	− 14.5	− 9.5	5.4	− 10.7	− 8.2	− 6.5
Colombia	0.4	− 6.1	− 10.1	− 9.8	− 6.8	− 3.9	1.6
Ecuador	− 7.0	− 10.0	− 11.5	− 1.2	− 2.4	1.1	− 6.3
Mexico	− 5.8	− 6.7	− 3.3	3.7	2.2	0.4	− 1.0
Venezuela	4.1	3.2	− 4.8	5.7	9.4	5.9	− 4.9

Source: International Monetary Fund.

Table 4.16   **Current Account Surplus or Deficit (−) in Selected Latin American Countries, 1981–86 (in billions of U.S. dollars)**

Country	1980	1981	1982	1983	1984	1985	1986
Argentina	− 4.8	− 4.7	− 2.4	− 2.5	− 2.4	− 1.0	− 2.6
Brazil	− 12.8	− 11.7	− 16.3	− 6.8	—	− 0.2	− 3.0
Chile	− 2.0	− 4.7	− 2.3	− 1.1	− 2.1	− 1.3	− 1.1
Colombia	0.1	− 1.7	− 2.9	− 2.8	− 2.1	− 1.2	0.5
Ecuador	− 0.6	− 1.0	− 1.2	− 0.1	− 0.2	0.1	− 0.6
Mexico	− 10.7	− 16.1	− 6.2	5.3	3.8	0.7	− 1.3
Venezuela	2.4	2.1	− 3.2	3.3	5.0	2.9	− 2.3

to adjust the nominal exchange rate when there is domestic inflation than to try to maintain an overvalued domestic currency.

Now, some authors argue that what really matters is external adjustment and balance of payments viability, and that as long as a country is able to meet its external obligations one should not be overly concerned about domestic inflation. But the question then arises about the fragility or precariousness of the external adjustment if internal imbalances are left uncorrected. And we have seen some examples of this.

Although one must be careful in drawing conclusions from changes in exchange rates, and there are many caveats that should be kept in mind,[5] I think it can be reasonably argued that what the numbers show is that policymakers in Latin America have learned a lot about the significance of this key price in their economies. Maybe more will need to be done to really set these countries on a long-term export growth strategy, but in any case what they have done so far is encouraging.

Current Situation and Pending Issues

Currently two major issues are pending in Latin America. The first one has to do with the difficulties of a number of countries to achieve more internal adjustment in terms of greater success in controling inflation and laying the basis for durable growth. The second one has to do with external financing, particularly the role to be played by the commercial banks which seem to have become increasingly reluctant to continue to provide financing.

The first issue is basic. In essence, it is the old question of how to eradicate high rates of inflation without having to go through a recession.[6] The two major monetary reforms adopted by Argentina and Brazil, the Austral and the Cruzado plans, ran into serious difficulties after some initial success. These two experiences suggest that transitional income policies and direct price interventions cannot substitute for correcting the underlying fundamental imbalances. This would involve a balanced government budget and a sustainable position of the current account balance of payments. Some authors argue that in the long run not only a balanced budget is required but also "a reduction in the size of the public sector" is necessary (Blejer and Liviatan 1987, 20).

Let me now move on to the related topic of structural adjustment, which in its most concise definition refers to the strengthening of growth through a more efficient use of existing resources. The basic question about structural change is not whether it is needed but how to implement it. We know the theory and we know the objectives, but that is not enough. We know that most public sectors should not continue to grow in relative terms, and yet fiscal deficits often are reduced not by cutting expenditures but by increasing taxes. We know that expenditure cuts should not take place in the investment budgets, and yet that happens with disturbing frequency. We know that trade liberalization will generally make economies more efficient, and yet we see that countries are reluctant to open up their economies. We know that overregulation is deleterious to growth, and yet governments end up unable to rid themselves of such restraints.

Why is the implementation of structural change so difficult? A large part of the answer lies in what Helen Hughes (1985, 19) calls "political obstacles" and in that power of vested interests.[7] The answer in my personal view lies in the strong political power of those who gain from large, inefficient, interventionist public sectors. There are strong political reasons that make it very difficult for policymakers to cut public spending, lay off workers, or lower barriers to imports. I place a lot of emphasis on the deliberate aspect of this type of measure to highlight the contrast between internal structural adjustment measures, on the one hand, and external adjustment policies, on the other.

In the first case, the policymakers cannot resort to the political protection offered by the argument that their policies are dictated by exogenous factors such as the fact that they have run out of foreign exchange. Here, policymakers are more vulnerable to political obstacles as they seem to be adopting policies that are their own creation and arising from convictions about some abstract theoretical model.[8] Ultimately, policymakers do choose implicitly or explicitly the level of domestic inflation that they have, while in the area of external adjustment countries cannot really choose between adjusting or not adjusting. In other words, internal adjustment is to some extent avoidable or at least postponable, while external adjustment is inevitable.

This argument takes me directly to the Baker initiative and its emphasis on structural adjustment. Is there not a contradiction here? I have said that the Baker initiative is right in focusing on structural change, and now I say that it is extremely difficult, for political reasons, for countries to implement comprehensive structural adjustment measures. I do not believe that is a contradiction. What I want to do is to add a word of caution about how much can reasonably be expected in the area of domestic structural change. It is important to avoid high expectations of quick results in the correction of internal imbalances through policy-based lending to remedy supply-side rigidities. Care must be taken to avoid the possibility of incurring a mistake similar to the one made in the years preceding the crisis, when bank commercial lending seemed a risk-free source of financing. The risk now is that some countries may give the appearance of adopting major structural adjustment measures in exchange for policy-based financing, when in fact they can deliver relatively little in this area in the short run.

Does this mean that policy-based lending for the correction of internal imbalances should not be increased by multilateral institutions and by official governments? Certainly not. But it should be done with full awareness that its conditionality will be more difficult to implement and to monitor than more traditional external adjustment performance criteria. What we must try to avoid is that, say, in 1990 and onwards we discover that the countries have become heavily indebted to, say, the World Bank and the IDB, but that commensurate progress has still not been achieved in structural areas.

The second unresolved issue at this juncture is the role expected of the commercial banks. The Chairman of Citicorp has stated that "capital will not be provided in any significant amounts unless the conditions of the financial markets are met" (Reed 1987, 27). On the other hand, the indebted countries argue that without additional financing they cannot service their obligations and maintain a modicum of growth (Funaro 1986, 4). Behind these positions is the issue of how to distribute the gap between the contractual value of the debt and the lower market value of those claims. For the commercial banks it is difficult to lend more money when the market discount is telling them that the new debt "will immediately fall to the same discount as the existing debt" (Dooley 1986, 3). For the debtors it is very difficult to service the obligations at their full contractual value when some of the corresponding assets are not performing for them either, at least not performing for their public sectors. Since the market has already established a discount, some believe that full service at the contractual value would mean a windfall profit to the banks.

Since all possible strategies[9] to manage the debt problem must involve some additional financing, this market discount is seen by many as a potential source of financing. The discount would provide debt relief to indebted countries and would cause the banks to realize the losses which the markets already have registered. All that is needed, some argue, is a mechanism or an institution to purchase the debt at the discounted market price.

On the surface this proposal looks appealing, but things are more complicated than that. In reality, there are no simple solutions to the debt problem (Mulford 1987), and there are a number of questions that need to be answered. First, from a distributional point of view, the question is: Who should gain the most from such debt relief, the countries that have the largest discount or the ones with the lowest discount? Is there not a "moral hazard" problem here? Granting more relief to those who have adjusted less may induce others to loosen their policies. A second question, from an efficiency point of view, is: Will this form of debt relief impair future international capital flows? Last and very important: Could debt relief be provided outside a policy framework of adjustment and structural change?

To this last question, the most realistic answer is that countries should continue to adjust and to improve the quality of their economic policies in spite of the tensions that exist in the system, including uncertainty about how this issue of debt relief will be settled. It would seem that countries have no better alternative than to continue their efforts to reduce their imbalances. After all, this is the only thing that they can really control. If the international economic environment were to turn inauspicious to the efforts of the indebted countries, even if the flows of external finance were to shrink, those countries that adopted the better economic policies would still be the ones able to avoid the most onerous forms of adjustment and would be the ones with better prospects for long-term growth.

If what the debtor countries want is more independence from the commercial banks or from external uncertainties that are beyond their control, such as changes in international real rates of interest or declining terms of trade or increasing protectionism, the best response lies in prudent economic policies. In spite of all the limitations and restrictions, this is what ultimately remains in their hands to a larger degree than anything else.

Possible Evolution of Latin America's Policy Response

Although it is difficult to say in which direction Latin America's policy response will evolve in the future, it may be interesting to look at some possible future policies somewhat apart from any particular solution of the debt problem. The idea is to focus on avenues of policy response that seem highly probable under most circumstances.

One area where policy response is not very difficult to visualize is that dealing with domestic savings. It would appear that debtor countries have little choice but to increase their domestic savings as the magnitudes of external savings that will be available to them will not grow very much over the next few years. This will not be an easy policy to follow, but it seems one that can hardly be avoided as countries will find that they must finance with a larger proportion of their own resources the investment necessary to achieve higher rates of growth over the medium term.

Since it would be difficult to finance large fiscal deficits without exacerbating inflationary pressures or without crowding out an already weakened private sector, it can be expected that, on the whole, the current fiscal effort to strengthen public finances will be maintained. While smaller fiscal deficits will contribute to a strengthening of domestic savings, it is not certain that this will also mean a reduction in the relative size of public sectors. That is, countries may be more inclined to reduce fiscal deficits by increasing revenues rather than by reducing expenditures. However, efforts can be expected to be made to increase the efficiency of public sectors, particularly of large public enterprises; how effective those efforts will be is very difficult to say.

Under most possible outcomes of the present problems faced in the debt strategy, it can be assumed that most Latin American countries will continue to pursue efforts to strengthen their external sectors. Policymakers are likely to continue to seek more competitiveness through their exchange rate policies and will seek to avoid overvaluations of their exchange rates. They will certainly work hard to strengthen their international reserve positions. Whether this will also mean a more liberal trade policy is not clear. This is a very sensitive political area. It could be assumed that with more depreciated exchange rates in real effective terms most countries would be more receptive to trade liberalization. And yet it may well be that policymakers will remain cautious on this front, as they seem concerned about the difficulty of managing a liberalization scheme at the same time they are trying to implement a stabilization program.

In terms of the sequence of liberalization, I have no doubt that the capital account will hardly be liberalized. The experience with capital flows has been rather negative in Latin America (Edwards 1984, 91), and there is also the question of whose risk would the possible new debt turn out to be. The debt crisis has sent Latin American policymakers the message that it is dangerous to open up the capital account. The experience of the last five years indicates that, at the end of the road, private risks tend to become public risks (Wiesner 1985). This is one area where many years will have to go by before liberal policymakers will be able to persuade public opinion about the alleged advantages of freely flowing capital resources. Those countries who in good faith followed that policy now find their public sectors and their fiscal positions burdened with those liabilities (French-Davis 1983, 25).

Given the recent experience with the emergence of the debt crisis, where external disturbances turned out to be so important, it can be expected that policymakers in Latin America will pay more attention to the international conditions in which they conduct their own policymaking. In other words, economic policymaking in Latin America will tend to improve as the authorities realize that they must look through the global interdependencies[10] to arrive at forecasts on, for instance, international interest rates or protectionist trends. Although these may be processes over which they have little control, or precisely because they do not control them, they will have to incorporate some assumptions about their possible behavior in their own policymaking exercises. This will be a salutary consequence of the debt crisis.

In brief, an overview of the possible policy responses of Latin America over the next years suggests that there will be, in global terms, an improvement in the quality of the economic policies. There will still be many flaws and setbacks but, on the whole, there will be more discipline in the public finances, better exchange rate policies, and some gradual advancement in structural change, but not much. This will be a positive balance. Although history is full of forgotten lessons, I believe that some of the ones learned from the debt crisis will long be remembered by Latin America.

Concluding Observations

Looking back on the past four years, the debt strategy that was put in place was effective in achieving its immediate objectives. Major individual country and systemic crises were averted and, most notably, a framework was established to coordinate the efforts of debtor countries, official and bank creditors, and international institutions. Nevertheless, it cannot be said that normal relations between debtors and creditors have been reestablished.

The policy response of Latin America to the debt crisis has been more effective in dealing with external imbalances than in controling domestic inflation or in laying the foundation for economic growth on a sustainable basis. It is a common experience that the reduction of external imbalances precedes that of reducing internal imbalances, perhaps because the former is viewed as inevitable and beyond the control of the authorities. Internal adjustment—namely, reducing inflation or the size of public sectors or making them more efficient—requires measures and policies that often are vigorously resisted politically, in part because they are not necessarily perceived as actions that are truly indispensable.

Structural change is certainly the long-term correct strategy to establish the conditions for durable growth, particularly when countries face the constraints of the need to (a) reduce fiscal deficits and (b) avoid incurring substantial additional external indebtedness. Although structural change is the right approach, it must be recognized that there will be strong political resistance to measures aimed at reducing the relative size of the public sectors or at opening trade or the capital accounts of the balance of payments.

The present debt strategy is under strain because one of its important components, namely additional commercial bank financing, has become increasingly difficult to obtain; it is noteworthy that in 1986 commercial bank flows to Latin America were negative (see table 4.13). Compounding this situation is the weakening of the adjustment effort in some of the debtor countries. In these circumstances, calls have been made again for some form of debt relief. The discount that the markets have established between the contractual value of the debt and its price in the secondary market is seen by some as the way both to provide debt relief and to allow the banks to present their situation in more realistic terms. However, there are difficult distributional and efficiency issues that need to be settled first. Beyond that there is also the key question of where the financing is going to come from for any institution to buy country debt, even at a discount.

Finally, it should be said that achieving economic growth on a sustainable basis is a very elusive and complex goal. Durable economic growth does not come about without a major effort of savings, investment, and technological and educational changes within a society. Sustainable growth does not follow automatically from the mere availability of additional financing, nor does it necessarily stop in response to a reduction in financing; it is the result of the quality of the policy mix put in place for a long period of time (Camdessus 1987). It is with this perspective in mind that the interrelationships between the debt strategy and economic growth should be contemplated.

Notes

The views presented here are those of the author and do not necessarily represent the position of the International Monetary Fund.

1. In only four years, from 1978 to 1982, the three largest countries—Argentina, Brazil, and Mexico—more than doubled the size of their nonfinancial public-sector deficits, which rose from the already high levels of around 6 percent of GDP to well over 15 percent.

2. For a different view, see Fischer (1986, 3). Fischer thinks that the rise in the ex ante real rate of interest was one of the major causes of the debt crisis.

3. IMF, *World Economic Outlook,* February 1987, p. 37.

4. For a discussion on the importance of resource efficiency see Guitián (1987), especially p. 15.

5. For a discussion of the major conceptual and methodological problems, see Maciejewski (1983, 491).

6. See Sourrouille (1987) for a discussion of the need to fight inflation without lowering real wages.

7. For a discussion of the power of interest groups, see Mueller (1986).

8. "Policymaking by conviction vis-à-vis policymaking by the inevitability of it all." This is the way Adolfo Diz, in a personal conversation, characterized this situation.

9. For an excellent discussion of options for new debt initiatives, see Feldstein et al. (1987).

10. For a discussion of this topic, see Dornbusch (1986).

References

Adams, Charles, and Daniel Gros. 1986. The consequences of real exchange rate rules for inflation. IMF Staff Papers, September.

Black, Stanley. 1985. Learning from adversity: Policy responses to two oil shocks. Princeton Studies in International Finance, no. 160.

Blejer, Mario, and Nissan Liviatan. 1987. Fighting hyperinflation: Stabilization strategies in Argentina and Israel, 1985–86. IMF Working Papers.

Camdessus, Michel. 1987. Opening Remarks at Symposium on Growth-Oriented Adjustment Programs, World Bank and IMF, Washington, D.C., February 25.

Cuddington, John T. 1986. Capital flight: Estimates, issues and explanations. Princeton Studies in International Finance, no. 58.

Dooley, P. Michael. 1986. An analysis of the debt crisis. IMF Working Papers.

Dornbusch, Rudiger. 1986. Impacts on debtor countries of world economic conditions. Seminar on External Debt, Savings, and Growth in Latin America, IMF and Instituto Torcuato di Tella, Buenos Aires, Argentina, October 13–16.

Edwards, Sebastian. 1984. The order of liberalization of the balance of payments. World Bank Staff Working Papers, no. 710.

Feldstein, M., et al. 1987. Restoring growth in the debt-laden Third World. Draft Task Force Report to the Trilateral Commission, February.

Fischer, Stanley. 1986. Sharing the burden of the international debt crisis. Paper presented at the Allied School Science Associations Meeting, New Orleans, December.

———. 1987. Economic growth and economic policy. Symposium on Growth-Oriented Adjustment Programs, World Bank and IMF, Washington, D.C., February.

Fishlow, Albert. 1986. Statement before the United States Senate, Subcommittee on International Economic Policy. Washington, D.C.: GPO.

French-Davis, Ricardo. 1983. Que pasó con la economía chilena? Estudios Públicos, no. 11. Santiago, Chile: Centro de Estudios Públicos.

Funaro, Dilson. 1986. Statement at the U.S. Congressional Summit on Debt and Trade, New York, December 5.

Guitián, Manuel. 1987. Adjustment and economic growth: Their fundamental complementarity. Symposium on Growth-Oriented Adjustment Programs, World Bank and IMF, Washington, D.C., February.

Hirschman, Albert. 1987. The political economy of Latin American development: Seven exercises in retrospection. *Latin American Research Review*
22 (3).

Hughes, Helen. 1985. Policy lessons of the development experience. New
York: Group of Thirty, OECD.

Maciejewski, Edouard. 1983. Real effective exchange rate indices. IMF Staff
Papers, September.

Mueller, Dennis. 1986. The growth of government: A public choice perspective.
IMF Departmental Memoranda Series, May.

Mulford, David. 1987. The international debt situation: Toward stronger growth,
trade and financial stability. Statement before the U.S. House of Representatives, Subcommittee on International Development Institutions and Finance, March 3.

Reed, J. 1987. The role of external private capital flows. Paper presented at
symposium, Growth-oriented Adjustment Programs, February. International
Monetary Fund, Washington, D.C.

Sourrouille, Juan. 1987. Minister of Finance's Buenos Aires Speech, February
25.

Wiesner, Eduardo. 1986. Latin America's debt situation. Paper presented at
the Symposium on The Debt Crisis: Adjusting to the Past or Planning for
the Future?, The Carter Center, Atlanta, April.

———. 1985. Latin American debt: Lessons and pending issues. *American
Economic Review* 75 (May).

5. R. T. McNamar

Evolution of the International Debt Challenge

This is no time to mince words. What today, at the inception of our
work, have we found? Well, in the first place, we see an impenetrable
and colossal fogbank of economic opinions, based upon premises of
fact which have changed so rapidly as to make the bulk of them seem
worthless, even if they were in agreement. With ail due respect to
the great ability of those experts who have wandered through this
gloomy labyrinth, they could not have failed to come out in the
opposite direction. They were confronted with the necessity of finding stable conditions where no conditions were stable.

In general, we have failed to find much value in economic arguments based on what ought to be instead of what is.

These are the words of Charles Dawes in Paris on January 14, 1924,
when he opened the meeting of the Committee of Experts that became
known as the Dawes Committee. At the time, Germany had defaulted
on its World War I reparation payments, and France and Belgium had
sent troops into the Ruhr. The British had taken exception to the French
and Belgian action, while the Germans threw up their hands and simply
asserted they could not pay.

And so Dawes was called to head a nongovernmental Committee of Experts to solve an apparently intractable situation. Well, by agreeing to stabilize the German economy (making what today the IMF would call structural adjustments), extending the time for reparations, and relating it to the German economy's ability to service the debt, Dawes developed a policy consensus that was implemented.

Today the question of repayments and debt service in each heavily indebted country involves both economic and political problems. And a permanent resolution necessitates a compromise between the economics and the politics, along the lines of expediency, which recognizes the real essentials of both. Again, Dawes's words summarizing his view of the situation after World War I may strike you as appropriate for today's challenges in resolving the overhang of international debt:

> In negotiating settlements of such a nature, men of official position, endeavoring to avoid offense to public opinion, tend to advocate proposals sacrificing economic principles for temporary political objectives, while economists, on the other hand, in applying economic principles tend to disregard existing public sentiments, which however prejudiced, ignorant, or temporary at first, must eventually determine the fate of the settlement.

These strike me as rather statesman-like words from a man who only a few years before had actually been the Comptroller of the Currency of the United States. Many people have forgotten that.

Let me talk about the evolution of the debt challenge. In August 1982, the international financial community was virtually paralyzed with fear. Mexico, Brazil, Argentina, and indeed Yugoslavia appeared on the brink of economic collapse. Although our European friends might not believe it, we in the United States were quite concerned about Yugoslavia.

In Toronto in September 1982, the mood of the meeting of the International Monetary Fund and World Bank was almost universally morose. Fear was widespread that the world's banking system would collapse, bringing an implosion of credit, then trade, and ultimately an inevitable worldwide depression.

Today we find ourselves in a different, rather improved world. Consensus has been reached on many points, yet the long-term solution is not evident, as real growth in the industrial countries appears fragile.

I shall ignore the origins of the problem, as they are well understood and chronicled. Indeed, I think Jeff Sach's paper (see above) was excellent on that point. Rather, I would like to review what I believe are the four phases of the debt problem's resolution and analyze some potential ideas that, with additional work, may have merit.

The four phases of the debt challenge that I have observed begins with Phase I, which was characterized by a crisis mentality and concern over liquidity. This was late 1982–83. Phase II was the period in which industrialized and developing countries alike came to grips with what had to be done to stabilize and strengthen the world financial system. That began sometime in 1983 and continued into the beginning of 1984 perhaps. Phase III, the period when orthodoxy and conventional solutions were applied with limited success and new approaches began to emerge, is where I would suggest we are today. Phase IV is, quite frankly, the next twenty-five years, when the problem will be resolved and be only of historical interest.

As Wilfred Gutt, the former chief executive of Deutsche Bank observed, in the life of every banker there is one event that leaves a permanent mark. For this generation of bankers that event appears to be the international debt crisis. Let's examine the management of that crisis, or challenge, as I prefer to call it.

Phase I: liquidity squeeze and crisis mentality. Throughout the spring and summer of 1982, the U.S. Treasury and the Federal Reserve had been concerned about the international debt situation. In the spring of 1982, the U.S. Treasury held a series of meetings with Mexican officials and repeatedly requested, but never received, an in-depth analysis of their economic and reserve situation or at least consultations with the then Lopez-Portillo Administration. In addition to Mexico, a very close watch was kept on Yugoslavia where the situation was deteriorating. And the Argentine debt situation was becoming critical as events led to the Malvinas conflict.

The debt crisis is usually considered to have begun on Thursday, August 12, 1982, when Mexico's newly appointed Finance Minister Silva-Herzog called the U.S. Treasury to say Mexico would completely exhaust its foreign exchange reserves by the following Monday. The next day, the Finance Minister flew to Washington. Over an intensive weekend (that I think might meet Mike Blumenthal's test of a period of exigency), the U.S. government arranged to prepay $1 billion in oil shipments for the strategic petroleum reserve, provide $1 billion to Mexico in CCC guarantees, and the Treasury, the Federal Reserve, and the BIS agreed to bridge loans totaling $1.85 billion, until Mexico could develop an approved economic adjustment IMF program.

Mexico squeezed by, but a crisis mentality among international bankers developed almost immediately. International confidence in the ability of the largest developing countries to service their debts had been dealt a staggering blow. With its vast oil reserves, Mexico had been considered among the most creditworthy of the developing nations. And I suspect that most people in this room would have shared the view that oil would go to $50 a barrel by now.

Within three weeks, the financial world was shaken again by similar problems in both Brazil and Yugoslavia. In Argentina the economic situation continued to deteriorate. By February 1983, some fifteen countries had encountered severe debt-servicing problems involving moratoria, extraordinary financing, forced reschedulings, and the necessity for an IMF program.

I think Phase I can be characterized first by the fact that there was an extreme liquidity problem for the debtors. Although their long-term economic prospects may have been positive, the sudden constriction of international lending caused a major shortage of hard currency for many developing countries. The so-called rollover assumption was shattered.

A second characteristic was the atmosphere of impending crisis. Genuine fear of a collapse of the banking system and subsequent collapse of trade and worldwide depression permeated the financial community. These fears were overblown and exaggerated by a press that did not understand the implications of the problem at first. I cannot overstate the morose atmosphere at the Toronto Bank-Fund meetings in September 1982.

The third characteristic of this phase, frankly, was a lack of global experience in dealing with such problems. Financial institutions and government leaders simply had not dealt with problems of this magnitude and number. No one fully understood the nature and dimensions of the problem. There was simply no briefing book, collected judgment, or historical precedent.

Phase II: coming to terms with the challenge. By February 1983, the monetary system had reached the brink and was coming back. Phase II had begun. Substantial progress had been made in settling the financial problems of key debtor countries, and our knowledge and understanding of that problem had increased dramatically. Plus, confidence had been restored so that we knew the world's financial system would not immediately collapse.

At the same time, G-10 agreed to a U.S. proposal to modify and expand the IMF General Agreement to Borrow (GAB). This was designed to serve as a standby borrowing arrangement for the IMF in emergency situations, which might threaten the stability of the system. For the first time there would be a safety net for the international financial system.

I might stop here for a second and say that I think this is an often overlooked event by the historians and the economists. There was no authorization to use the GAB for anything other than developed or industrialized countries who had balance of payments problems prior to this change. That fund is now available to assist a developing or developed country who gets into trouble because of an inability to service debt. There was no safety net at the beginning, now there is. It may or may not ultimately be used or be adequate, but at least a net is there.

Also by February 1983, our knowledge and understanding of the debt problem had improved. A process for handling the debt problems involving the IMF, the BIS, creditor governments, bank regulators, bank advisory groups, and debtor governments was emerging. I would say a fair characterization of the process would be to say that it was ad hoc, disorderly, poorly articulated, and minimally adequate. Indeed, I think that Charles Schultze's comment this morning that it was "muddling through" was probably fairly accurate.

Nonetheless, confidence had been restored. Indeed, the IMF meetings in 1983 were virtually upbeat by comparison to those in Toronto.

I think Phase II can be further characterized by what I call "country-specific" crises, or "mini-crises." Every deadline on a loan in a country seemed to bring a new problem. More country-specific problems erupted around the quarterly performance reviews at the IMF. Each of these were country-specific problems, not systemic threats, as in Phase I. Each was solved. And, I suggest that in the years ahead it's safe to predict that there will be more country-specific challenges. And they, too, will be managed.

A third characterization of Phase II was the rise and fall of ideas, such as a debtor's cartel or calls for global solutions. Debtor countries have come to realize that each country's situation is unique and requires a unique, appropriate domestic solution. In addition, developing countries, especially the newly industrializing ones, realize that their prospects for future growth are enhanced by continued cooperation with industrialized countries and the banking community rather than by confrontation and acrimony.

Similarly, global bailout schemes also emerged and declined in Phase II. These schemes, like the so-called debtor's cartel, failed to recognize the uniqueness of each debtor's situation and the importance of continued involvement and cooperation by creditor banks and governments on an individual country basis.

Key concepts were developed in Phase II. In 1983 some of these concepts emerged with the announced five-point U.S. strategy for resolving the international debt problem. This program consisted of adoption of policies by industrialized governments to promote sustained, noninflationary growth, encouragement of sound economic policies within debtor countries to allow them to live within their resources, strengthening of international financial institutions, encouragement of continued commercial bank lending, and continued willingness to provide bridge financing where necessary.

Phase III: convention and orthodoxy. Phase III has lasted from mid-1984 to the present time. This has been characterized by the application of conventional approaches or orthodox solutions for the debt challenges by the indebted countries, the IMF, and the commercial banks.

Probably the apex of this phase was the 1985 announcement of the Program of Sustained Growth at the IMF meeting in Seoul. This was a more positive and better articulation of the earlier five-point U.S. program. While sound from a policy objective standpoint, the so-called Baker initiative has simply not been implemented to date.

Further, the required preconditions of sustained, noninflationary growth and open markets for LDC exports are now, I believe, drawn into serious question. The Reagan Administration's trade actions have been mixed at best. By my own standards the Reagan Administration has been basically protectionist and inconsistent with its LDC debt strategy.

In addition, during this phase, as Sachs correctly points out, the free-rider syndrome—which has been mentioned by both Tony Solomon and Bill Ogden (see above)—has become quite acute among the small and regional banks. For example, but for the recent Brazilian announcement of a moratoria, the bank steering committee system would have probably collapsed because of the free-rider process and its cumbersome nature. That system plus the syndication process are proving increasingly cumbersome, ineffective, and perhaps simply unsustainable in their present form.

For example, 90 percent of the banks in the Brazilian syndicate provide only 5 percent of the money. And as Eduardo Wiesner (see above) pointed out quite correctly, the time lags between political consensus and the actual funding are increasing rather than decreasing. And, of critical importance to the developing countries and their ability to effectively implement change, political resolution must be followed by action. The current Mexican case is a perfect example of this problem when you consider the lag between the time the IMF-endorsed policy change was agreed to and the time the bank funding will actually take place. As that time lag is increased, the ability to affect policy change is reduced.

Last, during Phase III there have been tentative signs that the World Bank and the Inter-American Development Bank may begin to play a more active and forceful role in promoting policy-oriented and structural adjustment loans. Again, while the increased role of the MDBs is welcomed and necessary, I think it's questionable whether they will move quickly enough or effectively enough. And while they are a promising source of new financing, their future role is unclear and their response very uncertain.

Indeed, the U.S. position in the Inter-American Development Bank (IDB) as to the voting rights question has raised serious questions among Latin American countries as to whether the United States is in fact committed to an increase in IDB resources for structural adjustment loans. Many compromises were possible that would have met the basic U.S. policy objectives. All were rejected by Jim Baker. As a result of his actions, questions have been raised as to whether there is in fact a U.S. intention to push for the additional money in Congress or whether politically it's simply better to say "we couldn't reach a deal, so I didn't come up to Congress to ask for money." Indeed, the U.S. position was met with open cynicism in Miami. Read this week's *Economist* if you'd like a rather scathing review of the U.S. position on the IDB voting rights question. I think we are in an unfortunate situation.

As the recent Mexican loan package and the current Brazilian situation suggest, and as others have mentioned, debt fatigue is affecting all the parties. Capital flight and pessimism over economic policymaking are reinforced by the debt overhang. Few can see this current Phase III either as sustainable for many years to come or as solving the problem.

Indeed, can all the indebted middle-income countries always produce a trade surplus and continue net transfer of resources abroad indefinitely? Hardly not.

And on the horizon I suggest that the pending oil shock of the 1990s, while temporarily helping the oil-exporting LDCs, will in the current environment make the orthodox strategy ineffectual. International trade and world economic growth will suffer.

Let's consider some numbers so we have a background for the energy threat that is very near upon us. Every $1 increase in the price of a barrel of oil costs the oil-importing LDCs some $1.3 billion in foreign exchange. And there's a general assumption that you'll have higher interest rates with higher energy prices because of monetary policy responses. A 1 percent rise in interest rates is approximately $2.6 billion in additional foreign exchange to these countries.

So assume that oil were to rise from its current $15+ level back to about $30—a $15-a-barrel increase—but assume that interest rates only went up by 5 percent. The aggregate increase in LDC debt service would be $32.5 billion in addition to what they currently owe, on an annual basis. Let me suggest that this will certainly focus everyone's attention on the unsustainability of the present situation. The increase in interest rates would obviously offset any gains to the oil-exporting LDCs.

In short, new initiatives are needed to augment or supplement the case-by-case approach. To date we've only bought time, but we have no present solution.

Phase IV: the evolved process. The evolution of the debt challenge to date does offer some encouragement that new and more innovative approaches will ameliorate the difficulties of rescheduling and adjustment. However appealing, no global solution suggested to date appears feasible, negotiable, or to command a political consensus. Still the variety of new proposals indicates that reform and ultimately progress will continue to be made.

I would submit that there are nine points of general consensus:

1. Sustainable, noninflationary growth in the industrialized countries is a prerequisite.

2. Liberalized trade in both industrialized and developing countries must take place.

3. Moderate interest rates and realistic exchange rates must prevail.

4. Developing countries must have a positive inflow of net new capital.

5. Net new capital flows to developing countries must be invested in productive investments, not used for consumption or transfer payments.

6. Maturities on debt must be restructured into a realistic debt-service burden for those indebted countries.

7. Direct investment, debt-equity swaps, mutual funds, and other devices can all contribute to easing the short-term payments burdens and to stimulating economic activity.

8. Repayment in local currencies, interest capitalization, and similar schemes should all be judged by whether they will increase net new capital flows into productive investments. That is, if in fact they ultimately result in a decrease of net new capital flows, then they are inadequate schemes.

9. Domestic debt considerations will in fact have great influence on the industrialized countries' policies. One need only think of the Japanese national railway debt or the Farm Credit System in the United States and the interplay in our respective parliaments and congresses to see that there will not be any type of massive public subsidy of the debt. Indeed, the one point I would most strongly disagree with in Jeff Sachs's paper would be on the question of so-called debt relief for even the most extreme countries.

If what I have proposed is an accepted consensus (and it may well not be), then some recent developments suggest the outline of some events for Phase IV, which, again, I believe will last for twenty-five years.

First is the growth of domestic political pressures within the indebted countries. The political reality of rescheduling is that each indebted country must be able to show that it received as good or better terms than the most recently rescheduled loan. For example, the Philippines can point to its new package as being better than Mexico's 1986 rescheduling. In time, in my judgment, Brazil will undoubtedly do better still. Banks will have lower margins and fewer incentives to lend new money. This domino or contagion effect of extended maturities, lengthening grace periods, and local currency substitution on notes will all continue to rationalize the existing maturities and promote longer term syndicated loans or bond issues of ten, fifteen, even twenty-five years.

Second, the securitization of existing debt is beginning. A very thin secondary market is developing. Swapping of sovereign debt for project finance bonds is also beginning and offers good encouragement. The Philippine Investment Notes (PINs) provide a way for smaller banks to exit the syndication system and promote local investment. Mutual funds utilizing sovereign country debt to invest in local companies are being carefully studied and generally endorsed by debtor countries and investors alike. Indeed, those of you who have seen today's *Wall Street Journal* know that the Bank of Montreal has proposed a $100 million Brazilian mutual fund converting its debt.

Third, new options are being proposed that meet all the parties' needs. For example, one that I think deserves study (it's not new) is a split-currency interest rate to provide local capital. In this scheme, a rate of interest would be established that reflects a country's ability to pay, which conceivably could be below market rate; let's assume half of the market spread owed LIBOR. The difference between this rate and the market rate would be paid in local currency. This local currency interest rate payment would then be optionally relent to either the governments or the IDB, ADB, or World Bank to provide local counterpart funds for local projects. Again, recall that one reason for the decline in World Bank and IDB project lending is the lack of these funds.

The repayment terms on these local currency counterpart funds would coincide with the payment terms of the principle debt. These loans would be interest bearing. To avoid a foreign exchange loss to the commercial banks, these local currency loans, as well as the interest on the relent interest (that is, the part that is sent back for counterpart financing), could be indexed to the U.S. dollar or some other convertible currency and repaid by the debtor country in dollars at maturity, well into the future.

Let me say that I think people now realize that bank insolvency may not be substantially reduced from what it is today. The LDC debt problem for the banks is a funding or liquidity problem, not an accounting problem. So long as a bank can borrow profitably (that is, have an adequate spread either in the depositor market, the inner bank market, CDs, or international capital markets), it can tolerate the existence of loans that do not pay interest. Obviously, the higher a bank's asset quality, the better is its opportunity to manage its liabilities, that is, it can have longer term liabilities and be at the lowest rate over Treasuries or have an adequate spread to continue to make a profit.

So the term and spread over Treasuries can be better maintained, and the banks can fund themselves when they have higher asset quality.

By contrast, many analysts suggest that the money-center banks have already been discounted in the capital markets and that a further disposition of LDC debt will only injure their reported earnings, not further erode their bond ratings or funding costs. I'm sure there would be some erosion. I'm sure there would be some increase in funding cost or loss of ability to raise new capital.

But think about it. While the money-center banks in the United States today sell for about 40 percent of the price-earnings ratio of the Standard & Poor's 500, they're still able to raise capital and tolerate losses on LDC debt. I think this may, in some respects, suggest why you see a hardening of attitudes on the banks' parts. They're able to tolerate the losses and can increase their reserves. Remember, banks' reserves are counted as part of primary capital by a commercial bank.

Interest rate spreads and commissions will continue to narrow whether the banks like it or not. Commissions in 1982 were running 1.0–1.5 percent. By Mexico's 1984 rescheduling, it was 0.63 percent. And I don't hear a lot of talk about commissions today. Spreads have gone little less than 2.0–2.5 percent in 1982 to Mexico's 1984 rescheduling of 1.5 percent. Now we're down to the famous 13/16 percent. And the Philippines asserts it's doing a little better than that. I'm not sure I quite understand that, but I'm sure that it can be packaged for domestic consumption in Manila as being better than 13/16 percent. And again, I'm willing to predict that Brazil will ultimately find one way or another to come in at better than 13/16 percent.

The bank earnings from rescheduled loans are therefore going down, lowering return on LDC assets. As this happens, alternatives to redeploy these assets look more and more attractive to the banks. This is why you see the mutual fund proposal from the Bank of Montreal, a willingness to underwrite and participate in PINs, growth of swaps in Chile, and so on.

Let me say that I agree with Tony Solomon's view that the banks are incapable of a proactive solution where they come up with a proposal. They are basically going to continue to be in a reactive mode. I think, though, that time has brought a certain maturity to the bankers, to the IMF's understanding, to the World Bank, and certainly to the United States and other creditor governments.

And I also think there is some maturity in the debtor governments. I think that we will see exit vehicles for the smaller banks. I would hope that the World Bank in its structural adjustment lending will try to work with the IMF. However, I'm not encouraged by the current Mexican program. I have to tell you I'm quite disappointed in it. I think that the World Bank structural adjustment loan that was put together there can only be described as a pious hope, as opposed to a comprehensive program. That does not bode well.

One last comment: when people talk about U.S. government leadership, as Bill Ogden did, let me suggest that there is a background or set of criteria against which that leadership should be judged. It's very clear, or it should be very clear, that the IMF quota increase in 1983 was almost not passed by the U.S. Congress, despite the fact that it had been widely criticized internationally and by the banks as being inadequate in size. The United States has been too niggardly in terms of the access levels on the quota and other matters.

At the U.S. Treasury we found we were dealing with senators like the one who told us that the loan on his motel had been cancelled by his banker in a local small town because the banker told him he'd relent the money to big money-center banks, and they'd loaned it to Mexico, and he couldn't get it back. Well, I suggest there were probably other factors involved, but I don't know them. I do know I did not get his vote on the quota increase. And he's still there.

Let me suggest that you have to look at any of these global solutions, like an interest rate subsidy or an interest rate guarantee or anything else, in terms of the real politics of the United States. You have to look at it against the fact that we are currently having difficulty getting a replenishment of FISLC, our savings and loan guarantee fund. The analysis that I have personally participated in and have seen suggests that as of the third quarter last year, a minimal number for FISLC would require $35–$40 billion of new money—minimal. The Administration is pushing $15 billion, yet the Congress is talking $7.5 billion. We are not even addressing the problem. We can't even raise the money for a domestically supported program.

One must see debt release schemes for LDCs against the background of the current House Majority Leader's call for forbearance among the Texas savings and loans. You have to see it against the energy loans to the Texas, Louisiana, and Colorado banks, because I think the argument that there is a liquidity problem on these loans but that they're really good long term, because oil is going to be $30 or $40 a barrel, has a frightening parallel to the LDC situation. So I think it will be difficult, realistically, to expect the United States to continue to reduce its fiscal deficit, which we all agree it should, and at the same time to increase its subsidies, guarantees, or cash outlays on any type of global debt forgiveness scheme.

My conclusion is that it will take a variety of partial solutions acting in concert to "muddle through" Phase IV. Or we will need another Charles Dawes to provide a new consensus where neither economists nor politicians can currently forge one.

Summary of Discussion

Schmidt stated that progress can be made on the LDC debt problem only if the United States takes the initiative. He reiterated his belief that the Baker plan is a prophecy which the U.S. Treasury has yet to fulfill. Debtors will not be able to pay back the loans at face value; therefore, additional support must be forthcoming from either the IMF, the U.S. Congress, or a new international institution. In case this support is not forthcoming, banks should be setting aside reserves in anticipation of a substantial write-down.

Petty expressed the view that international financial cooperation between bankers, creditor governments, and international institutions occurs as the fear of failing grips them. To date, much more could have been done on the LDC debt issue. The Paris Club could have used reschedulings as an opportunity to offer more concessional terms, for example. *Anthony Solomon* agreed that the Paris Club has been niggardly, adding that it has offered no more leadership than the commercial banks themselves. Petty then suggested that guarantees on World Bank debt, which currently cover only principal, could be legally extended to cover interest instead. Asymmetric SDR allocations to the LDCs could be used to finance these countries and to encourage additional purchases from the developed countries. The debt problem will not be resolved in an international environment of slow growth.

Ogden concurred that leadership has been lacking and expressed disappointment that the U.S. government has not been more aggressive. The Bundesbank required West German banks to use the proceeds they earned on their rediscounts to supplement their loan-loss reserves. He thought it unlikely the Federal Reserve Board would mandate such a farsighted policy. Ogden found the inaction of the United States even more disappointing because a leadership role would not be very costly. For a time, the banks were close to setting a positive example with Brazil. A little bit of U.S. leadership would have gone a long way in helping to bring Brazil back into the international capital market and in persuading banks to resume voluntary lending. In view of Brazil's economic vitality, it is unfortunate that irresponsible Brazilian statements and policies were allowed to push the resumption of voluntary lending still further into the future. Ogden also expressed concern about the difficulty of keeping smaller banks involved in repeated refinancings. He felt this to be another area in which stronger government leadership would make a difference.

Carli argued that the huge U.S. capital account surpluses made finding additional financing for LDCs much more difficult. The $4 billion or $5 billion made available to LDCs pales in comparison with the U.S.

external borrowing requirements of $150 billion. As long as the United States absorbs so much of world savings, there is little opportunity for other countries.

Sachs pointed out that the discussion had focused on the financial implications of the debt for developed countries and had ignored the perspective of the debtor countries. From the point of view of the banks and creditor governments, the debt problem revolves around the question of whether the debts would be resolved without banks assuming large losses. But from the perspective of the LDCs, the debt problem has meant five years of misery: per capita income has fallen 20 percent, public services and infrastructures have deteriorated drastically, energy production is insufficient, and many public-sector corporations are bankrupt. Sachs argued that many proposals are simply financial band-aids and that the actors involved should be actively considering plans of selective debt relief. Bolivia had perhaps the most severe hyperinflation of the century: its terms of trade had fallen 20 percent with the collapse of tin and gas prices, and it was on the brink of complete financial collapse. Nevertheless, the IMF expected continued adherence to its program. This would have required Bolivia to funnel 60 percent of government revenues into debt service to banks. The IMF backed down, at last, but the incident indicates that bankers or IMF officials will continue to be surprised when defaults occur. The ultimate outcome could be a period of generalized debt moratoria. Sachs summarized empirical evidence that bank stocks were already discounted to reflect the price at which LDC loans are trading in secondary markets. A government-backed institution could purchase the debt from banks at current rates without a further loss to bank stockholders and give an enormous break to the debtors.

Feldstein held a different view from Sachs on the ability of the debtors to service the existing debts. He felt it was important to distinguish between larger countries, such as Mexico, Argentina, and Brazil, and some of the smaller ones, such as Bolivia and Peru. It is reasonable to be optimistic that these larger countries can maintain payments large enough to hold the nominal value of the debt constant, but small enough to allow for substantial increases in growth. He emphasized that political problems arise when different countries are treated differently. De facto, the Bolivias and the Perus will be allowed their conciliatory defaults. This kind of policy on the part of the banks is much less likely to be contagious to other debtor countries than a policy that officially condones such actions.

Wiesner disagreed with Sachs by saying that it was wrong to take the precrisis per capita level as the base for comparisons, since that particular base was not sustainable or realistic. Those high levels had been somewhat artificially raised by unsustainable external financial flows and by unsustainable fiscal deficits. To put it simply, these countries had been living beyond their means. The worst thing that could happen to Latin America was to come out of the debt crisis believing that wrong domestic policies had not been the principal source of its tribulations.

Petty reacted to the idea of debt relief proposals by pointing out that it is difficult to forecast the reaction of markets to a write-down of the debt to the levels at which it is traded in the secondary markets. He did not agree with Sachs's contention that the discount in bank stocks is completely attributable to the banks' LDC portfolios. Real estate, oil, and energy-related loans also have not performed well and contribute substantially to the present discount in bank stocks. Petty was skeptical that the U.S. government would ever guarantee the bonds of an institution charged with the responsibility of buying up LDC bank debt.

Ogden responded to Sachs by observing that Brazil's growth rate of 8 percent in 1985 and 1986 qualified it to resume borrowing, but that the irresponsible actions of its finance minister did not. He emphasized that the cases of Brazil and Bolivia should not be lumped together. The IMF's persistence in Bolivia was absurd, he felt, and the banks will write off the Bolivian debt. Similarly, banks will take a loss in Peru. If we are to avoid a bad outcome, other small countries, such as Ecuador, will need help from both creditor governments and banks.

Sachs went on to say that missing in the discussion of the case-by-case approach is the point that the banks and the IMF may agree to write off the debt, but they seem unwilling to forgive it, even in the case of Bolivia. We sacrifice Bolivia because we are worried about Brazil. This goes against the case-by-case approach to debt relief. He emphasized that de facto forgiveness is not the same as de jure forgiveness. Only with the latter do the debtors have the chance to be discharged from bankruptcy.

Greenspan viewed the case-by-case approach as a poor way of planning for bad outcomes. If the Brazilian situation were to collapse, serious fiduciary questions would arise if bank stock became worthless. Insufficient attention has been paid to the question of what we would do if widespread default actually occurred.

Anthony Solomon agreed that some de facto forgiveness will be required, but could understand why the banks have not yet moved in this direction. The banks do not underestimate the political bandwagon effects of country-specific debt relief. He called Sachs's emphasis on granting de jure as well as de facto forgiveness almost ideological: even with complete de jure relief, Bolivia would not be cleansed of its reputation as a bad debtor.

Frenkel underscored Feldstein's earlier point that Brazil and Bolivia should not be mentioned in the same breath. He was skeptical about the likelihood of a doomsday scenario. When Brazil announced it would not pay, Argentina, Chile, and the Philippines were quick to complete their financing agreements: the domino effect may in fact go the other way. On the issue of de facto and de jure forgiveness, he stressed that the key issue is the degree to which capital markets have memory. Capital markets that function well are likely to have good memory.

Ruggiero agreed with Solomon that a radically different strategy is not really needed. Much of the necessary structural adjustment in LDCs has already been achieved. Further advances for the debtors will be contingent on three things. First, more growth in the industrialized countries is necessary if the debtors can hope to grow out of their debts. Second, in order for LDCs to take advantage of the higher growth, free trade must not be compromised. Third, the debtors will require further liquidity, and this must be made available. Currently, the banks and creditor governments have not found a way to guarantee the flow of credit. Each participant should not pretend that the responsibility of solving the problem lies elsewhere. The risks of failure go beyond narrow economic considerations: many LDC democracies may be lost if the problem is not properly resolved.

McNamar expressed uncertainty about the possibility of determining how much of the discount at which bank stocks trade is attributable purely to LDC debts. Whatever the discount, whether banks can continue to fund themselves, given their current asset structures, remains a good question. He noted that bond rating services seem to have discounted the bad debts accordingly. McNamar also stressed the need for greater foresight in dealing with reschedulings. Over the next two years, Brazil is scheduled to transfer $15–$20 billion to the banks. It is in the interest of all the major players to replace the bunching of payments with a smoother repayment flow.

Fischer remarked that several improvements in the debt situation had not been mentioned. First, real interest rates have come down from the onset of the crisis in 1982. Second, banks have made substantial adjustments by building up their balance sheets. Third, LDCs have dramatically improved their current accounts and balance of payments. The problem is that these changes may not be sustainable and do not constitute a long-term strategy for the debt overhang. He argued that a third party, such as the IMF or a creditor government, needs to take the initiative for a comprehensive restructuring. Looking ahead twenty-five years, we certainly don't want development to be financed primarily by short-term floating rate debt. This implies that any voluntary lending must be in the form of equity, direct investment, and long-term bonds. Though debt-equity swaps are small flows, they will cumulate over time. But for many countries, these instruments will not be enough, and official flows must make up the difference. Such a change in the nature of LDC financing can be made only if better ways of monitoring LDC policies and imposing conditionality can be found, so that today's problems don't recur. Fischer also noted that the 20 percent reduction in per capita income of some of the debtors is measured since 1975, well before the debt crisis. In any case, a fall in real income should not be confused with the fall in absorption mentioned by Eduardo Wiesner.

Richardson suggested that we might use debt concessions to negotiate for trade consensus. The developed countries could insist on more restrictive rules governing the treatment of services, particularly intellectual property. The United States might ask for concessional treatment of U.S. multinationals in Mexico or Brazil in return for more generous debt relief.

Biographies

Jacques Attali is Special Adviser to President Mitterrand of France. He has held several positions within the French government, including Master of Requests at the Council of State, First Secretary of the Socialist Party, and Director of the Cabinet for Mr. Mitterrand when he was candidate for President.

W. Michael Blumenthal is Chairman and Chief Executive Officer of Unisys Corporation. He was Secretary of the Treasury in the Carter Administration. He was also Deputy Assistant Secretary of State for Economic Affairs in the Kennedy Administration, and Deputy Special Representative for Trade Negotiations under Presidents Kennedy and Johnson. He is a member of the Business Council and The Business Roundtable.

William Branson is Professor of Economics and International Affairs at Princeton University and Director of the International Studies Research Program at the NBER. He has been Senior Staff Economist at the Council of Economic Advisers, Deputy Director of the OECD Project Interfutures, and consultant to the World Bank. Professor Branson is also a member of the Council on Foreign Relations.

Guido Carli was Governor of the Bank of Italy and is currently a Senator of the Italian Republic. He is a member of both the Board of Directors and the Executive Committee of FIAT S.p.A. He is also Chairman of the Board of the Libera Universita Internazionale degli Studi Sociali.

Geoffrey Carliner is Executive Director of the National Bureau of Economic Research. Prior to coming to the NBER, he was a Senior Staff Economist at the Council of Economic Advisers working on labor issues and international trade policy.

Georges de Menil is Professor of Economics at the Institute for Advanced Studies in the Social Sciences in Paris, where he founded the Center for Quantitative and Comparative Economics. He was formerly head of the Quarterly Forecasting Model Group of the Ministry of Finance. Dr. de Menil is also

President of DEMVEST, a private investment firm, and a member of the Board of Directors of Schlumberger, Ltd.

Robert F. Erburu is Chairman and Chief Executive Officer of The Times Mirror Company. He is Deputy Chairman of the Board of Directors of the Federal Reserve Bank of San Francisco. He is also a member of The Business Council, The Business Roundtable, and a trustee of The Brookings Institution.

Martin Feldstein is the George F. Baker Professor of Economics at Harvard University and President and Chief Executive Officer of the National Bureau of Economic Research. He was Chairman of the Council of Economic Advisers from 1982 through 1984. Dr. Feldstein is a member of the Trilateral Commission, the Council on Foreign Relations, and the International Council of the Morgan Guaranty Company.

Stanley Fischer is Professor of Economics at the Massachusetts Institute of Technology and a Research Associate of the NBER. He has been a consultant to the Bank of Israel, the World Bank, the International Monetary Fund, and the State Department.

Earl W. Foell is Editor of *The Christian Science Monitor*. He previously served as a foreign correspondent, political reporter, and editorial writer for the *Monitor*. He is on the board of the World Peace Foundation and the Editorial Advisory Committee of the Foreign Policy Association.

Jacob A. Frenkel is the Economic Counsellor and Director of Research of the International Monetary Fund. Dr. Frenkel has been the David Rockefeller Professor of International Economics at the University of Chicago and a Research Associate of the NBER. He is also a member of the Advisory Committee for Studies on Debt and Development and Trade Finance—United Nations Commission for Latin America.

Kenneth Froot is the Ford International Assistant Professor of Applied Economics at the Sloan School of Management, Massachusetts Institute of Technology. He has served as an economist and consultant for the International Monetary Fund, the World Bank, the Board of Governors of the Federal Reserve System, and the Council of Economic Advisers.

David Gergen is Managing Editor of *U.S. News & World Report*. He has served with three administrations, most recently as communications director for President Reagan.

Alan Greenspan is Chairman of the Board of Governors of the Federal Reserve System. He served as Chairman of the Council of Economic Advisers in the Ford Administration and was Chairman of the National Commission on Social Security Reform from 1981 to 1983. He has served as a member of the Council on Foreign Relations, the Trilateral Commission, the Institute for International Economics, and the Hoover Institution.

Michihiko Kunihiro is currently Chief Cabinet Councilor on External Affairs in the Japanese Prime Minister's Office. He has held a number of positions in government, including Minister Plenipotentiary, Japanese Embassy, Washington; Counsellor, Embassy in the United Kingdom; Minister, Embassy in the Republic of Indonesia; and, Director General, Economic Affairs Bureau, Ministry of Foreign Affairs.

Richard C. Marston is the James R. F. Guy Professor of Finance and Economics at the Wharton School of the University of Pennsylvania and a Research Associate of the NBER. He has served as a consultant to the U.S. Treasury Department, the OECD, and the International Monetary Fund.

R. T. McNamar is Chairman of Gulf Pacific and Managing Partner of Conover & McNamar. He has been Executive Director of the Federal Trade Commission and Deputy Secretary of the Department of Treasury.

William S. Ogden is former Chairman of the Board and Chief Executive Officer of the Continental Illinois National Bank and Trust Company of Chicago. He is currently a member of The Conference Board, the Council on Foreign Relations, the International Institute of Finance, and the Private Export Funding Corporation.

John R. Petty is Chairman and Chief Executive Officer of Marine Midland Banks. He previously was Assistant Secretary for International Affairs in the U.S. Treasury Department under Presidents Johnson and Nixon.

Edmund T. Pratt, Jr. is Chairman and Chief Executive Officer of Pfizer Inc. He is Chairman of the Emergency Committee for American Trade and of the Advisory Committee for Trade Negotiations. Mr. Pratt is Co-chairman of The Business Roundtable and a member of The Business Council.

J. David Richardson is Professor of Economics at the University of Wisconsin and a Research Associate of the NBER. He has been a Visiting Scholar at the Board of Governors of the Federal Reserve System and has served as a consultant to the Economic Council of Canada.

Richard N. Rosett is Dean of the Faculty of Arts and Sciences and Vice Chancellor at Washington University in St. Louis. Previously, he was Dean of the University of Chicago Graduate School of Business. He is currently Chairman of the NBER Board of Directors.

Renato Ruggiero is Secretary General of the Ministry of Foreign Affairs for Italy. He has held a number of diplomatic positions, including Director General of Economic Affairs of the Ministry of Foreign Affairs.

Jeffrey D. Sachs is Professor of Economics at Harvard University and a Research Associate of the NBER. He has served as an economic adviser to several countries, including Bolivia, the Philippines, and Venezuela, and has been a consultant to several international organizations, including the International Monetary Fund, the OECD, and the World Bank.

Helmut Schmidt was Chancellor of the Federal Republic of Germany from 1974 to 1982. He is currently publisher of the German weekly *Die Zeit*. Chancellor Schmidt has also served as Minister of Defense and Minister of Economics and Finance.

Charles L. Schultze is a Senior Fellow at The Brookings Institution and Professor of Economics at the University of Maryland. He has served as Director of the U.S. Bureau of the Budget and Chairman of the Council of Economic Advisers.

Anthony M. Solomon is an economist and banker. He has served as Assistant Secretary of State for Economic Affairs, Undersecretary for Monetary Affairs of the U.S. Treasury Department, and President of the Federal Reserve Bank of New York.

Robert Solomon is a Guest Scholar at The Brookings Institution and President of RS Associates, Inc., publisher of *International Economic Letter*. He has served as a Senior Staff Economist at the Council of Economic Advisers, Director of International Finance at the Federal Reserve Board, and Vice Chairman of the Deputies of the Committee on Reform of the International Monetary System.

Robert S. Strauss has served as Chairman of the Democratic National Committee and was Special Trade Representative in the Carter Administration. He is presently a Director of Xerox Corporation, Archer-Daniels-Midland Corporation, Lone Star Industries, MCA, Inc., and Pepsico, Inc.

Eduardo Wiesner is Director of the Western Hemisphere Department of the International Monetary Fund. He has served as Director of Planning and Minister of Finance in Colombia.

Contributors

Jacques Attali
Conseiller Spécial auprès du
    Président du la République
Au Palais de l'Elysée
55 rue du Faubourg-St. Honore
75008 Paris
France

W. Michael Blumenthal
Chairman and Chief Executive
    Officer
Unisys Corporation
P.O. Box 500
Blue Bell, PA 19424

William Branson
Woodrow Wilson School
Princeton University
Princeton, NJ 08544

Guido Carli
via Due Macelli 9
Rome
Italy

Geoffrey Carliner
Executive Director
National Bureau of Economic
    Research
1050 Massachusetts Avenue
Cambridge, MA 02138

Georges de Menil
Suite 1506
One Rockefeller Plaza
New York, NY 10020

Robert F. Erburu
Chairman and Chief Executive
    Officer
Times Mirror Company
Times Mirror Square
Los Angeles, CA 90053

Martin Feldstein
President and Chief Executive
    Officer
National Bureau of Economic
    Research
1050 Massachusetts Avenue
Cambridge, MA 02138

Stanley Fischer
Department of Economics
Massachusetts Institute of
    Technology
E52–280A
Cambridge, MA 02139

Earl W. Foell
Editor
The Christian Science Monitor
1 Norway Street
Boston, MA 02115

Jacob A. Frenkel
Economic Counsellor and Director
Research Department
International Monetary Fund
700 19th Street, NW
Washington, DC 20431

Kenneth Froot
Massachusetts Institute of
   Technology
Room E52–430
50 Memorial Drive
Cambridge, MA 02139

David Gergen
Managing Editor
U.S. News & World Report
2400 N Street, NW
Washington, DC 20037

Alan Greenspan
Chairman
Board of Governors of the Federal
   Reserve System
Constitution Avenue and 20th Street
Washington, DC 20551

Michihiko Kunihiro
Chief Cabinet Councilor on External
   Affairs
Cabinet Office
1-6-1 Nagata-cho Chiyoda-ku
Tokyo (100)
Japan

R. T. McNamar
Conover and McNamar Inc.
707 Wilshire Boulevard
Los Angeles, CA 90017

Richard C. Marston
Wharton School
University of Pennsylvania
3404 Steinberg-Dietrich Hall
Philadelphia, PA 19104

William S. Ogden
1418 North Lake Shore Drive
Chicago, IL 60691

John R. Petty
Chairman
Marine Midland Bank
140 Broadway
New York, NY 10015

Edmund T. Pratt, Jr.
Chairman and Chief Executive
   Officer
Pfizer Inc.
235 East 42nd Street
New York, NY 10017

J. David Richardson
Department of Economics
University of Wisconsin
1180 Observatory Drive
Madison, WI 53706

Richard N. Rosett
Box 1133
Washington University
St. Louis, MO 63130

Renato Ruggiero
Secretary General of the Ministry of
   Foreign Affairs
Piazzia Dellas Farnesina
00100 Rome
Italy

Jeffrey D. Sachs
Department of Economics
Harvard University
Littauer M-14
Cambridge, MA 02138

Helmut Schmidt
Bundeskanzler a.D.
Bundeshaus
5300 Bonn 1
West Germany

Charles L. Schultze
The Brookings Institution
1775 Massachusetts Avenue, NW
Washington, DC 20036

Anthony M. Solomon
Chairman
S. G. Warburg (U.S.A.) Inc.
787 Seventh Avenue, 26th floor
New York, NY 10019

Robert Solomon
The Brookings Institution,
1775 Massachusetts Avenue, NW
Washington, DC 20036

Robert S. Strauss
Akin, Gump, Strauss, Hauer & Feld
Suite 400
1333 New Hampshire Avenue, NW
Washington, DC 20036

Eduardo Wiesner
Director of the Western Hemisphere
    Department
International Monetary Fund
Room 10–100
700 19th Street, NW
Washington, DC 20431

Name Index

Adams, Charles, 296
Adler, Michael, 130n.27
Ahearn, Raymond J., 183, 200n.36
Aho, C. Michael, 184
Akhtar, M. A., 87
Argy, Victor, 120
Aronson, Jonathan David, 184
Artus, Jacques, R., 129n.18, 132n.51
Atkinson, F. J., 129n.16
Attali, Jacques, 162, 166, 228–29, 321, 325
Axelrod, Robert, 198n.5

Balassa, B., 199n.26
Balassa, C., 199n.26
Baldwin, Richard, 90, 173, 184, 194, 197n.2, 198n.13, 199nn.20, 22, 24, 200n.39
Banks, Gary, 199n.18
Barro, Robert J., 40n.21
Bergsten, C. Fred, 91
Bergstrand, Jeffrey H., 128n.6
Blejer, Mario, 298
Bloomfield, Arthur I., 24, 119
Blumenthal, W. Michael, 75, 224–28, 321, 325
Brainard, William C., 41n.40, 60n.7, 131n.48
Brander, James A., 198n.5
Branson, William, 75, 93–94, 108, 129nn.14, 15, 130n.27, 131n.50, 226, 321, 325
Brooks, S. J., 129n.16
Buiter, Willem H., 40n.11, 91

Camdessus, Michel, 303
Camps, Miriam, 198nn.10, 14, 200nn.31, 37, 38
Canzoneri, Matthew, 40nn.11, 16, 17, 131n.44
Carli, Guido, 162, 166, 316–17, 321, 325
Carliner, Geoffrey, 321, 325
Clapham, John, 24, 41n.24
Clarke, Richard N., 173
Cline, William R., 253, 276
Coase, Ronald H., 198n.4
Cohen, D., 253
Cooper, Richard N., 40n.11, 59n.1, 60nn.9, 10, 172, 178, 197nn.1, 2, 198n.12
Cuddington, John T., 295
Cumby, Robert E., 130n.26
Curzon, Gerard, 200n.30
Curzon, Victoria, 200n.30
Cushman, David O., 87

Danker, Deborah J., 130n.28
Deardorff, Alan V., 176, 195
De Menil, George, 32, 41nn.35, 36, 48, 74, 162, 228–29, 321, 325
Destler, I. M., 183, 199nn.19, 20, 24
Diamond, Peter A., 194
Diebold, William Jr., 172, 198nn.10, 14, 200nn.31, 37, 38
Dixit, Avinash, 193
Dooley, M. P., 277n.5
Dooley, P. Michael, 299
Dornbusch, Rudiger, 304n.10
Dumas, Bernard, 130n.27

Subject Index